4th Edition

Creative Drama
for the
Classroom Teacher

Ruth Beall Heinig
Western Michigan University

PRENTICE HALL, Englewood Cliffs, N.J. 07632

Library of Congress Cataloging-in-Publication Data

HEINIG, RUTH BEALL
  Creative drama for the classroom teacher / Ruth Beall Heinig. —
4th ed.
  Includes bibliographical references and index.
  1. Drama in education. I. Title.
PN3171.H33   1993
372.6'6—dc20
  ISBN 0-13-189663-6   92-24359
                                              CIP

Acquisitions editor: Stephen Dalphin
Editorial/production supervision and interior design: Barbara Reilly
Copy editor: Nancy Savio-Marcello
Editorial assistant: Caffie Risher
Cover design: Ray Lundgren Graphics, Ltd.
Prepress buyer: Kelly Behr
Manufacturing buyer: Mary Ann Gloriande

For Mom and Dad
and Ed

 © 1993, 1988, 1981, 1974 by Prentice-Hall, Inc.
A Simon & Schuster Company
Englewood Cliffs, New Jersey 07632

Printed in the United States of America
10 9 8 7 6 5 4

ISBN 0-13-189663-6

Prentice-Hall International (UK) Limited, *London*
Prentice-Hall of Australia Pty. Limited, *Sydney*
Prentice-Hall Canada Inc., *Toronto*
Prentice-Hall Hispanoamericana, S.A., *Mexico*
Prentice-Hall of India Private Limited, *New Delhi*
Prentice-Hall of Japan, Inc., *Tokyo*
Simon & Schuster Asia Pte. Ltd., *Singapore*
Editora Prentice-Hall do Brasil, Ltda., *Rio de Janeiro*

Contents

Preface

Little did I imagine in 1974, when this text was first published, that it would be in a fourth edition almost twenty years later. Although originally designed to meet the needs of our students in creative drama classes at Western Michigan University, it appears to have met the needs of numerous teachers and students elsewhere.

For over thirty years I have taught creative drama to college students. Both pre-service and in-service teachers, as well as students from a variety of other fields, including special education, theatre, psychology, and recreation, are allowed to enroll in the course. Over the years we have bused demonstration classes from elementary schools to the campus so that our students can observe real classrooms of children being taught live. At the end of the semester course, students are placed in teaching pairs for a practicum experience. These practica take place in classrooms of all types, as well as in nursery schools, libraries, churches, and recreation centers. My constant interaction with children, college students, and classroom teachers has continually motivated me to develop and modify ideas and techniques of introducing the art of informal drama to children and youth.

This book is directed to the novice who is interested in teaching drama and who needs practical advice on how to begin. The aim is to guide students through a step-by-step explanation of numerous activities, ranging from the simple to the more complex. This does not mean, however, that the reader must cover each type of activity before proceeding to the next. In my own teaching, for example, I begin immediately with narrative pantomime in Chapters 5 and 6, completing the material in the first two weeks. The three introductory and theory-based chapters are covered next. Chapter 7 is then introduced and we continue through to the end of the book. Chapter 4, "Simple Drama Activities and Games," is sandwiched in by bits and pieces when it seems most appropriate to an individual class's needs. Since many of the activities are purposely familiar, they can be covered quickly. The section in Chapter 4 on the use of space is particularly crucial when students are preparing to teach their peers or children.

As in the previous editions of this text, I have focused on materials and methods for teaching drama rather than on discussions of various theories, history of the field, related arts, and so on. Also as before, I rely heavily on children's literature as the basis for drama. With the recent emphasis on literature-based teaching and the whole language movement, this approach should make drama even more consonant with other curricular aims.

Readers of the previous editions will notice several changes. Most notable is the addition of Chapter 11, "Leader-in-Role and Role Drama." This chapter, and related references interwoven throughout the text, is designed to introduce key features of the British approach to drama teaching. Since entire books have been written on this unique approach, readers will be referred to many additional sources for further study.

Chapter 9 in the previous edition, titled "Encouraging Creative Work," has been reorganized. The first half now appears in Chapter 4 and the second half is in the new Chapter 9 titled "Improvised Scenes and Stories." This new Chapter 9 also includes ideas previously contained in Chapter 7. Many sections of the text have been rewritten to include new examples and improve clarity. In addition, the many bibliographies of children's literature throughout the text have been thoroughly revised and updated and new photos have been added. Some older books have been retained in the bibliographies if they are considered classics or if publishers have recently reissued them.

It is truly impossible to thank personally all the people who have helped make this text a reality over the years. I must, however, recognize my colleague and coauthor of the first edition, Lyda Stillwell, without whose help this project might never have evolved. My mentor, former teacher, and friend, Dr. Barbara M. McIntyre of Victoria, Canada, deserves recognition for the unswerving faith she has had in me since the day she first introduced me to creative drama at the University of Pittsburgh. Thanks also are extended to Susan Pearson-Davis of the University of New Mexico for her invaluable assistance in reviewing this edition; to Prentice Hall Executive Editor, Stephen Dalphin, a mainstay on my writing projects for over fifteen years; and to production editor Barbara Reilly, who ably and with good humor guided this fourth edition into print.

Finally, deepest gratitude is extended to all the classroom teachers, college students, and children I have worked with over the years. They have taught me far more than I ever taught them. May this text stand as a tribute to their influence.

1

Introduction

We are looking in on three elementary classrooms during creative drama sessions.

In a first grade classroom the children are seated in a circle preparing to enact Eric Carle's picture book *The Grouchy Ladybug* (New York: Thomas Y. Crowell, 1977). The story has been read and some preliminary instructions given. Now the teacher is distributing colorful headbands of the various animals and insects in the story to children around the circle and in the order of their appearance in the story. Four children volunteer to form the whale. Three are placed under a rectangular, gray/blue scarf to form the head and flippers. A fourth is given a large plastic garbage bag stuffed with newspaper to represent the whale's tail. Several children who are playing fireflies are given pastel-colored chiffon scarves to use as wings. The rest of the children are put in charge of some special effects.

As the drama begins, a child turns off a light switch and the room is darkened, leaving a single ceiling light shining in the center of the circle. The teacher narrates the opening line about fireflies dancing under the moon. One child plays a wooden xylophone and two others swing wind chimes lightly. The fireflies enter the center of the circle and twirl about waving their wings as two children seated on the sidelines flick flashlights to create the fireflies' lights.

The lights come on to show daytime. Then, as the teacher narrates the lines which show the passage of time, two children move the hands of a makeshift clock. The teacher, with another child, now assists in playing the role of the grouchy ladybug encountering a friendly ladybug. Afterward, the

Paper headbands for *The Grouchy Ladybug* by Eric Carle (yellow jacket, praying mantis, gorilla, and lobster).

grouchy ladybugs go around the circle greeting each of the other insects and animals with the repeated lines, "Wanna fight?" "If you insist," and "Oh, you're not big enough." The teacher helps with the simple dialogue when needed, but allows the children to carry the scenes by themselves when they seem able. As the ladybug arrives at the noncommunicative whale, its tail swings and the ladybugs are "swatted" back to the center of the circle where they contritely share the aphids with the friendly ladybugs. The lights are turned off again and the opening line is repeated for the fireflies' dance.

After the story is played, the leader tells the children she is going to pretend to be the grouchy ladybug's mother and asks if the children can help her deal with her child's grouchiness. The children eagerly give their opinions and make suggestions, including "Don't let her watch so much TV so she goes to bed earlier at night." The discussion continues as we depart.

We move to a third grade classroom, where we learn that the children have been studying the subject of slavery and freedom. They have been interested in the story of Harriet Tubman and her work with the Underground Railroad, so the teacher has decided to guide the children in exploring what it would be like to be a slave seeking freedom. The children have already experienced writing secret messages of escape plans using code systems; learning the song "Follow the Drinking Gourd" (see book of same title by Jeanette Winter, New York: Alfred A. Knopf, 1988) and the significance of the gourd as a symbol of the Big Dipper or northward direction; and discussing situations encountered by slaves and the feelings generated: separation from family, traveling by night under cover, and being assisted by sympathetic people. Today, the children will experience the trip to freedom.

The classroom has been rearranged, and chairs have been pushed back against the walls. The children are sitting on the floor in the center of the room. The teacher specifies that one side of the room is a roadway, the adjacent side is designated as a marshland, the third is a forest, and the fourth side is a clearing and free territory. The window shades are pulled just enough to darken the room and to simulate night. A freedom song is being played softly. The children are just finishing group discussions about who they are planning to be in their drama and what they think will be their biggest difficulty on the trip. Some of the children are in groups of three and four; some are planning to work in pairs; and a few have preferred to make their freedom flight alone.

The teacher asks the children to decide the order in which they will progress around the room, and they organize themselves accordingly. They begin the experience by pretending to be asleep, waiting until it is dark enough to start the journey. One child, who has suggested that a hooting owl should be the signal for the action to begin, hoots softly on a cue from the teacher. The children, still in the center of the room, silently make their preparations to depart. The first few children start along the "roadway."

The teacher speaks softly as the action begins. She describes the surroundings and suggests the feelings that they might be having as they begin their adventure. She reminds them of the possible dangers. Suddenly she pops a blown-up paper bag, and there is no doubt that it is a gunshot. Everyone huddles closer to the floor, and they proceed even more cautiously. Some appear to have been wounded and are assisted by others.

Now most of them have reached the "marshland" area, and again the teacher quietly describes this environment and suggests the problems it offers. As most of the children approach the end of the trip, the teacher turns up the music and reminds them that they have almost reached freedom; it is only a short way off—within grasp at any moment. The children's faces bear encouraged looks; the walking wounded who are being aided by friends smile faintly. As they pass by the teacher, she turns up the music's volume and begins to sing, encouraging the children to join in. They return to their original places on the floor, singing until everyone is seated and the music fades out.

The leader talks briefly with the children about their escape and the particular problems each had. They also discuss the courage needed for a slave to escape. When some children mention the courage of those who harbored the runaway slaves, the leader asks, "Would you like to try a short drama about those people?" The children agree. She asks if they can pretend to be some sympathizers who have just hidden some slaves. She will be a law officer conducting an investigation. She stands, picks up a notebook from the desk, surveys the group slowly, and then addresses them authoritatively. "It has been reported to me that some runaway slaves are being harbored on these premises. I'm here to investigate. How do you answer to this charge?" A bold child says, "We have done no wrong." Others nod in agreement. She moves about the group, demanding explanations of their recent whereabouts and the contents of their "wagons outside the door." To some she says she has reports that they have been seen purchasing more supplies than their household would seem to need.

For several minutes, the children offer a variety of plausible explanations to the questions posed. The leader takes "notes," accepts the answers grudgingly and with some hesitation, and then ends by saying she will return later to investigate further. "Don't think you've seen the last of me," she warns. She returns the notebook to the desk, smiles at the children as she returns to her "role" as teacher. "Well," she remarks, "that officer certainly seemed determined to find evidence against those people. I wonder what he'll do the next time he comes back?" The session ends with the class suggesting ideas they would like to explore in subsequent drama periods.

Our third and final visit is in a sixth grade classroom, where we observe the following:

The students have been examining the scenes in Chris Van Allsburg's surrealistic picture book *The Mysteries of Harris Burdick* (Boston: Houghton Mifflin, 1984). The students have been divided into small groups and each group has selected one picture to explore. The teacher suggests that they develop a series of six frozen pictures (including the one they have selected from the book) to show what events came before or after the moment portrayed in the picture. The groups explore their ideas surrounding the scene and prepare to share them with the rest of the class. When everyone is ready, each group presents its scenes. The teacher instructs the audience to close their eyes in between each of the pictures so the presenters can set up their scenes in privacy and the illusion of six separate pictures is maintained. He rings a bell to signal each picture.

The first group of students has selected the picture entitled, "Under the Rug," with the caption, "Two weeks passed and it happened again." Their picture begins with the one in the book depicting a man holding a raised chair, ready to strike a lump under the carpet. The other students in the group form the family reacting in horror. The second picture shows a flattened lump and relieved onlookers. Thirdly the group shows a family sitting contentedly in the living room, each absorbed in a relaxing activity. The fourth picture repeats the first while the fifth looks the same except for a larger lump. The final picture shows an enormous lump and a flattened family. After the group finishes, the class discusses their interpretations of the presentations.

A second group has selected the picture entitled, "Uninvited Guests," with the caption, "His heart was pounding. He was sure he had seen the doorknob turn." The students' first picture shows the arrival of little gnome-like people through the basement door. Each of the next pictures shows the creatures creating destruction in various rooms of the house while the boy tries in vain to halt each disaster. In the final picture the little people are closing the small door behind themselves while the boy sits in the middle of the floor with his head in his hands. Behind him, his parents stand in the front door with suitcases in hand, one staring at the destruction in disbelief while the other is glowering at the boy.

After the other groups share their scenes, the teacher asks the students to write the story on their group's presentation, on one of the other presentations, or on one of the other pictures in the book. The children quickly set to the task of writing, overflowing with the ideas they've seen and discussed.

WHAT IS CREATIVE DRAMA?

The preceding examples describe only some of the many ways of working in drama in elementary classrooms. In the United States, the term *creative drama* is probably the most widely used, although other terms such as *informal drama, creative play acting,* and *improvisational drama* have often been used interchangeably. In Britain, Canada, Australia, and New Zealand, the terms *developmental drama, educational drama, role drama, leader-in-role,* or simply *drama* are more common.

The American Alliance for Theatre and Education (AATE) officially uses the term *creative drama* and defines it as "an improvisational, nonexhibitional, process-centered form of drama in which participants are guided by a leader to imagine, enact, and reflect upon human experiences."[1]

The definition further explains:

> The creative drama process is dynamic. The leader guides the group to explore, develop, express and communicate ideas, concepts, and feelings through dramatic enactment. In creative drama the group improvises action and dialogue appropriate to the content it is exploring, using elements of drama to give form and meaning to the experience.[2]

WHAT ACTIVITIES ARE INCLUDED IN CREATIVE DRAMA?

A multitude of activities and approaches to teaching those activities fall under the creative drama rubric. Among these activities are movement exercises and exploration, pantomime, theatre games, improvised story dramatization, discussions and debates in role, and group improvisations. An activity might be as simple as a game of "Statues," or as sophisticated as improvised group dramatizations on social issues related to the colonization of a new planet.

Many teachers, particularly as they gain experience and confidence, develop their own unique approaches to drama. These individual approaches must take into account the teachers' own personalities and styles of leadership as well as the needs of their particular students and the demands of the ever-changing school curricula, both in individual states and nationwide. Furthermore, new techniques of teaching drama emerge constantly and adaptations of older methods evolve. The result is a field in the midst of dynamic change and exciting experimentation. In spite of these many variances in the field, virtually all teachers of drama consider the arts essential to the basic curriculum and drama as an effective medium for teaching other curricular areas.

WHAT ARE THE GOALS OF CREATIVE DRAMA?

Referring again to AATE's definition of creative drama, "Participation in creative drama has the potential to develop language and communication abilities, problem solving skills, and creativity; to promote a positive self-concept, social awareness, empathy, a clarification of values and attitudes, and an understanding of the art of theatre."[3] Although several of these areas overlap each other, an examination of each follows.

[1]For a more complete discussion of this definition, see Jed H. Davis and Tom Behm, "Terminology of Drama/Theatre with and for Children: A Redefinition," *Children's Theatre Review*, 27, no. 1 (1978), 10–11.
[2]Ibid., p. 10.
[3]Ibid., p. 10.

Language and Communication

In the past, teaching language and communication in the schools usually meant the subjects of reading and writing. Most educators now accept the significance of oral language (speaking and listening) in the modern school curriculum. Recognizing oral language as the precursor of reading and writing, scholars and practitioners advocate its use as an underlying base for all language learning. Also stressed is the fact that oral communication skills are used on a daily basis more frequently than reading and writing.

Even more recently, the language arts field has introduced the concept of whole language, which emphasizes the integration of all the language arts and the use of language for real purposes in meaningful contexts. The whole language philosophy contends that the language arts are more effectively taught when they build on each other rather than when they are taught in isolation. Furthermore, language arts learning is more meaningful when it simulates everyday life experiences. Because language is used daily for the purposes of information, persuasion, imagination, ritual (social conventions), and affective communication (the expression of emotions), whole language proponents say these same functions should be emphasized in the classroom.

John Warren Stewig, a noted language arts educator and author as well as a past president of the National Council of Teachers of English, emphasizes the importance of creative drama as a means of enhancing reading, the study of literature, oral language and vocabulary development, nonverbal communication, listening ability, and creative writing.[4] Language arts specialists Fisher and Terry state, "The need for developing students' ability to use language orally in an effective way leads directly to increased use of dramatic activities in the classroom."[5]

Several studies have demonstrated that creative drama is useful in oral language development, reading, and writing. Stewig and Young found positive relationships between the use of creative drama and oral language growth in fourth and fifth graders,[6] while Stewig and McKee noted significant growth in oral language with seventh graders who participated in creative drama.[7]

Vitz demonstrated that creative drama improved oral language in grades one through three with a group of recent immigrants, predominantly Southeast Asian.[8] Snyder-Greco showed the usefulness of creative

[4]See especially John Warren Stewig, *Informal Drama in the Elementary Language Arts Program* (New York: Teachers College Press, 1983).

[5]Carol J. Fisher and C. Ann Terry, *Children's Language and the Language Arts: A Literature-Based Approach*, 3rd ed. (Needham Heights, Mass.: Allyn and Bacon, 1990), p. 284.

[6]John Warren Stewig and Linda Young, "An Exploration of the Relations between Creative Drama and Language Growth," *Children's Theatre Review*, 27, no. 2 (1978), 10–12.

[7]John Warren Stewig and John. A. McKee, "Drama and Language Growth: A Replication Study," *Children's Theatre Review*, 29, no. 3 (1980), 1.

[8]Kathie Vitz, "The Effects of Creative Drama in English as a Second Language," *Children's Theatre Review*, 33, no. 2 (1984), 23–26, 33.

drama in improving the functional language of children identified as ineffective communicators.[9] In the area of reading, an early study reported that creative drama sessions were important in developing readiness in kindergarten children,[10] while another study found that children who dramatized stories answered comprehension questions better than those who only read the story.[11] Dramatizing a story, according to Galda, results in a "greater understanding of cause and effect and the motivations and emotional reponses of the characters."[12] In the area of writing, Wagner found that the persuasive letter writing of children in fourth and eighth grades was significantly better after role playing than with lecture or no instruction.[13]

Children communicate in creative drama in a variety of ways as they discuss ideas, argue different viewpoints, share personal observations, and organize their dramatizations. They must find language that is appropriate to the characters and situations they are playing. Enacting dramatic scenes motivates them to become more effective in their use of language. For example, how can one persuade the Pied Piper to return the children to Hamelin town? What interview questions would be best to ask of a witness to a crime? What can a mayor say to appease two opposing factions within the city council?

By emphasizing self-expression, creative drama helps children form their self-concepts and expand their self-confidence. Their increased abilities in self-expression lead to better interpersonal communication skills in informing and questioning, in organizing and sharing ideas, and in enjoying the companionship and group interaction process with others.

Problem-Solving Skills

Because conflict is the basis for all drama, there exists strong potential for developing problem-solving skills. Through drama, children can be encouraged to hypothesize, test possible solutions and alternatives, and

[9]Teresa Snyder-Greco, "The Effects of Creative Dramatic Techniques on Selected Language Functions of Language Disordered Children," *Children's Theatre Review,* 32, no. 2 (1983), 9–13.

[10]JoAnne Klineman Tucker, "The Use of Creative Dramatics as an Aid in Developing Reading Readiness with Kindergarten Children" (unpublished doctoral dissertation, University of Wisconsin, 1971).

[11]L. C. Henderson and J. L. Shanker, "The Use of Interpretive Dramatics versus Basal Reader Workbooks," *Reading World,* 17 (1978), 239–243.

[12]Lee Galda, "Narrative Competence: Play, Storytelling, and Story Comprehension," in *The Development of Oral and Written Language in Social Contexts,* eds. Anthony Pellegrini and Thomas Yawkey (Norwood, N.J.: Ablex, 1984), 105–117. See also Mary Jett-Simpson, "Creative Drama and Story Comprehension," in *Using Literature in the Elementary Classroom,* eds. John Warren Stewig and Sam Leaton Sebasta (Urbana, Ill.: National Council of Teachers of English, 1989), 91–109.

[13]Betty Jane Wagner, "The Effects of Role Playing on Written Persuasion: An Age and Channel Comparison of Fourth and Eighth Graders" (unpublished doctoral dissertation, University of Illinois at Chicago, 1986). For more thorough documentation of research with drama and the language arts, see Wagner's article "Research Currents: Does Classroom Drama Affect the Arts of Language?" *Language Arts,* 65 (1988) 46–55.

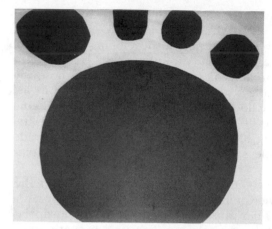

A cardboard footprint clue for the poem "Something Big Has Been Here" by Jack Prelutsky.

perhaps even redefine problems. As children struggle with the dramatic conflicts presented to them, what solutions will they discover? What ideas will they have for helping "The Old Woman in the Shoe" organize her household? What strategies can they suggest for helping a princess learn to cry? How will they solve the identity of the mysterious creature in Jack Prelutsky's poem, "Something Big Has Been Here" (35)?[14]

Children experience group problem solving in other drama learning as well. For example, how will a group demonstrate the working parts of a machine they create with their bodies? How will they choose to "stage" their drama, handling simple props or costume pieces for maximum effect?

In all of these experiences children are encouraged to seek answers, push for new ideas, generate and explore solutions, synthesize information, and exercise imagination. This is all a part of the problem-solving process which drama can stimulate.

Creativity

When children are presented with problems to solve, with open-endedness that requires a filling in of gaps, with information and ideas to synthesize into new relationships, they are learning creatively, according to Torrance.[15] Most researchers and writers on the subject of creativity believe that everyone has creative potential. In order to recognize each individual's full development and to foster independent thinking in a free society, our educational system has come to include this aspect of learning throughout the school curriculum.

The characteristics of creativity have been identified by a number of

[14]Throughout this text, numbers in parentheses correspond to the numbered anthologies and books listed in the final bibliography that begins on page 300.

[15]E. Paul Torrance, *Encouraging Creativity in the Classroom* (Dubuque, Iowa: William C. Brown, 1970), p. 1.

writers. Creative people are innovators, problem solvers, alternative testers, and adventurers. They are fearless, fluent, curious, unpredictable, constructively discontented, and sometimes even a bit "off center." But creative expression is necessary for the celebration of the individual, the one who will survive in a dehumanizing technological age and in a world that is so complex that its problems, let alone solutions, often elude us.

Although creative potential is present in each child, it needs to be released and given a nurturing environment to develop fully. Teachers can encourage creative thinking abilities by providing an accepting climate where children have the freedom to try and fail—where they are not afraid to take risks and explore. They can also nurture creativity by sensitizing children to environmental stimuli and by encouraging the spirit of play.

Although studies of creative drama's effect on children's creativity are limited both in size and scope, at least three can be noted. Karioth's 1967 study showed that creative drama could aid in developing creative thinking abilities in disadvantaged fourth graders as measured by Thorndike tests of creative thinking.[16] In 1971 Prokes reported that creative drama was useful in promoting the imaginative capacities of forty-five gifted junior high school students.[17] Finally, in a study by Schmidt, Goforth, and Drew, an experimental group of thirty-nine kindergarten students scored significantly higher than a control group on two creativity tests, one verbal and one visual.[18] This evidence seems to suggest that drama is an important vehicle for releasing and nurturing the creative potential of children.

Drama requires imagination and inventiveness. For example, how might students demonstrate the meaning of a particular proverb in group improvisational scenes? How will they express themselves in the role of a rat who refuses to be changed into a horse for Cinderella's carriage? What rules will they establish for their newly founded society on a remote island? These are not the usual workbook exercises associated with traditional classroom learning. They demand higher-order thinking processes that are at the heart of every creative venture.

Positive Self-Concept

Within each individual is a distinct being ready to emerge. Being creative, according to Moustakas, means continually evolving into one's own unique self—growing forward, responding to life, fulfilling one's maximum potential.[19] To be able to grow we must value and have faith in ourselves, for only then can we be secure enough to explore, experiment,

[16]Emil Karioth, "Creative Dramatics as an Aid to Developing Creative Thinking Abilities" (unpublished doctoral dissertation, University of Minnesota, 1967).

[17]Sister Dorothy Prokes, F.S.P.A., "Exploring the Relationship Between Participation in Creative Dramatics and Development of the Imagination Capacities of Gifted Junior High School Students" (unpublished doctoral dissertation, New York University, 1971).

[18]Toni Schmidt, Elissa Goforth, and Kathy Drew, "Creative Dramatics and Creativity: An Experimental Study," *Educational Theatre Journal,* 27 (March 1975), 111-114.

[19]Clark E. Moustakas, *Creative Life* (New York: Van Nostrand Reinhold, 1977). The theme of achieving a creative life pervades the entire book.

Drama can help develop a more positive self-concept.

and take risks in expressing ourselves. This self-expression, in turn, furthers the awareness and growth of the self.

In creative drama children's positive self-concept and self-expression are fostered by the leader who believes in each child's personal worth and creative potential. The leader's attitude produces a climate of psychological security in the classroom, so that the children are not afraid to be themselves, growing and searching for new awarenesses. The teacher who uses an activity like creative drama is often one who already believes in children's need for self-expression and is sensitive to the kind of leadership that encourages it.

An early experimental study on the effect of creative drama on personal growth was done by Irwin.[20] She demonstrated that third graders, receiving 40 minutes of creative drama each week for 15 weeks, improved in personal and social adjustment when compared with a control group. A study reported in 1982 by Huntsman demonstrated that 30 university students from introductory psychology classes made significant gains in self-confidence, self-worth, and spontaneity after participating in improvisational drama activities.[21] The classes were conducted in an 11-week period with 22 two-hour sessions held twice weekly. In a third study, 150-economically disadvantaged fourth, fifth, and sixth grade African-American and Hispanic schoolchildren participated in an improvisational

[20]Eleanor Chima Irwin, "The Effect of a Program of Creative Dramatics Upon Personality as Measured by the California Test of Personality, Sociograms, Teacher Ratings, and Grades" (unpublished doctoral dissertation, University of Pittsburgh, 1963).

[21]Karla Hendricks Huntsman, "Improvisational Dramatic Activities: Key to Self-Actualization?" *Children's Theatre Review,* 31, no. 2 (1982), 3–9.

dramatics program.[22] Results suggested that drama, in addition to improving reading achievement, also aided children's positive attitudes toward themselves and others. Students' attitudes and school performance were also rated more highly by their teachers after the program.

Among the kinds of anecdotal material most frequently shared by creative drama leaders are those which point to children's improved self-concept. Sometimes children feel better about themselves because of a certain role they have played that appealed to them: a powerful person, a brave person, an intelligent person. Or because self-expression has been encouraged and positive guidance rather than criticism has been the leader's method, children who might otherwise feel incapable of success now feel that their ideas have importance. The self can stand taller.

Social Awareness

It has often been said that drama is a rehearsal for living.[23] Through creative drama children can pretend to be the people or things they find interesting and significant. They can relive the experiences of others, of the various people that inhabit their storybooks, their history and social studies books, and their everyday life and fantasy world. They can experiment with societal roles and, in the process, identify and empathize with others, learning of their concerns, confronting their problems, and experiencing their successes as well as failures. Through drama children can begin to establish a tangible relationship with the human condition. What is it like to experience discrimination? What is it like to hold a particular political or religious view? What is it like to be a member of another culture or nation? Through drama children can discover the common bond of humanness that transcends time, age, and geographical boundaries.

Creative drama also provides learning experiences in social and group interaction. In many ways drama is a group art. Drama focuses on cooperative learning; the theatre requires the talents and skills of numerous artists. So, too, as children engage in drama, they must plan together, enact ideas together, and organize their playing space. Effective socialization becomes a high priority, and the rewards of cooperative group behaviors are often clearly demonstrated to even the youngest of children.

Empathy

Empathy is the ability to see life from another's perspective and to feel with that person. This "as if" feeling is similar to the one the Russian theatre director Konstantin Stanislavsky attempted to encourage through

[22]Annette F. Gourgey, Jason Bosseau, and Judith Delgado, "The Impact of an Improvisational Dramatics Program on Student Attitudes and Achievement," *Children's Theatre Review*, 34, no. 3 (1985), 9–14.

[23]For a wide array of anecdotal observations of children involved in dramatic play, see Virginia Glasgow Koste, *Dramatic Play in Childhood: Rehearsal for Life* (Lanham, Md.: University Press of America, 1987).

what he called "emotional memory." Actors were urged to sense and understand the character they were playing by recalling similar situations in their own lives.

Children begin to develop empathy as their thinking matures and they move away from egocentricity. A recent comprehensive study by Kardash and Wright analyzed sixteen studies of drama with children in kindergarten through seventh grade. Their results concluded that drama has "an extremely beneficial effect on role-taking ability."[24]

Through creative drama children have the opportunity to see the world from another point of view and to respond as that person would respond. If the inner attitudes of another can be identified and understood through creative drama, if children can experience "walking in another's shoes," more tolerant understanding of others and more effective communication will result.

Values and Attitudes

To deal with life's situations, we make decisions constantly, basing them on the values we hold. Yet if we are not sure what we believe, we may find it difficult to make the best decisions. In a world in which values are under constant scrutiny and appear to be changing at every turn, it is essential to help students develop the personal values that will affect their ways of behaving. While personal values may vary, certain values are generally accepted without controversy. Honesty and truthfulness, for example, are almost universally upheld though not always practiced. Schools have a significant role to play in helping children understand the values of our society.

Drama deals with people in action—facing life, making decisions, and dealing with the consequences of those decisions. In drama children are involved in situations and events they choose to experience, exploring the turn of events that evolve. They take on roles of various people, experiencing their attitudes and values and seeing life from their perspective. Through this process children may begin to understand some of the answers to universal questions. As Duke suggests, "When a person is required to act 'as if' he holds a certain belief, he is more likely to examine the application of that belief to his own life."[25]

In drama, alternative patterns of behavior can be explored. Children discover the results of their actions and behaviors without suffering the consequences real life hands out as a result of our mistakes and misjudgments. When children improvise drama, language and action are spontaneous—the way they happen in everyday life where there is no predetermined script. Children can experiment with alternatives, learning

---

[24]Carol Anne M. Kardash and Lin Wright, "Does Creative Drama Benefit Elementary School Students: A Meta-analysis," *Youth Theatre Journal* (Winter 1987), 11–18.

[25]Charles R. Duke, "Educational Drama, Role-Taking, and Values Clarification," in *Educational Drama for Today's Schools*, ed. R. Baird Shuman (Metuchen, N.J.: Scarecrow Press, 1978), p. 95.

firsthand which ways are most effective. As a result, they are able to increase their repertoire of communication and behavioral options and experience the self-confidence that comes from rehearsing life's situations before meeting them.

An Understanding of the Art of Theatre

In creative drama children learn about theatre in a way best suited to their developing talents and skills. Rather than focusing on the memorization of scripts and the elaborate production of a play, children are encouraged to improvise dramatic materials. Emphasis is placed on discussing and internalizing information and then playing it out, using self-expression rather than prescribed dialogue.

At the same time, children gain insights into the important elements of theatre, such as action, conflict, plot, mood, characterization, and spectacle. They will be exposed to plot structure and to the themes of stories. Their own interpretation of the characters will give them experiences in expression through movement and voice. They will begin to understand people better—not only how they appear on the outside, but how they think and feel on the inside. They will be more attuned to human motivations for behaviors and attitudes.

Children will also have the opportunity to experience the aspects of theatrical staging and, in modified forms, all the related spectacle of setting, props, lights, costumes, music, and dance. In bringing all the various art forms of the theatre together, students will learn the importance of working together to create a unified, artistic whole.

The basic concepts of creative drama are rooted in the art of theatre. (*Charlotte's Web* produced by Kalamazoo Civic Youth Theatre.)

The arts have traditionally provided a way for nations and cultures to develop, communicate, and preserve their identity. Because of the many interrelationships of the arts to the traditional disciplines of learning and because they develop intellectual and social skills, they are as basic to the curriculum as the three Rs.

A report from the National Endowment for the Arts, submitted to Congress in March 1988, asserts that education in the arts is integral to gaining a sense of what civilization is and how humans contribute to it.[26] Aptly titled *Toward Civilization,* the document gives four basic reasons for education in the arts: developing a sense of civilization; fostering creativity, particularly problem solving and reasoning; expanding effective communication, both verbal and nonverbal; and assessing products of the arts.

WHAT ARE SOME OF THE USES OF CREATIVE DRAMA?

Creative drama has been used in a variety of educational settings and with persons of all ages, including older adults. Many classroom teachers, who have either taken a preservice or an inservice introductory course in creative drama or have read about it in texts or journals, have tried it out for themselves. Some school districts, on either a temporary or permanent basis, have the luxury of educational-drama specialists who work with children in addition to serving as consultants to teachers in providing drama experiences. Some states, most notably Texas, have mandated the teaching of theatre arts at all grade levels, with regular classroom teachers serving as the instructors in the elementary grades.

Both recreational programs and library programs have long incorporated creative drama into their varied schedule of activities. Religious programs use drama as a more meaningful way to teach religious literature and ethical attitudes. In community theatre programs, creative drama is frequently offered to give children experience in informal drama and an understanding of the art of theatre.

Because of the therapeutic aspect of the arts in general, creative drama has been useful in a number of areas of special education. Even when the goals of creative drama are educational or aesthetic (stressing curricular information, encouraging imagination), the psychological well-being of the participants can also be enhanced. Some educators and specialists have found creative drama useful in alleviating emotional tensions that contribute to reading problems, speech and language disorders, and socialization difficulties, to cite only a few examples.[27]

---

[26]National Endowment for the Arts, *Toward Civilization: A Report on Arts Education* (Washington, D.C.: National Endowment for the Arts, 1988). For a summary article, see Frank Hodsoll's "*Toward Civilization:* Next Responsibilities," in *Design for Arts in Education,* 90, no. 3 (1989), 10–15.

[27]A distinction is made between *therapeutic* and *therapy.* Generally, any activity in which participants feel better about themselves can be termed therapeutic. *Therapy* is a more restricted term and is the domain of the trained professional whose responsibility it is to bring

Thus the uses of creative drama continue to expand, reflecting the growing recognition of the power of the drama experience to enrich learning and enhance living for all persons.

HOW DOES THE TEACHER INCORPORATE DRAMA INTO AN ALREADY FULL CURRICULUM?

Many educators feel that drama provides an essential style of learning for children. Since children naturally dramatize, the teacher who uses drama is simply capitalizing on what the children already know how to do innately. Through dramatization children use a wealth of information in more concrete and meaningful ways. When children play out an idea, they become an integral part of it. They become kinesthetically involved in experiences that might otherwise remain only words on a printed page.

Since it can incorporate so many desirable educational goals, drama is used in conjunction with many subject areas, such as language arts, science, social studies, and the fine arts. In history, for example, children might take on the role of early American explorers, facing the uncertainties of unknown lands; in literature they might explore the adventures of Alice in her land of wonder. In music, children might dramatize the folk song "Abiyoyo" or in science they might enact a day in the life of a kangaroo rat. For an oral language activity they might become lobbyists advocating their causes.

Creative drama can focus on specific facts and concepts as well as emphasize broader goals such as problem solving and creative thinking. Children can gain a better understanding of the various jobs in a logging camp through pantomime, or they may become members of the Continental Congress, arguing viewpoints and struggling with compromise as they attempt to draft the U.S. Constitution. They may also be encouraged to do further reading and research in order to play their ideas and roles with greater accuracy.

Drama experiences also provide a way of checking children's understandings of material covered. Suppose that after studying simple machines children pantomime some examples. As they play, it will be obvious what facts and concepts are understood and what misconceptions need correcting. Or as older children take on roles of Northern and Southern sympathizers during the Civil War period, one can assess their understanding of events and attitudes which led to the conflict.

Learning experiences can be previewed or reviewed through creative drama. In preparation for a field trip to a fire department, a simulated field trip can be enacted. Afterward the experience can be replayed, utilizing the information gained.

---

about behavioral change in a client. For a more complete discussion of this point, see Eleanor C. Irwin, "Drama Therapy with the Handicapped," in *Drama, Theatre, and the Handicapped*, ed. Ann M. Shaw and CJ Stevens (Washington, D.C.: American Theatre Association, 1979), pp. 21–30.

The drama corner of this classroom features a display of puppets, a reproduction of Shakespeare's Globe Theatre, and a *Hamlet* poster.

Finally, learning is made more enjoyable when it is dramatized. Often children who have difficulty with other classroom tasks find success and a place for themselves in drama, a discovery that gives them a renewed interest in learning. Those who need challenges beyond the traditional curriculum find an avenue of learning in drama that goes as deep as they are willing to probe. As Winifred Ward, a pioneer in creative drama in the United States once said as a final reason for engaging in classroom drama, "Fun—just plain fun! Is there any schoolroom which would not be better off with more of it?"[28]

WILL I BE ABLE TO DO IT?

For both the leader and the children, drama may be an adventure and an exploration into a new style of teaching and learning. It may take time to build the confidence needed to venture forth. But experimentation and the leeway to fail and try again are essential to the learning process. Just as we allow children to learn in this manner, we must allow it of ourselves, too.

It is hoped that this text will make classroom drama understandable, practical, meaningful, and enjoyable for everyone. Both the children's and

[28]Winifred Ward, *Stories to Dramatize* (New Orleans: Anchorage Press, 1952, 1981), p. 2.

the leader's needs have been kept in mind in order to ensure maximum success. The intent is to provide you with as many techniques, ideas, and materials as possible so that you will have many choices and alternatives. It is hoped that this approach will provide exciting learning experiences for your students and yourself. Welcome aboard!

FOR THE COLLEGE STUDENT

1. Using some of the materials in Virginia Koste's *Dramatic Play in Childhood* (Lanham, Md.: University Press of America, 1987), discuss your own observations of children or your recollections from your own childhood. What do these experiences and observations teach you about the use of drama in the elementary classroom?

2. Discuss with your classmates your early experiences with drama in school or in other settings. What are your remembrances of them? Are there both pleasant and unpleasant memories? Identify them as specifically as you can. How might you increase the pleasant experiences and diminish the unpleasant ones for your students?

3. Study the current curriculum goals and objectives in your state or local area. Is drama mentioned or implied in the teaching of basic skills, the fine arts, or other areas? What specific goals and objectives have been identified? Should others be added? What teacher resource materials in creative drama are made available from your state's department of education? Report on your findings in class.

SELECTED BIBLIOGRAPHY

Creative Drama

COTTRELL, JUNE, *Creative Drama in the Classroom, Grades 1–3 and Grades 4–6.* Lincolnwood, Ill.: National Textbook Company, 1987. These companion texts are theatre arts resource guides for the elementary classroom teacher.

HALL, MARY ANN, and PAT HALE, *Capture Them with Magic.* Charlottesville, Va.: New Plays, 1982. This small text is highly useful for teachers of young children, with many practical ideas for incorporating drama into language arts and science.

HEINIG, RUTH BEALL, *Creative Drama Resource Book for Kindergarten through Grade 3,* and *Creative Drama Resource Book for Grades 4 through 6.* Englewood Cliffs, N.J.: Prentice-Hall, 1987. These two companion texts are theatre arts resource guides for elementary teachers.

KASE-POLISINI, JUDITH, *The Creative Drama Book: Three Approaches.* New Orleans: Anchorage Press, 1988. This text, written by a widely respected leader in the field, explains three teaching methodologies of creative drama as currently practiced: playmaking, theatre games, and educational drama. An introductory text for students and practitioners alike, it encourages readers to develop their own unique style.

KASE-POLISINI, JUDITH, ed., *Creative Drama in a Developmental Context.* Lanham, Md.: University Press of America, 1985.

————, *Creative Drama and Learning.* Lanham, Md.: University Press of America, 1986. These two texts contain presentations made at five symposia on creative drama, sponsored by the American Alliance for Theatre and Education and held at universities in Canada and the United States over a five-year period.

McCASLIN, NELLIE, *Creative Drama in the Primary Grades,* and *Creative Drama in the Intermediate Grades.* New York: Longman, 1987. These two companion texts are theatre arts resource guides for the elementary classroom teacher.

————, *Creative Drama in the Classroom* (5th ed.). New York: Longman, 1990. This widely used introductory text on creative drama presents both theory and practical application. It covers the usual topics of pantomime, improvisation, story dramatization, and formal production. Other topics include such areas as theatre-in-education, clowning and circus arts, puppetry and mask-making.

POLSKY, MILTON, *Let's Improvise.* Lanham, Md.: University Press of America, 1989. This book gives many useful ideas for leading improvisation activities with a variety of groups and settings.

ROSENBERG, HELANE S., *Creative Drama and Imagination: Transforming Ideas into Action.* New York: Holt, Rinehart and Winston, 1987. Beginning with a historical overview of creative drama and a theoretical foundation in imagination, this text introduces the Rutgers Imagination Method (RIM) of teaching creative drama. Activities and examples of this approach, developed by Rosenberg and her associates at Rutgers University, form the second half of the book.

SALISBURY, BARBARA T., *Theatre Arts in the Elementary Classroom Kindergarten through Grade 3,* and *Theatre Arts in the Elementary Classroom Grade 4 through Grade 6.* New Orleans: Anchorage Press, 1986. These two companion books are specifically designed for the elementary classroom teacher who may be required to teach drama but who has little or no training.

SCHER, ANNA, and CHARLES VERRALL, *One Hundred Plus Ideas for Drama.* Portsmouth, N.H.: Heinemann Educational Books, 1981. This practical listing of numerous activities, including games, pantomimes, improvisations, and verbal exercises was followed by *Another One Hundred Plus Ideas for Drama,* 1987.

SCHWARTS, DOROTHY THAMES, and DOROTHY ALDRICH, eds., *Give Them Roots . . . and Wings!* New Orleans: Anchorage Press, 1985. This manual is the combined work of several creative drama leaders and is a useful resource for the beginning teacher. It covers creative movement and pantomime, characterization, improvisation, dialogue, and story dramatization, with many sample lessons.

SIKS, GERALDINE BRAIN, *Drama with Children* (2nd ed.). New York: Harper & Row, 1983. This presentation by a well-known drama leader and author focuses on her development of "process-centered drama" as a means of teaching theatre concepts to children. It includes numerous drama activities and lessons.

SPOLIN, VIOLA, *Improvisation for the Theatre.* Evanston, Ill.: Northwestern University Press, 1963. This well-known text is considered a classic in its presentation of improvisation. A section is devoted to working with children.

————, *Theatre Games for the Classroom: A Teacher's Handbook.* Evanston, Ill.: Northwestern University Press, 1986. This is an adaptation of Spolin's original work, made more accessible to the elementary classroom teacher.

STEWIG, JOHN W., *Informal Drama in the Elementary Language Arts Program.* New York: Teachers College Press, 1983. In this text the author presents his rationale for the incorporation of creative drama into the language arts curriculum. A number of language arts activities and references to children's literature are made throughout.

WARD, WINIFRED, *Playmaking with Children*. New York: Appleton-Century-Crofts, 1957. This text is the American classic in the field of creative drama written by "the first lady of child drama" in the United States. It discusses drama in elementary and junior high school as well as drama in recreation, religious education, and therapy. The emphasis is on story dramatization.

————, *Stories to Dramatize*. New Orleans: Anchorage Press, 1981. A collection of many fine stories and poems suitable for dramatization with children ages five to fourteen. A brief introduction explains the story dramatization procedure as Ward developed it.

WAY, BRIAN, *Development through Drama*. Atlantic Highlands, N.J.: Humanities Press, 1967. A well-known British drama educator presents his philosophy, focusing on development of the whole person. Included are a number of practical exercises and activities in sensory awareness, imagination, speech, and improvisation.

WILDER, ROSILYN, *A Space Where Anything Can Happen*. Charlottesville, Va.: New Plays, 1977. This guidebook is based on one leader's personal experience in a drama program in a middle school. Many techniques and ideas are presented in the author's description of her procedures.

Drama in Education

BOLTON, GAVIN, *Towards a Theory of Drama in Education*. New York: Longman, 1979. Using classroom examples, a well-known British drama educator presents his theories and outlines a drama approach which combines children's play and elements of theatre.

————, *Drama as Education*. New York: Longman, 1984. Subtitled "An Argument for Placing Drama at the Centre of the Curriculum," this text presents a British drama educator's theories as well as helpful analyses of a number of educational drama techniques.

CRANSTON, JERNERAL W., *Transformations through Drama*. Lanham, Md.: University Press of America, 1991. This guide to educational drama for kindergarten through grade eight acknowledges the influence of Dorothy Heathcote. Chapters such as "Learning and the Brain" and "Cooperative Learning" lend uniqueness. Sample drama lessons clarify the philosophy and provide practical material for curriculum integration.

DAVIES, GEOFF, *Practical Primary Drama*. Portsmouth, N.H.: Heinemann Educational Books, 1983. As its title suggests, this slim volume is practical and highly readable. The author studied with Dorothy Heathcote and presents a simplified version of a number of her techniques.

FOX, MEM, *Teaching Drama to Young Children*. Portsmouth, N.H.: Heinemann Educational Books, 1987. A highly practical and lively guide for teachers working in drama with the young. The Australian author is also a well-known writer of children's books.

JOHNSON, LIZ, and CECILY O'NEILL, eds., *Collected Writings on Education and Drama; Dorothy Heathcote*. Evanston Ill.: Northwestern University Press, 1991. Dorothy Heathcote is perhaps the most widely known drama educator in the world today. This is the only collection of her writings, originally published by Hutchinson & Co. in 1984.

MORGAN, NORAH, and JULIANA SAXTON, *Teaching Drama: A Mind of Many Wonders.* Portsmouth, N.H.: Heinemann Educational Books, 1987. The authors have presented a very clear description of the theories underlying teaching in role. Expecially useful for beginners are the many helpful tips on teachers' questions and answers and listing of various types of drama strategies and techniques.

NEELANDS, JONOTHAN, *Making Sense of Drama.* Portsmouth, N.H.: Heinemann Educational Books, 1984. This is a useful book in focusing on planning dramas, with examples from the author's own teaching experiences with students at the intermediate level.

O'NEILL, CECILY, and ALAN LAMBERT, *Drama Structures.* Portsmouth, N.H.: Heinemann Educational Books, 1982. This teaching handbook, developed by two British drama educators, is divided into four sections: theoretical basis, four drama structures, checklists for drama lessons, and encouragement for teachers to develop their own approaches to drama. Although focus is on the intermediate and secondary grades, the information is universal.

O'NEILL, CECILY, ALAN LAMBERT, ROSEMARY LINELL, and JANET WARR-WOOD, *Drama Guidelines.* Portsmouth, N.H.: Heinemann Educational Books, 1977. This handbook presents detailed descriptions of drama lessons taught by British teachers in kindergarten through grade 12. It includes a statement of the aims of drama teaching and examines the leader's role.

SHUMAN, R. BAIRD, ed., *Educational Drama for Today's Schools.* Metuchen, N.J.: Scarecrow, 1978. This book presents a variety of essays on some of the uses of drama—such as in language development and moral development—by several authors, including Dorothy Heathcote and Betty Jane Wagner. An extensive annotated bibliography is also included.

SWARTZ, LARRY, *Dramathemes: A Practical Guide for Teaching Drama.* Portsmouth, N.H.: Heinemann Educational Books, 1988. This very helpful beginning handbook for teachers uses a variety of literary sources. Each of the ten lessons presented focuses on a theme and provides a notion of how children have responded to the activities.

TARLINGTON, CAROLE, and PATRICK VERRIOUR, *Role Drama.* Portsmouth, N.H.: Heinemann Educational Books, 1991. This highly practical text gives an overview of role drama and includes descriptions of three dramas based on original and folk tale sources: "A Fierce Dragon," "Rumplestiltskin," and "The Pied Piper."

WAGNER, BETTY JANE, *Dorothy Heathcote: Drama as a Learning Medium.* Washington, D.C.: National Education Association, 1976. Wagner, an American language arts educator, wrote this early account of the procedures and techniques used in drama by British educator Dorothy Heathcote. The author carefully describes Heathcote's philosophy and practice with specific examples. Chapter headings focus on Heathcote's unique terminology, such as "edging in" and "dropping to the universal."

Drama in Special Settings or with Special Populations

BARRAGAR, PAM, *Spiritual Understanding through Creative Drama.* Valley Forge: Judson Press, 1981. With a particular emphasis on Dorothy Heathcote's methods, the author shows how to use drama in religious education.

BURGER, ISABEL B., *Creative Drama and Religious Education.* Wilton, Conn.: Morehouse-Barlow, 1977. The author's many years of work in creative drama and children's theatre bring much insight and practicality to this useful text.

————, *Creative Drama for Senior Adults*. Wilton, Conn.: Morehouse-Barlow, 1980. In this text the author applies her many years of work with creative drama to a different, but equally receptive, population.

JENNINGS, SUE, *Remedial Drama: A Handbook for Teachers and Therapists*. New York: Theatre Arts Books, 1974. This text was one of the first to explore, in readable fashion, the use of drama in therapeutic settings.

LANDY, ROBERT J., *Drama Therapy: Concepts and Practices*. Springfield, Ill.: Charles C. Thomas, 1986. This text is written for students preparing to work in the field of drama therapy.

NOBLEMAN, ROBERTA, *Using Creative Drama Outside the Classroom*. Charlottesville, Va.: New Plays, 1974. This practical guide explains how to teach creative drama in various community and recreational settings.

PEREIRA, NANCY, *Creative Dramatics in the Library*. Charlottesville, Va.: New Plays, 1974. Helpful tips are presented in this text for ways to begin drama, using time and space, handling groups of children, coordinating visual aids, and culminating activities in a library setting.

SCHATTNER, GURTRUD, and RICHARD COURTNEY, eds., *Drama in Therapy* (2 vols.). New York: Drama Book Publishers, 1981. This important collection presents the work of many practitioners and writers in the field of drama therapy.

TELANDER, MARCIE, FLORA QUINLAN, and KAROL VERSON, *Acting Up!* Chicago: Coach House Press, 1982. Written by the founding directors of a performing company, this text explains the improvisational techniques used by older actors who write and perform their own work.

THURMAN, ANNE, and CAROL ANNE PIGGINS, *Drama Activities with Older Adults: A Handbook for Leaders*. New York: Haworth Press, 1982. This highly practical text covers a multitude of activities for a special population.

WETHERED, AUDREY G., *Drama and Movement in Therapy*. London: MacDonald and Evans, 1973. This is a brief yet clear text on the therapeutic use of movement, pantomime, and drama. It provides a good introduction for the nonspecialist in this field.

2

Creative Drama Instruction
Some Basics

As has already been stated, the focus in creative drama is on the creative process of drama rather than on some finished product such as a well-mounted play. How does drama instruction, in practice, differ from "putting on a play"? What is it that the drama leader does when guiding children in creative drama? This chapter will explore some of these basic questions.

CREATIVE DRAMA GOALS

In creative drama, as with many other curricular areas in the elementary school, there are multiple goals that can be identified. Generally these include the following:

1. Drama–theatre goals (for example, pantomime, dialogue improvisation)
2. Personal development goals (for example, creativity, self-control, cooperative group work, self-confidence)
3. Additional curricular or other subject-matter goals (for example, career education, health and safety)

Any one of these goals can be a justifiable reason for undertaking creative drama. But to maximize limited teaching time in the classroom, teachers usually try to identify and emphasize several goals and objectives in each lesson.

Notice also (again, as with other areas of the curriculum) that the goals and subgoals can easily, and often do, overlap and intertwine. For example, some leaders might list creativity under drama–theatre goals rather than under personal development goals, whereas others might place it under all three goals. We need not become overly concerned about our labeling of goals and subgoals and what gets placed where. All of them are important, and we will want to see that they are a part of the curriculum in whatever way they can be covered.

DRAMA–THEATRE GOALS

Many of the drama goals are derived from formal theatre. You need to be familiar with them, as they will guide you in constructing drama activities and lessons.

Dramatic Structure

The basic components of a play are plot line, character, and setting. A plot develops with a beginning, which introduces the story with its characters and setting; a middle, which presents the problem or conflict the characters face; and an ending, which contains the resolution to the problem and brings the story to a close. In drama children can learn to recognize this dramatic structure. They should have opportunities to enact characters in a variety of situations and stories, experiencing their conflicts and their attempts to deal with them. They will also be creating and enacting their own plots.

Conflict

Conflict, or the struggle between opposing forces, is the main ingredient in dramatic structure. This struggle, whether comic or serious, arrests our attention and sustains our interest in the plot until it is resolved and the story ends.

Generally, there are five kinds of conflict. Characters may struggle *against nature,* as does the little spider in the simple action song "The Itsy Bitsy Spider," who is washed down the drain spout. A character may struggle *against another person*—as does Tom Sawyer, who has differences with both Aunt Polly and cousin Sid. An example of struggle *against society* would be Andersen's "Ugly Duckling," who is faced with the dilemma of living in a society that does not accept him. There are characters who struggle *against technology,* as Homer Price does when he cannot get the doughnut machine to stop. In the final and perhaps most abstract and complex type of conflict, characters may struggle *against themselves,* as does Pinocchio, whose goal to become human is thwarted by his own internal weakness.

Conflict is also needed to create suspense and dramatic tension. Suspense keeps us in a state of anticipation over the outcome of the problem. It causes us to wonder what will happen next and keeps the drama interesting.

In creative drama you will consider conflict and dramatic tension repeatedly, searching for ways to incorporate them into each activity and each lesson you teach. Children should learn to identify, enact, and see alternatives for various kinds of conflict and their resolutions. Younger children can identify conflict as a "problem to be solved" and should be able to understand the four simpler types of conflict. Older students will be able to understand the more abstract, fifth (internal) type of conflict.

Movement and Pantomime

The plot of any dramatic story is carried out by the characters' actions. Movement and pantomime help to express that action. In drama children are encouraged to move rhythmically, freely, and creatively, but with attention to thought and discipline.

Pantomime is detailed movement which expresses specific ideas, emotions, characters, and situations. In drama, children will communicate through pantomime for their own expressive satisfaction as well as to convey meaning to others.

Younger children, whose bodies are often in constant motion, need the frequent physical activity that drama provides. Older children, who have been conditioned to sitting at desks and saving physical movement for the gymnasium, may be somewhat self-conscious about movement and pantomime activities in the classroom. Eventually, both younger and older children should feel comfortable and successful with their expressive abilities in movement and pantomime.

Sensory Awareness

Sensory awareness is central to drama, as it is to all learning. Our basic knowledge of the world around us is derived from our sensory experiences with it. Through our senses we make observations, comparisons, and discriminations, and form our perceptions about the nature of things. We store our sensory experiences and retrieve them when we use expressive language and movement and when we listen to or read the thoughts of others. Drama should expand children's sensory awareness and strengthen their imaginative powers. As a result, it should increase their abilities to experience life with greater meaning.

Emotional Attitudes and Behaviors

In drama children have many opportunities to interpret and express feelings and emotions. They should be exposed to a wide range of emotions, experiencing them through facial expression, body movement and pantomime, vocal tone, and improvised speech. They will also need to play a variety of roles, taking on the emotional attitudes of others. All this should progress toward a greater understanding of what motivates behaviors and why people behave as they do.

Characterization

In a play, it is the characters who initiate and carry out the plot. They must be believable in order that we may identify with them and care about what happens to them. As children are exposed to various characters in literature and the roles people play in life, they will take on their physical, mental, and emotional attitudes. Younger children should be able to portray successfully the actions and attitudes of simple characters, including animals, personified objects, and people. As children mature and grow in awareness of other points of view, their interpretations and portrayals should demonstrate more sophisticated understandings. By playing different roles in a variety of situations, their insight into others' feelings, attitudes and behaviors should also increase.

Verbal Skills and Dialogue

Characters express meaning through verbal and nonverbal interaction with others. In drama children will be expressing their own ideas and attempting to understand the messages of others. This wide range of experiences will incorporate pantomime, vocal sound effects, and vocal interpretation. Imitative speech will be used as children reenact familiar scenes from stories.

Drama also offers opportunities in improvised speech and dialogue interaction. These language experiences evolve when children reenact situations in stories, expressing their interpretations of those scenes. Language is also explored in drama when children take on the roles of people thrust into a variety of predicaments. How they work themselves out of those dilemmas often depends on the language strategies they use.

GUIDING CREATIVE DRAMA

Working with children in creative drama requires the constant use of skills in group management. Many of the skills can be fairly easily acquired with practice, whereas others may take a longer time to master. We will take a beginning look at the leader's role in the next section; a more thorough presentation will be given in Chapter 3.

The Leader's Role

Because creative drama is a planned learning experience, the leader has the responsibility of designing and organizing the lessons. Inexperienced leaders are often not sure they should plan, direct, or even incorporate disciplined attitudes into creative drama lessons for fear of stifling their own and the children's imagination. But groups need organization, people need limits, and creativity needs disciplined structure.

In addition, the leader must design and organize the lessons according to the group's abilities. The group's personality, age, needs, and interests must also be considered. To tax children beyond their capabilities frustrates them; to underestimate their abilities stifles their thinking and leads to boredom.

At the same time, leaders must consider their own personality, style of teaching, and feelings of confidence. They must continually assess their own progress as well as that of the group so that they can guide with the greatest sensitivity and flexibility.

Children's Participation

Children may participate in creative drama in several ways. They may participate as observers, discussants, analyzers, or players. Their participation will vary according to their interest in the topic, their mood, their confidence, and their awareness of their own needs.

Shy Children.   There is a natural tendency for many leaders to feel that children will want to participate immediately in all drama activities. Some may feel that if children are not actively participating, they are not benefiting from the activity or even enjoying it. However, shy children are often more comfortable watching their peers for a while before joining in. Forcing reticent children to participate before they are ready only increases their reluctance. The leader's understanding of children's hesitations and acceptance of the fact that some children need time will eventually give reluctant ones the courage to participate.

Forcing shy children to participate only increases their reluctance.

Outgoing children often want immediate and continuous involvement in drama.

Outgoing Children. On the other hand, many children want to be involved in as much of the playing as possible rather than watching their classmates. They often have difficulty waiting their turn. Although they can appreciate each other's contributions and can work together cooperatively, the fun of the activities is so compelling that they usually want immediate and continuous involvement.

These children may need frequent reminding of the limits and rules in playing. Sometimes their involvement is superficial and they need to be cajoled and pushed toward higher achievements. This can be done good-naturedly, but then with quiet seriousness if the point is missed.

DRAMA ACTIVITY VARIABLES

This text is designed to help beginning drama leaders progress through the activities and related teaching skills step-by-step, from the easier to the more difficult. The activities that are easier for the children to play are usually easier for you to teach; the same is true for the more difficult activities. To help you see this progression, eight drama activity variables have been identified. They are listed in the chart on page 28 on a continuum of easier to more advanced, with the variables in the left-hand column *generally* being easier than the more advanced ones in the right-hand column.

The qualification "generally" is made since there can be exceptions. For example, older children who are highly verbal but self-conscious about their bodies' rapid changes may find it easier to undertake verbal activities before pantomime. Likewise, they may feel more comfortable playing in groups (rather than engaging in solo or individual playing in unison) because of their strong need to be with peers. A leader's own degree of skill or natural ability with any one of the variables may also affect the general continuum indicated in the chart. Some leaders, even if they are beginners, will have no trouble keeping groups organized in space; others will find it a real challenge. Nevertheless, the chart is useful as a general guideline.

Continuum of drama activity variables

Easier	*to more* Advanced
1. Use of desk area	Use of larger areas of space
2. Teacher direction	Creative or independent thinking
3. Pantomime	Verbal
4. Solo (individual) playing	Pair and group work
5. Unison playing for one's own satisfaction	Playing to share or communicate with observers
6. Humorous or "light" material	Highly dramatic or "serious" material
7. Minimal information content	High data content
8. Run-through playing	In-depth playing for greater involvement

In the next section these variables will be discussed in detail. They will also be referred to throughout the text and should become increasingly clear as you move through it.

The Use of Space (Variable 1)

One of the basic concerns in working with groups is keeping them organized physically. One of the simplest remedies is to limit the space in which they are allowed to work. Contrary to many other books on creative drama, this one does not encourage a beginning drama leader to use large areas of playing space. Teachers are frequently told to use gymnasiums or activity rooms for creative drama, but having a gymnasium to work in can be more of a curse than a blessing. The space is so open that voices echo and meaningful communication is lost. Furthermore, children usually associate a gym with active sports and the chance to blow off steam. Their anticipation of doing that rather than experiencing drama can be frustrating to them, which causes more problems for you. Large all-purpose rooms can create similar problems. More often than not, the regular classroom provides sufficient space for the beginning teacher, and even the use of that fairly well-defined space requires a number of considerations.

Playing at the desk area provides control as well as psychological security.

For many drama experiences the children's desks are the most logical playing area. In fact, desks have important psychological advantages. First of all, the desk area is a convenient and concrete tactile boundary that defines the working space, separating the children from each other and minimizing distractions. The desk is also a comfortable territory for shy children who may need the security it provides.

Using the desk area is important for assuring initial teaching success. Most beginners would agree that it is difficult enough to concentrate on the drama lesson itself without the additional worry of keeping thirty active children organized in space. In fact, using a desk activity as a warm-up before moving to larger areas of space will often be a helpful procedure in each drama lesson you teach—even after you become skilled.

Directed–Creative Activities (Variable 2)

The activities the leader uses for creative drama fall on a line that might be called a continuum of creativity. At one end of this continuum are the activities that tell children what to do and have strong structure built in. At the other end of the continuum are the activities the children create on their own with minimum guidance from the leader.

Eventually a leader is able to determine how much direction or creative latitude a particular group needs. Challenges are offered, but the leader also knows how to change to an easier activity if a creative one just will not work. The leader also learns how much independence a group can handle and how much organizational help it needs.

Pantomime—Verbal Activities (Variable 3)

For young children, movement is their natural means of exploring and discovering. They integrate themselves physically with whatever interests them; rarely do they passively observe. Language development progresses rapidly, and the verbal skills of older elementary children are quite advanced compared with the younger ones. With all this in mind we cautiously make a very general assumption that pantomime activities are easier than verbal activities.

The exception to this rule, however, is that some older children may feel more comfortable with verbal activities than with pantomime not only because of their advanced verbal skills but also because of possible concerns about the physical changes their bodies are going through. Furthermore, since older children are usually given less opportunity for physical activity in the classroom than are younger children, they may consider movement and pantomime activities somewhat foreign. Therefore, flexibility and caution are needed with this variable.

Solo (Individual)—Pair and Group Playing (Variable 4)

As a general rule it is important to involve as many children in the playing as possible while still maintaining order and control. At times, the children will all work solo (individually) without interacting with others, which provides privacy and minimizes distractions. Both of these factors are essential for concentration.

Children may also work in pairs and in small groups, engaging in important social and cooperative learning. They can stimulate each other's thinking, integrate ideas, lend support, and experience compromise. Al-

Individual or solo playing lets students work by themselves and enjoy their own ideas.

though group process involves trials in power struggles and personality conflicts, it also affords the opportunity to combine the creative thoughts of several. Individual efforts thus become part of the greater whole.

Unison–Shared Playing (Variable 5)

Unison playing means that several or all of the children in the class are pantomiming or talking at the same time, whether by themselves, in pairs, or in groups. Each individual, pair, or group works privately, independently concentrating on their own ideas. This is true whether children are pantomiming the actions of a character in a story, interviewing each other in pairs, or planning a group scene.

Unison playing allows children the chance to enjoy their ideas without worrying about peer evaluation from the group as a whole. It gives them an opportunity to sort out their own thinking and to rehearse and polish their ideas before sharing them with classmates.

Another benefit of unison playing is the reduction in time spent waiting to take turns. Particularly for younger children and for older active ones who cannot bear to sit and wait—convinced that their turn will never come—unison playing is very satisfying.

Even though the major purpose of creative drama is to promote the development of the players rather than entertain an audience, children do share their ideas in the classroom, serving as an audience for each other. For some children, the knowledge that they may eventually share something with others sparks their interest and motivates them to do their best work. While they need an outlet for their creative expression, they also want someone to view their work and to respond. There may also be times when the children have a collective desire to share a particular activity with others outside the classroom community. And if an activity has so captured the attention and interest of the children that they have spent a great deal of time on it, it may even appear to be as rehearsed and polished as a formal production.

Humorous Material–Highly Dramatic Material (Variable 6)

As a general rule it is usually easier to work with materials that are humorous. Lighthearted activities and situations relax everyone and help build group rapport. If the characters are amusing, there is less pressure on the children to play the roles in a polished or formal way.

Yet, playing material rich in dramatic tension or conflict is often the most rewarding experience children can have. After all, life is not always a joke; there are many sad and hurtful times to balance the pleasant ones. There is no question that it is worth the time it takes to understand more serious material and to work at becoming involved in it. Surprisingly, the most unlikely children (for example, class clowns) are sometimes the ones who lead in the requests for challenging material once they have had a successful experience of being involved in it.

Minimal Information Content–High Data Content (Variable 7)

This variable, quite simply, refers to the amount of curricular information the leader wishes to incorporate into an activity. If children are asked to pantomime "something you like to do" as opposed to "an export from Chile," there is obviously a difference in the amount of information recall involved. Or, when working with historical data, there will be a need to check accuracy of facts, perhaps even stopping to research needed information before continuing the drama.

Run-through Playing–In-depth Involvement (Variable 8)

In rehearsing a play, the term *run-through* is often used. As its name implies, the purpose is to get an overview or a total picture of an idea rather than to focus on a concentrated or intense study of it. An analogy might be made to the subject of reading. At times, we skim printed material; at other times, we read for greater understanding. In-depth involvement, on the other hand, requires the expending of greater effort.

Generally speaking, the success of drama experiences, as measured by both the leader and the children, is dependent on the degree of the players' involvement in their work. The leader's encouragement of children's concentration and involvement in drama is crucial in helping them go beyond a superficial level of playing to more meaningful experiences. Since this variable is so important and will require many skills from the leader, this special section is devoted to a more complete exploration of it.[1]

Identifying Involvement

According to one writer, there is an aesthetic dimension which distinguishes many play activities and is crucial to validating the claim that creative drama develops the whole person. "At the moment of doing," she states, "when nothing outside the situation matters, there emerges a sense of ultimate integration: a fusion of the person with his or her surroundings."[2] A distinguished researcher in psychology, comments on the "autotelic" (meaning that goals are self-contained in the activity) nature of drama, describing it this way:

> When everything is right—the challenges and skills are well meshed, the concentration deep, the goals clear, feedback sharp, distractions minimized, self-consciousness absent—actors and spectators achieve ecstasy. That is, they step outside accustomed reality, and feel with all possible concreteness an-

[1]Dorothy Heathcote made famous the terms *building belief* and *commitment to the drama*, which have similar meanings to the term *involvement* described here. For an extended discussion of her methods in achieving this goal, see Chapter 7, "Building Belief," in Betty Jane Wagner, *Dorothy Heathcote: Drama as a Learning Medium* (Washington, D.C.: National Education Association, 1976).

[2]Maureen Mansell, "Dimensions of Play Experience," *Communication Education*, 29, no. 1 (1980), 48.

Involvement means believing what you are doing.

other dimension of existence. For all they know at the moment, they are in a different reality. This feeling is what drama is about.[3]

It is this experience the leader constantly assesses in the children's playing and assists them in achieving.

Even the beginning teacher knows when children are engrossed in any classroom work. One can see the furrowed brow of concentration, the oblivious attitude to disruptions, and the look of pleasure and satisfaction that acknowledges a job well done. Similar moments in drama show children so absorbed and engrossed that they are unaware of anyone observing them. Perhaps they enjoy the material so much that they forget about everyone else, or perhaps they are able to block out distractions successfully.

When they are involved, children often demonstrate a detailed awareness of the experience they are enacting. For example, suppose children are asked to pretend they are walking a tightrope. We may observe a child stepping very carefully, placing one foot exactly ahead of the other, balancing the body with outstretched arms. Then she stops momentarily, gently swaying, eyes fixed straight ahead, arms moving as if in an attempt to regain a temporary loss of balance, and then slowly moves ahead. All these movements demonstrate that the pantomimer is very much aware of the

[3]Mihaly Csikszentmihalyi, "What's Interesting in Children's Theatre," in *Children's Theatre Creative Drama and Learning,* ed. Judith Kase-Polisini (Lanham, Md.: University Press of America, 1986), p. 14.

narrow rope suspended high above the ground and of the skills required of one who performs on it.

Another clue to involved playing is the spontaneous addition of details that the activity has not specified. The child mentioned above might also pretend to hold an imaginary umbrella for balance while bowing and throwing kisses to an enthusiastic but imaginary audience. Involved players concentrate intently and are usually highly pleased with their work. They may ask to repeat an activity and seem to be revitalized with each playing.

Involvement is also demonstrated when children eagerly enter into discussions, freely offering their opinions and ideas. They take on roles naturally, assuming the behaviors and attitudes of all manner of persons as well as animals and even inanimate objects.

When children are not absorbed, they may exhibit showing-off behavior. They often overact in a "hammy" way with physical and vocal exaggerations or make jokes and side comments in discussions. Being shy or insecure can also stand in the way of concentration and involvement. These children often giggle frequently, crowd against others in an attempt to disappear in the masses, or hesitantly look at other classmates to see what they are doing. They are silent during discussions or may offer only a few nervously mumbled words.

To complicate matters, there are times when the entire classroom responds as one person, all with the same depth of involvement or lack of it. At other times part of the class is involved while some children are only superficially involved.

The leader can be instrumental in making a drama experience as meaningful as possible. From the selection of the topic until the group's final playing of it, the leader has the opportunity to affect the involvement the children will have in it. A discussion of these points follows.

Selection of Topics

The first consideration is the selection of appropriate and meaningful topics. Children work best when they are intrigued. No one can respond to or concentrate on an idea that seems to be a waste of time. Leaders usually have to learn from their students what topics they find most appealing. Sometimes the easiest approach is to simply ask the children, "Would you like to do this?"

Groups also vary in personality. Some are satisfied only when topics amuse them. Others prefer to be involved in more serious encounters. Some groups have eclectic interests; others are quite finicky. Tastes and interests can be expanded, but that may take time.

Literature that captures children's attention may be something that thoroughly entertains or that encourages intense discussions and stimulates sincere concerns. Although many listings of books specify the age groups they are suited for, these are only guides and not sacred rules. You need to gauge which material is most interesting and meaningful for your particular group, regardless of its age level.

Topics should also appeal to you as leader, since your own involvement is usually contagious. Select ideas to which you can be committed and with which you feel confident, since you may need to "sell" it to a group who need additional proof that the subject is worth their attention.

Your choice of topics will naturally reflect your personality and interests. For this reason, you should periodically examine the nature of your favorite materials to see if they are meeting the needs of the children. You may discover that children have other interests, values, or concerns. And, you may need to reach beyond a limited sphere of interest in order to keep alert to new materials, and to listen with a sensitive ear to both the spoken and implied interests of the children.

Presentation of Materials

All material—whether it is music, props, pictures, literature, or simply an idea—is only as good a stimulus as your presentation makes it. As you tell a story, lead a discussion, or simply give directions, your overall attitude can establish the appropriate atmosphere for the playing.

Establishing Mood. You can convey the mood of certain materials with appropriate reactions. One may smile and laugh along with a humorous story or tell it in tongue-in-cheek fashion. In playing music the sensitive leader carefully fades it in and out rather than treating it abruptly. In showing a curious prop you can react with a measure of surprise in your voice when you ask, "Who do you suppose this could belong to? Have you ever seen anything like it before?"

A good story that is presented well captures attention.

Vocal quality, pitch, timing, and intensity of voice are all tools you can use to contribute meaning and understanding. Some leaders are able to convey a quiet, soft quality when describing the feel of a kitten's fur. They say the word *warm* and children feel it, or *tangy, crisp apple* and they almost taste it. A voice can creak like the door of a haunted house, moan like the wind, or boom like thunder. While there is no need to overdramatize or sound phony, one should be aware of the voice as a human musical instrument that has potential waiting to be tapped.

Aiding Concentration. To aid children's concentration it is wise to make appropriate room arrangements. For example, have children remove extraneous items from their desktops so they are not distracted by them. Arrange the room to accommodate both the presentation of the material and the playing. For example, don't move the class to the story corner to listen to a story if you intend to have them play it at the desk area. Shuffling them back and forth can break the mood of the story and the children's involvement in it.

It is imperative to be thoroughly familiar with literature you present. Even if a poem or story is well known or you have used it several times before, it should always be reviewed before presenting it again. Familiarity with the material eliminates the irritating tendency to omit crucial points, to mispronounce words, or to be halting and hesitant in delivery. Preparedness also frees you to concentrate on developing rapport with the children and judging the material's effect on them.

It also helps children's concentration if you prepare them for listening. Some leaders are particularly adept at captivating children's attention with storytelling. They begin a story and allow the first sentence or two to calm down a wiggly group or entice a listless one. Most teachers establish the rule that a story will not be shared until the children show they are ready to listen. Then they wait a moment or two until the children settle down. Or, children might be asked to lay their heads on their desks and close their eyes as aids to listening.

Discussions

Discussions are invaluable in drama. They focus the group's attention, probe its thoughts, and establish a questioning stance. Discussions often focus on universal questions:

"How does peer pressure affect a person's behavior?"
"What kind of person would it take to confront a giant?"
"What concerns would a pioneer have in starting life in a strange, new place?"

Analyzing Literature. Discussions can also help children understand and identify with specific characters or roles. Some literary characters are very simply drawn and may even be stereotypes. Folk-tale characters, particularly, are often one-dimensional, such as "wily fox," "curious child," or "proud king." Because of their simple characters, folk tales are usually the easiest type of literature to dramatize; they also offer the widest latitude of interpretation.

Generally speaking, the more complex the literature, the more developed the characters. It may take the author the length of a book to show us the many facets of a character. Charlotte the spider in *Charlotte's Web* or Johnny in *Johnny Tremain* are characters we learn a great deal about and are not likely to forget.

In playing different roles we may reflect on the ways others are similar to or different from us. Much of this information is revealed in the things that happen to the characters and how they feel and react to those events. Through discussion questions such as the following, students examine how they would react in similar instances:

> "The story doesn't tell us, but I wonder how 'Gertrude McFuzz' [see bibliography on p. 117] has her temper tantrum. What does she do, do you suppose?"
>
> "How do you think Johnny Tremain [65][4] felt when Isannah screamed that his scarred hand was 'dreadful'? If you were Johnny, how would you have felt?"
>
> "In *Shadow of a Bull* [87] there is one scene when all the boys merrily jump from a wagon of hay. All but Manolo; he's too afraid. What thoughts do you think are in Manolo's head when the boys suggest jumping? How do you think he feels? When have you been afraid of doing something the way Manolo is afraid of jumping?"

Discussion are often important if an experience is a culturally different one for the children:

> "Before we dramatize some scenes from *Call It Courage* [see bibliography in Chapter 6], let's talk about courage. What is courage to you? What are some things you think a courageous person might do? What is courage to Mafatu?"
>
> "James Huston vividly describes a very dramatic moment when Tiktaliktak [see bibliography in Chapter 6] gives up hope of surviving and builds himself a coffin. Why does he do that? What are his last thoughts as he carefully arranges his weapons by his side? Why does he want his relatives to understand the reason for his death?"

Discussion of literature is helpful in clarifying language and perceptions and in bringing experiences closer to the children's own. For example, in the poem "Foul Shot" (see bibliography on p. 113), the basketball player "measures the waiting net" and is "squeezed by silence." Children, asked to explain in their own words, might respond as follows:

> "He 'measures the waiting net' by holding the ball up to his eyes and aiming it really carefully."

[4]Throughout this text, numbers in parentheses correspond to the numbered anthologies and books listed in the final bibliography that begins on page 300.

"'Squeezed by silence' means you feel cramped inside because it is so quiet and everyone's watching you."

Through discussion children often discover that others share their ideas and their powerful feelings. They realize, "I guess I'm not the only person in the world who has felt that way." Besides clarifying ideas and feelings, such discussions also help set the mood for the playing.

Stimulating Awareness. Often you will be acquainting children with topics that are new to them. If you show them pictures or objects related to the topic, understanding and involvement will be reinforced. Before playing an experience on scuba diving, for example, you might show some fins, a mask, an oxygen tank, and perhaps some shells and a piece of dried seaweed, allowing the children to examine them and talk about them. Or before children role play young Helen Keller, you may ask them to close their eyes and explore various objects through their other senses.

As other examples, a film such as *Dream of the Wild Horses* (Contemporary Films, McGraw-Hill, 9 minutes, color) can illustrate the beauty of slowed movement. Or pictures from Edward Steichen's *Family of Man* (New York: Museum of Modern Art, 1955) can demonstrate the universality of human emotions. Such materials can create images and awareness that words alone cannot communicate.

PLAYING THE MATERIAL

A frequently asked question is, "How do you keep the kids from acting silly?" Most of the time children act silly because they do not know what to do, or because they are being asked to do something too difficult, or because they have not been fully prepared. The silliness simply comes from embarrassment. Without understanding this, it is easy to lose patience. And that adds to, rather than solves, the problem.

As was stated earlier, it is usually helpful to begin with humorous materials. In addition to its previously mentioned benefits, a little silliness or laughing when playing humorous material does not destroy the mood as easily as it does with dramatic material.

Playing Dramatic Material

Working with highly dramatic material does take additional and special considerations. Following are some suggestions.

Clarify the Nature of the Material and the Expectations You Have. Sometimes teachers assume that if children are told certain material is serious they will automatically respond appropriately. Many times this is not the case. Alerting and preparing children at the outset can save time later. For example, a teacher might say:

We've been studying about the relocation of Native Americans, and I thought we might be able to understand this idea a little better if we make a drama about it. This could take some real work on our part because it's not an easy topic. What do you think? Shall we try?

Encourage Quiet Reflection of Feelings.   Before children begin playing, ask them to speak aloud a brief thought their characters might be thinking. This technique is even more effective if you speak in a quiet voice and ask the children to close their eyes or cast them downward to avoid eye contact with others. Then go around the room placing a hand on each child's shoulder to cue him. This procedure lends a solemn ritual to the experience and helps curb giggling responses. The thoughts the characters speak may be very simple, "I'm afraid"; "I wonder what will happen now?"; "Is he really the person I think he is?"; "Why are we being called to this meeting?"; or any similar comment that relates to the scene.

At First, Play Briefly.   For initial attempts at in-depth involvement with dramatic material, it is best to keep the playing fairly brief. This can help children be less anxious about participating since the experience will be over before they have time to be embarrassed by it.

Brief playings are also easier on leaders since they will not have to work so long and hard at creating and sustaining the mood. An initial success will also bolster both the teacher's and the students' confidence for a longer playing another time.

Create the Appropriate Mood.   The vocal quality you use to introduce, discuss, and side-coach the material will make a great difference in conveying and sustaining the appropriate mood.

As in the theatre, the use of music, lights, and sound effects can also affect the mood, create a wealth of pictorial images, and stimulate the imagination. Numerous selections of music—both classical and popular—can lend sadness, intrigue, and suspense and provide appropriate background for your voice. When the room is dimmed, children can more easily imagine dark tunnels, mysterious underwater worlds, ancient ruins, or the Arctic. Quickly flashing classroom lights on and off can simulate lightning, neon signs, the glitter of an ice world, and the like.

Sound effects can have a similar influence. In some social studies books it is noted that the sound of fife and drum accompanied Nathan Hale to his place of execution. If children were to dramatize this moment, it might be intensified by the ominous sound of drumming of fingers on the desktops.

Create a Good Working Climate by Limiting Distractions.   Separating students from each other can lessen distractions and aid concentration. Dimmed lights can, in addition to providing a mood, help students focus on their own work.

Keeping your eyes closed can help focus your thinking.

Another aid is having students close their eyes. (Particularly when they are playing individually and are in limited space, having their eyes closed will not pose a problem.) Not only does this help block out distractions, it helps children visualize the experience. Often children adopt this aid on their own after realizing its usefulness in making the playing more involving and hence more satisfying for them.

Ask children what helps them concentrate and what distracts them. Even young children can list such things as "having other kids too near me, especially touching me"; "my best friend making faces at me"; or "I don't like it if someone watches me." This information can be helpful to you in making working conditions more favorable to individual students as well as to the whole class.

After children have given behavioral evidence that they were involved in their playing, it is helpful to have them describe it.

"When I was being the bird with a broken wing, I remembered how hard it was to do anything with my right arm when it was in a cast all last summer."

"When I was being one of those explorers on the *Kon-Tiki* [see bibliography in Chapter 6], I remembered what it was like when my dad and I were in a canoe

Distractions can keep a person from concentrating fully.

and it capsized. If we had been closer to the rapids, we might not have made it. I wasn't scared then, but I was afterward when I thought about it."

Select Volunteers for Initial Playings.   Although you will want to let as many students as possible participate in drama activities, in some cases it is a wise precaution to start with just a few who can be the most easily involved. Particularly when trying out new material and the group's response cannot be predicted, there is no point in taking chances with an entire class. The first players can be a model for subsequent replayings and can set a mood for others to build on.

You might also ask for volunteers "who can really concentrate on this idea and be involved in it." Sometimes children who already have their hands raised for volunteering will think again about this requirement and wait it out. This gives them the chance to self-evaluate and avoid for the moment what they think they are not yet ready to handle. Surprisingly, many students do have an awareness of their own limitations and are willing to approach a task with caution.

Build Belief and Commitment over Time.   Particularly for extended dramas, such as themed lessons and role dramas, it will be necessary to keep involvement sustained over a long period of time. Typical activities that assist in bonding children to extended drama experiences might include brainstorming and listing ideas; writing autobiographies of characters or roles being played; drawing pictures; writing letters or newspaper articles; interviewing characters; and the like.

Side-coaching

Side-coaching is a technique in drama in which the leader gives suggestions or comments from the sidelines to heighten and advance as well as control the playing. It is literally "talking the children through" an experience and is an indispensable aid to encouraging concentration and involvement. Side-coaching can also fill in awkward silences, giving security to those who are unsure and guidance to those who might need calming down. Frequently a group's lukewarm response to an idea changes to excited involvement with expert side-coaching from an enthusiastic leader.

There are many occasions for side-coaching, although you will probably never know exactly how much and what kind of side-coaching will be necessary until you see the children's response. Side-coaching is a skill that will grow with experience and with your own sensitivity to your students' needs.

Leader Participation

A leader actively participates in many drama activities. At first this may sound as if you are taking something away from the children. However, the leader plays roles to facilitate the drama, provide a model of commitment, lead communication toward deeper levels of meaning, and shape the dramatic structure. This is true no matter if the children are creating an improvised play from a story or are engaged in role drama. When you play a role, you give students a character or situation to respond to. It helps set the scene, create the mood, and highlight the dramatic tension. In a story dramatization, you can play a role to assist children with dialogue and mapping out the scene locations. By playing with the students you also demonstrate a willingness to accept the same challenges you are offering them.

EVALUATION AND REFLECTION

When you and the students evaluate your work, you increase the possibility of deeper involvement in subsequent playings. When students are asked to say what they liked about their playing, they are verbally reinforcing themselves.

When you evaluate what students have done, be as specific as possible. Saying "good," although it is nice to hear, does not really give the students enough information. However, if you say, "Good ideas! Your advice to the queen shows your concern for her problem," or, "Good control. You stayed right with the music," students understand your judgment better and also know what to repeat in further playings.

Believability is an important goal: "Good pantomiming; I could really see some zoo animals that time" or "Your robots were so believable, I almost wondered for a minute if my fourth graders had disappeared!" These comments place a premium on the look of reality, achieved only by disciplined imaginative thinking.

Evaluation of the drama's effectiveness can also be measured by a reflective discussion afterward, exploring the broader questions raised by the drama. For example, after playing a drama about solving a mystery, a class discussed the recent discovery of new evidence to explain aviatrix Amelia Earhart's disappearance in 1937. With the leader they reflected on the nature of mysteries, why they intrigue us, how clues may be contradictory, and how some mysteries may never be solved conclusively. Students are better able to relate such discussions to their own lives after experiencing them in drama.

Without students' self-evaluation, the leader's evaluative guidance, and reflective discussions, drama work will usually be superficial in the long run. Only when careful attention is given to all aspects of the playing will the best results occur.

REPLAYING

Often you will be replaying drama activities. Seldom does the best creative thinking and the deepest understanding emerge in a first playing of a drama game, a dialogue scene, or a story, even if you and the students are experienced in drama work.

You may play some activities three times, even in one session. The first playing might be a run-through in order to get a total picture. In a second playing students may add new ideas, drop out less effective ones, and do further refining and polishing. A third playing can produce a final synthesis of ideas.

It is helpful for you and the students to realize that your best work may not be achieved immediately. Taking an experimental viewpoint is comforting to anxious students and will allay your own fears, too. It is equally important to *verbalize* this concept—for your own sake as well as the children's.

"We've never done this before. Let's just try it and see what happens."

"I thought we did well for our first time with this scene. What did you think was particularly good—and where might we make some changes for the next time?"

All the techniques just discussed will play an important part in helping you lead children to greater involvement in their playing over time. Sometimes you will be amazed at how easily it happens; at other times you will be disappointed because you are not getting the response you expected immediately. But once students have experienced in-depth involvement in drama work, they will often not be satisfied with superficial playing again. They may still need assistance in arriving at that goal. But with everyone working toward it, many more enriching experiences will be possible.

VENTURE FOR FREEDOM

The following is an extended example of a thirty-minute activity with a fifth grade class during their fourth session of creative drama. It demonstrates many of the techniques for encouraging involvement.

Noteworthy is the fact that there was lengthy preparation in order to guide the understanding and to establish a strong, serious mood and a sense of deep involvement. The physical activity itself involved walking only about six feet. The drama event was focused literally on only about three sentences of text. But the understanding of the event, as well as the emotions involved, required much discussion and work.

The leader guided the children through three discussions and three playings. After thirty minutes of work, all the children had become involved in what developed into a very moving experience.

The children and the teacher grouped themselves on the floor at one end of the room. The teacher introduced the book *Venture for Freedom* (93), explaining that it was a true story based on the experience of a captured African tribe and of an African king's son whose English name was Venture Smith. She read short, specific episodes describing the fatal beating of Venture's father; the day Venture sneaked down to the ship's hold to find his mother; and the moment the Africans disembarked into the blinding Barbados sun and slavery.

Then the teacher and the children discussed the following questions:

"What kind of people do you think they must have been to have a king who would die rather than betray his tribe?"

"The story gives us some idea of the grim condition in the ship's hold, but expanding on that with your imagination, what do you think the hold was like?"

"How must Venture have felt, knowing his mother was in that hold?"

"His mother told him to go back on deck and stay alive. How do you think she felt, saying that? How did Venture feel?"

"What do you think it was like to come out of the ship's hold, after so many weeks in the dark, into the blinding sun? What thoughts and feelings do you think they had?"

"How must Venture have felt, knowing that this would be the last time he would see his mother and his people?"

During the discussion the leader played the song "Sometimes I Feel Like a Motherless Child." She explained that it grew out of and reflected the sorrow of the slave-trading days.

The teacher asked the children to put themselves back into this time and into the lives of these Africans. The lights were turned off. They were to imagine that they were in the ship's hold and that the two chairs she had placed close together in the middle of the room represented the ship's disembarking plank. Slowly, one at a time or in pairs, they were to come out of the hold, walk the plank, and then sit and wait for their brothers and sisters.

She told them to think about who they were, their physical conditions, their attitudes about seeing land again, about the slave seller who would bark his orders to them as they slowly emerged into the day, their feelings about each other, and their feelings about slavery.

To help establish a mood, the teacher asked the children to close their eyes and softly hum "Motherless Child" as they thought about the situation. After a few moments the teacher stood and in a rough and callous voice growled, "All right, look lively! Come on out!"

As the first children reached the plank, the teacher threw open the classroom window curtains to reveal the very bright sunlight. The children slowly walked between the chairs, some seriously involved in the activity, some snickering to their partners. After they had all assembled, the leader turned on the lights.

She talked to them for a few moments, commenting objectively. Quietly and in the mood of the material she said, "As we played this the first time, some of you were involved in the moment, and some of you found it difficult. It's not easy to play something as serious as this, but I think we can do it if we work at it some more. Let's try it again. Now that you know what this situation is about, let's have you decide if you think you can remain involved in it this next time. If you think you cannot, you may sit and watch quietly."

Six children chose to watch. The activity was repeated. The involvement was stronger the second time, but the leader suggested that the children might be able to "feel the moment" even more deeply on a third playing.

"What do you think? Shall we try it once again?" she asked. They all agreed they wanted to try one more time. The leader gave them the option of playing or watching. All the children indicated readiness to play. This third playing was the most successful, and the children spontaneously expressed their satisfaction with it.

FOR THE COLLEGE STUDENT

1. Select some material or topic suitable for dramatization. Have in mind a particular group of children who will play it. Consider the following questions:
   a. What are the drama–theatre, personal development, and additional curricular goals you would emphasize?
   b. What considerations will you make for each of the drama activity variables? Explain your answers.
   c. What do you personally like about the topic or material? What is your own commitment to it?
   d. How will the material serve the interests, needs, and concerns of the group of children who are to play it?
   e. What will be important for you to consider in your presentation of the material to the children?
   f. What methods might you use to assist the children in understanding the material or the topic? Be specific.
   g. Outline your plan for playing the material or the topic.
   h. What special effects might be used to enhance the discussion or the playing?

2. Select a humorous piece of literature. Practice reading it aloud or telling it, using your voice to convey the mood. If you wish, you may select music to accompany the material. Rehearse the music with your reading until they flow together smoothly. Share the selection with your classmates.

3. Select some material rich in dramatic conflict. Follow the same procedure as in Exercise 2.

4. Using the extended example *Venture for Freedom* (pp. 44–45), enumerate all the techniques used by the leader to aid involvement. What other techniques might have been employed?

3

Working in Groups

In traditional classroom teaching, children are most frequently an *assembled* group, working individually on their own seatwork activities or projects. Generally, it takes considerable training and experience for classroom teachers to learn how to work with their students as an *interacting* group. As noted in Chapter 2, managing children in creative drama requires special skills. An important part of this management includes guiding children to be self-seeking, self-directed, authenticated individuals capable of integrating themselves into a democratic, cohesive group. In this chapter, some of the basic concepts regarding the nature of groups and group process, as applied to creative drama in the classroom setting, will be explored.

THE NATURE OF THE CLASSROOM GROUP

Every classroom is composed of a group, including the teacher, organized for the express purpose of education. To accomplish this most effectively, a high degree of cohesive interaction is required. It is the leader's responsibility to guide the group toward this goal.

The methods of achieving group interaction are not easily described because of the variables involved in the nature of groups themselves. No two children, leaders, or groups are alike. Neither do they remain consistent in their differences from day to day or even minute to minute. As every

Leadership in creative drama is an experience in group management.

experienced teacher knows, variations in demeanor and attitude can be caused by such factors as weather, time of day and year, physical aspects of the environment, material presented, presence or absence of individual members, age, sex ratio, cultural and ethnic mix, and size of the group. Furthermore, every individual in the group, including the teacher, is a constantly growing and evolving human being—never static. Being aware of these variables is necessary to guide the group most effectively.

Likewise, each person in the group is unique because of different experiences and background. Yet each member is equally important, and each one's individuality makes its own special contribution. Leaders also play a role as a group member. Their backgrounds, with their unique experiences, have contributed to the persons they are. When leaders examine the source of their ideas, values, feelings, and behaviors, they will develop a greater awareness of why they favor certain curricular subjects; enjoy working on particular pet projects; like or dislike certain personalities; have a personality that can be labeled "jovial," "sensitive," or "demanding"; or value certain ideas above others.

In all classroom learning, the leader's total personality will probably influence the children more than any subject matter taught. Especially in experiences dealing with human emotions and interpersonal relationships, the leader's own behaviors will serve as a strong example. Examining and understanding our own sensitivities as human beings will be required if we are to teach human interaction through drama with honesty and relevance.

The leader is responsible for establishing a secure climate in the classroom.

POSITIVE CLASSROOM CLIMATE

The emotional climate in the classroom is determined by the overall feelings experienced by the group members. In a positive environment the students and the teacher have a mutual trust and respect for each other, an essential ingredient in facilitating the development of self-esteem and optimal learning. Individuals make their best contributions when they feel confident and possess a positive self-image. This attitude develops in a climate of *acceptance, psychological freedom,* and *open communication.*

Acceptance is the belief that all people are worthy individuals. Although certain behaviors and actions may be disapproved of, there is a recognition of a person's basic self. Acceptance forms the very foundation for successful group interaction which creative drama attempts to foster. The leader initiates acceptance and becomes the model for it by demonstrating acceptance of each child as a human being with important feelings and ideas. The leader's guidance also reflects an understanding of children's various stages of growth and development as well as their interests, needs, and concerns. The right of every child to be treated with equality is respected, and this attitude is taught to the group by example and practice.

Psychological freedom allows a person to be secure enough in the social, physical, and emotional environment to operate with relative ease. Everyone has known the feelings of fear and anxiety in uncomfortable and tense situations. At such times all the eyes of the world appear to be staring at us, making impossible demands. Our insecurity may cause us to become shy and withdrawn or hostile and aggressive, making it impossible for us to operate with maximum effectiveness.

The leader is responsible for establishing an atmosphere of psychological freedom and creating the secure climate in which children can express their thoughts freely, without fear of reprisal. Not only is this condition important for positive self-growth, it is crucial for encouraging the risk taking that creativity demands.

Creative drama is a natural medium for the free expression of ideas, feelings, and attitudes. Fostering *open communication* becomes fundamental and paramount in the leader's successful guidance of creative drama. Leaders must value and respect the sincere, open, and honest communication from children that drama can engender. Furthermore, they must be ready to communicate their own thoughts and feelings with equal sincerity.

Conveying Acceptance

Conveying acceptance to children is one of the most important factors in fostering their self-growth. We convey acceptance both openly and subtly by our general attitudes, our nonverbal behaviors, and our verbal comments.

Self-acceptance.   The first step in being able to accept another person is to accept oneself. Essentially, when we recognize our own humanness, we are accepting of others. Leaders who expect perfection from themselves and from their students will continually be frustrated, a condition which builds more unacceptance. These accumulating, unaccepting behaviors are then translated into a negativism which can pervade the entire classroom.

When we are aware of our personal makeup and our feelings, we can more easily reflect them in our verbal comments. For example, the teacher who says "I get really upset when I hear so much chattering" rather than "You're the noisiest bunch of kids I've ever seen" has owned up to personal feelings and has taken responsibility for them. Since the same amount of noise might not be bothersome to another person, the feelings lie in the speaker. By speaking I-statements, we can get in touch with our personal feelings and values, making them clear to ourselves and to others. With I-statements we can also be more exact in expressing our needs: "This noise may not be bothering anyone else, but it's interrupting my thinking. Please hold it down."

Our You-messages, on the other hand, place blame and negative judgment on the other person, often causing guilt and resentment. Probably the last thing it will accomplish is the change of behavior we had hoped for. Saying "You're rude" seldom generates politeness.

Children sometimes have a difficult time accepting themselves. Often it is their own self-rejection statements we are most tempted to censor.

> "That's a pretty sweater you have on, Mark," said the leader at the beginning of the session.
> "I don't like it. I hate myself in it," said chubby Mark, who had not yet played with his classmates in creative drama, although he had been attending the sessions regularly.

The leader was tempted to say, "Well, I don't know why you don't like it. It really is a pretty sweater" or "You shouldn't hate anyone, not even yourself." But she knew that these statements would have rejected Mark's feelings. And because she also recognized that Mark's weight problem may have caused his concern over his appearance, she simply made no further comment. As it turned out, Mark played that day for the first time and continued to participate on succeeding days.

Accepting Ideas and Behaviors. Students assess their worth as human beings by the verbal and nonverbal statements communicated to them. Most children flourish under accepting comments like flowers responding to a warm spring rain. In fact, we all appreciate acceptance demonstrated by a nod, a pat on the back, a smile, a kind word about our efforts and thoughts, and an understanding of feelings.

In verbally accepting children's ideas and behaviors, we might say

"That's a good idea."

"Nice work!"

"I think all this noise means you're excited."

By hearing accepting statements children will often begin to express acceptance and appreciation also.

"Mr. Burns, what music were you playing when we were pretending? It's super."

"I liked watching Jim when he pretended he was that stubborn donkey and rolled on his back."

"Clever, Annette."

Although it is important to be accepting of ideas, there is no need to claim creative genius for a good but rather ordinary idea. Children have an awareness of what is pretty good and what is outstanding, and exaggerated praise is usually recognized as phony. One leader discovered this fact from the children themselves. She had the habit of being overly enthusiastic with everyone and everything. When a group of children spontaneously praised one child's ideas in playing a scene, the child expressed delight and was very pleased. The children reminded him that the teacher often praised his work, but his response was "Oh, she says *everything's* good." The child viewed his classmates' praise as more discerning and therefore more meaningful than the teacher's constant global praise.

Accepting statements may be particularly difficult to give when one appears to be under direct attack.

One seven-year-old boy in an early session in creative drama said to the leader, "You're stupid." Although stunned, she probed, "Why do you think so, Rocky?" "Because you pretend and make up things. That's stupid," was his reply. The leader reflected his feelings: "It's true that I do like to pretend and make up things. You feel that pretending is stupid."

Creative drama fosters the expression of ideas.

Possibly Rocky has heard a similar statement himself. Perhaps he did not want to risk pretending if someone might call *him* "stupid," so in defense he applied it to someone else before anyone had the chance to label him. In being allowed to express his concerns and in hearing that someone had understood them, Rocky's anxiety may have been relieved. Interestingly, he continued to attend the voluntary sessions and in time participated freely.

Understanding and Accepting Feelings.   Every experienced teacher knows the importance of a learner's healthy emotional outlook. Without a feeling of well-being, learning is not possible. If for no other reason, emotions must be dealt with because of their effect on learning.

Throughout all drama experiences sincere and honest expression of ideas and feelings is encouraged. If they are rejected, the open channels of communication are at risk. Consider the following examples.

> A group of fourth graders were pretending to be robots. In the first playing they were robots working at their jobs, performing a variety of tasks. For the second playing, the leader suggested that they be robots enjoying themselves on a night off. In the discussion that followed the playing, one boy said, "I had a fight with my wife and went to the gasoline station and got oil and got drunk."

The child's answer was logical for the situation and, more important, was delivered sincerely. The answer was accepted with a simple nod of the head. If the leader had given a shocked look or rejected the answer as inappropriate, he would have given reproof to a child's honest expression. From a pragmatic point of view, he could also have triggered other children into creating "drunken robots" too, if they thought it would get attention.

In another instance, a six-year-old, pretending to be a witch casting an evil spell, said fervently that he was "turning all the parents in the world into furniture." The leader, playing the "oldest and wisest" witch, merely cackled and said, "I see." If the leader had remarked "Are you sure that's what you'd like to do to parents?" or "You shouldn't say things like that," she would have rejected the child's strong feelings. Apparently he felt secure enough to express his thoughts in what he assumed to be a safe environment, and the leader verified his assumption by accepting his statement.

Creative drama, as an enjoyable, active experience, creates by itself a positive emotional atmosphere. The strong movement of marching around the room to a bouncy rhythm can help a child achieve a fresh and renewed outlook on the rest of the day; or pretending to be on a raft with Tom Sawyer floating down the Mississippi may help children forget, if only temporarily, their own struggles with life.

Drama leaders can deal even more directly with the subject of emotion. They can help children understand what emotions are, how they are expressed, why people behave as they do, and how emotional responses differ. Such topics are also a part of other curricular areas, such as social studies, literature, or health.

The subject of emotions is also dealt with every time the leader guides the children in a discussion of the characters in stories and the motivations behind their behaviors. Children readily identify with certain characters. These are often the ones they choose to play, and through these characters they have the opportunity to release important feelings. They feel safe under the guise of the character to express feelings that may not be allowed them otherwise.

Many drama leaders have noted shy students suddenly becoming assertive in a particular character role, or aggressive ones becoming subdued. One leader tells the following:

> I remember distinctly the overly feminine youngster who pleasantly surprised her classmates (who were usually put off by her phoniness) and me by playing Tom Sawyer with great honesty and believability. I also remember the rather aggressive boy who was a class clown but who asked to play a wish-granting sprite in a story we were dramatizing. I threw caution to the winds and allowed him to do it, and was amazed to find a caring and kind personality emerge in the playing. Both these students apparently felt safe in expressing their emotions through the characters they chose to play.

When students discuss people, situations and emotions, they often draw upon their own experiences. You need to be aware and accepting of these comments without showing judgments so that students realize that they, and the feelings they are experiencing, are normal.

STUDENT: I hate his guts!
TEACHER: You're really angry with him.

STUDENT: My sister's dumb.
TEACHER: You seem to be upset with your sister.

Said objectively, these statements reflect the emotions the students are expressing, letting the children know they have been heard. This is often all that is needed to assist them in handling their feelings.

Although we think of feelings as good (happy, excited, loving) and bad (angry, lonely, unhappy) because of the effect they have on us, having a particular feeling is neither good nor bad in itself. It used to be thought (and some people still think) that we should be able to keep ourselves from having "bad" feelings. That is why many people say "Don't be unhappy" or "You shouldn't be afraid" or even "You must never hate anyone." But all feelings are normal and just *are*. We cannot keep ourselves from having them. What we *do* with our feelings is what makes a difference.

Often children have been denied normal emotions by such statements as "Big boys don't cry" or "It's silly to be afraid of the dark." But rejection of feelings only causes one to be defensive or to question one's perceptions of the world. Rather than rejecting feelings, it is more helpful if we acknowledge that they are normal, allowable, and have a reason for being. "Sometimes crying helps us feel better" or "We're sometimes afraid of the dark because we can't see what's there" are statements that encourage positive emotional growth.

We will want children to understand that people all over the world share emotions of fear, love, hate, and joy. When students hear someone expressing understanding of their emotions, they know their feelings are normal. For some children it can be particularly helpful for the teacher to identify with them in the experiencing of common human emotions with statements such as "I know how you feel," "I can understand how you must have felt," or "I felt the same way when I was in that situation."

We will want children to understand that even though feelings are neither good nor bad in themselves, some can be troublesome or painful:

"No one likes to be called names."

"Yes, you can feel hurt if someone won't let you walk with him to school."

Learning to cope with emotions may mean learning to understand that feelings are normal and have a reason for existing. Instead of rejecting them we try to understand why they occur and what causes them.

Differences of emotional expression are influenced by the concepts and values held by different cultures and subcultures. No doubt it is surprising for some children to learn that in some parts of the world men greet each other by kissing, or that fist fighting in some cultures is a shameful way to express anger. Even within the classroom community there may be some dissimilar practices or values. Children may be surprised to find that a classmate does not like ice cream—something they think is universally liked. Or they may find it curious that some children say they are not afraid of thunder and even like the sound of it. Understanding and appreciating

Expressing surprise and anger with expressionless masks.

these differences is a valuable learning experience that begins with the leader's interaction with the children.

> A leader was guiding a class of third graders in creative drama. She noticed one boy's negative response to physical contact when she took his hand to form a circle and later when she unthinkingly gave him a friendly pat on the head. She made a mental note that Tom did not like contact and that she should not touch him.
>
> But the very next time she met the children, she forgot her intentions. This time she was playing with the children, pretending to be smoke rising. The mood was quiet and mysterious, but it was quickly broken for Tom when her smoke movements accidentally touched him. The teacher stopped playing and said quietly, "Tom, I know you don't like for me to touch you. I'm sorry that I did just now. I've told myself not to do it, but I seem to be having a hard time making myself mind."
>
> There was a moment of absolute silence. By now everyone was aware of what was happening. Tom's face changed from one of real disgust to one of surprise. Then the eight-year-old said, "That's all right, I understand." Tom obviously appreciated her concern for his feelings and, in turn, was able to understand hers. At that moment a bond of understanding and respect was formed between them.

Many children have difficulty dealing with emotions. Realistically the teacher will not be able to solve many of the child's problems; neither can one legitimately assume the role of a therapist or a counselor who diagnoses and treats specific emotional disorders. But simply in the number of waking hours spent together, perhaps the teacher, of all the people in the child's world, is in an ideal position to help the child understand and cope with human emotions.

Accepting Creativity and Imitation. Beginning leaders are often so concerned about evoking creativity in children that they expect immediate and outstanding results. But we all have rather ordinary ideas at first until we have had the chance to experiment further and probe deeper. Some leaders express their disappointment openly or with thinly disguised, forlorn facial expressions when students give initial responses. However, one needs to be accepting of these first attempts at creative thinking and to continue to be supportive to keep the flow of ideas coming.

In drama activities, children will often imitate each other or even repeat a previous response, particularly if the leader has praised it. This is normal and natural; imitation, after all, is a basic mode of learning. Yet some feel that imitating is similar to cheating and convey this attitude to children. As a result, children may express considerable concern about imitative behavior in classmates:

> "Kim's doing *my* idea!"
> "Tom's copying!"

In response to these protestations, one can communicate an acceptance of imitation in a way that protects the child who is imitating yet reassures the child who has originated the idea.

> "When people see an idea they like, they enjoy using it. Tom must have liked your idea. . . ."

Acceptance through Leader Participation. Acceptance is also demonstrated when the leader participates and plays with the children. At first you may feel reluctant or even a little nervous (perhaps *vulnerable* is a better word) in playing. But in time and as experience is gained and you become more relaxed, participation usually becomes more comfortable. It is not important to be skilled in playing; in fact, one could intimidate some children by being too accomplished. Participation should therefore emphasize entering the spirit and enjoyment of play rather than skill. Many children will find your participation encouraging, and will more readily participate and relax and enjoy themselves also.

Whether leaders play a role in a story or role drama, the communication bond is strengthened. One becomes a contributing member of the group and establishes a meaningful working relationship with it. As a result, we learn to understand ourselves and the other members more clearly. This insight can be valuable in assisting effective classroom interrelationships in all learning activities.

Accepting Mistakes. The process of learning involves experimenting, often accompanied by uncertainty and mistakes. But many adults and children are conditioned to feel that mistakes indicate failure. And since, in their minds, failure cannot be tolerated, they become unduly distressed by mistakes.

One of the most effective ways for drama leaders to help children realize that mistakes are natural and normal for everyone is to acknowledge their own.

Acceptance is demonstrated when the leader plays with the children.

"Boy, this isn't working, is it? Let me try another idea. . . ."

"I think I should have explained the directions differently. It was my fault we had a mixup."

And just as we can stop and acknowledge our own difficulties, we can guide children to do the same.

"I sensed that some of you had second thoughts about the way your scene went. Would you like to try again?"

"Some people seemed to forget the rules. Let's try it again, and remember this time that you are to use only the space at the side of your desk."

SETTING LIMITS

Even though we accept the children's ideas and feelings, limits must be set on negative behaviors. We obviously cannot allow them to fight with each other, hurt each other's feelings purposely, shout obscenities, or refuse to follow rules. Children need guidance in learning that the blatant expression of all feelings and actions can get them into trouble. A person who acts out aggression by kicking someone, for example, will certainly be avoided or possibly even kicked in return.

It is important to disapprove of behaviors and actions without rejecting the individual who expresses them. Notice how the following statements acknowledge the children's feelings but reject the behavior accompanying them.

"I know that you're angry, but fighting is not allowed in the classroom."

"All your talking lets me know you're excited. But you know the rules. We can't begin playing until everyone has settled down. I'll know that you're ready when everything is quiet. . . ."

"I know you're disappointed that you can't all play this first time. But in just a few moments we'll be repeating it, and everyone will have a chance."

There may be times when children's behaviors become disruptive to the rest of the class. When this happens, rules for participating should be reinforced as objectively as possible. It is also helpful to speak to children privately so they are able to "save face."

"Please sit down. When you feel that you can follow the rules to remain by yourself and not disturb others, you may rejoin the group."

Children's behavior is sometimes such that they cannot be allowed to participate with the group at all for an entire session.

"I'm sorry. I know you are disappointed. But I cannot allow you to poke and pinch other people who are trying to do their work. Perhaps it will be easier for you to follow the rules tomorrow. For the rest of today, just watch."

Although the other children will enjoy playing their activities in a quieter setting after disruptive children have been removed, it is important for the offenders to be returned to drama as soon as possible. It is within the framework of drama itself that children have one of their best opportunities to learn social interaction skills and to get along with one another.

A simple ignoring of unwanted behaviors will sometimes serve to diminish them. Consider the following:

As an only child of career parents, David was often left on his own and craved attention. Although bright and likable, he was unusually outspoken and aggressive. He also had the annoying habit of contradicting the leader's remarks or pointedly doing the opposite of everything that was requested in order to draw attention to himself. The leader, who often gave in to his demands, decided to change tactics.

LEADER: I'll be the North Wind that blows all the Snow People inside the house. Here we go!

DAVID: *I'm* not going inside.

LEADER: OK. The rest of us will go inside and you can stay outside.

DAVID: I'm coming! I'm coming!

GROUP DYNAMICS

Learning to function in a democratic society is an educational priority. While we encourage each child to develop individual expression, we also emphasize the value of social interrelationships. Ultimately the leader guides the group to learn that it functions best when everyone contributes. Organization, cooperation, group problem solving and decision making thus become an integral part of the group experience.

The dynamics of group behavior are interesting. Although a group may be composed of a wide range of individuals, it has a personality all its own—as if it were one huge and unique individual embodying the separate members. A common saying among professional group leaders is "The group contains all the people in the group plus one more." Teachers note this phenomenon of group behavior when they make such statements as "My class is so rowdy this year!" or "My class would really like that," as if the class is a person by itself.

Creative drama encourages group interaction. When activities are carefully planned, when instructions are clearly given, and when the group knows what is expected of it, group work should pose few problems. If organization is not handled carefully, however, there can be problems, especially for the beginning leader. When the group is given too much independence before it is ready, it can develop a life of its own and may even get out of control. Beginning leaders who have not had much experience with group work may panic at seeing this unleashed power, particularly if they see their own contact and control diminishing. (Even experienced leaders can find such moments threatening and traumatic.) This panic may freeze leaders into inaction at a time when their leadership is most needed.

Fortunately, no group really wants to get out of control; in fact, group members themselves feel panic at a group's uncontrolled power. It is much more comfortable to be a part of a group that is organized and on course. Strong direction, as well as support from the leader, is usually welcomed until children feel confident working more independently.

Some children have an easy time cooperating and integrating themselves within almost any group. They obviously enjoy working together and demonstrate the maturity, as well as a readiness, to accept one another. For them group involvement is natural:

"Maria and I have an idea. Can we do it together?"

"John and I are going to be the ticket sellers and Alonzo and Mack are going to buy tickets from us. What are you guys going to do?"

They have ideas for facilitating organization and interaction:

"I think we should put our hand up if we want to say something."

"I think each group should have a corner of the room to plan our scenes so we can work in private."

"Oh, I know how we can do this story, Mrs. Hackett. You be the old lady and we'll be the rabbits."

They listen to each other with understanding and empathy:

CHILD 1:   I know how the boy in that story felt. The saddest time for me was when my dog died. He was run over by a car.

CHILD 2:   That's sad.

They are interested in each other and spontaneously comment on, and question further, the ideas of their peers:

CHILD 1:   I wanted a horse.

TEACHER: Did you get one?

CHILD 1:   I'm too little. If I rode it, I'd fall off.

CHILD 2:   Oh, you're crazy. You can't have a horse because you gotta have a ranch to have a horse and you gotta have a saddle and you gotta have a bridle and you gotta have horseshoes and you gotta have a lot of food to feed 'em.

CHILD 1:   Oh, no. You don't have to have all that stuff for a horse.

CHILD 2:   Well, maybe you're right.

CHILD 1:   If I could have my wish, I'd go to another planet and help start a new civilization there.

CHILD 2:   Like the boy in our story.

CHILD 3:   You'd have to get used to living in pressurized buildings all your life.

CHILD 2:   Yeah. And maybe you'd even save the spaceship like that kid did.

On the other hand, some children have difficulties in group interaction. Some are ignored by the group. Some choose to avoid any group, hesitating to participate or to contribute an idea or opinion. Still others with personal ego needs demand undivided attention from the group, refusing to listen to others, to compromise, or to cooperate. For these children and their leader, group work will take time and effort.

The seemingly simple act of dividing the larger group into pairs and smaller groups can be a particular problem for beginning leaders. Although children often work best when they are allowed to choose their coworkers, you will want to avoid the formation of cliques. Some children are mature enough to handle this on their own. They can pair and group themselves with few arguments and no hard feelings, rotating their choices of classmates.

Most children, however, will need your assistance in rotating group membership. Quickly counting off and placing 1s together, 2s together, and so on is a common way to mix the group. Not only does this system prevent petty squabbling over who plays with whom, it gets to the excitement of playing sooner. With some planning ahead, you can easily vary your grouping methods to keep interest high.

No matter what your procedures, some children are never satisfied. Yet if you allow the voicing of too many complaints, the playing is usually held up and little is solved. For this reason, many leaders say that if they keep the activities moving forward and act as if they assume the children can get along together, the children soon learn to live up to the expectation.

Leaders often find it helpful to formulate a list of rules for working in groups. One class collectively listed the following:

Because I like to have people listen to me, I will listen to others.

Because I wouldn't want anyone to say my ideas are stupid or dumb, I won't say that about anyone else's.

Because I don't want anyone to make fun of the way I feel, I won't make fun of anyone else's feelings.

Because I don't like being disturbed when I'm doing drama, I won't disturb others.

Because I want people to be a good audience for me, I will be a good audience for them.

Because I don't like being left out of a group, I will include others in my group.

General discussions about group cooperation and compromise can also help, stimulated by such questions as

"When people cooperate, what do they have to do?"

"How can a group decide what ideas it will use?"

"How can a group make certain that everyone has a chance to speak and contribute?"

"When only a few members in a group do all the talking, how do the other members feel? What can they do?"

The subject of group cooperation and compromise can even be the basis for drama experiences:

TEACHER: What examples can you think of to show the importance of compromise and cooperation?

CHILD 1: Every summer my family decides where we'll spend our vacation. My mom and dad tell us how much money we can spend and how far that will take us, and then we vote. Before we voted we used to argue a lot. My sister always screamed about going to the lake because she had a boyfriend there. I always vote for camping.

CHILD 2: Well, this isn't about compromise, just the opposite. My brother's in Mr. Bender's class, and when the art teacher wanted groups to make a mural, they couldn't do it. They couldn't agree on anything. One of the kids even ripped up the paper. My brother said Mr. Bender just flipped and really got mad at them.

CHILD 3: Our committee had a hard time planning the class Halloween party. Not to mention names, but *someone* wanted to bring in *real* eyeballs and guts for kids to touch when they had their blindfolds on. He was going to get them from a butcher. Some kids said they'd get sick, so we made him take a vote.

TEACHER: I can see you have lots of ideas. We'll divide into groups of five. Each group will dramatize a scene to show the importance of cooperation and compromise. Be sure everyone has a part to play, and be sure to have an ending so you know when to stop.

Group Decision Making

It is necessary to a democratic society and to children's growth and development that they learn to handle their own problems and make their own decisions in drama. The decisions they make may not always be the ones the leader would have made, but the process of thinking through an idea and experimenting with trial and error is an excellent learning experience.

Children can be granted the opportunity to be self-directed in many ways:

"Let's see, how can we do this? Does anyone have a suggestion?"

"We've been playing this drama for quite a while. Are you still interested in it or should we go on to something else?"

"Do we need a preview playing this time?"

"Do you think everyone can play at the same time, or should we start out with just a few people first?"

"How much space do you think we can handle today?"

Of course, whenever children make their own decisions they must also accept the consequences. If things don't work out, the playing will have to be stopped and the situation reanalyzed. Just as the leader can make mistakes and miscalculations about what a group is ready to do, so can the children in managing themselves. The more important point is that they have had a hand in the decision-making process.

The group may also deal with its own problems of personal interaction in everyday classroom living. In the example below, a teachable moment was used to help a group of second graders see alternatives in handling a particular behavior problem. The class had just begun a discussion when a rather constant and irritating problem reoccurred.

GEORGE: Troy's hitting me again.

TEACHER: Troy seems to be a problem for you, George. What are you going to do about it?

GEORGE: What am *I* going to do about it?

TEACHER: Yes. How are you going to solve your problems?

GEORGE: Well . . . I'll . . . (shouts at Troy) STOP DOING THAT!!!!

TEACHER: (musingly) That's one way. Is there anything else you could do?

GEORGE: I'd hit him, too.

TEACHER: Hmmm, that's another possibility. Do you think it will work?

ANGELA: Troy would hit you back, wouldn't you, Troy? (Troy doesn't respond.)

MARNIE: Ask him nice to leave you alone.

TEACHER: Yes, that's another idea. Are there any others?

JAMES: Just don't play with him anymore.

RUSTY: Go sit by somebody else.

TEACHER: Since you have so many ideas, let's take a few minutes to have you work together in pairs. Decide on the best way you can think of to handle a problem like George's without any hitting. George and Troy, you watch with me and see what ways you think would work best. (After the playing, the group returns to a discussion of the most workable ideas they saw.)

Democratic living is not easy! Cooperative interaction takes time, and social maturation is not necessarily correlated with chronological age. Furthermore, the group's personality and behavior will fluctuate and change. There inevitably will be days when both the leader and the children wonder how they will ever be able to work together or why in the world they would even want to! These seemingly backward steps are a natural part of the group process and the group's growth toward cohesiveness. The children are constantly growing in awareness of themselves as individuals and as a part of the group.

Yet, the group is powerful, and the need to belong to a group is strong. Usually you can count on this need to motivate children to continue to make attempts at integrating themselves. For children who do have difficulties, you will need to give emotional support; and for those trying times, you may need an extra dose of patience and understanding to survive.

The need to belong to a group is strong.

CREATIVE DRAMA FOR ALL CHILDREN: CONSIDERATIONS
FOR CHILDREN WITH SPECIAL NEEDS

A child in a wheelchair plays a role in a story dramatization; he is aided in moving about the room by a classmate who is double-cast in the same role. A drama leader tells a story, making sure that her lips and face can be seen by a child wearing a hearing aid. A child with special talents has written a story that a small group of her classmates are dramatizing. And a child with behavior difficulties is making a noticeable effort to restrain his outbursts in order to play a drama activity with his classmates and be a part of the group. Today's elementary classroom has students with a multitude of different needs, and individual children may have multiple handicaps. Addressing these needs is mandatory if we are going to provide equal opportunities for all.

In conducting drama activities we consider, without overreacting to, children's special needs in order to help them participate as fully as possible. Although there may seem to be certain aspects of drama some handicapped children cannot participate in fully, the children themselves will frequently see ways to solve the problem creatively on their own. Focusing on the children's abilities rather than on their inabilities will encourage these attempts.

It is generally assumed that the leader is the one responsible for implementing compensatory learning experiences. However, the classroom can also become a community of learners who willingly assist each other and help each other succeed. Many goals can be achieved by establishing a "buddy" system. A child who speaks a different language, for example, can be aided by the child who is bilingual. The academically gifted, in addition to pursuing their own interests, may be able to assist others. Children can aid handicapped classmates; in fact, some handicapped children can assist others whose handicaps are different from theirs. All these experiences can give children a needed sense of responsibility and importance in serving the classroom community.

Although each child is special in some way, many children come to school with preconceived notions of their abilities. A child with a minor handicap may come from an overprotective environment; a gifted child may have been told that he is superior to his classmates and should not pay attention to them. Such conditions will obviously complicate matters. It also means that there will never be just one answer to a problem or just one way to deal with it. The following general guidelines are presented for consideration.

General Drama Techniques to Consider

A basic axiom to remember is that drama is a group art. Unlike the musician who can perform solo or the artist who paints pictures alone, the actor generally must work with other actors as well as with "behind the scenes" artists. The same is true of creative drama. Therefore, attention is not, and should not be, placed on single individuals. Furthermore, there is an obligation to work together as a group to make the most successful dramatization. This philosophy leads to some specific techniques employed throughout the text that will be particularly beneficial in working with children who have special needs.

One of these techniques is *simultaneous* or *unison playing*. When all children are playing or discussing an idea at the same time, they are automatically part of the group. They can also see other children participating and learn from this modeling and demonstrating. Yet, there is no undue attention on the children themselves, and they can participate and blend into the activity at their own pace.

A second technique is *multiple casting of roles*. Almost any role in a story can be double-cast, allowing two children to work together, each supporting the other. Some parts can be played by even more than two players. This technique allows any child to play virtually any role because of the assistance from a partner.

Multiple casting is also used with other drama activities. Consider, for example, the simple debate (p. 196). The class is divided into two roles. Yet, even if children choose not to say anything, they are still included in the playing experience. For many children, this is as much participation as they want or can handle. And, again, they can increase that participation at their own pace.

There is one final point in the overall consideration of children with special needs. Drama encourages participants to get *outside themselves*. Much of the stress we feel in our lives is the result of inward focus, and children who have been made aware of their special differences undoubtedly carry an extra burden. By extending ourselves into the world around us and "losing ourselves" in activities like drama, we can experience a therapeutic

Drama is a group art.

release. This release can help us put life back into its proper perspective and render us healthier for future tasks.

Additional Suggestions for Specific Special Needs

Following are some additional suggestions for working in creative drama with children of varying needs and abilities. They are not all-inclusive but are merely intended to encourage your thinking. Eventually you will discover many more options yourself that will fit your own and your classroom's particular needs.

Multilingual-multicultural

1. Many drama activities in this text are based on folk literature, a universal literary form. Some folk-tale plot lines (for example, "Cinderella") have been found to exist in almost every language and culture. Take special note to include stories from your classroom's language and cultural heritage. Encourage the children to bring such stories to your attention for drama activities.
2. Movement, pantomime, and nonverbal communication are also universal languages. They can take over when words fail or are inadequate to express needs. Bilingual children will particularly enjoy the focus on pantomime activities.
3. Incorporate references to special cultural holidays, customs, and experiences in drama activities, from simple sensory activities to more elaborate dramatizations. Utilize the rich multiethnic resources your students can provide for you and for each other.
4. Many story dramatizations can be a good vehicle for learning vocabulary. Headbands or name tags can be made for characters (for example, dog, king, and man) using both the English words and native language words. (See Chapter 10.)

Mentally handicapped

1. These children will need to have as many concrete experiences as possible. Pictures, props, character headbands, and other similar aids will be necessary for them to understand information and concepts.
2. Pantomime is also valuable for the slow learner, whose verbal skills may not be advanced enough to engage fully in the dialogue and improvisational activities. Include plenty of pantomime activities in each drama lesson.
3. The graded materials in this text should assist in finding literature these children can handle successfully.
4. The roles these children play in drama activities should not tax them beyond their academic skills; and at the same time, they can often surprise us with their concentration and involvement, their careful observation of classmates, and their contentment in participating with their peers in a group activity. Be sure to reinforce the things they can do well.

Academically gifted and talented.
Academically gifted children, those who have high IQ scores, are ahead of their classmates mainly in the use of language. However, there are other talents that children can be gifted in,

such as music, athletics, or even interpersonal skills. Therefore, children can be gifted or talented in some areas but not in others.

Enriching experiences are usually required for gifted and talented youngsters, who can bypass the kind of skill-building work other children may need.

1. In drama some gifted children will excel in dialogue and improvisation. They will particularly enjoy verbal encounters and debates. And it may be easy for them to invent all manner of dialogue in story dramatization and role drama.

2. Some gifted and talented children may be interested in creating drama materials. They may even wish to develop some of the activities discussed in this text, from narrative pantomimes to sequence games to segmented story activities. Encourage these activities, perhaps letting them work with the many bibliographic references in this text.

3. Gifted children may also want to try their hand at leading drama activities. They may wish to narrate a narrative pantomime story for the class or for a small group to perform. They may show directorial skills by visualizing interesting ways for their classmates to interpret stories. They may even play a leader role in role drama.

4. Gifted children may also be encouraged to try their hand at playwriting, creating puppet shows, or even leading a small group to perform dramas for other classrooms in their school.

5. Other avenues of enrichment for these children may include working with film, television, or appropriate community theatre activities. They may be interested in reading further about theatre and sharing their findings with the rest of the class.

6. Because they have often pursued their interests as lone individuals, some academically gifted children may have difficulty integrating themselves into a group. Drama as a group art should make this easier, but be alert to the uncomfortableness they may feel at first.

Physically disabled

1. Limited space activities will be easier for these children to manage. However, a partner can assist in moving a wheelchair or in making an area accessible to children with limited mobility.

2. These children may be partial to verbal and dialogue activities if they are limited in bodily movement. Give plenty of opportunity for such activities in each lesson.

3. Remember that nonverbal communication (pantomime) is conveyed by all parts of the body—from body posture to facial expression and from hand gestures to the way we move our feet. Depending on the impairment, focus on pantomime activities that can be done with the children's most mobile parts of their body. Facial expression can be focused on for those whose arms and legs are impaired. Or gestures can be emphasized if the hands and arms are mobile.

4. People in wheelchairs tend not to receive as much supportive touch as other children, probably because the chair itself acts as a barrier. Be alert to this fact and give reassurance and emotional tactile support to these children as often as you do to the rest of the class.

Visually impaired

1. Limited space activities will be easier for these children. However, with a sighted partner they can explore expanded areas of space gradually.
2. Try to paint word pictures and clear details of what you are talking about. Describe pictures, props, and tell stories with great detail to create mental pictures for the visually impaired.
3. Music is valuable in aiding the mood or environment you are trying to create.
4. Let visually impaired children explore through touch as much and as often as possible. If you are using props, for example, they will want and need to handle them.
5. Abstract concepts and ideas may not be easily understood by these children. Consider this as you plan a lesson to make sure you cover all points clearly.
6. Touch, if carefully monitored, can assist in calming, directing, or assisting the child and can give moral support and encouragement.
7. Use a "buddy system." A partner can help explain quietly any points that may be missed.

Hearing impaired

1. Be sure these children can see your face and particularly your lips if they are trying to lip read. There is no need to exaggerate your speech; in fact, that will distort the sounds they have been trained to observe. Also try not to stand with a window behind you, as this will cast a shadow over your face.
2. Repeat comments made by children whose voices are too soft to be heard easily.
3. Visual cues, pictures, props, gestures, and directions on cards are very helpful for these children. Use them generously.
4. In general, these children particularly enjoy, and are successful with, pantomime activities.
5. A partner can repeat directions or explanations quietly whenever the child needs additional assistance.

Speech impaired.   Speech impairments generally include articulation disorders, stuttering, phonation problems, and delayed or limited speech.

1. Generally the classroom teacher can assist with speech difficulties by providing an open and relaxed atmosphere that encourages, rather than inhibits, these children in their speech. Since children usually consider drama fun, they tend to forget about their speech difficulties during drama class.
2. Pantomime experiences will be particularly enjoyable for these children.
3. Being able to play with oral activities is useful for speech-impaired youngsters. They need opportunities to speak and to hear others engaging in language.
4. Engaging in rhythmic activities, choral speaking in unison, and character role playing often lessens stuttering behaviors.

Emotionally handicapped.   Some emotionally handicapped children have difficulty controlling themselves, but others are very quiet and withdrawn.

1. Because these children often have short attention spans, they will need to move frequently from one task to another. Be alert to their responses and to the fact that you may need to cut an activity short and go to another for variety's sake.
2. At the same time, extending their periods of concentration on a task is also desirable. Move by slow increments in this goal for maximum success.
3. Movements of larger muscles are often successful. Body-movement activities and pantomime should be particularly useful for them.
4. A secure, consistent, and supportive environment is important for these children. They also need to experience success and to feel good about themselves. Initially, using a series of short activities that they can feel competent in doing should provide a good foundation to build on.

As a final word, remember that there are more similarities than differences between children with "special" needs and their classmates. We are all human, and we all have the need to love and be loved, to communicate, to learn, and to feel successful.

The subject of drama is the subject of life. And because it provides a variety of avenues for all to express their specific talents in unique ways, drama has often been called a great leveler of persons. No one is considered any greater or lesser than anyone else in drama. And this is also as it should be in life itself.

Throughout all experiences in drama, the goal is to help children understand and empathize with others—to learn to put themselves into other people's shoes. We want them to discover the common bond of feelings with people they know, people they read about, historical or famous personalities, and people of other countries and cultures. We want them to know each other better and to appreciate themselves as viable human beings. This understanding and awareness is the essence of drama. And it is this understanding that frees us from alienation in a world where the quality of life depends on the quality of human relationships.

FOR THE COLLEGE STUDENT

1. After reading this chapter, consider your own individual uniqueness. What are some of the values, feelings, likes, dislikes, and so on that are predominant in your personality? Discuss and share ideas with a small group of your classmates.
2. Discuss with your classmates those specific incidents during your elementary years when a teacher demonstrated acceptance of you. Recall specific incidents when you felt rejected. What conclusions can you draw?
3. Brainstorm with a group of your classmates some situations involving children's expression of ideas and feelings in the elementary classroom. What specific verbal statements can you think of to demonstrate acceptance of children's ideas and feelings in these situations?
4. Consider situations in which children demonstrate negative behaviors. Practice giving statements that reject the behavior without rejecting the child. Take turns

giving your statements and have classmates listen as if they were the children receiving them. What reactions and emotions do the listeners feel?

5. Make a list of situations that involve groups working together. Which ones might be suitable material to use for drama enactment in the classroom?

6. Read Chapter 9 of Elizabeth George Speare's *The Witch of Blackbird Pond* (97), in which Kit leads children in a dramatization of the parable of the Good Samaritan; or read the episode in Chapter 7 of Louise Fitzhugh's *Harriet the Spy* (New York: Harper & Row, 1964), in which the gym teacher attempts an enactment of Christmas dinner. Analyze the problems each teacher faces. What suggestions can you offer?

7. Examine some of the many books that deal with emotional situations in the classroom. Share one or two of your favorites in a classroom discussion. How might the material be suitable for a creative drama activity?

SELECTED RESOURCES TO USE WITH CHILDREN

The following materials are a selection of the many that are available dealing with interactions. You will find them interesting just for children to read on their own or to use for reading and discussion with the entire class. Many will also provide material for drama lessons.

ADOFF, ARNOLD, *Outside/Inside Poems*. New York: Lothrop, Lee & Shepard, 1981. This collection of poems sensitively describes feelings we have on the inside that do not often appear on the outside.

ALIKI, *Feelings*. New York: Greenwillow Books, 1984. These are brief stories and sketches of childhood feelings.

BERGER, TERRY, *I Have Feelings*. New York: Behavioral Publications, 1971. This useful text presents black-and-white photos covering seventeen different feelings, giving a situation for each followed by an explanation. See also *I Have Feelings, Too* (1979).

BROOKS, GWENDOLYN, *Bronzeville Boys and Girls*. New York: Harper & Row, 1956. African-American children express their feelings in this sensitive poet's classic work.

BUSCAGLIA, LEO, *Because I Am Human*. Thorofare, N.J.: Slack, 1982 (distributed by Holt, Rinehart and Winston). Black-and-white photos illustrate this simple text which describes all the things children can do because they are human—from rolling down a hill to chewing five sticks of bubble gum all at once. Younger children will love doing this one as a narrative pantomime (see Chapter 5) or as a count-and-freeze pantomime (see Chapter 7).

GRIMES, NIKKI, *Something on My Mind*. New York: Dial Press, 1978. This book, illustrated by Tom Feelings, presents descriptions of many inner emotions not often expressed.

SCHULTZ, CHARLES, *Love Is . . . Walking Hand in Hand*. San Francisco: Determined Productions, 1983. This "typically Peanuts" collection has many pantomime possibilities for twos and threes to play.

SPIER, PETER, *People*. New York: Doubleday, 1980. A well-known author-illustrator presents a delightful celebration of differences in people the world over.

VIORST, JUDITH, *If I Were in Charge of the World and Other Worries.* New York: Atheneum, 1983. With humor the poet touches on children's deep-seated concerns.

YASHIMA, TARO, *Crow Boy.* New York: Viking Penguin, 1955. In this classic book, a young Japanese boy is rewarded for six years of perfect attendance in school. Yet he is an outsider to the other children in the classroom until a sensitive teacher finds a way to give him the recognition he deserves.

SELECTED TEACHER RESOURCES

AMIDON, EDMUND, and ELIZABETH HUNTER, *Improving Teaching.* New York: Holt, Rinehart and Winston, 1966. This valuable text was one of the first ever devoted to helping teachers be aware of their specific verbal behaviors and the consequences of them in seven teaching categories: motivating, planning, informing, discussing, disciplining, counseling, and evaluating.

COOPER, PAMELA J., *Speech Communication for the Classroom Teacher* (4th ed.). Scottsdale, Ariz.: Gorsuch Scarisbrick, Publishers, 1991. This text gives a thorough treatment of several topics including listening, small group communication, and communication barriers.

CULLUM, ALBERT, *The Geranium on the Window Sill Just Died but Teacher You Went Right On.* New York: Harlin Quist, 1971.

———, *Blackboard, Blackboard on the Wall, Who Is the Fairest One of All?* New York: Harlin Quist, 1978.
    The author of both books, a teacher of drama, presents poems that reflect the feelings of students and teachers. The poems are amusing, yet poignant and thought-provoking.

GINOTT, HAIM G., *Between Teacher and Child.* New York: Macmillan, 1972. Here is a classic, highly readable book for strengthening interpersonal relationships in the classroom.

JOHNSON, D., and F. JOHNSON, *Joining Together: Group Theory and Group Skills* (3rd ed.). Englewood Cliffs, N.J.: Prentice Hall, 1987. A basic text devoted to the subject of how groups work.

4

Simple Drama Activities and Games

When both the leader and the children are new to drama, it is helpful to use some simple activities first, such as drama games, action songs, and brief pantomimes. These activities can also be used as warm-ups and for building commitment in longer drama periods. Often they involve some skill building or rehearsing that is useful before playing more challenging material. Simple activities are also good for ending a drama period, particularly if they have a calming effect on the group.

THE GOALS OF BEGINNING ACTIVITIES

One goal of beginning activities is to create the appropriate climate for psychological security. They can relax the class, generate good feelings, and promote a sense of group cohesiveness. Often they unite the children in a common effort, which becomes strong enough that individuals forget themselves and participate freely.

Other important goals of these beginning materials are that they encourage movement, focus and concentration, imagination, social cooperation, and self-control of the players, necessary skills in other areas of learning as well as in further drama work. Although not all the activities presented in this chapter will achieve each of these goals equally, consider for example the intense concentration little children exhibit in mastering the movements in a simple finger play, the imagination required in inventing different ways to move about the room to a musical stimulus, or the discipline required to mirror a partner's movements.

Another value of these materials is that they almost organize themselves. When the children learn the rules of a game or activity, they help monitor each other. The student teacher who has not had much experience working with groups of children will usually find it easier to begin with these activities.

However, the beginning leader must recognize and accept the responsibility for guiding and controlling even the simplest activity. It does not happen magically or automatically. Giving directions, rearranging the classroom, and keeping order and control are tasks that require some planning ahead. This chapter is designed to help the inexperienced teacher learn some initial skills in leading simple activities.

DIRECTED ACTIVITIES

The kind of activity that keeps the most control, is the easiest to organize, and is the simplest for the children to play is one in which a leader tells or shows the children what to do. Another value of such activities is that the children can play many of them seated or standing in one location while still being actively involved in a movement experience. Following is a discussion of several kinds of leader-directed activities.

Finger Plays

Finger plays—little rhymes, songs, or chants that the children act out as they recite them—are very popular with young children. Some classic

Finger plays are a good warmup for more challenging activities.

examples are "The Itsy Bitsy Spider" and "I'm a Little Teapot." Traditional finger plays are readily available in numerous sources. Many can be created from favorite nursery rhymes.

Single-Action Poetry

Some poems suggest single rhythmic movements—such as running, hopping, or galloping—that are fun to act out. While the leader reads the poem, the children simply perform the actions seated at their desks or standing at the side of them. Actions are done *in place*. Following are some examples.

"A Farmer Went Trotting upon His Grey Mare," Mother Goose (3).[1] Trotting can be done standing or sitting at the desk. The "bumps" and "lumps" can be acted out in various ways of your choice.

"The Grand Old Duke of York," Mother Goose (3). With this rhyme, march in place. Then, at the same time, stand for "up," crouch for "down," and half crouch for "halfway up."

"Grandma Bear from Delaware," Jack Prelutsky (27). Rocking action can be played at the desks.

"Hoppity," A. A. Milne (3,18). A little boy hops everywhere he goes. Children can "hop" this one on their bottoms at the desk. For variety, on the line beginning "If he stopped hopping," slow down your reading like a record player running out of electricity. Let your voice get lower and slower until you and the hoppers come to a "sitstill" on "couldn't go anywhere." Then pick up the tempo again at "That's why he always goes. . . ." One class decided to add "Pop!" at the very end.

"Jump—Jump—Jump," Kate Greenaway (3). Children can jump three times on the first line of each stanza. Do this *in place*. Children hold crouched position while you read the next three lines. On the last two lines they sit.

"Justin Austin," Jack Prelutsky (27). This short jump rope rhyme can be sung to the tune of "Yankee Doodle" as the children jump.

"Merry-Go-Round," Dorothy Baruch (3). Children can go up and down like the horses on a merry-go-round. As you read, the lines (and the horses) gradually go faster and then slow down to a final halt. Try adding music such as "Carousel Waltz" from Rodgers and Hammerstein's Broadway musical *Carousel*.

"The Swing," Robert Louis Stevenson (3,22). Swinging can be acted by leaning forward and backward in seated position or by taking four small steps forward and back for each two lines.

"Trot Along, Pony," Marion Edey and Dorothy Grider (3). Trot and clap thighs in rhythm to this poem. The last line takes the pony home to supper, so you can finish off by feeding the pony and bedding him for the night. (Children can pretend they are feeding an imaginary pony, or *they* can be the pony that *you* feed.)

---

[1]Throughout this text, numbers in parentheses correspond to the numbered anthologies and books listed in the final bibliography that begins on page 300.

Action Songs

Action songs such as the following are also fun to sing and act out: "Did You Ever See a Lassie?" "Here We Go 'Round the Mulberry Bush" (or "This is the Way We Wash Our Clothes"), "If You're Happy and You Know It," "She'll Be Comin' 'Round the Mountain," and "This Old Man, He Played One."

Some songs can easily be made into action songs. For example, the traditional African folk song "Kum Bay Yah" has a very strong and steady rhythm. The words are repeated in the different verses with little variation. Simple gestures of singing and crying can be added to the song, along with clapping and swaying that is usually inevitable with such a song. *Very simple* dance movements are also easily added if the group is strongly moved by the song.

Another example is the song, "Michael, Row the Boat Ashore." One teacher discussed with the children all the activities that sailors must do on a ship. Verses were added that included the children's names and various tasks that everyone mimed: "Sally, help to swab the deck," "Andy, pull up the anchor slow," and so on.

Traditional songs that lend themselves to simple dramatization include, "Frog Went A-Courtin'," "I Know an Old Lady Who Swallowed a Fly," "Old MacDonald Had a Farm," "Sing a Song of Sixpence," "Twelve Days of Christmas," and "Waltzing Matilda."

Action Stories

Action stories are well known in recreational circles, and many are taught by word of mouth. They are narrated by a leader, with children performing specified actions or sounds or both. You may already be familiar with such traditional stories as "Lion Hunt," "Bear Hunt," or "Brave Little Indian."

You can easily make up similar kinds of action stories by narrating a brief version of a folk tale. Young children will enjoy a story like "The Three Billy Goats Gruff," with actions and sounds for each of the billy goats ("trip trap"), the troll ("grrr"), and even the bridge ("creak, creak"). Older children enjoy stories with more "sophisticated" subject matter such as melodramas (complete with moustached villains and swooning lasses), spy and detective stories, or cowboy and rustler adventures.

Assign parts to small groups. Or for greater challenge to listening skills, the entire class can perform them all. Here is one example of an action story based on a folk tale.

JACK AND THE BEANSTALK

JACK:	Hey, nonny nonny! (snap fingers)
JACK'S MOTHER:	Who, me? (point to self)

BEANSTALK:	Flutter, flutter. (wiggle fingers at side of body for leaves)
GIANT:	Fee, fi, fo, fum! (stamp feet)
GIANT'S WIFE:	Oh, dear! (hand to forehead)
HEN:	Cackle, cackle! (flap wings)
HARP:	Twang, twang! (pluck nose to make nasal sound)
BAGS OF GOLD:	Clink, clink! (assume shape of lumpy bag)

Story. Once upon a time there was a poor boy named *Jack* who lived with his *mother.* One day he traded their cow for a handful of so-called magic beans. His *mother,* angered with his stupidity, threw the beans out the window. That night a huge *beanstalk* grew up into the sky. The next morning *Jack* climbed the *beanstalk* and found a castle belonging to a *giant. Jack* asked the *giant's wife* to let him in, and she did. But when the *giant's wife* heard the *giant* approaching, she hid *Jack* in the oven. The *giant* ate his breakfast and asked for his *hen* that laid the golden eggs. "Lay an egg, *hen!*" growled the *giant.* Then he called for his *harp.* "Play a tune, *harp!*" growled the *giant.* Then he called for his *bags of gold.* He counted the *bags of gold* until he grew sleepy. As the *giant* slept, *Jack* crept out of the oven and grabbed the *hen,* the *harp,* and the *bags of gold* and climbed down the *beanstalk.* But the *hen,* the *harp,* and the *bags of gold* made so much noise that the *giant* woke up. The *giant* and the *giant's wife* chased *Jack* down the *beanstalk.* When *Jack* reached the bottom, he called to his *mother* to bring an ax. With the ax he chopped down the *beanstalk* and the *giant* and the *giant's wife* fell to their deaths. And *Jack* and his *mother* lived happily ever after.

The End—Everyone takes a bow!

Children can even make up their own stories. A third grader wrote the following:

CINDERELLA
by Corby T. DeBoer
(Mattawan, Michigan)

CINDERELLA:	Work! Work! Work! (say with hand motions for type of work)
STEPMOTHER:	Cinderella! (say gruffly)
STEPSISTERS:	We're so beautiful! (say slowly and higher pitch)
BALL:	La! La! La! La! La! (sing this)
FAIRY GODMOTHER:	Bibbety, boppety, boo! (pretend to have magic wand)
PRINCE:	Charming! Charming! Charming! (bow as this is said)
GLASS SLIPPER:	Ting! Ting! (say in high voice)

Story. *Cinderella* lived with her *stepmother* and her *stepsisters.* One day when *Cinderella* was washing the floor, the doorbell rang. She opened the door and saw a messenger from the *Prince.* He said, "There shall be a *ball!*"

When the day of the *ball* came, *Cinderella* was too busy getting her *stepsisters* ready. She could not get herself ready, and besides, she had nothing to wear and no way to get to the *ball*. When her *stepmother* and *stepsisters* left, *Cinderella* began to cry. "Oh, how I wish I could go to the *ball!*" she cried. Suddenly an old lady appeared! *Cinderella* asked, "Who are you?"

"I'm your *fairy godmother*. I've come to see you off to the *ball!*" When *Cinderella* was about to leave, her *fairy godmother* said, "You must leave before the clock strikes twelve for everything will turn back as it was!"

The *Prince* was dazzled. He said, "Please dance with me!" And she did, but the clock struck its first strike—DONG!

"I must leave!!" When she was leaving, her *glass slipper* fell on the steps.

The *Prince* found it and said, "Whoever has the foot that fits this small *glass slipper,* I will marry."

Finally, the *glass slipper* came to *Cinderella*'s house. Her *stepsisters* said, "OOH, AHHH!" Then, *Cinderella* tried it on. It's a perfect fit! And that very day, she married the *Prince*. And they lived happily ever after!

SIMPLE PANTOMIMES

Simple pantomimes are brief vignettes children act out at their desks. They require children to concentrate on remembering past experiences, recall information, and form mental images. These skills are necessary for most learning tasks and can be sharpened through exercises that simple pantomime activities provide.

Variety of action is useful. Notice how the whole body is involved in the following activity:

"Wonderperson! There isn't a thing you can't do! You can leap tall buildings . . . run faster than a speeding bullet . . . break chains with a snap . . . hang by your teeth . . . twirl a rope on the end of your little finger . . . now with both hands . . . and rotate a hula hoop around your neck at the same time!"

Movements can involve a variety of levels and directions: up/down, back/forth, left/right, bending over, turning around, going in reverse, and so on. Note this as children act out the movements of a power shovel in operation:

". . . you drive over to your job. Now swing the cab around to the left and lower the dipper [outstretched arms] to that mound of dirt. Slowly now . . . scoop up the dirt. Now raise the dipper and swing back to the right. . . . That's it. . . . Now very slowly and carefully swing the dipper over the dump truck. . . . Now open the dipper and drop the dirt in. . . ."

Try changes of tempo. Actions can be done in double time, triple time, or speeded up like an old-fashioned movie. Or use slow-motion time, as with television replays of sports action.

"Pretend you are a bow-legged cowboy walking down a frontier town's dusty main road. . . . Now do that same walk a little faster . . . a little faster . . . Now stop! In slow motion take your pistol out of the holster. . . . Now reverse that action. . . . Take out the gun even slower. . . . Now reverse that action just as slowly. . . . Practice taking the gun out in double time . . . triple time. . . ."

Role-Playing.   Simple pantomimes can focus on different characters and topics.

Community helpers

"First pretend you are a doctor, giving someone a shot to fight disease.. . . Now you're a mail carrier, driving a mail truck and stopping to deliver some mail. . . . Now you're a city forester carefully sawing limbs from a tall tree. . . ."

Literary characters

"Pretend you're the wolf, sneaking through the woods, looking for Little Red Riding Hood. . . . Now you're the giant in "Jack and the Beanstalk" sitting down to dinner and eating a mountain of food. . . . Now you're Pecos Bill lassoing a cyclone to ride. . . ."

The Senses.   Pantomimes may focus on sensory awareness.

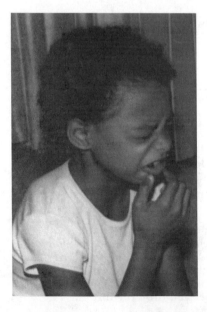

Pretend to eat a sour pickle.

 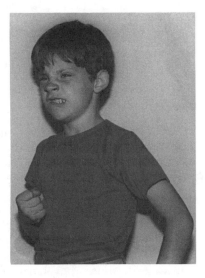

Expressing emotions: surprise . . .   . . . and anger.

Pretend that you are:

Tasting	Taking a dose of bitter medicine Biting into your favorite dessert Eating a dill pickle
Touching	Threading a needle Shuffling cards Playing a musical instrument
Hearing	A bird listening for a worm Asleep and the alarm rings and wakens you Suddenly aware of a small voice coming from your shirt pocket
Seeing	Observing the actions of a small insect on your desk Peeking through a knothole in a board fence Flipping through a magazine looking at food ads
Smelling	Opening a carton of milk and finding it sour Peeling onions Smelling smoke coming from inside your desk

Emotions. Pantomimes may also emphasize emotions.

Pretend you are:

All alone watching a scary television show

A cautious rabbit, eating a carrot for the first time

A crafty witch mixing a powerful brew in your cauldron

Conflict. Many of the above pantomimes have conflict in them to heighten their dramatic impact. Notice how the addition of conflict makes the following pantomimes more intriguing:

Pantomime	Addition of conflict
Eat an ice cream cone . . .	and the temperature is 100°.
As you read a book . . .	a pesky fly bothers you.
You're listening to a very boring speech . . .	being given by your boss.

GAMES

Games are also useful for beginning drama work. In fact, games have been used extensively in the work of Viola Spolin. (See the bibliography at the end of Chapter 1.) Many traditional games are also usable, provided they involve action or the development of some skill needed for drama. Many games can also serve double duty in the classroom with the incorporation of additional curricular concepts.

There are some cautions about traditional games. Those that eliminate players do not give children a chance to practice the skills they need to master. Eliminated players understandably become bored watching classmates excel where they have failed. Games that encourage competition often cause children to be more concerned about winning, gaining points, or teasing those who lose than about mastering the game's skills. Such games should be avoided or redesigned.

Miming Games

Traditional games that encourage imitative actions are Follow the Leader and Simon Says. Both can be played at the desk area. Instead of eliminating players in Simon Says, just note "ah, a few were caught that time" and continue the game. Older children can take turns being leaders for these games.

Games can be varied to incorporate other curricular concepts. One teacher reviewed sizes and shapes: "Simon says: Make yourself shaped like a box; walk in place taking giant steps; shape yourself like a piece of pie; become as small as a mouse," and so forth. Another used it to review foreign language words: "Blink your *yeux;* clap your *mains;* stamp your *pieds.*" Still another used it for the names of bones: "Shake your cranium; wiggle your ilium; rotate your clavicle"; and so on.

Sensory Games

Games that emphasize the development of sensory awareness are useful in drama work as well as many areas of the curriculum, such as science and language arts. Following are some examples.

Seeing

Who started the motion?   Players form a circle. One child is "it." A leader in the circle performs a series of actions that the other players must imitate. Imitators must try to stay with the leader without directly looking at the person. "It" must guess who is the initiator.

Scavenger hunt   The children are given a list of articles to collect within a given time limit. The articles may be a green pencil, a paper clip, a book with a picture of a Toltec temple, a paragraph with the word *magnet* in it, or a picture of a scientist conducting an experiment. The children may work on their own, in pairs, or in groups. After, discuss which method worked best and why.

Concentration   (1) Arrange a variety of items on a tray and allow the children to study them for a minute. Then have them recall the items from memory. (2) For variation, remove one or two items while the children close their eyes and see if they can guess which have been removed. (3) Rearrange the sequence of items after children have observed them and see if they can replace them in the original order. (4) For a variation of this game, have children face a partner whom they observe carefully. While observers' backs are turned, partners change one thing about themselves (for example, untie a shoe or take off a piece of jewelry). Observers must identify the partner's change.

Hearing

Guess the sound   Tape record a number of familiar sounds or make sounds behind a screen. Examples of sounds might be tearing a piece of paper, snapping fingers, the sound of a vacuum cleaner, or a running faucet. As the children listen to the sounds, they are to guess the source.

Who's my partner?   The leader distributes to each child a slip of paper with directions for a specific sound, such as "mew like a cat" or "whistle a bobwhite call." Each sound has two (or more) children performing it. On a signal everyone begins making the sound softly, repeating it until the partner is found. When the partner is located, the sounds stop, and the pairs wait where they are until all partners are discovered.

Touching

Guess the object   Have the children try to identify numerous items by their shape and texture. The objects might be in paper bags, the children might be blindfolded, or they might sit in a circle and have the objects passed behind their backs. Objects might be a fingernail file, a toy truck, a key chain, and so forth.

Leading the blind   Have children work in pairs, one with eyes closed and the other as leader. They explore the classroom, discovering that what is usually taken for granted is different when "viewed" in this way. Usually it is best not to allow any talking during this activity in order to aid concentration. Discuss safety precautions beforehand.

Tasting   Discuss the differences in tasting and smelling with such items as onion, chocolate, peppermint, and potato. We taste only sweet, sour, salt, and bitter. We smell rather than taste foods we eat. By holding the nose when tasting, it is difficult to guess a number of foods and flavors.

Smelling   Put a variety of items with distinctive odors in small containers. Have the children guess the items by sniffing *gently.* Items might be vinegar, ammonia, turpentine, Coke, banana oil, vanilla, cedar wood, and onion.

Imagination Games

Many drama leaders consider imagination as a muscle that needs frequent exercising. Games which focus on stimulating children's imagination may be played.

Pass the object I   Children sit in a circle. Pass a simple object such as a ball or a pencil and suggest that it is "a bird with a broken wing," "a very sharp knife," or another significant item. Silence is required so that the children can concentrate on the object, handle it, and respond to it before passing it on.

Pass the object II   Without using a prop the children pass an "object" of their own choosing. After the first child responds to the teacher's suggestion, (ice cube) he or she gives a new suggestion (sticky taffy) to which the next child must respond, and so on. The suggestions should remain an appropriate size for passing hand to hand.

Mystery box   Bring an imaginary box of any size into the center of the circle. For a very large box, several children may help carry it in. Volunteers, singly or in pairs, may open the box, which might become a packing carton, an elaborately wrapped gift, a cage, and so forth. Children take the item out of the box, handle or use it in some way, and then return it. The item should be appropriate to the size of the box.

Props to stimulate ideas for the game "What Could It Be?"

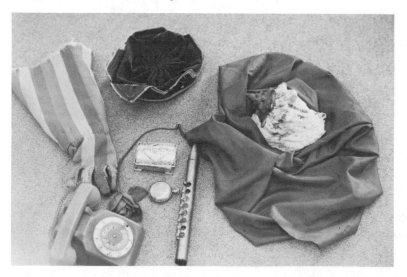

What could it be? Show children objects which they are to imagine might be something else. For example, a pair of scissors might become a dancing puppet, a spear for catching a fish, or a lorgnette. An interesting piece of driftwood might take on a variety of shapes as it is turned in different ways and examined. A conch shell might become a large rosebud, a horn, or a fairy's palace.

Communication Games

Some games help children increase their communication skills, both in speaking and in listening. Such games are designed to help children realize the importance of sending and receiving messages as accurately as possible.

What's this? One person describes an object—such as a safety pin, a paper clip, a light bulb, or an article of clothing—without naming what the item is. The listeners must draw each part of the object as they listen to the description. They cannot ask questions. Whenever listeners think they know what the object is, they may guess.

Giving directions This game is similar to the previous one. Two children stand back to back with a desk or table in front of each of them. Several items, such as a pencil, an eraser, and a book, are on each desk. Children take turns arranging the objects and then telling the partner how to arrange his or her items in the same pattern. Again, the listener cannot ask questions.
Variation: To help children see the importance of questioning for clarity, one partner—or both children—may be allowed to ask questions as the game is played.

Character voices Different types of people speak with different voices. Even an inanimate object might have a voice that is affected by the material it is made of: Tin produces a metallic sound, whereas cotton has a muffled quality. Place a number of simple sentences ("Good morning," "Hello," "How are you?" "Why me?") on cards and distribute them. On another set of cards a variety of characters (Papa Bear, Paul Bunyan, a grandfather clock, a tin soldier, a weeping willow, or a wooden spoon) are listed. Children say the sentence as the character might sound.

The olde junke shoppe Children pretend to be items in an old junk shop. They create sounds for each item to make as it moves. Children may choose to be a squeaking old rocking chair, a scratchy gramophone, an out-of-tune music box, and so on. The leader browses through the shop checking the various items. A child may play the store owner.

Movement Games

The following games encourage a variety of movements. The goal is to work toward relaxed and free movements within the specifications of the games. They all can be played at the desk until you and the students become accustomed to using more space.

Move to the beat   The children sit at their desks. The leader beats a drum, while the children move in as many different ways as possible. They may move *only* when the drum beats, so you should vary the beats, halt suddenly, and the like, so that the children are encouraged to listen closely.

Balance movement game   While standing by the sides of their desks, children perform a variety of movements that you call out. For example, they can stand on tiptoes, crouch and touch both knees, or take one step forward and one step back. The challenge: All the actions are to be done while they balance a book on their heads!

Painting   Children pretend to paint with a small brush that grows into a larger and larger brush until it is the size of a broom. Then it shrinks again. Children move from painting on their desk top to painting in the air and then at the side of the desk. They return to a seated position as the brush shrinks back to its original size. Encourage children to think of themselves as famous artists painting with great skill. Waltz music encourages free movements.

Activities with a ball   Children pretend to bounce different-sized balls: a basketball, a volleyball, a tennis ball, and so forth. Change the weights of the balls: The ball is heavy, and then it is light. The Harlem Globetrotters' theme, "Sweet Georgia Brown," is wonderful background music for this one.

GROUP MANAGEMENT IN LARGER AREAS OF SPACE

Foresight and preparation are needed in managing any group. Interestingly, when operating as a group, adults actually behave very much like a classroom of children. If you have gained experience leading a group of your own classmates in an activity, you will probably have fewer difficulties with a classroom of children. Following are some tips to keep in mind.

Giving Directions

Word directions explicitly and carefully. Children will usually do what is asked of them if it is clearly and firmly stated. Unfortunately, they usually cannot tell you when they do not understand. They simply go ahead and do something—even if it leads to chaos. That is your clue that your directions were unclear, and that you need to intervene before it is too late to rectify the situation.

As much as possible, give directions while children are seated and you have their attention. Once any group gets up and begins moving, you will have difficulty getting their attention again without reseating them—and that's not easy for you or them. (It's a little like the old song "How ya gonna keep 'em down on the farm, after they've seen Paree?")

How to Manage Rearranging the Room.

Always make sure you really need more space and that changing the classroom arrangement is really necessary before you go ahead and do it. If more space is needed, the desks can be moved to the edges of the room.

In many classrooms, a usual procedure in expanding space is to move the furniture against the walls. Experienced teachers can make it look ridiculously easy, but for a beginner it can be an awesome experience. Frequently a novice will tell an entire class to "quietly push your desks against the wall" and then expect it to be done in absolute silence. The sound of thirty desks scraping and thirty pairs of feet scuffling, added to spontaneous whispering and chattering, may be enough to convince the neophyte that experienced teachers possess supernatural powers. Furthermore, if one's voice lacks assurance, the verbal directions can sound more like a question than a command. This, in itself, can cause perfectly normal children to take advantage and "cut loose." They never hear the pandemonium they create with zestful abandon, but the rest of the school probably will!

What the casual observer often does not realize is that the seasoned teacher usually has previously set up an efficient procedure for moving desks which the children have followed many times. It only *seems* spontaneously organized. Until a beginning teacher has set up a similar procedure, there is no substitute for caution. It is much wiser to take a little more time and proceed step by step.

> "Row one, pick up your desks and place them here." (When they have finished and are seated, continue.) "Row two, over here" (and so on).

Avoid Sugarcoating Directions in Fantasy.

Inexperienced teachers are often afraid to make rules and give directions because they think children will not have as much fun. As a cover-up they sugarcoat directions in fantasy. For example, some leaders try to make a game out of moving desks, suggesting that the desks are "explosives" which the children have to move carefully so they do not blow up. However, such directions are too tempting for some children. "Exploding" one's desk may be even more interesting than the planned activity! It is usually best to be straightforward about getting the furniture arranged.

As another example, suppose you want the children to remain in a designated area, yet you warn:

> "You're like sticky gum, so don't touch anyone or you may stick together."

For most children this statement is like a Wet Paint sign; it becomes an interesting possibility and announces itself as a challenge to be tested. Ironically, they are then beguiled into doing exactly what you are trying to avoid. Not only do they touch each other; they clump in a huge mass before you ever figure out what happened! Being straightforward is usually safer.

> "During this activity you are to remain in your own space. Give yourself enough room so that you do not touch anyone."

It is always best to be explicit about no talking. You may be tempted to downplay directions. For example, you are doing a poem about snowflakes, and you say (quite creatively, you think):

> "Remember now, snowflakes don't talk."

But if children can imagine being a snowflake, they can also imagine that their snowflake is capable of speech. (In fact, you just might ask for this kind of imagination on another occasion.) So they begin chattering, rationalizing in their own minds that they are using "snowflake voices," and your good intentions have backfired. It is generally best to just say simply and directly:

> "For this activity I want you to move as silently as possible. There should be no talking at all. When everyone is quiet, we shall begin."

Repeating Directions.   Do not assume that once you give directions children will automatically understand and remember them. It may be difficult, for example, for children to stay in their area once the playing begins. Usually they mean well, but it is natural to gravitate toward friends, and soon social interaction completely overshadows the activity. Of course, concentration is usually lost.

It may take practice for children to learn to stay in separate playing areas, particularly young ones, whose bodies are constantly in motion. You may need to repeat your directions and your reasons for your rules—patiently—several times before children can follow through successfully. When children see how your rules help their concentration and make the playing more interesting, they will be able to follow them more readily.

Staying in Control with Nonverbal Directions.   Look for ways to maintain control without constantly scolding and nagging children about their behavior. Much of this control can be done nonverbally. Experienced teachers can do much with a glance, a definite shake of the head, or other simple tactics that convey as strong a message as a verbally stated one—such as waiting with folded hands or a finger to the lips for a group to settle down before trying to talk above their chattering. Many of these gestures will take time to learn and perfect, but you will do well to think of some possibilities for yourself.

One student teacher who was having a difficult time getting the children's attention because of her soft voice drew a large, colorful sign with

Cool It! written in bold letters. Whenever she wanted the group to be quiet and listen for further directions, she simply held up the sign and waited for a few seconds until everyone saw it. Then she proceeded with the activity. For her it worked.

You can often stop negative behaviors, such as disturbing chattering or minor horseplay, if you simply move in the direction of the offenders. The close proximity of the authority figure speaks for itself. If needed, a hand on the shoulder can be an additional nonverbal reminder of the rules.

Getting the Group's Attention.

Getting the Group's Attention. When any group moves out into larger areas of space, they make some noise just in their moving about. They also pay more attention to each other than to you and may even begin to talk. If you try to shout above the group's noise to get their attention, it only adds to the din and confusion. The children often are too engrossed in their activities to be aware that you are talking at all. Furthermore, when you raise your voice's volume, your pitch usually rises, too. As the situation escalates, you begin to sound like a screaming banshee. This obviously contributes to cacophony, to say nothing of causing a loss of dignity!

Visual and auditory cues are usually more effective. These may include the ring of a small bell or a beat on a drum; the flicking of lights or the raising of a hand.

Some commands can be fun, challenging, and effective. For example, children usually like the word *freeze* to call them to attention. It seems to them more of a game rule than a command. Other signals might be "Cut!" "Lights, camera, action!" "Quiet on the set!" "Roll tape!" or other commands from theatre, film, or television that children are familiar with. It makes them feel more professional.

Be careful, however, of overusing any one signal; they are more effective when used judiciously and sparingly. As you become more skilled and develop a rapport with the group, and as they become sensitive to your procedures and expectations, you may need only say

Attention-getting devices are useful.

"Groups, go to your areas. When you're settled, I'll give you further directions."

Taking Action.   When things go wrong, it is best to take direct action. Inexperienced teachers are often hesitant to do this, and instead try to muddle through or look the other way rather than face a problem. This usually makes an already bad situation even worse. Although there are many minor situations that can be overlooked because they will diminish on their own, a whole session can deteriorate quickly if serious problems are allowed to continue.

You may even need to stop the activity to sort out what has happened and find a way to remedy it. Even the children are aware that this procedure can be helpful. Once some kindergarten children were pretending to be baby animals and suddenly turned into ferocious tigers and lions, fighting one another. The student teacher stood in a near daze until, "out of the mouths of babes," a five-year-old tugged on her skirt and suggested, "Teacher, I think we need to sit down in a circle."

Understanding Problems

Children often get excited as they get ready to participate in drama. Excitement leads to whispered talking. Suddenly they are moving about, and disorganization sets in. It is not necessary to scold children for something that is a natural response. Just say good-naturedly,

"Whoops, I can see we've got a problem. Let's work on it."

Problems may also occur in spite of your best planning and intentions. You may get excited and rush the children before they are ready, thus

Problems can occur despite your best planning.

contributing to their hyperactivity. Or you may do too much discussing of an idea, and the children begin to get restless.

Recognizing and admitting one's own mistakes is important so that children know that the difficulties may not have been their fault:

> "I think I've kept you sitting a long time while we've discussed this. . . ."

> "Sometimes I get so excited about what we're doing that I rush you too fast. I think that may be what happened just now. We were really getting ahead of ourselves."

For your own emotional health, verbally acknowledging the problem is usually more helpful than silently blaming yourself or the children. Once, in trying to organize a group the author became exasperated with one child who was talking with a friend. Accusingly she asked, pointing a finger at him, "Can you do this?" He, puzzled but cooperative, nodded his head and pointed his finger also! At a time like this, a sense of humor is the best antidote.

These hints, though not all-inclusive, should help keep order and control, so that everyone can focus on the drama activities rather than on discipline problems.

SIMPLE CREATIVE MOVEMENT ACTIVITIES

Many children are able to create ideas easily and freely while others need stimulation and encouragement to develop into creative thinkers. In this section we'll look at some fairly simple creative movement activities and techniques you can use to guide the playing. Some can be played at the desk while others will be more effectively played in larger areas of space.

Creative movement activities may be played by the children in solo, in pairs, or in small groups. The ideas may come from a variety of topics. Following are some examples:

Exploratory movement　"Squeeze into the smallest (or roundest, hardest, fastest) thing you can be. What are you?"

Literature　"Let's pretend you are a gingerbread boy and have just come to life in the oven. The door is still closed and you're waiting to get out. I'll be the person who baked you, and when I open the door, you jump out and do one thing you think the gingerbread boy would do in his first moment of life *before* he runs away. . . ."

The study of shapes　"This time, pretend you're using something that is in the shape of a circle; maybe you'll ride a bicycle, eat a doughnut, or swing a lasso."

The interpretation of a musical selection　"Now that we've listened to some of George Gershwin's *An American in Paris,* let's act out some ideas to go with it. What are some of the things a visitor to Paris (or any other new place)

"Be as small as you can be. What are you?"

might do? I'll play part of the selection again and whenever I say 'Now,' change what you're doing and try something else."

Similar activities may be played in pairs and groups:

Being shadows in pairs   "Decide between you who will be the shadow and who will be the person the shadow is following and imitating. You'll have to decide who the person is and what he or she does during a day's activities."

Being robots in groups   "After you divide into groups, you'll need to decide what sorts of jobs your robots are working on: Are they painting a house or working in a restaurant? Then once you've decided on the job, you'll need to plan all the things you robots do."

Aids in Guiding Creative Work.   Children need an accepting, non-judgmental environment to feel free to create. All the following techniques are useful in helping children feel as comfortable as possible in their work.

1. Brainstorm some ideas with the whole group verbally before playing. ("What kinds of community helpers are there?")
2. As the children play their ideas, go around and check what they are doing. But keep the ideas private. If it seems appropriate, have them "freeze" while you go around and quickly interview a few. Your responses need only accept the idea: "Ah, that's interesting." "Um, hum." "Really?" and so forth. No judgments of relative worth need be made.
3. The climate needed for creativity is similar to that needed for encouraging involvement discussed in Chapter 2. Therefore unison and brief playing will be helpful at first. Use side-coaching to remind children of the different ideas they mentioned in discussion. Note some of the ideas you see being played, or

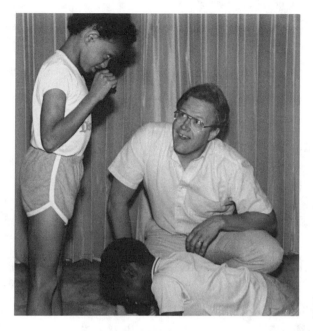

Leader listens appreciatively
to children's ideas.

suggest other possibilities for them to consider. Again, music will be helpful in stimulating students' thinking and providing a filler for any awkward silences.

4. When the playing is ended, comment on what some of the ideas were without identifying the players. ("I saw some people putting insulation in the attic, closing drapes to keep out the heat or cold, turning off lights—all kinds of ways to save energy.") This technique shows acceptance of the students' ideas and lets the rest of the class learn what the various ideas were.

5. As children become confident in creating, they will want to share their ideas with each other. Those who wish may do so, either by telling what they did or by demonstrating their ideas.

Control Techniques in Creative Work. Beginning leaders are sometimes afraid to let students be creative in their playing for fear they will get out of control. Providing a definite structure or framework for creative work can keep the class organized and lessen your anxiety. The following tips are useful:

1. Use topics with a built-in control. Children are usually more motivated to play quietly if they are secret agents doing undercover work, museum statues which come to life when all is dim and quiet, or elves secretly doing good deeds or slyly making mischief.

2. Always be definite about when the children should start and stop their pantomiming. Following are some suggestions:
   a. You may simply say, "Begin. . . . Freeze."
   b. You may count, saying for example, "Think of three things you can do as I count to three." Then count slowly, pausing in between counts.

    c. "When the music (or drum, tamborine, and so on) begins, you may move; when it stops, you freeze."

    d. As you become more confident, your language can be more descriptive. After explaining instructions, you can say mysteriously:
"When the lights go off, that will be the signal that Halloween night is here. And all you little hobgoblins will come out from your hiding places [desks] to dance your own little dance [solo at the side of the desk] in the moonlight. But when the clock strikes five o'clock [hammer on a small gong], you must return to your hiding places again where no human eye can see you."

    e. Children's inventiveness and length of playing time needed will vary with each individual. Therefore, it is helpful to tell the children that they are to sit down when they have played their idea and wait quietly for others to finish.

ACTIVITIES FOR SELF-CONTROL

Although games in themselves have a built-in control, there are several games and activities which particularly focus on building self-control and self-discipline. Children need to learn that self-discipline is necessary for artists to perform at their best—just as sound minds and bodies are important to athletes.

For these activities you will eventually want to guide older groups to let their physical needs and their ideas determine the use of space. They may move wherever they feel they need to and wherever their ideas take them, provided they can remain absorbed in their work and can be aware of the others in the group. Such an experience in democratic responsibility is extremely valuable but may need to be approached systematically.

The student leader will find these games helpful in enticing children to work at developing these important skills. The repeated playings of the exercises should result in increased skills. Many similar games are practiced continuously by professionals, so they provide constant review material.

The solo materials will be the easiest for younger children, though a few of the paired activities are also possible. Group activities are reserved for older or more advanced players.

Solo Work in Self-Control

Parades   Young children love parades. They are fun, but they are also controlled and precise. Children can be assigned parts or may decide who they want to be. Begin marching in a circle with a few children, and then add on in ones, twos, threes, or more.

Parade ideas can come from music, literature, or other sources of stimulus. Following are a few ideas.

Music

"Parade of the Wooden Soldiers," Leon Jessel. Stiff, wooden movements are encouraged. This music is good also for a parade of marionettes, robots, and windup or mechanical toys.

"March Past of the Kitchen Utensils," Vaughan Williams. This is fun for physical characterization of various cooking tools.

"Baby Elephant Walk," Henry Mancini. Other animals, in addition to the elephants, can take part in this parade.

"Circus Music," from *The Red Pony,* Aaron Copland. A circus parade is always good fun.

Literature

And to Think That I Saw It on Mulberry Street, Dr. Seuss. New York: Vanguard Press, 1937, Marco makes up a story about what he sees after being asked daily "What did you see today?" See also (32).

"Skeleton Parade," Jack Prelutsky (18). Skeletons are out on Halloween night.

The Snow Parade, Barbara Brenner. New York: Crown Publishers, 1984. Young Andrew Barclay creates a parade with animals, people, and "hundreds more." Try using Leroy Anderson's "Sleigh Ride" for accompaniment.

The Wedding Procession of the Rag Doll and the Broom Handle and Who Was in It, Carl Sandburg. San Diego: Harcourt Brace Jovanovich, 1922, 1978. An unusual procession is made up of many unlikely characters—such as Spoon Lickers, Easy Ticklers, and Musical Soup Eaters—that offer ideas for different movements.

Walking game Establish the point that space must be used responsibly. Play "walking" music with a lively $\frac{2}{4}$ beat. Children simply walk about the room sharing space. There can be no bumping into anyone. Begin with a few children, and then add on more. A group discussion with the children might be helpful at some point, asking children to share their observations on "What do people do in order to share space with each other?" (They watch each other; they have to vary their speed or even stop in order not to bump into anyone; sometimes you pass around them, moving sideways.)

In-service teachers practice moving in slow motion.

Slow-motion and fast-motion activities Slow motion is an excellent exercise in disciplined, thoughtful movement. And when slow motion is mastered, it can be as fascinating to watch as it is to perform. Since almost any activity can be played in slow motion, this technique will be mentioned frequently throughout the text.

Children will first need to learn the concept. Compare slow motion to moving underwater or through heavy syrup, to the television replays of sports events, or to time-lapse photography.

Moving in slow motion is not always easy and requires the guidance of the leader. Children have to be reminded to keep the movement slow; in the excitement of moving, the tendency is to speed up.

> That's it. Keep it slow. Freeze. Now this time go even slower—three times as slow as you just did. [Give these directions in a slow-motion voice, like a record playing on slow speed.]

Music can be helpful. Try selections such as Debussy's "Clair de Lune" or "Afternoon of a Faun." Slow-motion effect can be gained by playing almost any slow selection at a slower speed.

Fast motion can also be an exercise in self-control. Encourage students to move like people in an old silent film. Because the effect is amusing and everyone looks a little ridiculous, it helps ease the tension of performing in a sophisticated manner. Often older students feel more comfortable moving in this fashion. Scott Joplin tunes provide excellent musical background.

"Freeze" game encourages physical control and self-discipline.

Freeze game   This game establishes the fact that space must be used responsibly. Children may move about the room quickly in any way they wish (without bumping into each other), but on signal (drum beat, ringing bell) they must freeze. Specify certain movements, such as hopping or skipping. They may also be directed to freeze into a position or an expression, such as looking funny or becoming an animal.

Be sure to give a definite signal for freezing and test it out first with just a few children. It is also better to begin with only a few children at a time and gradually add on more. The goal is to have the entire class playing the game at the same time, but this will probably not happen the first time you try it.

Variation: Children move only when you beat a drum or while the music plays. They must stop when you do.

Circle game   Two concentric circles are formed. They rotate in opposite directions. Players are to remain equally spaced as they march around the circle to lively music. When the leader calls "Change," the players must reverse directions.

After this much of the game is mastered, another challenge can be added: The leader moves around the circles and taps players on the shoulder. The tapped person moves into the opposite circle and changes directions while still marching. Other players must adjust the spacing so that the space is still equidistant between players. The leader can continue to call "Change" at any time.

Caught in the act   In this game children move in any way they wish while their feet are "glued" to the floor. A signal is given to freeze into position. Another signal is given and they move about the room *in the position they were frozen in.* Another signal stops them, roots them to the spot, and the game repeats.

Be careful!   Pantomime walking over stepping stones, on a tightrope, or on a fence top, retaining balance. Do this at the side of the desks or have small groups go from one end of the room to the other.

Conducting an orchestra   All the children are orchestra leaders and must keep with the beat of a particular piece of music. Try a variety of music with different rhythms and moods—from classical to the latest hits.

Spies   In groups (one group at a time), be spies sneaking through a building guarded by an electronic eye. Children must move as rapidly as possible from one side of the room to another but must go down to the floor whenever they hear the sound cue which indicates activation of the electronic eye. (An alarm-clock bell or buzzer works well for this.) The objective is to move quickly *and* quietly. Groups can work to improve their speed.

I won't laugh   Several students at a time sit facing the class. They cannot close their eyes or plug their ears. The rest of the class volunteers to tell jokes, make faces, or whatever else they can think of (without touching the contestants) to make them laugh. Again, groups or individuals could work to increase the length of time they can hold out.

Interrogation In each group, one child is the questioner. He or she focuses on one person, but it is the person on the right of the questioned person who must answer, and with a straight face. The questioned person must maintain eye contact with the questioner and not laugh. Whoever in the group cannot remain solemn throughout the proceedings becomes the next interrogator. For an added challenge, if the questioner points a finger at a subject, the person on the left must answer. Try going fast.

Falling Children love to fall. Suggest that anyone can fall, but that it takes real skill to do it with control. Caution them not to fall on unprotected parts of their bodies like elbows, knees, and heads. Think of different kinds of objects that fall: a leaf, a balloon losing air. Fall in slow motion. No one can reach the ground before you count slowly to ten. Have them close their eyes so they concentrate only on their own work.

To tire out an overactive group, make them fall in a variety of ways very quickly: "Up again. This time fall quickly like a falling star. Now!" (They fall.) "Up. This time you're a feather. Fall on the count of five." (They fall.) "Up again. . . ."

Making noiseless sounds Children pantomime making a vocal sound by using their face and body but not their voice. Try it in slow motion. Cough, sneeze, gulp, gasp, sigh, and shout.

Pair and Group Work in Self-Control

Many groups of children need assistance and motivation in order to work together. The games in this section are useful in achieving this goal.

Sound pantomime One child pantomimes while another creates the sound effects. At first, the sound effects should fit the timing of the pantomime. Then let the pantomimer fit movements to the sound effects. Use simple ideas at first: someone sneaking across a creaky floor trying not to be heard; sawing a piece of lumber; cutting down a tree with an ax; trying to start an old, junky car; a robot moving with creaking joints.

Two-person jobs Select a task which requires two people to perform. Pretend to fold a flag or tablecloth; saw wood with a lumberjack's saw; play seesaw. Pairs must concentrate on the pantomimed object and cooperate to make the object appear real.

Mirroring Two people face each other. One is the mirror, and the other the person using the mirror. The mirror must follow the leader in putting on makeup, face washing, shaving, and so on. Consider possibilities with a full-length mirror also, as in practicing a dance step. Switch parts. Try this in slow motion to keep the actions carefully "mirrored."

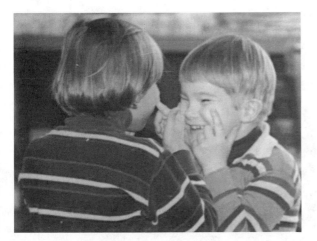

Kindergartners play the "Mirror Game."

Sculpturing   One person is the sculptor, and the other a piece of clay. The sculptor molds clay into a statue, giving it a particular stance or emotional attitude. The statue must allow itself to be moved about. Nontouchers and the ticklish will find this a real challenge.

Group jobs   Five people are carrying a large piece of glass from one side of the room to the other. The five people must coordinate their movements so that the imaginary piece of glass really seems to exist. As the group walks, the pane of glass must stay in one piece! As an added challenge have the group walk as fast as possible, "upstairs," "downstairs," and the like. Other group jobs might be firefighters carrying an extension ladder, pirates carrying a large treasure chest, or police moving a very tall murder victim.

Tug-of-war   Two teams of three or more pretend to pull on an imaginary rope. The rope must seem to exist. The leader needs to side-coach the game: "Team 1 is ahead. . . . Now it's team 2. . . ." On the leader's signal the rope breaks and the players fall in slow motion. Players cannot reach the floor until the leader, who is counting slowly, reaches the count of ten.

Conducting an orchestra   This time the children are in groups pantomiming to music. One is the conductor, while the others are playing specific instruments. Drums, cymbals, violins, and trombones are particularly good because they require large movements. March music (Sousa) is easiest to begin on. For further self-discipline stop the music periodically so players have to freeze.

Mirroring in groups   After experiencing a pair mirroring, the children can try pairs mirroring pairs. For example, a person at a beauty or barber shop is mirrored; then the hairdresser or barber is mirrored. A manicurist and shoe shiner, both mirrored, may even be added for a total of eight people.

"Tug of War" encourages concentration and focus.

One at a time   Several players pretend to be in a given setting, perhaps a living room. They are seated randomly. They may move about the room as they like, but they do not interact. However, only one person may move at a time. The action of the next person moving freezes the first mover in place until that player decides to initiate movement again. For example, person 1 gets out of a chair and turns on an imaginary TV set. Person 2 picks up a newspaper from a table, which freezes person 1 at the TV. Perhaps person 3 crosses her legs and freezes person 2. Then person 1 might decide to return to his seat, and so forth. Children must become very sensitive to each other's movements or the game fails. They must also be assertive if they want to move. The leader monitors and coaches: "Only one person can move at a time. . . ."

To help children learn the game, it is useful to give players a number. You call the numbers at random to indicate when the children may move. Once the children understand how the game is played, they initiate their own actions.

Variation: Have children sit in a circle and not move from their seats. All initiated action must be in a seated position. Work toward using smaller and smaller actions. Groups of five to ten work best, but more than one group may play at a time. (Note: The spontaneity of this game makes it fun for the rest of the children to watch. Dramatic tension is added if children pretend to be undercover detectives.)

Mechanical movement   The movement of robots, windup or mechanical toys, music boxes, and so forth, combines creative work and controls very nicely. The leader is the operator who manages the "on" and "off" switches.

Players create a machine by adding on parts, one by one.

In pairs and groups children create machines with interacting parts. The machines may be real (household appliances, indoor and outdoor machinery of all sizes) or imaginary (homework machine, wake-up machine that also gets you out of bed, or a dream machine). Other mechanical group work might include clocks with characters that move as the hour strikes (Leroy Anderson's "Syncopated Clock"), a mechanical circus, or a merry-go-round (Aaron Copland's "Circus Music" from *The Red Pony*). Again, you can be the operator who manages the "on" and "off" switches.

Children may also enact invented story lines. For example:

Story A. The toys in Santa Claus's workshop are helping to make new toys. But their batteries run down and they slowly come to a stop. You (as Santa's chief elf) recharge them, one by one, so that they can continue their work and return to the shelf before Santa awakens.

Story B. Robots are going on a picnic. It rains, and the robots all "rust" and are "frozen." You (as a garage mechanic) can oil them up, one by one, so that they can finish the picnic and get home.

Machine ideas can come from literature. Consider such stories as the following:

"The Doughnuts," Robert McCloskey (61). A doughnut machine goes haywire and cannot stop making doughnuts. Children will probably suggest creating "the part that squeezes out the dough," "the flipper to turn the doughnuts over," "the paddle that keeps pushing the doughnuts along," and "the chute where they come out."

Mr. Murphy's Marvelous Invention, Eileen Christelow. New York: Clarion Books, 1983. Mr. Murphy, a pig inventor, creates a unique housekeeping machine for his wife, but it cannot do anything right.

"The Sneetches," Dr. Seuss (33). Children can create both the "Star-On" and "Star-Off" machine. What parts are needed in these fanciful machines that can put stars on and take them off Sneetches' bellies?

CONTROLLING FIGHTS AND BATTLES:
STAGE COMBAT

Perhaps one of the greatest challenges in control work is staging combats. Fight scenes are found in many stories and in other curricular materials. These are always exciting to play, but it would obviously be foolhardy to let a group of children enact a fight scene without some previous preparation. If you choose to play such scenes, students need to learn how to "stage" fights as they are in fact handled in movies, in the theatre, and on television. (For an alternative method of depicting fights see "Frozen Pictures" in Chapter 7.)

Fighting is of interest to many children. They are usually intrigued and impressed with the fact that the realistic fights they see in dramas are really artful pretense and organized with great care. They like to learn, the way actors and stunt people do, how to throw a punch without making actual physical contact with the partner. They also like the challenge of pretending to receive a blow in a convincing manner. Be sure they understand that it is the victim who makes the punch seem real.

Throughout all stage combat work it is wise to focus on the challenge of skill development: "Anyone can shove and push people around and even hit them. But it takes skill and concentration to make pretend fighting look real so that no one gets hurt." When students are capable of working out combat ideas in cooperation with each other and rehearsing "staging" techniques, they are often greatly pleased. It takes far more skill than an ordinary playground brawl, and is certainly more satisfying for all.

The following procedure is recommended for teaching this kind of lesson:

1. First children work alone, pretending to be a victim receiving a blow. You call the blows by counting. You might also tell them where the punches will be: (a) stomach, (b) chin, (c) left shoulder. Allow them to include moans and groans as long as they can hear the cues. You can eventually pretend to be the one giving the blows with some dialogue: "One. Take that! Two. And that! Three. That'll teach ya, ya orn'ry varmint!"

2. Next the children work alone, imagining the partner they hit. They must practice and perfect their skill in stopping the blow at the precise moment before contact. The point of contact they aim at may be imagined or may be a wall, their desk, or the palm of one hand. Again you call the blows. This time you might pretend to be the one receiving the punches and give appropriate verbal response: "One," (Pause for the hit.) "Ugghh! Two," (pause) "Ooh, you got me there" (and so on).

3. Now they can work in pairs, but again you count. They may decide on

Pretending to hit; pretending to be hit. Learning to master the pretense of fighting.

five punches. Go slowly, perhaps even freezing after each count to make sure all rules are being followed.
4. Speed up *only* when they exhibit appropriate skill and sensitivity to each other. If you see any problems at all, stop immediately!

When children have shown real skill and care in their work, they may be allowed to try some scenes of fights from different sources: social studies, science, or literature. The fights may be between people or animals. Along with these dramas there might be valuable discussions on historic weapons or animal armor.

Selected Stories with Fight Scenes

The Elephant's Child, Rudyard Kipling. New York: Walker, 1970. After the elephant's child gets his trunk, he goes home and spanks all his relatives (various animals) the way they used to spank him. How can children show both spanking scenes in pairs? Before playing you might discuss the different ways the various animal relatives (giraffe, ostrich, hippopotamus, baboon) would spank. See also (14).

The King's Stilts, Dr. Seuss. New York: Random House, 1939. The Nizzards (large birds) and the Cats have a battle. The story says that "the fur flew fast but the feathers flew faster. It took only ten minutes."

The Knight and the Dragon, Tomie de Paola. New York: Putnam Publishing, 1980. A knight and a dragon fight each other unsuccessfully in this picture book with very little text.

Millions of Cats, Wanda Gág. New York: Coward-McCann, 1928, 1977. The cats all "bit and scratched and clawed each other" and finally ate each other up. How can they show this in pairs?

"The Mungle and the Munn," Jack Prelutsky (17). This is a fight for pairs. The two make a decision to meet again, since the fight was so much fun.

"Robin Hood's Merry Adventure with the Miller," Howard Pyle (36). Robin Hood and his men want to play a joke on the miller, but their plan backfires. The fight begins with the miller opening his bag as he pretends to search for money, continuing with the blows he gives the flour-covered men, and ending when Robin gives three blasts on his horn.

The snow sculpture melts slowly. A quieting activity to close the drama session.

QUIETING ACTIVITIES

These simple activities are useful in ending a drama period. After children have been involved in a lot of action and concentration it is often helpful to calm them down rather than let them go to their next task at a high pitch.

One technique is to narrate a quieting selection in which the subjects are relaxed or tired and the actions subdued. The literature listed below is suitable for this purpose. Children may close their eyes as they enact a selection. Try to capture the quieting mood in your voice or use some quiet music for accompaniment.

> "Fatigue," Peggy Bacon (20). The subway ride home at night features tired workers.
>
> *Grandfather Twilight,* Barbara Berger. New York: Philomel, 1984. A grandfatherly figure is shown going through his nightly ritual, putting the world to sleep.
>
> "Grandpa Bear's Lullaby," Jane Yolen (24,31). Bear cubs settle down for a long winter's sleep.
>
> "Keep a Poem in Your Pocket," Beatrice Schenk de Regniers (22,24). A poem will sing to you at night when you are in bed.
>
> "Lullaby," Robert Hillyer (26). We are in a rowboat, drifting along peacefully.
>
> *Moonsong Lullaby,* Jamake Highwater. New York: Lothrop, Lee & Shepard, 1981. Select excerpts from this long poetic description by a Native American author.
>
> "Snow toward Evening," Melville Crane (3,22). A calm, peaceful snowy night is described.
>
> "Sunning," James S. Tippett (3,24). An old dog sleeps lazily on a porch.
>
> "Tired," Shel Silverstein (15). A child enumerates the many tasks accomplished while lying in the grass.
>
> "Tired Tim," Walter de la Mare (3,18,24). Poor Tim is just too tired to move.
>
> "Who Has Seen the Wind?" Christina Rossetti (18,22,24,31). Leaves hang trembling and bow their heads when the wind passes by.

Leaders may also create their own simple quieting activities by narrating a few sentences about a candle burning and slowly melting or by having children pretend to be a leaf floating on calm waters.

The purpose of the quieting experience is to relax the group and to calm down any hyperactivity. Perhaps more importantly, however, it helps the children to absorb the concepts, experiences, and feelings covered during the drama period.

FOR THE COLLEGE STUDENT

1. Collect or design each of the following:
   a. A finger play
   b. A single-action poem

    c. An action song
    d. An action game
    e. An action story
    f. A quieting activity

2. Find a game or design one of your own that has action in it but can be played at the desk.

3. Select a game to lead your classmates in. Give the directions for playing the activity. Organize the group for playing the game. Bring the playing to a close. Afterward discuss with your classmates what your strengths and weaknesses were. Brainstorm ways to improve the activity.

4. Select or design a game that illustrates the use of controls.

5. Find or create a game to develop children's imagination.

6. Select or design five sensory games, one for each of the senses.

7. Select or design a communication game, emphasizing either speaking or listening skills.

8. Write a pantomime, of at least fifty words, which emphasizes a variety of actions.

9. Write five sensory pantomimes, one for each of the five major senses.

10. Write a pantomime emphasizing emotions.

11. Make a list of three brief pantomimes; then in a second list add conflict to each.

12. As a class, play some of the games for self-control. Afterward discuss your reactions. Were you able to improve your skills as a result of the playing? How do you think this was accomplished?

13. Discuss various physical features of the classroom environment. Consider such factors as fixed desks, rows of desks on runners, large rooms with movable furniture, small rooms with tables and chairs, carpeting, thin classroom partitions and walls, skylights, and shades. Consider ways to accommodate any of these physical features. Include selection of material, planning and organizing space, and giving directions.

14. Brainstorm a list of different machines to use for mechanical movement. Consider literature and curricular sources. Try creating some with your classmates in small groups.

15. With a partner, go through the steps in staging combat. Suggest other literature or curricular sources.

5

Literature for Narrative Pantomime
From Solo Activities to Improvised Plays

A number of years ago, while searching for an easy way to help teachers get started in creative drama, we discovered that many excellent pieces of children's literature centered primarily on action. We found that if such pieces were narrated, children could play along, pantomiming the actions. We called both the materials and the technique of playing them narrative pantomime. Some of the most familiar pieces include Paul Galdone's version of *The Three Bears,* Beatrix Potter's *The Tale of Peter Rabbit,* and Dr. Seuss's *How the Grinch Stole Christmas.*[1]

THE VALUE OF NARRATIVE MATERIALS

Narrative pantomime provides an expedient, efficient, and enjoyable way to dramatize excellent literature. It is a useful activity regardless of the amount of experience you and the children have had in creative drama. Since pantomime materials are usually easier to enact than dialogue materials, narrative pantomimes are useful for beginning groups as well as for warm-ups with experienced groups.

Narrative materials also provide a foundation for further creative work. There are a variety of ways to elaborate on them, as you will see.

[1]All materials referred to in this chapter are listed in the bibliographies in this chapter.

Children are also introduced to basic dramatic structure: a plot with a conflict and a beginning, a middle, and an ending.

The Value to Children

Narrative pantomimes provide a way for children to experience excellent literature, trying on favorite characters and joining them in their adventures. Through this process they interpret the literature and increase their understanding of it. Particularly with the stories, children feel a sense of accomplishment and satisfaction in being able to enact completed little dramas early on.

Children are able to be successful in narrative activities, since they need only follow the actions the literature prescribes. This gives children security and self-confidence to try more challenging drama work later. At the same time, they must also listen carefully to know what to do and when to do it. This helps them focus their concentration and develops listening skills.

The Value to the Leader

Because children must follow the literature's directions in narrative pantomime, there is built-in organization, an important aid to the beginning leader. By narrating the action, you give the cues for playing and have control of the dramatization.

As you become proficient in narrative pantomime, you will quickly learn what literature works best and will soon find yourself being able to edit material easily and even to write some of your own materials. (This will be discussed further in the next chapter.) Narrative pantomime will also help you in developing descriptive commentary, useful in the technique of side-coaching in other activities.

THE TYPES OF NARRATIVE PANTOMIME MATERIAL

Narrative pantomime literature may have one character (solo or individual playing), two characters (paired playing), or even several (group playing).

Material for Solo or Individual Playing

In solo material the character may live alone, as does Henry the Duck in *Henry's Awful Mistake.* Or the character may be alone on an adventure, as is Harold on his many purple crayon adventures. (See *Harold and the Purple Crayon, Harold's Circus, Harold's Fairy Tale,* and *Harold's Trip to the Sky.*) Some material has two or more characters who act independently of each other. In such material the child can play all the parts, changing from one to the other with relative ease. *The Pond,* for example, describes the movements of several characters, one at a time: the water, a dragonfly, shadows, and so forth. Or in the poem "Foul Shot" by Edwin A. Hoey, the students can first be the ballplayer, then the basketball, and finally the crowd watching the basketball game.

Material for Paired Playing

Stories or poems with two fairly equal characters are played in pairs. Such a story might be Beatrix Potter's *The Tale of Two Bad Mice*. Paired playing can be used with stories in which one character goes on an adventure and meets different people along the way. One child plays the adventurer, and the partner plays all the people who are met. Or in a story like "Gertrude McFuzz," the same child who plays Lolla-Lee-Lou can also play Uncle Dake.

Material for Group Playing

Material which has several characters (or has the potential for adding characters) can be played in groups. Some of the characters in group stories have small parts, but if they are interesting ones, the children will want to include them all. For example, in *Ittki Pittki* there are, in addition to the title role, the prince, the wife, four sons, the prince's messenger, the doctor, the funeral director, and all the customers and mourners. Although some appear only briefly, they all are important to the plot.

As you become more familiar with narrative pantomime, you will want to try many varieties. This chapter will cover techniques for playing narrative pantomime. Within the chapter there are extensive bibliographies, listed in three groups according to the playing that the literature is most suited for: solo, pair, and group playing. Let us first look at the general considerations you will need to make in playing narrative pantomimes.

GENERAL CONSIDERATIONS FOR PREPARING NARRATIVE PANTOMIMES

Selecting and Editing the Material

Material used for narrative pantomime must have enough continuous action to keep children actively involved from beginning to end. The selections in the bibliographies in this chapter are some of the easiest to use. But since most authors and poets have not written their materials for narrative pantomime purposes, almost any selection can benefit from minor editing. Some material benefits from tightening the physical action, even to the extent of omitting some words or even sentences, as long as the plot is not destroyed.

The most dramatic materials build to a climax and have a quieting ending. Many stories and poems even have the character in a settled position at the end. This is a welcome aid in getting the students back in their seats or in a stationary position after playing. In some cases you will want to add this feature with an added line or two or a simple rewording. For example, even though you read the entire story *The Snowy Day* to children, you might end their *playing* of it with Peter going to bed and dreaming of tomorrow and another day in the snow. This way the children are seated and sleeping at the end, rather than waking and going outdoors again as the book's ending does.

You will sometimes find that additional action is helpful, particularly in picture books, where much of the story is told through the artwork. Adding descriptive detail to action can also enrich the drama experience. For example, a line may read, "The farmer worked in the field all day long." You might add the words "cutting and stacking the hay." Or if you want to give them something to do without being too active, you might narrate "The bears became tired and sat down under a tree to rest and enjoy the scenery."

Editing Dialogue

Some stories have brief lines of dialogue. If they are short, the children will enjoy repeating them. It is almost crucial, for example, to let children say "Gwot, I ate it!" the final line of George Mendoza's "The Hairy Toe." Or in Russell Hoban's *The Little Brute Family*, the lines "How nice" and "May we keep it?" are fun to repeat. Longer lines can be dropped.

Some dialogue is easily pantomimed (for example, "No," "I don't know," or "Here"), but generally the mouthing of words is distracting. Therefore, if you see the children doing this as you narrate, it probably means that there is too much dialogue and it should be cut (or that children are ready to add dialogue, which will be discussed later in this chapter).

Presenting the Material

There is no one way to present the material before enacting it. You might want to read the story first and discuss it to make sure the children understand it and know what they are to do. Other times you might want to read a story "cold" and have them improvise on the spot. In any event, you will always want to be sure they know what they are to do, have ideas for doing it, understand how to use space, and can handle any physical action safely. It is sometimes helpful to have competent students demonstrate to the others how to play difficult or problem situations.

Creative Interpretation of Movement

Although narrative materials have many actions to perform, there is no one way to interpret a particular action. Children may interpret their ideas in whatever way they choose. Even with a fairly explicit line such as "frogs hop," there is room for creativity. Some children may choose to enact their frog in an upright position, hopping on hind legs. Others may want to be on all fours, perhaps even crooking their arms to represent the frog's bowed front legs.

Some actions are more challenging. For example, in Carl Sandburg's "Lines Written for Gene Kelly to Dance To," the children are asked if they can dance a question mark. This could be interpreted in a variety of ways: The feet might draw a question mark on the floor; the hands might inscribe one in the air; or the whole body might form one, dissolving and reforming in a rhythmic dance.

Encourage students to find their own ways of performing an action. The ideas can be discussed prior to the playing and perhaps tried out and demonstrated before the entire selection is played.

Limiting Space

As discussed earlier, it is most useful to keep the students working at their desks or in a designated place on the floor. The desks can often become part of the drama if you refer to them as a bed, a car, a table, or whatever the material calls for.

For pair and group playing, be sure the children understand the limits of their space. In some cases it may also be necessary to let only half the class play while the other half observes. (Observers might help with the sound effects or other technical aspects.)

Narrating the Material

Much of the artistic burden of narrative pantomime depends on the narrator's reading abilities. You need to practice giving a good oral reading interpretation. Know the story well enough to be able to keep an eye on the class's performance and to time the pauses for playing.

One student teacher learned the value of good narrating most graphically. She began by selecting a short poem that was too difficult for her kindergartners to understand. Then she read the poem, haltingly and without once glancing up. The children stood patiently, listening, but had no idea what to do. At the end of the poem and after a moment's silence, one little voice piped up, "Is that it?" Although the student had made an error in selecting inappropriate material, she should have realized the children were doing nothing. A couple of glances up from the page would have made this clear.

Experiment to determine your vocal capabilities. Even when children are pantomiming, they are moving about and making some noise in the process. If you have a soft voice, it may be necessary to allow only half the class to play at a time in order that your voice may be heard.

Timing and vocal intensity can also control the action and the noise level. Although you should not rush your narrating, it is generally better to use shorter pauses rather than longer ones until you are sure the children are filling in the time with meaningful actions. Also, if the students should get a bit too noisy, just pause. As they quiet down to hear the next cue, speak in a softer voice. This should help calm their playing down.

It is usually best not to let the students be the narrators, particularly at first. Later, when they become familiar with narrative pantomime, you may

A small group rehearses its play with a student narrator.

find superior readers volunteering to narrate and doing an excellent job. (One of our best narrators was a second grader who read *Seven Skinny Goats* for his classmates to play. His only problem was keeping from laughing at the antics of the players!)

If you have several talented readers, you might want to let them all be narrators for one selection. Just divide the material at logical intervals. This technique is then very similar to "reader's theatre."

It should be added that when children see the importance of the narrator's role and have a desire to try it, they are often motivated to perfect their reading skills. The narrator's role then becomes as significant to them as the major characters in the story.

Using Music

Some materials benefit from musical background, which lends atmosphere, sustains involvement, and encourages ideas. Some suggestions are indicated in the bibliographies in this chapter. You will need to rehearse the narration with the music before trying it with the class to be sure it will enhance the playing.

Evaluating

Both you and the students will be evaluating the playing throughout. Acknowledge the good work you see them doing, noting the playing and the students' management of themselves:

"You had so many interesting and different ways of being a cat. I saw some washing themselves; some were sitting on their haunches; and I think I even heard some quiet purring."

"I liked the way you were able to stay in your own space and not interfere with someone else's work."

Self-evaluation is also important and can be encouraged by asking

"What's one thing you did that you liked the best?"

"What do you think you might do differently the next time we play it?"

Some may like to share their ideas for interpretation, both in telling about it as well as in demonstrating.

Replaying

If students have enjoyed the material and their own expression of it, they may ask to repeat it. In repeated playings they can perfect their ideas with your encouragement and guidance. New goals may be established.

"This time you may want to try some new ideas."

"I'll slow down this time in the part where you thought I read a little too fast for you to act out all the ideas you had."

In replaying, children might wish to add characters. They may ask to add Thayer in *Beady Bear* or Peter's dog in *Whistle for Willie.* They might want to add several of the characters in *Smedge,* including Smedge's owners, the limousine driver, and the President of the United States, making it into a group story.

The cat licks its fur to clean itself.

A BIBLIOGRAPHY OF NARRATIVE PANTOMIMES
FOR SOLO PLAYING

At first, young children generally prefer narratives that are solo, or individual. Since each child can be the "star" in his or her own little drama, it is a very satisfying experience. But they will eventually find paired and group playing fun to try, too, as long as they can take turns and play every part.

Older students, on the other hand, may at first prefer enacting the narratives that have two or more characters since these materials resemble a short play. But as they begin to understand what narrative pantomime is and become more comfortable in their pantomiming abilities, they will also enjoy the materials that feature one character.

The following stories and poems are suitable for solo playing. They are arranged alphabetically by title. Numbers in parentheses correspond to numbered anthologies listed in the final bibliography that begins on page 300. The following symbols are used to indicate the age level the material might be best suited for:

Y   Young children in kindergarten, first, and second grades
M   Middle-grade children in third and fourth grades
O   Older children in fifth and sixth grades

Y   *The Adventures of Albert the Running Bear,* Barbara Isenberg and Susan Wolf. New York: Clarion Books, 1982. An overweight zoo bear escapes when his food is restricted. Edit for solo playing and shorten the story considerably.

M–O "Base Stealer," Robert Francis (18,24,26). In this poem, a baseball player's actions are described. Experiment with slow motion. Students should run in place on the last line. You call "Safe!" to end the playing.

Y   *Beady Bear,* Don Freeman. New York: Viking Penguin, 1954. A stuffed toy bear thinks he should live in a cave. Can be played solo or in pairs.

Y–M *The Bears on Hemlock Mountain,* Alice Dalgliesh. New York: Charles Scribner's Sons, 1952. Jonathan discovers a unique way to hide from bears in this story based on a Pennsylvania pioneer folk tale. Chapter 4 and part of Chapter 8 can be spliced and adapted easily.

Y   *Bearymore,* Don Freeman. New York: Viking Penguin, 1976. A circus bear must think of a new act to perform before hibernating. Edit for solo playing.

Y   *Ben's ABC Day,* Terry Berger. New York: Lothrop, Lee & Shepard, 1982. Colored photos show the action words Ben does in one day.

Y   *Bunnies and Their Sports,* Nancy Carlson. New York: Viking Penguin, 1987. Simple text lists various sports humanlike bunnies do. Discuss what children would do for the last sentence to show they "feel good." Sequels may also be of interest.

Y–M "Cat," Mary Britton Miller (3,24). A cat's movements are detailed. For playing, I change the last two lines to read, "And sits on her rug with her nose in the air" to end in a seated position.

Y   *Corduroy,* Don Freeman. New York: Viking, 1968; Puffin, 1976. A teddy bear searches for a button for his overalls. Sequel: *A Pocket for Corduroy.* Both available in Spanish: *Corduroy* and *Un bosillo para Corduroy.*

Y–M *"Could Be Worse!"* James Stevenson. New York: William Morrow, 1977. Grandpa tells an incredibly tall tale. Everyone plays Grandpa when his adventure begins.

M "Dainty Dottie Dee," Jack Prelutsky (17). Dottie is so clean she even washes her garbage.

Y *Fish for Supper,* M. B. Goffstein. New York: Dial, 1976. Grandmother's fishing day is described.

Y *Flamboyan,* Arnold Adoff. San Diego: Harcourt Brace Jovanovich, 1988. A day in the life of a young girl in the Caribbean is poetically described in this brilliantly colored picture book. Her fantasy of flying comes true this day as she soars with the birds over her island home.

M *Fortunately,* Remy Charlip. New York: Four Winds Press, 1980. Good fortune and bad fortune go hand in hand in this adventure.

M–O "Foul Shot," Edwin A. Hoey (24,26). This poem gives a detailed description of a basketball shot. Students are the player and then become the ball. For a final touch, they are a person in the crowd giving a *silent slow-motion* "roarup," and then freeze (as a newspaper photo that might appear on the sports page the next day).

M–O "The Hairy Toe," George Mendoza (10). In this deliciously weird adaptation of an old tale, everyone will want to say the line "Gwot, I ate it!" all together at the end.

Y–M *Harold and the Purple Crayon,* Crockett Johnson. New York: Harper & Row, 1955. A little boy has many adventures to draw with the help of a purple crayon. In all the Harold stories, edit to clarify that Harold is drawing the details shown in each picture. Try also *Harold's Fairy Tale* (1956), *Harold's Trip to the Sky* (1957), and *Harold's Circus* (1959).

Y–M *Harry the Dirty Dog,* Gene Zion. New York: Harper & Row, 1956, 1976. When Harry gets so dirty that his family does not recognize him, he realizes the importance of cleanliness.

Y *Henry's Awful Mistake,* Robert Quackenbush. New York: Parents' Magazine Press, 1980. When Henry the Duck prepares dinner for his friend, his effort to get rid of an unwanted ant causes one disaster after another.

Y–M *Henry's Important Date,* Robert Quackenbush. New York: Parents' Magazine Press, 1981. Henry runs into one difficulty after another getting to his friend Clara's birthday party—only to find he's a day early.

M–O *Hidden Treasure,* Pamela Allen. New York: G. P. Putnam's Sons, 1986. A selfish man spends his life trying to guard a treasure from imagined dangers.

Y–M *Hildilid's Night,* Cheli Duran Ryan. New York: Macmillan, 1971, 1986. A woman tries everything she can think of to get rid of the night, until she becomes so exhausted she falls asleep just as day returns. Check out the spitting line before playing.

Y *I Was a Second Grade Werewolf,* Daniel Pinkwater. New York: E. P. Dutton, 1983. A second grader's imagination turns him into a werewolf, but no one seems to notice. Edit for solo playing. Extra characters can just be imagined.

Y–M *I Will Not Go to Market Today,* Harry Allard. New York: Dial Press, 1979. Day after day, Fenimore B. Buttercrunch's attempts to go to market for strawberry jam are thwarted. After months of trying, his persistence pays off.

Y "The Journey," Arnold Lobel (16). A mouse goes off to visit his mother, using various forms of transportation.

Y "Jump or Jiggle," Evelyn Beyer (3). A brief poem that names different animals and their ways of walking.

Y–M *Just Suppose,* May Garelick. New York: Scholastic, 1969. Suppose you were a number of animals, doing what they do. There is plenty of opportunity to explore animal movement and habits in this experience.

M–O "Lines Written for Gene Kelly to Dance To," Carl Sandburg (42). This poem asks the famous dancer to dance such ideas as the alphabet and the wind. The first section is the easiest to do, ending with "such good feet," but the entire poem offers wonderful possibilities. Try it with a musical background such as Leroy Anderson's "Sandpaper Ballet." (Say a line, turn up the music's volume for the miming, fade down and say the next line, and so on. Maintain a rhythm as you do this.)

Y *Little Black Bear Goes for a Walk,* Berniece Freschet. New York: Charles Scribner's Sons, 1977. A little bear goes off on an adventure and is rescued by his mother.

Y *Martin's Hats,* Joan W. Blos. New York: William Morrow, 1984. Martin experiences a variety of occupations by trying on different hats while playing in his room.

Y *Monday I Was an Alligator,* Susan Pearson. Philadelphia: J. B. Lippincott, 1979. A little girl pretends to be a different animal for each day of the week.

Y–M "My Brother Built a Robot," Jack Prelutsky (17). A robot goes haywire with no off switch. Plan an ending.

Y–M "My Snake," Jack Prelutsky (35). A snake performs various letters of the alphabet but cannot dot an "i."

Y *Owl at Home,* Arnold Lobel. New York: Harper & Row, 1975. Try "The Guest" in which winter pays a visit and "Strange Bumps" in which Owl discovers bumps in his bed.

M–O "The Passer," George Abbe (34). This brief description of a football pass is best played in slow motion. A college fight song playing in the background (at slow speed) lends atmosphere.

Y–M *The Patchwork Cat,* Nicola Bayley and William Mayne. New York: Alfred A. Knopf, 1981. A cat's search for her blanket the family has tossed out takes her to a garbage dump.

M–O *The Pond,* Carol and Donald Carrick. New York: Macmillan, 1970. This sensitive poem describes movements of water and all life near and in a pond. Students can switch from one character to another. Try Debussy's "La Mer" as background music. Effective also as a shadow dance behind a backlit sheet.

M–O "Rodeo," Edward Lueders (26). This poem describes a cowboy readying to mount and ride a Brahma bull. Use slow motion.

M *Salt Boy,* Mary Perrine. Boston: Houghton Mifflin, 1968. A young Indian boy gets his wish: learning to rope a horse. Edit for solo playing of the boy.

Y–M *Smedge,* Andrew Sharmat. New York: Macmillan, 1989. A dog, with briefcase, suit, and limousine, has a second life as a diplomat in Washington, D.C.

Y *The Snowy Day,* Ezra Jack Keats. New York: Viking, 1962. Young Peter plays in his first snow. End with Peter in bed at the desk, dreaming of more snow. (Also available in Spanish, *Un Dia De Nieve.*)

M *Sometimes I Dance Mountains,* Byrd Baylor. New York: Charles Scribner's Sons, 1973. Ideas for dance pantomime are presented in this long poetic work. Select excerpts. Photographs of a girl illustrate movement ideas. Simple instruments (wooden xylophone, tambourine, drum, and so forth) can provide background effects. Try it as a shadow dance behind a backlit sheet.

M–O *The Sorcerer's Apprentice*, retold and illustrated by Inga Moore. New York: Macmillan, 1989. The young apprentice to a magician remembers only part of a magic spell and finds himself in much trouble. Begin the action where the sorcerer leaves. Try the music of Paul Dukas written for this story for background. It can also be played in groups. See also (36).

Y–M *The Story about Ping*, Marjorie Flack. New York: Viking Penguin, 1933, 1961. This is the adventure of a little duck on the Yangtze River in China. Edit to shorten and to focus on Ping's experiences.

M "There's No One As Slow as Slomona," Jack Prelutsky (35). Slow motion is required for this one. After a pause, all say "Ouch!"

Y *Third Story Cat*, Leslie Baker. Boston: Little, Brown, 1987. An apartment cat escapes for an adventure in the park. It's probably best just to imagine the tiger cat.

Y *Today Was a Terrible Day*, Patricia Reilly Giff. New York: Penguin Books, 1980. A second grade boy has a series of problems at school. Edit for solo playing.

M–O "Trinity Place," Phyllis McGinley (20). This poem compares the actions of pigeons in a city park to humans. Although brief, it suggests wonderful possibilities for sophisticated movement.

Y *The Very Hungry Caterpillar*, Eric Carle. New York: Philomel/Putnam, 1969, 1986. A voracious caterpillar prepares for eventual change into a butterfly. Emphasize variety of action in eating the different foods.

Y *Whistle for Willie*, Ezra Jack Keats. New York: Viking, 1964. Peter learns how to whistle for his dog. Available in Spanish, *Silba por Willie*, 1992.

NARRATIVE PANTOMIMES FOR PAIRED PLAYING

Unless they are very little or socially immature, young children can also successfully play stories that have two characters, as long as each character has a similar amount of action to perform. (Most children want equal stage time!) A good example of such a story is Margaret Wise Brown's *The Golden Egg Book*, which features a bunny and a duck.

As stated earlier, older elementary students will particularly enjoy enacting stories that have two or more characters, since these stories resemble a short play. (An example might be George Mendoza's "The Crack in the Wall," the story of a hermit whose house falls apart because of a crack that will not stop spreading.) They feel a sense of accomplishment in creating their own dramas quickly and easily without having to memorize a script. Older students also prefer interacting with classmates and do not feel as isolated as they might with solo stories.

Remember that paired playing can also be done with stories that have one character meeting several other characters during an adventure. One student can play the major character, while the second one plays each of the other characters. This procedure is often preferred by the students, as it gives them the opportunity to enact more roles.

In paired playing, the entire class (or as many as you can handle) are paired and the pairs play simultaneously. This procedure allows more students the opportunity to participate.

Stories with two or more characters may have physical interaction or fighting as part of the plot.

Physical Contact in Paired and Group Playing

You will quickly note that when a story has two or more characters, the characters frequently interact socially and even physically. For example, in *The Golden Egg Book,* the bunny rolls the duck (who is still inside the un-hatched egg) down a hill. "The Crack in the Wall" is fun to play with one student being the hermit and one being the expanding crack. But the hermit pounds and kicks the wall. (Obviously you must make sure the children can perform such actions appropriately and safely before you let an entire class enact the story. A preview demonstration with a pair of trustworthy and competent children will probably be required.) The actions in "The Crack in the Wall" can be done *close* to the "wall" without actually touching it. This means the players will have to use caution in judging their distance from each other, and the "hermits" will have to control their actions. Such physical contact has to be faked, as is done in the movies and on television. (See p. 100 for more detailed instruction on stage combat.)

A BIBLIOGRAPHY OF NARRATIVE PANTOMIMES
FOR PAIRED PLAYING

The following stories and poems are suitable for paired playing. They are arranged alphabetically by title. Numbers in parentheses correspond to numbered anthologies listed in this text's final bibliography. Suggested grade levels are listed at the left margin.

M *Alistair's Elephant,* Marilyn Sadler. Englewood Cliffs, N.J.: Prentice-Hall, 1983. An elephant follows Alistair Grittle, a busy little boy, home from the zoo and causes many problems. Sequels available.

M *Andy and the Lion,* James Daugherty. New York: Viking Penguin, 1966. A young boy reads about lions and imagines himself in an adventure similar to that of the fabled Androcles. You may prefer to begin with Part II. Use desks for the rock.

Y *Bear Shadow,* Frank Asch. New York: Simon & Schuster, 1985. A little bear learns about his shadow in this picture book. Other books about Bear may also be of interest.

Y *The Beast in the Bathtub,* Kathleen Stevens. New York: Harper & Row, 1987. A child imagines a beast as he gets ready for bed. Could play in threes if you want two children linked together for a large beast.

M–O *The Boy Who Would Be a Hero,* Marjorie Lewis. New York: Coward-McCann, 1982. A lad who sets off to become a hero meets a witch who wants him for a hero *sandwich* to celebrate her birthday. Try this first with pairs—the boy and witch who can also play minor characters. Since the witch's body appears in parts and later becomes disassembled, the story could be played in groups. Edit out the simple dialogue.

Y–M *Caps for Sale,* Esphyr Slobodkina. New York: Scholastic, 1968. Thieving monkeys take a peddler's caps in this perennial favorite. Use one monkey to one peddler.

Y *The Chick and the Duckling,* Mirra Ginsburg. New York: Macmillan, 1972. A follow-the-leader game ends with a swimming duckling but a wet chick.

M–O "The Crack in the Wall," George Mendoza (5). A hermit loses his house to a crack in the wall that will not stop spreading. The second player is the crack that starts out "knife-thin, the length of the hermit's hand." Plan carefully the hermit's examination of the crack. Let everyone fall at the end, but in slow motion to a count of three.

M "Gertrude McFuzz," Dr. Seuss (32,43). Gertrude discovers that a big tail may not be what she really wants after all. The second child plays Lolla-Lee-Lou and Uncle Dake.

Y *Gilberto and the Wind,* Marie Hall Ets. New York: Viking, 1963. A young boy learns all the things the wind can do—and cannot do. Discuss and try out some of the more abstract ideas before playing the entire selection. (Available in Spanish, *Gilberto Y El Viento,* 1967.)

Y *The Golden Egg Book,* Margaret Wise Brown. Racine, Wisc.: Western Publishing, 1975. A bunny and a newly hatched duck discover each other. Plan the interaction carefully.

M–O *Gone Is Gone,* Wanda Gag. New York: Putnam, 1935, 1960. A man swaps chores with his wife. Another version is "The Husband Who Was to Mind the House" (3,29). Edit to combine the best features of both stories.

Y *Harry and the Terrible Whatzit,* Dick Gackenback. New York: Clarion, 1977, 1984. A little boy shrinks an imaginary monster down to size. Can be played in threes since the Whatsit has two heads. Available in Spanish *Harry y el Terrible Quiensabeque* (New York: Scholastic, 1992).

M *How the Grinch Stole Christmas!* Dr. Seuss. New York: Random House, 1957. A spiteful character learns the true meaning of Christmas giving. The second player is Max the dog and the Who child. See also (32).

M *How the Rhinoceros Got His Skin,* Rudyard Kipling. New York: Walker, 1974. A Parsi gets revenge on a rhinoceros. See also (14).

H *Humphrey's Bear,* Jan Wahl. New York: Henry Holt and Company, 1987. A boy and his teddy bear go on a nighttime adventure.

M   "I Wish My Father Wouldn't Try to Fix Things Anymore," Jack Prelutsky (35). While one plays Father, the other becomes all the things that are "fixed."

Y   *If You Give a Mouse a Cookie,* Laure Joffe Numeroff. New York: Harper & Row, 1985. This cautionary tale enumerates all the additional things you must do if you give a mouse a cookie. See sequel, *If You Give a Moose a Muffin,* 1991.

M–O   *The Knight and the Dragon,* Tomie dePaola. New York: Putnam Publishing, 1980. After a knight and a dragon fight each other unsuccessfully, they open a barbecue restaurant together. There is little text, but you and the students can create your own. This can be a drama for three, should you want to add the princess. See page 100 for techniques in mock battling.

M   *Lizard Lying in the Sun,* Bernice Freschet. New York: Charles Scribner's Sons, 1975. A lizard has a peaceful day in the sun until an eagle flies by. One child is the lizard; the second child plays each of the other animals.

M   *Mrs. Gaddy and the Ghost,* Wilson Gage. New York: Greenwillow Books, 1979. Mrs. Gaddy decides to move when she fails to get rid of a ghost. Mrs. Gaddy talks to herself, but the children can just mime it.

M   *The Night Before Christmas,* Clement C. Moore/Tasha Tudor. New York: Macmillan, 1975. See also James Marshall's humorous illustrations of the same title from Scholastic, 1989. Students may wish to have more than two characters.

Y   *The Tale of Peter Rabbit,* Beatrix Potter. New York: Frederick Warne, 1901, 1987. This is the timeless story of a misbehaving bunny who finds adventure in Mr. McGregor's garden. Can be played solo, but most children will want to include Mr. McGregor. The second player could also be some of the other minor characters. You will need to simplify and shorten the text for the playing, but children should hear the inimitable Beatrix Potter language the rest of the time. See also (29,36).

Y–M   *The Tale of Two Bad Mice,* Beatrix Potter. New York: Frederick Warne, 1932. Two mice find a doll house and create havoc when they discover the play food is not edible. Edit out the minor characters.

M   *Two Bad Ants,* Chris Van Allsburg. Boston: Houghton Mifflin, 1988. Two ants go off on their own and narrowly escape many dangers in a kitchen. While the text tells the story from the ants' point of view, the large, photo-like illustrations explain the story from a human's perspective.

M   "What Was I Scared Of?" Dr. Seuss (33). A typical Seuss character is frightened of a pair of pants with nobody in them until it finds the pants are afraid of it!

GROUP STORIES INTO PLAYS

Some narrative pantomime stories have three characters, and some have an unlimited number of characters. Younger children can play short stories with three to five characters fairly easily. From second grade up, students will want to make these stories into informal plays.

Some stories have a small cast. Oliver Herford's "The Elf and the Dormouse" has the two title characters and a mushroom. *The Little Brute Family,* by Russell Hoban, has a mother, a father, and three children. By dividing the class into small groups, it is possible to let several casts play the story simultaneously. Young children are often quite happy doing this. At first it may seem a little like a three-ring circus, but it does give more children a chance to play. The remainder of the class who are watching can see different interpretations of characters and lines. Older students are especially interested in this latter feature.

Some stories have entire villages or crowd scenes included in the cast of characters. In this case, an entire class can often play in one of these group stories. For example, in *The Beast of Monsieur Racine,* by Tomi Ungerer, there are crowds in both the railway scene and in the auditorium at the Paris Academy of Science. The picture book shows numerous interesting characters which the students can develop in greater detail. The same is true of Tomie de Paola's *Strega Nona,* which features an entire town inundated with spaghetti from a magic pasta pot.

With older children you may prefer to divide the class into small groups and let each group act out a different play, working out their own portrayals. The working groups should probably not be larger than five to seven students, including the narrator, to keep the decision-making tasks easier. Students may draw lots to see who plays which part. If there are several minor parts in a story, they can often be played by one person. (Some students are especially adept at changing characters quickly and love the idea of having several parts to play in one story.) An informal drama festival, with each group sharing its performance with the rest of the class, can be the end result of this more elaborate procedure.

Adding Dialogue

If a class enjoys a group story and likes replaying it, they may begin to perfect it much as they might in rehearsing a play. They may even begin to add dialogue in repeated playings. This happens because these stories develop so easily into a play format.

Consider for a moment that when you put on a play, the first step you take is to select a script. And a script is mainly the dialogue or speeches of the characters. Actors must memorize the speeches (or script) and then add the action (stage directions) so that the plot unfolds.

However, in the process being recommended here, we begin with the pantomimed action first, organizing and rehearsing it. As the students work with the story they may see opportunities for dialogue. The narrator may pause in the appropriate places and allow the actors to improvise their dialogue. In some cases the students may carry the story along so completely that narrating will be needed only sporadically. It may even be eliminated in time.

Adding Technical Aspects

Students will enjoy adding technical aspects to their plays, particularly if they are planning to share them with classmates. It is best to keep these

Costumes used in formal plays provide ideas for classroom use. This dragon costume can be imitated with a decorated grocery bag (stuffed with newspaper), three yardsticks with cross-pieces, and a long strip of material. (Kalamazoo Civic Youth Theatre)

additions simple and not clutter or overpower the most important part of the drama: the actors and the story.

Costumes can be simple pieces of material draped or tied around any child of any size. Cast-off curtains, blankets, tablecloths, and fabric remnants do nicely. Hats and scarves are also useful. Some stories are particularly suited to the use of masks, which can be made of paper bags, paper plates, or other simple materials.

Props should be made of simple materials. Many can still be pantomimed. And indeed, this procedure is sometimes more aesthetically pleasing than using real objects. Children have played the pasta pot (three on their knees with arms encircled) and also the pasta (bubbling up and over the pot and even slithering on the floor) in *Strega Nona*.

You and the students can also find ways to use objects creatively. Some fourth graders once played a version of "Jack and the Beanstalk" and for the beanstalk used a broom and a chair. Jack stood on the chair and held the broom high. Then as he "climbed the beanstalk," he went hand over hand along the broomstick. As the broom lowered to the floor, the illusion of climbing was cleverly, yet simply, executed.

Scenery is usually never required. Students can get very literal about what is needed and should instead be encouraged to use their imaginations. Again, simplicity is the key: Children have often created their own scenery by physically being doors that open and close, trees waving in the breeze, machines, vehicles, or whatever their imagination has inspired.

A bright light behind the actors casts shadows on a sheet for a shadow play.

Some of the stories in the bibliography can be played as *shadow dramas*. For this you need a darkened room and a floodlight behind an old sheet. The actors move behind the sheet in front of the light, and interesting shadows are the result.

Music and sound effects, if they aid the interpretation of the story, can also be added.

Finally, some students will enjoy working on the technical aspects of the production more than performing the story itself. Some may even show abilities in managing, designing, and executing these simple technical aspects. Encourage this and give as much attention to these technical artists as to the actors. You may even find some students exhibiting excellent directing and overall management skills.

Sharing with an Audience

As students gain more confidence in themselves and in their work, they may ask to share it with an audience. However, sharing should be the collective desire of the group rather than being imposed by you.

Students often have more success sharing these narrated materials than they would a scripted play. Fear of forgetting lines, usually the biggest worry in performing a play, can be eliminated, since the dialogue is not essential to these stories. There is less pressure than with a scripted play, since these plays go on as long as the narrating and pantomiming continue. If some students are hesitant with dialogue, they can still participate in the playing, and those who are ready for improvising can add it.

Older elementary students may find it a rewarding experience to perform their stories for students in the lower grades. Of course, they should perform the stories that are most appealing to that age group and ones younger children will understand.

When sharing the play with classmates, you have an excellent opportunity to emphasize what an audience is and how it shows its appreciation of theatrical events. An audience watches to learn and enjoy; it is polite and shows respect for the actors. Those students who form the audience should be as courteous to their classmates as they will want their classmates to be when their roles are reversed.

"URASHIMA TARO AND THE PRINCESS OF THE SEA"

The following is a description of the development of a group story into a classroom play with a fourth grade class. The narrative was condensed from the Japanese folk tale "Urashima Taro and the Princess of the Sea" (3,7), which the students had read in their basal reader. In this story, a young man who saves a turtle is rewarded with a trip under the sea. While enjoying himself there for what he thinks are three days, many years pass on earth. One day he asks to return to visit his parents. He is given a box which he is told not to open so that he may use it to return to the sea again. When he finds that he is in another time period on earth, he opens the box and is transformed into an old man.

A narrative pantomime was developed from this story for the entire class to play. The story was shortened, the action tightened, and all but the simplest of dialogue was edited out. The major characters in the story were Urashima Taro, the princess of the sea, and the turtle. Other characters were added by focusing on the underwater sea life (crabs, fish, octopuses, and so on) which Urashima passed on his ride to and from the sea on the turtle's back. Then when the princess showed Urashima the seasons, several children pantomimed actions appropriate to each—swimming in summer, skiing in winter, and so forth. Other characters were a group of children who taunted the turtle in the opening scene, courtiers under the sea, and a couple who greeted Urashima at the end of the story.

The action of the play began at the front of the room, moved around the side, and then to the back of the room for the princess's palace. The return trip was made on the other side of the room, and the story ended in the front of the classroom again.

For the costumes, pieces of sheer pastel fabric were used, mainly of green and blue shades, to represent the underwater world. The only scenery was crepe-paper streamers of various colors which were twisted slightly. With one child at each end of a streamer, several streamers were alternately raised up and down. The effect was of sea waves, so that as Urashima and the turtle moved in between the two streamers, they appeared to be swimming in the sea. At the back of the room the same technique was used with various colored streamers depicting the seasons—red and orange for fall, blue and white for winter, and so on. The pantomimes of the seasons were enacted between the streamers. A small jewelry box, serving as the princess's gift to Urashima, was the only prop used.

The actions under the sea, as well as Urashima's turning into an old man at the end of the story, were done in slow motion to add to the mood. For background music, a recording of Orff instruments was used.[2] With more time, the children could have played the instrumental music themselves.

The entire lesson took only about forty minutes to complete. At the end, the children expressed pleasure with their work and thought that the story was a beautiful one.

The major objective was to enhance a reading lesson, not to prepare a play for performance. However, if the children had wished to share it with an audience, this could easily have been done.

[2]Carl Orff and Gunhild Keetman. English version by Margaret Murray, *Music for Children* (Angel Records, 1959).

A BIBLIOGRAPHY OF NARRATIVE PANTOMIMES FOR GROUP PLAYING

The following literature, suitable for group playing, is arranged alphabetically by title. Numbers in parentheses correspond to numbered anthologies listed in this text's final bibliography. Suggested grade levels are listed at the left margin.

M–O *Abiyoyo*, Pete Seeger. New York: Macmillan, 1986. The author has adapted this tale from a South African lullaby and folk story. A boy and his magician father are banished from a town but are welcomed back when they make the giant Abiyoyo disappear. Requires some editing. The song is included.

Y–M *The Bears Who Stayed Indoors*, Susanna Gretz. Chicago: Follett, 1970. Five bears and a dog named Fred spend a rainy day playing spaceship. The bears' actions are so cleverly written and fun to play that even older students should enjoy this one.

M–O *The Beast of Monsieur Racine*, Tomi Ungerer. New York: Farrar, Straus & Giroux, 1971. A retired French tax collector discovers a rare beast, befriends it, and takes it to the Academy of Sciences. It may be played in threes (two are the "beast") or with the added crowd scenes. Try a series of frozen pictures (see Chapter 7) for the line "Unspeakable acts were performed."

M–O *The Big Yellow Balloon*, Edward Fenton. New York: Doubleday, 1967. With his yellow balloon, Roger manages to lure an unlikely parade of a cat, a dog, a dog catcher, a lady, a thief, and a police officer. Organize this one carefully. Precise timing is required for maximum effect.

M *Blueberries for Sal*, Robert McCloskey. New York: Viking Penguin, 1948; Puffin, 1976. Little Sal and her mother get separated on a blueberry hunt, as does the bear cub from its mother. Sal and the bear cub mix mothers for a very amusing story. Four players.

M–O *Casey at the Bat*, Ernest Lawrence Thayer. Boston: David R. Godine, 1988. This is the classic American poem of the ballplayer who strikes out and causes Mudville to lose the baseball game. This edition has wonderful gay-nineties illustrations by Barry Moser. The poem should not be edited, so action needs to be created in several sections. Another effective way to do it is through a series of frozen pictures (see Chapter 7). The frozen pictures might also be done as a shadow play. An edition by Patricia Polacco (New York: Putnam Publishing, 1988) has additional text that changes the setting to a Little League game.

Y–M *Chipmunk Stew,* Beth Weiner Woldin. New York: Frederick Warne, 1980. Two chipmunks open a restaurant and hire a chipmunk chef, Pierre La Chippe. Dialogue can be mimed or easily edited out. Extra characters can be imagined or perhaps added in replayings.

Y–M *Crictor.* Tomi Ungerer. New York: Harper & Row, 1986 (renewed). Madame Bodot's pet boa constrictor goes to school with her by day and protects her from burglars by night.

Y–M *Curious George,* H. A. Rey. Boston: Houghton Mifflin, 1941, 1973. This is the original story of the curious little monkey who cannot stay out of trouble. Edit for solo playing at least once to give everyone a chance to be George. Sequels available.

M–O *Drummer Hoff,* Barbara Emberley. Englewood Cliffs, N.J.: Prentice-Hall, 1967. This a simple cumulative story of a cannon being loaded and fired off. Older students will like the challenge of mechanical movement in this one. You might like to watch the Weston Woods film company's animated version for movement ideas.

Y–M *The Duchess Bakes a Cake,* Virginia Kahl. New York: Charles Scribner's Sons, 1955. A bored duchess tries her hand at baking and winds up on top of a huge cake. There are numerous characters in this rhyming tale. The dialogue can be pantomimed.

Y "The Elf and the Dormouse," Oliver Herford (24,36). In this brief poem an elf borrows a dormouse's mushroom shelter on a rainy day and invents

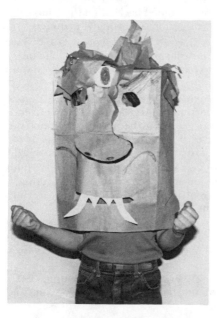

A grocery bag makes an oni character for *The Funny Little Woman* by Arlene Mosel.

umbrellas. One child can be the mushroom. For an illustrated version see *The Elf and the Dormouse and Other Faerie Stories* illustrated by Bob Petillo (New York: Unicorn Publishing House, 1990).

M–O *The Funny Little Woman,* Arlene Mosel. New York: E. P. Dutton, 1972. A giggling little woman in Japan chases a rolling rice dumpling underground and is captured by wicked Oni. There is some dialogue, but it can easily be mimed.

Y–M *The Goblin under the Stairs,* Mary Calhoun. New York: William Morrow, 1967. A boy and his parents each have a special way of viewing the goblin who lives in their house—and the goblin lives up to each one's expectations. The narrator can also play the neighbor.

Y *The Great Big Enormous Turnip,* Alexei Tolstoy. New York: Franklin Watts, 1968. It takes the whole family, some animals, and a mouse to pull up a monstrous turnip. One or more children can be the turnip. Encourage physical differences in the various characters. See also *The Turnip,* Pierr Morgan. New York: Philomel, 1990.

Y–O *Horton Hatches the Egg,* Dr. Seuss. New York: Random House, 1940, 1968. Horton, the elephant who is "faithful, 100 percent," hatches an egg for the lazy Maizie bird. Mime the dialogue but let everyone repeat Horton's chant.

M *Imogene's Antlers,* David Small. New York: Crown, 1985. Imogene's family tries many suggestions to cope with the antlers she grew suddenly. They disappear on their own—only to be replaced by a peacock tail!

M *Inspector Aardvark and the Perfect Cake,* Kathy Caple. New York: Windmill Books, 1980. Aardvark, with his two rat friends, searches for the perfect cake. Try this in threes. Those who play the rats can also play the waiter, the police, and other minor characters.

O *It Could Always Be Worse,* Margot Zemach. New York: Farrar, Straus & Giroux, 1976. A rabbi advises a crowded, irritable family to bring animals into their house. Then when he advises taking the animals out, the house seems spacious and quiet. Freeze the mayhem in the house each time the father visits the rabbi.

M–O *Ittki Pittki,* Miriam Chaikin. New York: Parent's Magazine Press, 1971. Ittki Pittki, a Mideastern cloth merchant, fears he has been accidentally poisoned at the prince's palace and returns home to wait for death. This funny tale has a moral as well: Life is precious and should be enjoyed.

M–O *Jabberwocky,* Lewis Carroll. New York: Harry N. Abrams, 1989. Illustrations for this nonsense poem from *Through the Looking Glass* are by Graeme Base. See also (3,18,24,29).

O *Lentil,* Robert McCloskey. New York: Viking Penguin, 1940, 1968. A boy saves the day for a small town when he greets the town's generous benefactor at the train with his harmonica music. There are plenty of characters, minimum dialogue, and lots of opportunity for improvisation.

Y *The Little Brute Family,* Russell Hoban. New York: Macmillan, 1966. A family consistently has grumpy and unpleasant days until a little lost feeling enters their lives. A child can play the little lost feeling, or music can be played to represent it.

M–O *Ming Lo Moves the Mountain,* Arnold Lobel. New York: Greenwillow Books, 1982. This is a good narrative pantomime for three. Note the varying positions the wise man sits in.

M–O *The Money Tree,* Sarah Stewart. New York: Farrar, Straus & Giroux, 1991. Miss McGillicuddy discovers a money tree in her yard but has such a "rich" life, she gives the money away and uses the tree for firewood. There is room for much sophisticated interpretation in this one. Note the possibility for a shadow scene.

M *The Mouse and Mrs. Proudfoot,* Albert Rusling. Englewood Cliffs, N.J.: Prentice-Hall, 1985. Mrs. Proudfoot and Miranda try to get rid of a little mouse in their cottage by bringing in a series of animals.

M–O *Mrs. Beggs and the Wizard,* Mercer Mayer. New York: Parent's Magazine Press, 1973. Many strange events happen in Mrs. Beggs' boarding house when a strange renter comes. Try a quick blackout for the ending.

M–O *My Grandpa Is a Pirate,* Jan Lööf (English translation by Else Holmelund Minarik). New York: Harper & Row, 1968. A boy and his grandfather have a pirate adventure while Grandma takes a nap. There are lots of characters and exciting action in this one.

M–O *Oté,* Pura Belpré. New York: Pantheon Books, 1969. In this humorous Puerto Rican folk tale, a family is plagued by an unwanted, nearsighted little devil.

M–O *Paper John,* David Small. New York: Farrar, Straus & Giroux, 1987. John makes everything out of paper. When the devil plays his trick of commanding the four winds, John refolds his paper house into a boat to rescue everyone.

Y–M *Peter and the Wolf,* retold and illustrated by Michele Lemieux. New York: William Morrow, 1991. This picture book tells Sergei Prokofiev's classical orchestral tale.

M–O *The Pond,* Carol and Donald Carrick. New York: Macmillan, 1970. Movements of water, insects, and all life near and in a pond are sensitively described. Try some simple choreography with a shadow drama. Debussy's "La Mer" works well for background music.

College students enact "The Sneetches" in garbage bag costumes.

Y *Roll Over!* Mordecai Gerstein. New York: Crown Publishers, 1984. Ten various animals are in bed, and roll out one by one.

O *Saint George and the Dragon,* Margaret Hodges. Boston: Little, Brown, 1984. A retelling, in picture book format, of a portion of Edmund Spenser's *The Faerie Queene.* George, accompanied by the fair maiden Una, slays the dragon in a three-day fight. The fight scene itself can be played in groups of five: Una, George, and three for the dragon (one each for the head, wings, and tail).

M *Seven Skinny Goats,* Victor G. Ambrus. San Diego: Harcourt Brace Jovanovich, 1969. Jano, a young goat herder, does not realize that his flute playing, which causes everyone to dance, is not appreciated. Control the scenes of frenzied dancing with music cues and the technique of dancing with one foot "glued" to the floor. Music played at fast speed adds to this.

M *The Sneetches,* Dr. Seuss. New York: Random House, 1961. Sneetches with stars on their bellies feel superior to those without until an enterprising salesperson takes advantage of the situation. Children enjoy becoming the machine. (See "Mechanical Movement," Chapter 4).

M–O *The Stonecutter,* Gerald McDermott. New York: Viking Penguin, 1975. This well-known Japanese folk tale is simply told with numerous characters and no dialogue. McDermott's illustrations inspire shadow drama possibilities.

M *The Story of Babar,* Jean de Brunhoff. New York: Random House, 1933, 1961. The classic tale of a little elephant who is taken care of by a kind and generous woman in Paris and returns to the jungle to become king.

M–O *The Story of Ferdinand,* Munro Leaf. New York: Viking Penguin, 1936; Puffin, 1977. The classic story of Ferdinand, the bull who would rather smell flowers than fight in the bull ring, gives children the opportunity to learn about

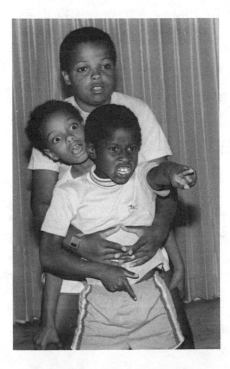

Three Poor Tailors (story by Victor Ambrus) ride off on a goat to seek adventure in the city.

Frog, Rabbit, and Elephant are surprised to find that it is only Caterpillar in Rabbit's house. (*Who's in Rabbit's House?* by Verna Aardema)

bullfighting customs. A parade of bulls, matadors, picadors, and others is always fun to add before the bullfighting scene. Available in Spanish, *El Cuento de Ferdinando.*

M—O *Strega Nona,* Tomie de Paola. Englewood Cliffs, N.J.: Prentice-Hall, 1975. Strega Nona, or "Grandma Witch," has a magic pasta pot which Big Anthony misuses, and the town is flooded with pasta. There are numerous characters to play, including the spaghetti and the pot.

Y *The Three Bears,* Paul Galdone. New York: Seabury Press, 1972. This version of the classic tale works nicely for a narrative pantomime. Although it can also be played solo with everyone being Goldilocks, most children will want the bears, too.

M—O *The Three Poor Tailors,* Victor G. Ambrus. New York: Harcourt Brace Jovanovich, 1965. Three tailors go off on the back of a goat to see the city and find fun, adventure, and trouble. It is more fun just to imagine the goat.

M—O *The Way the Tiger Walked,* Doris J. Chaconas. New York: Simon & Schuster, 1970. Porcupine, zebra, and elephant try unsuccessfully to imitate tiger's regal walk while monkeys watch the show. When tiger imitates *their* walks, they return to their natural movement. Subtle humor underlies this story that deserves to be perfected into a finely tuned precision piece, perhaps with rhythm instruments for sound effects.

M—O *Who's in Rabbit's House?* Verna Aardema. New York: Dial Press, 1977. In this African Masai tale, Caterpillar hides in Rabbit's house and scares all the animals away. Although there is dialogue, the narrator can still read while actors mime in masks as the illustrations show.

M—O *Yeh-Shen,* Ai-Ling Louie. New York: Philomel, 1982. In this Chinese Cinderella story a fish replaces the fairy godmother. Action dominates; the dialogue is easily mimed. Free-flowing illustrations suggest stylized pantomime, aided by flowing scarves and masks. A shadow play is also possible.

FOR THE COLLEGE STUDENT

1. Select a story and a poem suitable for a narrated activity. Prepare it to read aloud to your classmates. Practice and experiment with pauses, timing, and vocal pitch and quality to make the selection as interesting as possible. Find some background music suitable to the mood of the selection and play it as you read.

2. Select a narrative poem or story suitable for individual playing. Lead your classmates through a playing of the material you have selected. Consider whether or not a discussion will be necessary and whether demonstration playing is required. Give all the necessary instructions for organizing the playing. Consider the possibility of special lighting effects, sound effects, and so forth. Evaluate the playing.

3. Select a narrative poem or story to be played in pairs or groups, following the format in Exercise 2.

4. Divide into groups. Select several group stories for each of the groups to prepare. Rehearse and arrange the story as a play, perhaps adding simple costumes and props. Share your stories with the class.

5. Find as many other suitable materials for narration as you can. Keep a file of these materials. Select from reading books and trade books used in the classroom.

6

Writing Narrative Pantomime

Once you have become familiar with narrative pantomime, you will quickly see that there are many other uses for it. You have probably already discovered a number of your own favorite stories and poems suitable for narrative pantomime.

In addition, many action episodes from longer books can easily be adapted or spliced together for narrative pantomime. For example, Michael Bond's Paddington (47)[1] stories for younger children have many wonderful episodes useful for solo pantomime. This popular little bear frequently undertakes an adventure, such as wallpapering a room or cleaning out a chimney, and, of course, runs into all sorts of difficulties along the way. For older children, there are numerous episodes in Armstrong Sperry's *Call It Courage* or Scott O'Dell's *Island of the Blue Dolphins*—two books about young people who face a lone existence—that can easily be excerpted or spliced together for excellent narrative pantomime experiences.

Narrative pantomime is also useful in additional curricular areas of study. The topics are almost limitless. Science stories about animals or experiments, biographical data on historical or modern-day figures, informa-

---

[1]Unless otherwise indicated, literature mentioned in this chapter can be found in the bibliography at the end of this chapter. Numbers in parentheses correspond to the numbered anthologies and books listed in the final bibliography at the back of this text.

tion on various occupations, and stories about people in other times and geographical and cultural settings are just some of the many possibilities. By enacting these materials and the facts and concepts presented in them, the children should be able to internalize the information more completely than if they simply read about it.

A number of excellent curricular stories already exist. At the end of this chapter is a bibliography of stories covering animal life cycles, career education, biography, history, and so forth. You can use these materials as they are, with editing in some cases, or as a stimulus for your own writing.

Although the length of narrative pantomimes can vary from a brief paragraph to a story of several hundred words, the techniques remain the same. This chapter will examine and consider the dramatic principles in narrative pantomimes. Understanding and applying these principles should help you in selecting and adapting, as well as in writing your own materials.

FOCUSING ON ACTION

Action is always the central focus of narrative pantomime. To achieve this, several cautions and considerations are in order.

Action in Poetry

Although there are some excellent poems you can use for narrative pantomime, such as Edwin A. Hoey's "Foul Shot" (p. 113) or Byrd Baylor's *Sometimes I Dance Mountains* (p. 114), poems are not as readily available as prose selections. By its very nature, the language of poetry often does not focus on a continuous, forward-moving action that can be performed logically. Complete sentences may be lacking and wording may be convoluted. The rhythm and rhyme may be so exact that even minor editing is difficult, if not impossible. Therefore, it is best to use caution in selecting poetry and to become comfortable with prose first.

Inanimate Objects

Inanimate objects must have enough action to make them interesting for children to play. Generally it is easiest to play an inanimate object if it is going through a process of some sort. Sam Rosenfeld's *A Drop of Water* takes us through a water drop's many changes, at times being part of the ocean or fog or rain. As another example, a tree may be cut down and the log sent to a paper mill, where the bark is removed and the log chipped, blown, soaked, cooked, beaten, and finally rolled into paper. Players can react to these various processes and pantomime the various shapes the wood is put through. Similar topics might be the journey of an egg through a modern-day processing plant, the recycling of glass or cans, the adventure of a tomato from the vine to the soup can, or the steps a letter goes through getting mailed.

Editing Dialogue

Because the emphasis in narrative pantomime is on action, dialogue should be nonexistent, or almost so. In searching for narrative material, a helpful first clue is the absence of quotation marks. Keeping this in mind you can flip through the pages of books rather rapidly, eliminating unlikely candidates.

Condensing Action

As a general rule, action should be condensed in time. When spread out over a period of time, action tends to lose its dramatic impact.

The action should also be as continuous as possible. Flashbacks, reflective thinking, or additional information will interrupt the flow of action and usually require the players to wait before they can continue pantomiming. Be careful also of narrative that shifts back and forth in time.

Chronological Word Order

The cues for action should always follow chronologically. If they do not, players may be misled. For example:

> She left the apartment and went down to the first floor. When she got off the elevator and entered the lobby, she . . .

Players following this narration might *walk down steps* rather than ride an elevator, since this information is not specified until the second sentence.

Immediacy of Action

A sense of immediacy in narrative pantomime is aided by the use of present tense and the wording "you." "You," of course, may also be implied.

"You get up in the morning and wash your face. . .

. . . and brush your teeth. . .

Now (you) run your hand along the bark of the old tree. (You) Lean forward and smell the mossy dampness. . . .

Robert McCloskey has incorporated this wording in his award-winning book *Time of Wonder.* A few other books also use this technique. For example, Roger Caras's *Skunk for a Day* begins "Today you are a skunk. . . ." and Joan Ryder's *The Snail's Spell* opens with these words "Imagine you are soft and have no bones inside you." But you will not see this style of writing frequently.

Although it is not necessary to change all narrative pantomime literature into this wording style, children do respond more naturally to this direct wording, feeling that the action is happening right now and to them.

Because you are not used to reading stories in the present tense and with "you" wording, it may be difficult to write your stories in this fashion.

. . . and do your exercises."

It is a good practice experience to try it, even though other styles will also work. Note the different styles in the following examples.

> *Third person, present tense.* As the sun shines, the Athenian citizen gets out of bed and folds a piece of wool cloth around himself, pins it at the shoulder, and ties a sash around his waist. Then he sits down to breakfast and drinks a cup of wine mixed with hot water and honey and eats a dry barley cake.
>
> *First person plural, present tense.* We begin cleaning out the horse's stall, shoveling the old straw into a wheelbarrow and wheeling it carefully outside the barn. We empty it into a large pile. The pitchfork is used to bring fresh straw to the horse's stall and spread it evenly over the floor.
>
> *Third person, past tense.* To build his wigwam, Running Bear first had to find a level surface. He marked a groove in the ground with a sharp stick. Then he made an oval shape about twice as long as it was wide. . . .

Whatever person and tense you use in your story, it is important to remain consistent throughout and not shift back and forth.

Descriptive Language

Language that is descriptive paints the mental images of sensory and emotional detail. It artfully compels the children to be aware of the setting and environment and invites their involvement. In the story of Goldilocks and the Three Bears, for example, the scene of eating the porridge might be narrated as follows:

> You see three bowls of porridge, and you are so hungry. You taste the porridge in the great big bowl. Ouch! That's too hot! Well, maybe the porridge in the middle-sized bowl will be better. Scoop up a big spoonful. Take a big bite and . . . oh, no! That one is too cold. And LUMPY! Well, there's one bowl left. Take a tiny spoonful of porridge and check it with the tip of your tongue first. Ahhh, perfect. What good porridge; not too hot, not too cold. So you eat . . . and eat . . . until there is nothing left. Ummmmmmm . . . good!

Amount of Action and Description

The amount of action and descriptive language you use in narrative pantomime, and in side-coaching, depends on the children's needs. Some children will be able to elaborate on ideas more easily than others. For example, a line may read, "They prepared their equipment for the camping trip." Some children may be observed packing numerous items and making considerable preparations, whereas other children quickly finish only one idea. Detailed, descriptive, and compelling narration may be needed to involve some children in playing it. On the other hand, too much narration can interrupt or hold up the inventive children's own ideas. Therefore, one must be flexible and let the needs of the *majority* dictate the amount of action and description used. With practice and by knowing your material so that you can observe the class carefully, you should become skilled quite quickly.

STORY FRAMEWORK

The overall outline of a narrative activity, no matter what its length, should have a beginning, a middle, and an end for a sense of completeness. One clue is the sense of progression or chronological order in wording such as "First . . . and then . . . finally . . . ."

> The marionette's strings are breaking one by one. First to go is the string on the right arm . . . then the left . . . then the right leg . . . then the left . . . and finally their heads droop. Now they are as limp as the rag dolls on the shelf above them.

Longer narratives are often built around a framework such as the performance of a task, the setting of a goal and its accomplishment, or starting out on a journey and returning home. There is one episode in Scott O'Dell's *Island of the Blue Dolphins* in which Karana builds a house for herself. The process of a day's work is covered in Chapter 5, "A Climbing Boy's Day," in *Chimney Sweeps;* part of a mole cricket's life cycle is described in Jean George's *All Upon a Stone.* These "rounded out" experiences are generally the most satisfying to play.

Suspense and Conflict

Many narrative stories are based simply on an interesting or satisfying experience. It may be a pleasant one, as in Donald Hall's *Ox Cart Man,* or a humorous one, as in Peggy Parish's *Amelia Bedelia* stories. Most dramatic

"Don't forget to put suntan lotion on your nose." Getting ready to go to the beach.

"At the fair you eat some salt water taffy—and it gets stuck in your teeth. . . ."

stories, however, have some conflict in them, so you should be familiar with the various ways to include it.

Children usually enjoy and want plenty of exciting action and conflict in drama. They will sometimes add it, even if you do not. A line says to smell a flower; they do, and a bee stings them. Or a line says, "He walked carefully so he would not slip"; they walk carefully but slip, too! For some children there can never be too much excitement in their stories.

As we learned in Chapter 2, there are many types of conflict. Strong conflict is obvious in fights, chases, or the meeting of an enemy face to face. Conflict is also present in nature. A threatening storm begins slowly. Winds blow, lightning flashes, and thunder crashes until a dramatic climax is reached. When the storm subsides, the conflict of nature is resolved. George Maxim Ross's *The Pine Tree* demonstrates the drama in nature most graphically.

Conflict can be present in the daily struggle of life. Even if a task is a rather ordinary one, it may be crucial to continued survival. Gary Paulsen's *Hatchet* details many such experiences of a young boy who manages to survive in the wilderness after a plane crash.

Suspense can sometimes be additionally implied in the language. If an action is performed "cautiously" or if a line reads "He held his breath as he lifted the cargo," an imminent problem is suggested.

Conflict in narratives not only makes them more dramatic and suspenseful, it usually creates physical intensity in the playing. Movements may become stronger or more energized as the players exert themselves to solve the conflict. Perhaps one must swim rapidly to escape a shark. Meeting a deadline, getting to work on time, or finishing a sports event before it rains all are conflicts that create hurried action. This physical exertion then more logically leads to the restful conclusion of the story.

Beginnings and Endings

It usually works best if children begin a narrative in a quiet position and are calmed down again at the end. This structure is invaluable in keeping a classroom of children controlled in their playing.

Notice how frequently many stories include calm beginnings and endings. For example, an animal lies in quiet wait for a prey. After eating, it often rests. In writing your own materials, you will want to model this structure for maximum effectiveness.

WRITING ORIGINAL MATERIALS

Creating original materials need not be a difficult experience. Many ideas are readily available in literature such as those listed in the bibliography at the end of this chapter.

Finding an Idea

Let us consider a simple example. We are told in one sentence of Milne's *Winnie-the-Pooh* (96) that this famous teddy bear does "Stoutness Exercises." This suggests an interesting pantomime activity. All we are told is that Pooh tries to touch his toes, but a simple conflict is implied if we remember that he has a protruding tummy that probably makes bending over a bit of a problem.

Elaborating on this idea, you might write a narrative taking Pooh through an entire fitness program, doing all sorts of body building exercises. There might be some jogging, weight lifting, pushups, and hitting of a punching bag. The sense of completeness is the exercise program itself. The beginning might be a slow warm-up, exercising just the paws. (After all, Pooh would not want to overexert himself!) As the activities progress in intensity and difficulty, Pooh Bear will become tired and eventually need a rest—with the reward of a bit of honey perhaps.

Playing Space

As you design your narratives, consider the use of playing space. The desk, for example, may be an exercise bike for Pooh, a rowing machine, or the overstuffed chair he relaxes in at the end.

Leader-in-Role

Often it adds to the fun as well as to the meaning of the playing if you play a role in narrating. Generally, this character is an authority figure or one who can legitimately direct and guide the actions of the children.

For example, in the Winnie-the-Pooh exercise, you might play Christopher Robin, the teddy bear's owner. The wording of the narration can reflect this role as follows:

"Now, Pooh Bear, I know you have good intentions, but sometimes you need a little help. It's time for your exercises, and I shall watch to see that you do them correctly. In fact, I'll even count for you. We'll begin with the first one. . . ."

The children often get more enjoyment out of following a character–narrator's rules and comply with them more willingly. Being Pooh following Christopher Robin's directions is usually more fun than simply doing what the teacher says.

Sources for Materials

In addition to the curricular materials in the bibliography, another very good source is your own personal experience. Various occupations experienced by you or people you know offer stories for career education. Grocery checkout cashier, construction worker, camp counselor, table waiter, dental assistant, truck driver, and tour guide at a cereal factory are just some of the many jobs students have written about.

Sports have been another popular topic for narratives, including skiing, sky diving, scuba diving, hiking, and aerobics. Pets such as hamsters, turtles, and guinea pigs have also had stories told about them that children have enjoyed playing. Younger children like to be the pet, while older children like to be the one caring for the animal. In the process they have learned about how the animals must be cared for, an important part of nature study. Stories have been written about maple sugaring in Vermont, touring a family's dairy farm, and going through army basic training with the leader as a drill instructor.

The details you can bring to these activities are a direct result of your own involvement in them. In addition, you usually feel comfortable with and enthusiastic about these topics which, of course, adds to the children's enjoyment in playing them.

Finding Material through Research. Materials for narratives can easily be found through research. Trade books, encyclopedias, and information magazines supply a wealth of subjects to draw from. The sources in the bibliography at the end of this chapter give only a sampling of the materials that exist.

Often these materials have a framework such as "A Day in the Life of _____" that focuses on an occupation, a child in another country, an historical figure, an animal, or an insect. Consider "The Process of Making _____," and select a product, food, shelter, or clothing to write about. For "Journey to _____," you can select a particular building, historical sight, city, country, or even another planet to build the story around.

In the following story an unusual species of spider called *Argyoneta aquatica* lives underwater by building air-filled bubbles. It must struggle to keep the captured air bubbles anchored and to pull itself with guidelines. It is alert to the vibrations in the water and aware of its need to secure food. The story ends with the satisfying completion of a project and a deserved rest.

A WATER SPIDER'S DAY

Narrator: You're in the process of building your web for the air bubbles you will soon capture. You move from one plant stem to another, throwing from your spinnerets silken web strands. . . . Deftly your legs secure the threads to the plants . . . and you carefully move back and forth from stem to stem until you have a finely meshed web. This web will become your summer bell home; later you'll build another for winter.

Now for the air bubbles. . . . You swim to the top of the water. . . . Once there, you turn over and with your back legs you grab a bubble of air, pulling it gently toward you so that it covers the breathing pores around your abdomen. . . . Now your legs search for the silken guidelines you set earlier . . . there you are! . . . and holding securely to the line, you begin to pull yourself down to the new web. It's a difficult feat . . . for the air bubble is heavy and would rise to the surface if you didn't pull. . . . At the web you release your air bubble . . . and it rises into the web—captured!

You take more trips to the surface for air . . . and soon your home contains several bubbles and is completed. Now it is time for a rest. . . . You carefully enter your air-filled home . . . and hang head downward. . . . As you rest, the water house sways to the rhythm of the moving water . . . its vibrations can communicate that danger or a potential meal is near. . . . It's vibrating!

Your eight eyes signal food. . . . You emerge from your bell, carefully carrying an air supply with you. . . . A tiny fish swims near . . . you lunge . . . grab . . . sting with your poison . . . and carry the dead fish into your new home. You'll eat it in a while . . . but now you'll rest. The spider's day has been a busy one.

Fantasy and Reality in Science Topics

For curricular subjects such as science, topics must be handled realistically, as in the preceding story. Animals and plants have often been personified in literature and given human senses, feelings, and cognitive ability. Although there can be humor in a story about a crayfish who needs a squirt from an oil can to unstick a stubborn antenna, this is fantasy that is more appropriate as cartoon material and cannot be considered a science lesson. As much as possible you should have faith in the information itself to create the drama.

Compare the following two passages and note that even a few words can make a difference in writing that leans toward fantasy and writing that is more scientifically stated. The excerpt is based on the life cycle of a dragonfly.

> You spy a crack in your old skin and struggle to squirm through it. It's hard work and you're glad this is the last time you'll have to shed it. You push and push until you get rid of the clumsy thing. Now you admire your slim, new body. But it's still stiff, and your joints creak as you slowly try it out. The sun feels warm and you decide to unfold your wings. . . .

Note that the words *glad, clumsy, admire,* and *decide* all attribute human understanding and emotional feeling to an insect and therefore make the material less scientifically accurate than the following:

> You wiggle and squirm through the crack in your old skin. It's hard work, but this will be the last time you will have to shed it. You push and push until you are freed. Your slim, new body is still stiff, and your old shell clings to the stalk below you. The sun is warm and your four wings start to unfold slowly. . . .

There are writers of excellent literature who are also knowledgeable about scientific information. Jean George (see *All Upon a Stone, Moon of the Winter Bird,* for example) and Miska Miles (*Fox and the Fire, Wharf Rat*) have created nature stories that are accurate in their information and dramatically captivating as well. You would do well to select such literature for

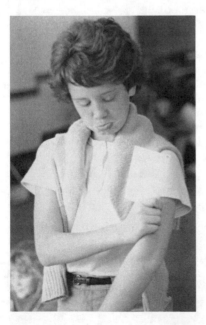

"The dragonfly's skin cracks and begins shedding."

narrative pantomime and to use it as a model for your original narrative writing.

Science Fiction

The combination of accurate information and a fictional setting is, however, a valid kind of writing and extremely useful for a number of curricular topics. Children frequently enjoy, for example, the idea of being made small in order to make explorations of various environments, such as a beehive, the workings of a watch, the inside of a tree, or the human eye. One leader took her class on an exploration of the ear, which they had been studying. Not only were they delighted to experience such events as bouncing trampoline fashion on the tympanic membrane, they also found it difficult to forget such an adventure and all the related information. Joanna Cole's *Magic School Bus* series is a good example of this kind of writing.

The following is an excerpt from an exploration of the parts of a flower:

EXPLORING A FLOWER

Narrator: Today we're going to look at the construction of a flower, but we're going to pretend that it is the year 3001 and scientists have developed some new ways to conduct scientific explorations. You are a special consultant who has been called in for this mission. But it is a secret mission, so you will be given your instructions at special points along the way. Let me know when you're ready for your mission by sitting at attention, saluting, and reporting for duty. (The children respond.)

Good. (The leader now speaks in an impersonal voice, as if over an intercom.) *Good morning, scientists. Please check your equipment.* You notice that you've been issued a very tiny notepad, a very small pencil, and very tiny (handle them carefully!) special pollen-resistant goggles. There is also a capsule, but it is unmarked. Everything is encased in plastic to keep it clean.

Now enter the greenhouse. Inside you will be given additional equipment. As soon as you open the door you sense the cool, damp atmosphere. *In front of you there is a small box on the table. Add it to your equipment. In a moment you are to drink the contents of the vial, which will make you small enough to explore the flower from the inside. Now drink the special formula.*

You do and notice that it is a tasteless clear liquid. Very quickly and painlessly your body shrinks. Your clothing shrinks with you. Your head swims and you feel the slightest bit of nausea. You look around and calculate that you must be about one inch high, the perfect size for this assignment.

Now open the box. Inside you find a laboratory coat, just your new size. *Remove any jewelry and anything that protrudes sharply or has a rough texture. You must leave the scientific environment exactly as you have found it: no marks, no telltale signs of human intrusion.* Inside the box you also find a pair of soft cloth slippers. *Put on the laboratory coat. Remove your shoes and put the slippers on. Now the goggles. Check that you have the notepad and pencil and you are now ready to begin. . . .*

Stories for Pairs and Groups

Although it can present an additional challenge, you may want to try writing activities for pairs and groups. Each character in the narrative, of course, must have action to perform. The activity of Winnie-the-Pooh exercising (p. 137), for example, could easily be played in pairs, since Pooh does his exercises before a mirror. A partner could thus play the mirror image.

Other topics that lend themselves to paired playing are tasks that require more than one person, such as dentist and technician, pilot and flight attendant, or disc jockey and radio engineer. A scientist building and testing a robot, a plant competing with a weed, or red and white corpuscles working together in the bloodstream are other possible ideas.

The following is a narrative for paired playing:

A PLANE RIDE

Narrator: Today we're going to pretend to be Amelia Earhart or Charles Lindbergh flying our planes. The desks will be the airplanes. You'll be playing with partners. One partner will be the pilot; the other will be a student who is learning to fly. We'll play twice so each person will have the chance to play both parts. Choose a partner and decide between you who will be the pilot first. (Pause for organization.)

Now, in our plane, the Stearman biplane, the pilot sits behind the passenger–student. So arrange yourselves accordingly. (Pause again.)

You're going to take a ride across the mountains and land on the other side. This is going to be a dangerous trip because of the bad weather through the mountains, and the landing will be very difficult, owing to the rugged mountains surrounding the landing field. Because this is a dangerous trip, you will have to listen to directions carefully.

The Stearman biplane needs its propeller twirled to help the pilot start the engine. Student, you need to learn this, so you stand at the side of the plane by the propeller. Now, pilot, fasten your seat belt and shoulder harness. Make sure they're on tight. You'll have to take your signal from the control tower. I'm operating the control tower, and you will get your signal from me. Put on your earphones so you can make contact with the control tower and make sure everything is all set for takeoff. (The children pantomime earphones. The teacher holds hand to mouth to make a rather muffled sound as if speaking over the radio transmitter.) *Biplane NC 211, cleared for takeoff.*

OK, pilot, adjust your engine controls. Student, spin the prop to start the engine. Whoops. Guess the old plane will need several spins to get started. You'll have to try again. (Pause) There! The engine throbs to life. Pilot, apply the brakes. Student, pull out the wheel chocks. Now climb aboard. Fasten your seat belt and harness.

Students, listen carefully. In front of you is a stick that controls the plane's direction. It is connected to the pilot's control stick. By placing your hands lightly—I repeat, lightly—around it, you will be able to follow the pilot's sensitive control. In this way, you can get the "feel" of controlling the plane.

Both of you be sure your goggles are in place. Now let up on the brake and taxi down to the end of the runway. You'll have to zigzag so that you can see beyond the nose of the plane.

You're almost at the end of the runway now, so quickly pull the stick toward you. Remember, student, when the stick is forward, it makes the plane go down, and when the stick is pulled toward you, the plane goes up. Now the plane is rising off the ground. Up you go! Check your compass to make sure you're going north toward the mountains. Look down below you. The airport is small and far away.

You're going through the mountains now. It looks like you're going into a storm. Be sure to bank the plane so the wings don't tip too much one way. They should be kept level with the body of the plane. It's starting to rain hard now. Reach up to the top of your control panel and press the blue button on the right to start the windshield wipers.

If you look over to the left you'll see the flash of lightning. Don't look too long! Keep your eyes on the altimeter to be sure you stay well above the mountains.

Keep watching for the mountain tops so you can be sure to pass over them. Careful! There's a peak right in your course. Quickly bank the plane or you'll hit it. Whew! That was a close call.

It looks like you're passing through the storm safely. You're almost on the other side of the mountains now, and the landing field is coming up on the right. Pick up your radios and let's make contact with the control tower and let them know you're coming in for a landing. (The teacher as control tower) *Flight NC 211. Cleared for approach to landing. Approach from the southeast.* Now check your seat belts and prepare to circle the landing field until we can come in for a safe landing.

Now let's bring the plane down easy. You have to go slow because the fog is thick and you might miss the field. There it is! You're right on course. Stand by for a landing. Check the air-pressure meter next to the lever control. Now get ready to pull back the brake lever when you touch ground. You're down. That was a good landing. Pull back on the brake lever and let's bring it to a stop. A perfect three-point landing! Congratulations!

Narratives can also be designed for groups. Again, tasks that require input from several persons are useful topics: an operating team, a group of elves in charge of certain tasks in toy making; the expedition team in Thor Heyerdahl's *Kon-Tiki* adventure. Group narratives might also be based on the workings of a car engine or the human heart, with children playing the various parts of each.

In the following story, students work in groups of four pretending that they have been newly hired as cookhouse helpers for Paul and the head cook, Hot Biscuit Slim. They should find a space that four can work in comfortably but without interfering with other groups. They should decide who will play cookhouse helpers, or "cookies" 1, 2, 3 and 4.

COOKING FOR PAUL BUNYAN

Paul Bunyan was a lumberjack whose logging camp was the biggest in the world. His mighty deeds are known from Maine to California. According to some of the legends about his logging camp, it took 200 cooks to feed all the men, and the tables were 6 miles long.

Narrator: It's early in the morning and you're still sound asleep in your cots. Suddenly you're awakened by the clanging of the bell. Jump out of bed and quickly pull on your clothes. You're excited about your first day at work for Paul Bunyan. Your first job is to make pancakes for breakfast! Run to the 10-acre griddle pan. Help each other strap the flat sides of bacon on your feet to grease the pan. Make sure they're on tight. Good. Now line up in a row and begin skating back and forth over the hot griddle. Remember that Hot Biscuit Slim told you to stay together and skate carefully so you don't miss a spot. But soon you notice that some of the other cookies are playing tag. It looks like fun so the four of you begin playing tag with each other. Ah, but since this is your first time on the griddle, you don't realize how hot it can get. Cookie 1 falls and burns his pants. Ouch! Help him up. Now, take it easy and do it the way Slim told you to. That's better.

As you skate you notice the steam from the hot grease makes a thick cloud over the griddle. It's hard to see. Watch out! Here comes a flood of pancake batter pouring out onto the griddle. Quick! Skate to the side of the griddle and grab a large, flat shovel. These hotcakes are so big it takes five men to eat one, so it will take all four of you to turn it over. You watch to see when the pancake has baked. (You'll know when you see bubbles on the top.) Now, it's ready. Get on one side and together lift it carefully with your shovels and flip it over. Ah, it's done to a crispy brown—and smells delicious. But there's no time to waste. The lumberjacks are sitting at the 6-mile long table and are very hungry.

Take off the bacon slabs and put on your roller skates to serve the men. You'll be loading the pancakes onto a large horse-drawn wagon. Together you lift and toss. Lift and toss. Good. Now get on the four corners of the wagon and skate down the length of the huge table to serve the men. Be sure you stay together! Flip the pancakes onto the men's plates. By the time you get to the end of the table, all the pancakes are gone. These loggers eat a lot, but they work hard, too. After breakfast the men can rest, but a cookie's work goes on, because now you must get lunch ready. Take off the roller skates and get over to the soup kettle.

The huge kettle holds 1,100 gallons of soup and the water is already boiling in it. You'll be using a rowboat to get to the center of the soup, but first you have to load the ingredients in the boat. Cookies 1 and 2 will row the boat, so 3 and 4 can hand you the ingredients: three bushels of carrots, two bushels of peas, a bushel of onions, two bushels of turnips, and fifty heads of cabbage. Cookies 1 and 2, sit down in the boat while 3 and 4 tie a raft, loaded with potatoes and four roasted pigs, behind the rowboat and sit on top. Now, 1 and 2, row toward the middle of the kettle. Careful, this water is even hotter than the griddle was. When you get to the middle, 1 and 2 will keep the boat steady while 3 and 4 throw in the carrots, one bushel at a time. Careful, don't let the hot water splash on you. Unload the boat carefully so it doesn't get unbalanced. That's it. Steady. Now the cabbage. Cookies 1 and 2, take a taste of the soup from your dipper. Um . . . not bad. Cookies 3 and 4, now slowly and carefully shove the potatoes in. Good. Now carefully drop in the four pigs, one, two, three, four. Uh! Whew! What a job this is!

Now, all of you taste the soup again. Ummm, delicious. After it simmers for a few hours it will taste even better. The men will love it. Now row the boat back to the edge of the kettle. It's really hot and steamy now. Whew! Get the raft and the rowboat out of the soup. Someone else will clean them up for the next time. You're off duty now. So you drag yourselves back to the bunkhouse where you collapse on your cots. Feeding those hungry lumbermen is a hard, but important job! Someday you'll be included in those tales about Paul Bunyan, but for now all you can think about is sleep. Pleasant dreams!

With experience you will become more flexible in narrating by ad-libbing and expanding or condensing the material according to the children's responses. The experienced leader may even be able to incorporate some of the children's spontaneous ideas into the story as it is being played. It is this kind of give-and-take between the leader and the children that makes the strongest, most meaningful drama experiences.

FOR THE COLLEGE STUDENT

1. Write a 300- to 500-word narrative pantomime on any of the following subjects. Underline the action words. Label the conflict. If appropriate, indicate the leader role you might play.
   a. Select a short folk tale or fairy tale and rewrite it as a narrative pantomime. Be sure the story you select does not depend on extensive dialogue to be understandable.
   b. Select a topic from social studies or science or another curricular area appropriate for narrative pantomime.
   c. Use a job or a personal experience you have had that you can describe realistically and in detail.
   d. Write a story about an insect or animal without giving the subject human characteristics.
   e. Write a story specifically designed for pairs or groups.
2. Narrate your story for your classmates to enact. Discuss together the story's strengths and possible areas for improvement.

BIBLIOGRAPHY OF NARRATIVE PANTOMIMES
FOR ADDITIONAL CURRICULAR SUBJECTS

The following symbols are used to indicate the age level the material might be best suited for:

Y   Young children in kindergarten, first, and second grades
M   Middle-grade children in third and fourth grades
O   Older children in fifth and sixth grades

(*Note:* The materials focusing on animal and insect life are often of more interest to children from kindergarten through third grade. Students in fourth through sixth grades generally are more interested in the materials focusing on people. However, you will be the best judge for your own particular class.)

Y–M   *All Upon a Sidewalk,* Jean Craighead George. New York: E. P. Dutton, 1974. A yellow ant has an important mission to carry out. (Any of George's writings are superior science lessons and always dramatically written.)

Y–M   *All Upon a Stone,* Jean Craighead George. New York: Thomas Y. Crowell, 1971. A mole cricket searches for and finds his fellow crickets. After a brief meeting, he returns to his solitary life once again. Solo playing is recommended.

Y–M   *Amelia Bedelia,* Peggy Parish. New York: Harper & Row, 1963; Scholastic, 1970. Amelia Bedelia, a housekeeper, takes all her instructions literally. This makes a humorous lesson in language, but children must be old enough to understand double meanings. Edit for solo playing. There are many sequels to this popular book.

M   *And Then What Happened, Paul Revere?* Jean Fritz. New York: Coward-McCann, 1973. This is an accurate and amusing story of a national hero by one of the most popular history writers for children. Check other *And Then . . .* books by Fritz.

Y–M   *Authorized Autumn Charts of the Upper Red Canoe River Country,* Peter Zachary Cohen. New York: Atheneum, 1972. Two canoe trips are described, telling the reader exactly what to do.

Y–M   *The Bakers,* Jan Adkins. New York: Charles Scribner's Sons, 1975. This is a detailed description of bread making.

M–O   *Balloon Trip: A Sketchbook,* Huck Scarry. Englewood Cliffs, N.J.: Prentice-Hall, 1983. In this book we travel on an extended balloon trip, discovering the many intricacies of this exciting sport.

M   *The Barn,* John Schoenherr. Boston: Little, Brown, 1968. In an old barn a skunk searches for food; yet to the mother owl, the skunk is food for her babies. Solo playing is probably best.

Y   *Bear Mouse,* Bernice Freschet. New York: Charles Scribner's Sons, 1973. A meadow mouse hunts food for her young, escaping a hawk and a bobcat. Solo playing is easiest.

M   *Beaver Moon,* Miska Miles. Boston: Little, Brown, 1978. An old beaver is forced out of his lodge and searches for a new home.

O   *The Black Pearl,* Scott O'Dell. Boston: Houghton Mifflin, 1967. Ramon tells of his adventures with Manta Diablo, a fearsome fish, and of the search for a black pearl in Mexican waters. Many excerpts from this longer novel are useful.

M–O *BMX,* Dave Spurdens. New York: Sterling Publishing, 1984. This book presents excellent data and photos (both color and black and white) on bicycle motocross. There are story possibilities in the sections on riding, stunts, proper clothing, and maintenance.

O *Call It Courage,* Armstrong Sperry. New York: Macmillan, 1940. A South Sea Island boy, son of a tribal chief, has many fears of the sea and sets out to conquer them. Numerous solo excerpts from this book are usable.

M *Cassie's Journey: Going West in the 1860s,* Brett Harvey. New York: Holiday House, 1988. A pioneer girl tells of her wagon train journey to California. Excellent detail is taken from actual accounts.

Y–M *Catching the Wind,* Joanne Ryder. New York: William Morrow, 1989. The author describes a girl's experience of changing into a Canadian goose in order to imagine the world from the bird's perspective.

Y *"Charlie Needs a Cloak,"* Tomie de Paola. Englewood Cliffs, N.J.: Prentice-Hall, 1979. The process of making a cloak is demonstrated from sheep shearing to final sewing. Little tension, but it can be a satisfying story.

Y *A Chick Hatches,* Joanna Cole. New York: William Morrow, 1976. Color photographs document the process.

Y–M *Children of the Earth and Sky,* Stephen Krensky. New York: Scholastic, 1991. Five brief stories describe some of the daily activities of Hopi, Comanche, Mohican, Navajo, and Mandan children.

M–O *Chimney Sweeps,* James Cross Giblin. New York: Thomas Y. Crowell, 1982. A 900-year history of chimney sweeps is presented with illustrations and photographs. Chapter 5, which takes the reader through a day in the life of a chimney boy in nineteenth-century London, is perfectly written for narrative pantomime if edited for length.

Y–M *Clem: The Story of a Raven,* Jennifer Owings Dewey. New York: Dodd Mead, 1986. A baby raven is rescued by a family and raised to adulthood when it is returned to the wild.

Y–M *Cosmo's Restaurant,* Harriet Langsam Sobol. New York: Macmillan, 1978. A young boy experiences a typical day at a family-owned Italian restaurant. Black-and-white photos add to the information.

M *Coyote for a Day,* Roger Caras. New York: Windmill Books, 1977. A coyote searches for food and experiences several adventures in this story which begins, "Today you are a coyote. . . ."

M *A Day in the Life of a Firefighter,* Betsy Smith. Mahwah, N.J.: Troll Associates, 1981. A firefighter's day is documented with color photographs and text centering on rescuing a young child and putting out a dangerous fire.

O *A Day in the Life of a Forest Ranger,* David Page. Mahwah, N.J.: Troll Associates, 1980. A forest ranger goes through a typical day, which involves everything from paperwork to relocation of animals. Photographs are included. Other titles in this series focus on occupations such as marine biologist, police detective, meteorologist, and basketball coach.

Y–M *A Day in the Life of a Sea Otter,* Kay McDearman. New York: Dodd Mead, 1973. A mother sea otter spends her day with her baby searching for food, playing, and escaping dangers. It is easiest to play solo and should be edited to shorten. Black-and-white photographs illustrate.

O *A Day in the Life of a Television News Reporter,* William Jaspersohn. Boston: Little, Brown, 1981. This book, complete with photographs, shows a typical day of a television news reporter in Boston, from an early morning call about a robbery to the evening news broadcast.

Y–M *A Day in the Life of a Veterinarian,* William Jaspersohn. Boston: Little, Brown, 1978. This book documents a vet's many interesting duties, illustrated with black-and-white photos.

O *A Day in the Life of an Emergency Room Nurse,* Margot Witty. Mahwah, N.J.: Troll Associates, 1980. A nurse, through text and photographs, demonstrates her experiences in an emergency room.

M *Doctor in the Zoo,* Bruce Buchenholz. New York: Viking Penguin, 1974. A fascinating account of the many duties of a zoo doctor is presented with black-and-white photos.

M–O *The Dream Is Alive: A Flight of Discovery about the Space Shuttle,* Barbara Embury. New York: Harper & Row, 1990. Based on an IMAX film, this book provides detailed descriptions and full-color pictures of all aspects of space travel.

Y–M *A Drop of Water,* Sam Rosenfeld. New York: Irvington-on-Hudson, 1970. A drop of water is followed through its many changes in the environment.

O *Exploring the Titanic,* Robert D. Ballard. New York: Scholastic, 1988. A famous marine geologist recounts his experiences in discovering the sunken ocean liner *Titanic.* Sequel is *Exploring the Bismark,* 1991.

M *Felipé the Bullfighter,* Robert Vara. San Diego: Harcourt Brace Jovanovich, 1967. A young boy in Spain tries his hand at fighting a small bull. The beautiful color photographs add to the understanding of the story. Little editing is needed, although it will be more dramatic if the action is condensed into one day's time.

Y *First Comes Spring,* Anne Rockwell. New York: Thomas Y. Crowell, 1985. Good ideas for seasonal pantomimes.

M *A First Guide to Horse and Pony Care,* Jane Kidd. New York: Macmillan, 1991. Detailed descriptions of the layperson's work involved in caring for horses and ponies.

M *The First Travel Guide to the Moon,* Rhoda Blumberg. New York: Four Winds Press, 1980. A detailed tourist's guide for a flight to the moon in the year 2000. It requires editing to shorten for one playable trip.

M–O *Flying to the Moon and Other Strange Places,* Michael Collins. New York: Farrar, Straus & Giroux, 1976. This is a firsthand account of space from one of the early astronauts. Excerpts are usable.

M *Fox and the Fire,* Miska Miles. Boston: Little, Brown, 1966. A young red fox searches for food and is interrupted by a barn fire.

Y–M *The Golden Book of Space Explorations,* Diane L. Moché. Racine, Wisc.: Western Publishing Company, 1990. The section entitled "Liftoff!" begins "Imagine you're an astronaut," and presents excellent material if edited to sequence chronologically.

M–O *Gorilla, Gorilla,* Carol Fenner. New York: Random House, 1973. This is a poignant description of a gorilla's life in the zoo, with flashbacks to his earlier life in the jungle.

O *Great Survival Adventures,* ed. Robert Gannon. New York: Random House, 1973. A collection of nine true stories told by the people who survived their adventures despite great odds. Settings cover the desert to the Yukon, a bailout from a jet fighter to a rowing adventure across the Pacific Ocean. The stories need considerable editing to shorten.

O *Hatchet,* Gary Paulsen. New York: Bradbury Press, 1987. A thirteen-year-old boy survives fifty-four days in the wilderness after a plane crash.

M–O *Hiroshima No Pika,* Toshi Maruki. New York: Lothrop, Lee & Shepard, 1980.

A retelling of the events during the bombing of Hiroshima from a survivor's viewpoint.

Y *How Animals Sleep,* Millicent Selsam. New York: Scholastic, 1962. Descriptions of the sleep habits of several animals are given. This experience is also useful for a quieting activity.

Y–M *How to Dig a Hole to the Other Side of the World,* Faith McNulty. New York: Harper & Row, 1979. Detailed instructions are given for taking an imaginary 8,000-mile journey, beginning with a shovel and a soft place to dig to a "no-spaceship" with supercooling system, fireproof skin, and a drill on its nose.

M *How Do You Go to the Bathroom in Space?* William R. Pogue. New York: Tom Doherty Associates, 1991. An astronaut answers children's questions about space travel.

M–O *i am the running girl,* Arnold Adoff. New York: Harper & Row, 1979. In this story, told in poetic form, Rhonda trains for a running meet.

Y–M *In the Driver's Seat,* Ron and Nancy Goor. New York: Thomas Y. Crowell, 1982. Through black-and-white photos and text, this book guides us through the steps in driving a front-end loader, combine, blimp, M60 tank, race car, Concorde Jet, 18-wheel truck, crane, and train. The "you" wording makes it perfect for narrative pantomime.

M–O *Indian Hunting,* Robert (Gray-Wolf) Hofsinde. New York: William Morrow, 1962. The author describes Indian weapons, hunting methods, and the ceremonial rites of the hunt. Other books by this Native American may also be of interest.

O *Island of the Blue Dolphins,* Scott O'Dell. Boston: Houghton Mifflin, 1960. A California Native American girl is left alone on an island in the Pacific and manages to survive. There are many episodes to use from this exciting book based on a true story.

M *Joshua's Westward Journal,* Joan Anderson. New York: William Morrow, 1987. In black-and-white photos, actors portray a fictional account of a family traveling westward from Indiana in a Conestoga wagon.

O *Julie of the Wolves,* Jean Craighead George. New York: Harper & Row, 1972. An Eskimo girl must choose between the world of her ancestors and the world of modern white people. Her sensitivity to the wolves and time spent with them comprises much of the story. Many episodes are usable.

M–O *The King's Day: Louis XIV of France,* Aliki Brandenburg. New York: Thomas Y. Crowell, 1989. An illustrated description of a day in the life of the monarch known as the Sun King.

O *Kon-Tiki and I,* Erik Hesselberg. Englewood Cliffs, N.J.: Prentice-Hall, 1970. This is the account by one of the six explorers in Thor Heyerdahl's expedition that sailed a small raft from Peru to the Polynesian Islands. Excerpts are usable.

Y–M *The Last Dinosaur,* Jim Murphy. New York: Scholastic, 1988. A speculative account of what the last dinosaurs might have experienced. Use a series of frozen pictures (see Chapter 7) for the fight.

Y *Lizard in the Sun,* Joanne Ryder. New York: William Morrow, 1990. The author transforms the reader into a green anole to experience life from the animal's perspective.

M *Lone Muskrat,* Glen Rounds. New York: Holiday House, 1953. An old muskrat survives a forest fire and makes a new home for himself.

M–O *The Long Ago Lake,* Marne Wilkins. New York: Charles Scribner's Sons, 1978.

Fascinating data is presented in this book on outdoor life in the Wisconsin north country in the 1930s.

M–O *Lucky Chuck*, Beverly Cleary. New York: William Morrow, 1984. Teenage Chuck, who has a job pumping gas, gets a traffic ticket in an accident with his motorcycle. It teaches a good safety lesson along with the fun of pretending to ride a motorcycle.

M–O *Lumberjack*, William Kurelek. Boston: Houghton Mifflin, 1974. The author describes his personal experiences as a young lumberjack in Canada.

M *The Magic School Bus Inside the Earth*, Joanna Cole. New York: Scholastic, 1987. A teacher takes her class on field trips in an exciting and unusual manner. See other adventures in *The Magic School Bus Inside the Human Body* (1989), *The Magic School Bus Lost in the Solar System* (1990), and *The Magic School Bus at the Waterworks* (1986).

O *The Man Who Was Left for Dead*, Jenny Tripp. Milwaukee: Raintree Publishers, 1980. This is a true story of Hugh Glass, who in the early 1800s was badly wounded by a giant grizzly bear, yet made a 100-mile journey back to his fort. Chapters 4 and 5 form the basis for an exciting solo pantomime adventure.

Y–M *Maple Harvest: The Story of Maple Sugaring*, Elizabeth Gemming. New York: Coward-McCann, 1976. A detailed description of the steps in the process of maple sugaring is presented.

Y–M *The Moon of the Winter Bird*, Jean George. New York: Thomas Y. Crowell, 1970. This lengthy story details the dramatic experiences of a sparrow trying to survive in Ohio's winter weather.

O *My Side of the Mountain*, Jean George. New York: E. P. Dutton, 1959; 1988. The various adventures of a young boy who tries his hand at living by himself in the Catskill Mountains provide an excellent nature study.

M–O *Night Dive*, Ann McGovern. New York: Macmillan, 1984. A twelve-year-old girl accompanies her mother, a marine biologist, on nighttime scuba-diving adventures. Several stories show undersea life, exploring an old shipwreck, as well as the rigors of scuba diving. Color photographs illustrate.

Y–M *Nobody's Cat*, Miska Miles. Boston: Little, Brown, 1969. The adventures of an alley cat in the city and his struggles are told in a dramatic way.

Y–M *Octopus*, Evelyn Shaw. New York; Harper & Row, 1971. An octopus needs to find a new place to live.

Y–M *The Old Bullfrog*, Bernice Freschet. New York: Charles Scribner's Sons, 1968. On a hot summer day, an old bullfrog sits on a rock looking asleep, but knows the exact moment to escape from a hungry heron. Play in pairs or with a third player to enact all the other animals and produce sound effects for them.

M–O *One Day in the Desert*, Jean George. New York: Thomas Y. Crowell, 1983. Description of how members of the Papago Indian thrive and desert animals survive the record-breaking heat. See also *One Day in the Alpine Tundra* (1984), *One Day in the Prairie* (1986), and *One Day in the Woods* (1988) for other dramatic nature stories in this series.

M *Ox Cart Man*, Donald Hall. New York: Viking Penguin, 1979. This beautiful picture book depicts day-to-day farm life in nineteenth-century New England. Although more focus is on the father, we see the duties of each member of the household, so it can be played in a group. There isn't a strong conflict, but it is a satisfying experience to play because of the completion of the seasons' cycle.

Y–M *Pete's House,* Harriet Langsam Sobol. New York: Macmillan, 1978. This text, illustrated with black-and-white photos, details the steps in the building of a young boy's new house.

M–O *The Philharmonic Gets Dressed,* Karla Kuskin. New York: Harper & Row, 1982. Over 100 members of an orchestra, including the conductor, are shown getting ready for a performance. At the end you can play a short, symphonic piece and let the orchestra be conducted. (See "Conducting an Orchestra," p. 97.)

M *The Pine Tree,* George Maxim Ross. New York: E. P. Dutton, 1966. A pine tree struggles for survival. Although this is a basically simple story, it is beautifully written and highly dramatic.

M–O *The Plymouth Thanksgiving,* Leonard Weisgard. New York: Doubleday, 1967. The details of the events leading up to the first Thanksgiving are presented simply. There are numerous characters for small groups to play simultaneously or for the entire class to play as one presentation.

M *A Prairie Boy's Winter,* William Kurelek. Boston: Houghton Mifflin, 1973. This picture book gives separate descriptions of the many rigors and pleasures of living on the Canadian prairie in the 1930s. Sequel *A Prairie Boy's Summer* (1975) is equally enchanting.

O *The Printers,* Leonard Everett Fisher. New York: Franklin Watts, 1965. This is one of a series of over a dozen handsomely illustrated books on colonial craftspersons, including blacksmiths, glassmakers, wigmakers, cabinetmakers, and homemakers.

M *Rattlesnakes,* G. Earl Chace. New York: Dodd Mead, 1984. A prairie rattlesnake is followed through her life cycle. The story contains good detail with black-and-white photos and may be excerpted from the section where the snake first makes her move into the world through the end of Chapter 3 after she eats her first meal.

Y–O *Roadrunner,* Naomi John. New York: E. P. Dutton, 1980. The hurrying desert roadrunner, a comic figure, spends his day running, chasing, and racing with twists, circles, and sudden stops.

O *Robinson Crusoe,* Daniel DeFoe. New York: Charles Scribner's Sons, 1983. A man is shipwrecked and lives for years on a lonely island. There are many episodes to choose from in this novel.

M–O *Rodeo School,* Ed Radlauer. New York: Franklin Watts, 1976. A detailed narrative account of the training rodeo riders undertake and the techniques they must know.

Y–M *Sarah Morton's Day: A Day in the Life of a Pilgrim Girl,* Kate Waters. New York: Scholastic, 1989. With full-color photographs of the reconstructed Plimoth Plantation, we follow a typical day in the life of a young girl who came to New England on the *Mayflower.*

M–O *Shackleton's Epic Voyage,* Michael Brown. New York: Coward-McCann, 1969. The true story of the 800-mile voyage of Captain Shackleton and five men to get help for the rest of his crew stranded on an Antarctic island. It can be played solo or in small groups. The text is simple and short.

O *Shaw's Fortune: The Story of a Colonial Plantation,* Edward Tunis. New York: Collins Publishers, 1966. Data on all facets of plantation life are beautifully and carefully illustrated.

Y–M *Skunk for a Day,* Roger Caras. New York: Windmill Books, 1976. Illustrated with black-and-white drawings, this book begins, "Today you are a skunk" and then details the day's events.

O *Slake's Limbo,* Felice Holman. New York: Charles Scribner's Sons, 1974; Aladdin, 1986. A thirteen-year-old boy escapes with his troubles to live under Grand Central Station for 121 days.

Y *The Snail's Spell,* Joanne Ryder. New York: Frederick Warne, 1982. This short experience of pretending to be a snail is perfectly written for a narrative pantomime. It begins, "Imagine you are soft and have no bones inside you."

Y–M *Space Travel: Blastoff Day,* Janet McDonnell. Elgin, Ill.: The Child's World, 1990. The voyage is described simply and can be narrated without much editing.

Y–M *The Spider Makes a Web,* Joan M. Lexau. New York: Hastings House, 1979. The story of a shamrock spider and how it builds its web is told through text and drawings.

M *Sugaring Time,* Kathryn Lasky. New York: Macmillan, 1983. Through words and pictures, this book follows a family in Vermont during the maple-sugaring season.

M *Tarantula, the Giant Spider,* Gladys Conklin. New York: Holiday House, 1972. In this explanation, tarantulas are presented as useful insects that need not be feared.

Y *This Is the Way We Go to School,* Edith Baer. New York: Scholastic, 1990. Children around the world are shown going to school in different ways and with varying transportation.

Y–M *Three Days on a River in a Red Canoe,* Vera B. Williams. New York: Greenwillow Books, 1981. A young boy tells of his camping adventure with his mother, aunt, and cousin. With little editing this can be played in groups of four with second and third graders. Some rewriting is necessary for solo or paired playing.

O *Tiktaliktak,* James Houston. San Diego: Harcourt Brace Jovanovich, 1965. An Eskimo boy is trapped on a rocky island and must make it back to food and safety.

Y–M *Time of Wonder,* Robert McCloskey. New York: Viking Penguin, 1957. This is a sensitive description of a summer's experiences in Maine. Detailed information on many aspects of summer life in this part of the country, including a storm, is given.

M–O *The Tipi: A Center of Native American Life,* David and Charlotte Yue. New York: Alfred A. Knopf, 1984. This book presents excellent data with illustrations on tipis, the sophisticated dwelling of the Great Plains Indians. Story material is possible in the tipi construction and the role of women in the task.

O *To Build a Fire,* Jack London. Mankato, Minn.: Creative Education, 1980. A man in the Yukon, after a brave struggle, loses his battle against the 75-degrees-below-zero temperature. This story can easily be shortened.

Y–M *The Web in the Grass,* Bernice Freschet. New York: Charles Scribner's Sons, 1972. This colorful picture book tells the story of a little spider's dangerous and friendless life.

M–O *A Week in the Life of an Airline Pilot,* William Jaspersohn. New York: Joy Street Books, 1991. A description of a flight crew's experiences from New York to New Delhi. Black and white photos illustrate.

M–O *Westward with Columbus,* John Dyson. New York: Scholastic, 1991. Description of a journey aboard a replica of the *Nina.*

M *Wharf Rat,* Miska Miles. Boston: Little, Brown, 1972. This is a realistic portrayal of a rat's survival when threatened by an oil slick near the docks.

Y–M *When Bastine Made Bread,* Treska Lindsey. New York: Macmillan, 1985. In this lovely picture book, six-year-old Bastine spends an entire day baking bread, including such steps as threshing the wheat.

Y *Where Butterflies Grow,* Joanne Ryder. New York: E. P. Dutton 1989. The reader is asked to imagine being a caterpillar turning into a butterfly.

Y–M *White Bear, Ice Bear,* Joanne Ryder. New York: William Morrow, 1989. A boy imagines himself transformed into a polar bear.

Y–M *Window into an Egg,* Geraldine Lux Flanagan. Reading, Mass.: Addison-Wesley, 1969. A detailed account, with black-and-white photos, of the development of a chicken egg which has had a "window" cut into it. Play the end section, entitled "Hello, Chick."

O *Wolf Run: A Caribou Eskimo Tale,* James Houston. San Diego: Harcourt Brace Jovanovich, 1971. Rather than face certain starvation, a young Eskimo boy sets off to find caribou against almost hopeless odds.

M *The Wounded Wolf,* Jean Craighead George. New York: Harper & Row, 1978. Roko, a wounded wolf in the Alaskan wilderness, is saved from death by Kiglo, the wolf pack leader. This story is based on fascinating research of wolf behavior. Solo playing is probably best.

O *Wrapped for Eternity: The Story of the Egyptian Mummy,* Mildred Pace. New York: McGraw-Hill, 1974. This presents fascinating information about a fascinating subject, particularly for older children. For a simpler version, see *Mummies Made in Egypt,* Aliki Brandenberg, New York: Thomas Y. Crowell, 1979.

Y–M *Your First Airplane Trip,* Laura Ross. New York: William Morrow, 1981. This is a useful description of an airplane trip. There is little conflict except for a bit of bumpiness in the ride, but it is a satisfying experience for younger children to play.

7

Pantomime
Guessing Games

In the previous chapters, pantomimes were designed for the players' self-expression and self-satisfaction. The children often played in unison with no audience observing. While there were opportunities for voluntarily sharing ideas, there was no obligation to do so.

Even so, anyone watching the playing probably would have been able to understand what the children were doing and "saying." In fact, as leader you may have been translating many nonverbal ideas in side-coaching: "I see some happy people," "That's it. Nice and slow," "Oh, you must be tired," and so forth. Pantomime communicates many messages to observers, whether intentional or not.

This chapter covers a variety of ways to use pantomimes for communicating messages. In these activities and guessing games, pantomimers are encouraged to communicate their feelings and ideas through actions and facial expressions. The audience, through analysis and synthesis, interprets and translates the messages. The challenges and learning experiences thus are shared equally by both pantomimers and guessers.

Because children's verbal language increases each year, they tend to forget how much communication can be accomplished nonverbally. Pantomime encourages them to stretch, and in some cases recapture, their ability to communicate without words. Pantomime also encourages them to pay attention to each other, a valuable experience in itself. I discovered this once in working with a group of gifted children. All were highly verbal and so used to being leaders, they found it difficult to listen to each other or even acknowledge each other's presence. I restricted their work to pantomime for an extended period of time so they were forced to look at each other. Eventually, they were ready to give and take in cooperative experiences.

Children usually find these activities highly entertaining as well as challenging, whether they are doing the pantomiming or the guessing. You will also find it <u>easy to incorporate numerous curricular</u> topics into these activities for additional learning benefits. These activities can also be incorporated into story dramatization, role drama, and extended drama lessons.

GUIDING PANTOMIME PLAYING

Player and Audience

Since pantomimes for guessing require an audience-and-performer arrangement, it is best to avoid having only one child pantomiming for any length of time in front of the rest of the class. Such procedure places too much pressure on the performer, causing embarrassment or showing off behavior. And if the rest of the children have to wait too long for their turn, they become bored and restless. Therefore, all of the activities presented in this chapter are designed to involve several children at a time in pantomiming.

Pantomime is ambiguous, as is all nonverbal communication. This is its fascination; we speculate on it, guess, and test our accuracy constantly. Therefore, pantomimers should be encouraged to communicate their ideas as clearly as possible and the guessers encouraged to observe closely.

To guess a pantomime, you have to watch closely for clues.

Children will also need to understand that it may take a little time to figure out what a pantomimer is doing. Furthermore, a pantomime may appear to be entirely different from what the player is intending. All these considerations will take some time and effort on everyone's part.

The guessing aspect of pantomimes can cause various reactions in children. For example, shy students may be disappointed or think they have been unsuccessful if their pantomimes are not guessed immediately. They may even say the audience has guessed their idea correctly when, in fact, they have not. If observers cannot guess what these children are pantomiming, it may help if you say, "That's a hard one! You have us stumped; I guess you'll have to tell us what your idea was." This should help them feel more comfortable as well as reinforce the ambiguity of pantomimes.

Outgoing students may be disappointed, angry, or may think they have been unsuccessful if their pantomimes *are* guessed right away. Often they want to confuse an audience so they can continue performing. They may even say a guess is not correct or not accurate enough, while changing their idea subtly to avoid being guessed. For these students it is helpful to say, "You gave us such good, clear details that we were able to guess it right away." This comment reinforces the importance of pantomiming good clues.

Guessing the Pantomimes

The major goal of using pantomime guessing games is to help children become more aware of nonverbal communication and its use in conveying feelings and ideas. While guessing often adds fun to the game, it should never supercede the process of exploring and sharing ideas.

Limiting the guessing is a good way to challenge the performers and the guessers to do their best work. As a rule of thumb, there is little justification for allowing more than three guesses for any pantomime. After children are familiar with drama work, frequently only one guess is allowed. In fact, guessing can be eliminated altogether for some of the activities. Whenever a pantomime cannot be guessed, the players simply state what they were doing.

If guessing is allowed to continue at length, there can be problems. For example, a second grader was once performing something extremely elaborate. The directions were to continue pantomiming until the idea was guessed. The child kept saying no to each guess, yet he continued pantomiming very intriguing actions. Finally the leader said, "I guess you'll have to tell us what your idea was, Billy." Billy thought for a moment and then answered somewhat sheepishly, "I forgot."

Some children simply do not realize that their full idea cannot always be guessed with total accuracy. They hold out for specific guesses as a kindergartner once did: "You're a lion." "No." "A tiger." "No." "You're a panther." "No, I'm a *lioness with green eyes.*"

Evaluating

In discussing pantomimes, the leader should give verbal feedback on the various clues the children were giving:

"Sandy, I knew immediately that you were a tiny spring in the clock. You stretched, and then relaxed and jiggled. And each time you did exactly the same movement."

"I can tell you have really been studying that book on armor. All five of you were pantomiming so believably I could practically feel the weight of each article of clothing you put on."

During the playing side-coaching may be useful. Speculate out loud on your thinking process in making a guess, perhaps even giving a possible idea or two. This is helpful both to the players and the guessers.

"I wonder what David and Chris are carrying. It must be something that's too big for one person to lift. It looks as if it's heavy, too. I wonder what could it be?"

Discuss particularly careful pantomimes, pointing out the details that help the audience understand the actions.

TEACHER: What do you suppose Cliff was doing when he moved his hands like this? (He demonstrates.)
CHILD 1: Taking the cap off a tube of toothpaste.
TEACHER: How did you know it was toothpaste? Couldn't it have been hair gel? Or first-aid cream?
CHILD 1: No! He squeezed it on his toothbrush and brushed his teeth!
TEACHER: Cliff used a special kind of toothbrush, didn't he? What kind was it?
CHILD 2: Electric.
TEACHER: How do you know?
CHILD 2: 'Cause he plugged it in and he jiggled.
TEACHER: What was Orlando doing?
CHILD 3: That's easy. Peeling an onion.
TEACHER: How could you tell?
CHILD 3: Because he peeled it and cried.
TEACHER: Cliff and Orlando were very careful in their actions. They added details that helped us know what they were doing.

Of course, you should be careful about implying that a child is unskilled in pantomiming. No doubt some children will be more successful than others, but it is important to encourage continued work. Discussions should not be allowed to become boring or overly critical. The greatest improvements will come about through practice and through doing, rather than through the extended evaluation of others.

A class plays a Half-and-Half Pantomime.

DESCRIPTIONS OF PANTOMIME GAMES

Half and half

This game is based on a children's game called by various names: New Orleans, Trades, or Lemonade. Divide the class into two groups. They line up and face each other. Traditionally, occupations were acted out for the opposing group to guess. The first group to play walks up to a designated middle line while chanting

TEAM 1: Here we come.
TEAM 2: Where you from?
TEAM 1: New Orleans.
TEAM 2: What's your trade?
TEAM 1: Lemonade.
TEAM 2: Show us if you're not afraid.

Team 1 pantomimes an occupation or a trade. Team 2 calls out its guesses, and when the guess is correct, Team 1 must run back to its original place without being tagged by anyone from Team 2. Tagged members, in the traditional game, must join the opposite team. For classroom playing, the chasing and tagging should be eliminated. (Or children could hop on one foot to slow down.)

Variations

1. The game, of course, can be played with topics other than "occupations." See the listing of additional topics on pages 167–71.
2. The rhyme may also be changed. For example, the following could be used with seasonal activities. "Here we come." "Where you from?" "Kalamazoo." "What do you do?" "Depends on the weather." "Well, give us a clue."

Sequence game

For this game, pantomime activities are written or pictured on cards. Since the pantomime cards are to be played in sequence, a written cue precedes the pantomime. Suspense is created in the quiet and careful watching and waiting for one's cue.

The cards are shuffled and distributed. Each child receives a card. (Or two or three children may share a card.) The first card might say:

> (You begin the game.) Pretend to mount a motorcycle. Rev it up and cruise around the room once. Sit down.

The pantomime must be interpreted correctly by the player who has the next card that reads:

Cue: Someone pretends to ride a motorcycle around the room.
You: Pretend to be a police officer driving in your patrol car. You spot a speeder. Chase the speeder with your siren turned on. Go around the room once and return to your seat.

It is helpful to have the cues and the pantomimes written in different colors. For example, the cue may be in red (stop and look) and the pantomime in green (go ahead). The directions for standing and sitting are useful the first few times the game is played.

The pantomimes can be unrelated, or they may tell a simple story. The following is an example of a modern Inuit-Eskimo seal hunt.

Card 1:   (You begin.) Stand and pretend to put bundles of heavy clothes, sealskin boots, and boxes of food into an umiak in the middle of the circle. Sit.

Card 2:   (Cue: Someone pretends to put supplies in an umiak.) Go to the center of the circle and pretend to step carefully into the umiak. Then sit in the umiak.

Card 3:   (Cue: Someone sits down in the umiak.) Sit down behind the person in the umiak.

Card 4:   (Cue: Two people have seated themselves in the umiak.) Pretend to start the small motor that propels the boat. After a few moments the motor "catches." Sit down as if you are ready to steer the boat . . . [and so on]

It is wise to prepare a master sheet for yourself, with all the pantomimes in their proper sequence, in case the group gets lost.

Once children are familiar with sequence games, they can help transcribe the material on cards or even create their own games. One group of sixth graders worked diligently on a sequence game based on the process of preparing an Egyptian mummy, while another created its version of a Spanish bullfight.

Variations

1. A sequence game might give practice in learning directions: "Fly south," "Swim east," "Roll a ball northwest," and the like.

2. Pictures can be used in place of words. Animals, people performing various tasks, or portrayals of different emotions are all possible. One teacher used pictures of various body parts (head, hand, leg, and ear) her kindergartners were learning. They were simply to move the body part pictured on the lower half of their card after someone performed the cue pictured on the upper half of the card.

3. Activities which follow a step-by-step sequence work well: performing a task, following a recipe, or tracing the steps a letter goes through being mailed are all fun to do. Similarly, the actions of a simple, familiar story can be made into a sequence game. For example, the narrative pantomime stories in Chapters 5 and 6 work well.

4. An alphabet sequence is another possibility. An "A" word (*alligator, angry*) is followed by a "B" word (*bear, bashful*) and so forth. You may choose to just let the alphabet itself be the cue to the next pantomime. See *The Marcel Marceau Alphabet Book,* by George Mendoza (New York: Doubleday, 1970), for an excellent example of this. Numerous other alphabet books also exist.

5. As a final variation, prepare two or three sets of cards of the same game. Divide the class into two or three smaller groups to play the game simultaneously. Prepare a master sheet for each group and let a child from each group monitor.

Add-on pantomimes

Add-ons are played similarly to the sequence game. As before, one player's pantomime is the cue to the next player's pantomime. In this game, however, each child invents an idea to fit the selected topic.

One person begins by pantomiming an idea, while the audience guesses *silently.* The guesser (checked by you) joins the first player and assists. For example, one child may pretend to cook dinner. The second player may decide to set the table, another may make a salad, and so on. The players add on until they run out of ideas or until everyone who wishes to has contributed.

Variations

1. Show various people at an event by gradually adding on individuals, pairs, or small groups to the scene. For example, the Indianapolis 500 pit crew, drivers, fans, owners, flag signalers, and so forth could take their appropriate places and perform their activities.

2. Try creating objects, with players becoming the various parts. Several players might form a castle, a bicycle, or a clock.

3. Older children might like to add on in interacting pairs. For example, the topic might be "cooking breakfast." One player fries eggs, while the partner *becomes* the eggs cooking. Other partners for cooks might be bubbling oatmeal, sizzling bacon, browning pancakes, and the like.

Build a place

In still another variation of the add-on, children can create a room or location, equipping it with appropriate furnishings or objects. A space is marked off on the floor, with doors or entryways indicated. The players bring one item at a time into the specified area. The goal is to create a complete imaginary environment; therefore, players must remember where each item is placed so they do not walk over or through it. Children can furnish a modern living room, a covered wagon, an Egyptian tomb, a science lab, Heidi's grandfather's alpine hut, or a grocery store.

For an added challenge, after players pantomime an item, they are required to use one of the previous items in some way. For example, after bringing in test tubes to the scientist's laboratory, the player lights the Bunsen burner brought in previously. This serves as a review of what is already in the room and keeps the image of the room and all its furnishings in mind.

Often the created place becomes so real to the students that a ritual is necessary to end the playing. Sometimes the leader (in mime) erases the room, or folds it up and puts it on a shelf for another day. When the children have worked hard to maintain a group imaging project, it seems only fair to honor their efforts.

Variations

1. Try building an entire shelter, following appropriate procedures. Children may build a log cabin, a wigwam, an igloo, or a modern-day house, constructing walls, roof, and windows in addition to furnishing the shelter.

2. Build a city, state, or country. Put masking tape on the floor in the appropriate shape. Children place the locations by pantomiming actions appropriate to them. A city, for example, may be known for a particular sport, industry, or product. As an added challenge, place the locations appropriately, observing directions and distance relationships. Books that are useful for this activity would include David Macaulay's *Castle* (Boston: Houghton Mifflin, 1977), in which he details castle construction in thirteenth-century Wales. In *Underground* (1976) he pictures sewers, telephone and power lines, cables, pipes, and tunnels—all the underground elements of a large city. And in *Unbuilding* (1980), he imaginatively reverses the building process and dismantles the Empire State Building, step by step. *Simple Shelters*, by Lee Pennock Huntington (New York: Coward-McCann, 1979), presents simple data and sketches of eighteen various kinds of houses, such as igloos, teepees, stilt houses, and Masai houses. *Skara Brae: The Story of a Prehistoric Village*, by Oliver Dunrea (New York: Holiday House, 1986), outlines the archaeological discovery of a village on an island north of Scotland, showing how stone houses were built and rebuilt.

Count-and-freeze pantomimes

Select five to eight volunteers to pantomime simultaneously in front of the class while you count to, perhaps, ten. (The counting may be as slow or as fast as is needed. If players are having a difficult time, a fast count is more comfortable. If the players are involved and the audience is interested, the counting can be slowed.) Call "Freeze" and then let the audience guess the pantomimes. Players may sit down when they are guessed.

The ideas may be as simple as "something you like to do" or as complex as "connotations of words" (for example, adventure, discovery, sacrifice, freedom, dreams, happiness, invention, or serendipity).

This game is useful when space is limited or when you want only a few

Second graders play a Count-and-Freeze Pantomime.

children to play at a time. However, since it has the largest audience for an extended period, the guessing should be kept moving as quickly as possible.

Variations

1. Combine ideas: "Pack something to take on a camping trip; the first letter of your item should be the same as the initial of your first or your last name." Or, "Act out an invention; the audience must guess the invention *and* name the inventor."

2. Ideas may be pantomimed in pairs. The topics might be "two-person" mimes (playing catch, pulling taffy) or "compound words" (break-fast, light-house).

Pantomime spelling

Similar to count-and-freeze is spelling out words. For example, players can spell out a city's name by simultaneously acting out animals whose names begin with the appropriate letters. *New York* might be spelled out by seven players pantomiming *n*anny goat, *e*lephant, *w*alrus, *y*ak, *or*angutan, *r*hinoceros, and *k*angaroo. Other possible categories of words to mime include action words, occupations, foods (those that are usually eaten in a distinctive way), sports, musical instruments, and so on.

The audience can try guessing the words even if they are not sure of each letter. (The procedure is similar to working a crossword puzzle.) For a good cooperative learning experience, children can guess in small groups, pool their interpretations, and make a group decision.

Variation.   Young children can spell out simple words by forming letters with their bodies. Some letters will require more than one child.

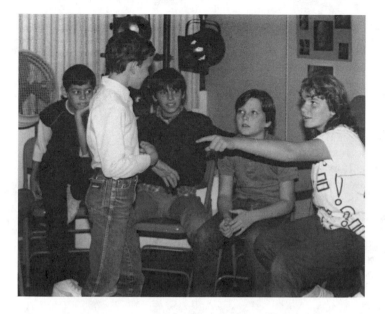

A game of charades is good practice for perfecting pantomime skills.

Count-and-freeze charades

As a variation of the traditional game of Charades, several children at a time act out words of a title (omitting the articles *a, an,* and *the*). For "Row, Row, Row Your Boat," three people could pantomime rowing, a fourth might point to the audience ("your") and the fifth might mime seasickness.

Longer names can be divided and acted out by groups also. "Washing-ton," "Indian-apple-us," and "Robin-son Crew-sew" are some possibilities.

Charades

This age-old game can be played by older elementary students. Once the game is learned, it is probably best played in small groups so that more students have a chance.

Two teams are formed. One team gives its topic to one of the players from the opposite team to enact for his or her team to guess. A time limit is imposed, though you may wish to deemphasize this feature.

Traditionally, players are given song, play, book, film, or television titles as well as common sayings to act out. Usually the words are acted out one at a time, although they need not be acted out in the order in which they appear in the title. Sometimes only one syllable at a time is acted out.

The pantomimers have several aids they can use:

1. They may tell the guessers, "This is a _____ (title or saying). There are _____ words in it. I'm going to act out the _____ word."

2. The player may say, "This is a short word." The guessers then simply call out as many short words as they can think of until the correct one is called. Words such as *a, an, the,* or various pronouns and prepositions can be handled quickly in this manner.

3. The pantomimer may act out a word that *sounds* like the original word if that would be easier to guess. The word *car*, for example, might be easier to act out and guess than the word *far*.

For additional curricular emphasis, story titles might be from literature. Sayings might be historical quotes, such as "Walk softly and carry a big stick" (Theodore Roosevelt), "Give me liberty or give me death" (Patrick Henry), or "A house divided cannot stand" (Abraham Lincoln).

Frozen pictures

For this game, players select a scene, decide what parts they will play, and then freeze into position. They might freeze into pictures with titles such as "The Night the Ghost Visited," "Pony Express Ride Breaks Record," or "Napoleon Defeated at Waterloo."

Variations

1. Art masterpieces can be recreated: Seurat's *Sunday Afternoon on the Island of La Grande Jatte,* Daumier's *Accident at the Zoo,* or Picasso's *Guernica.* Statue or museum groupings are also possible.

2. Scenes from favorite stories and books or scenes of historical or current events might be created. Students could also imagine and create the paintings made by Little Gopher in Tomie de Paola's *The Legend of the Indian Paintbrush* (New York: Aladdin, 1988). Or, with a book like Trinka Hakes Noble's hilarious *Meanwhile Back at the Ranch* (New York: Dial Press, 1987), the uneventful scenes in Sleepy Gulch can be alternated with the amazing events occurring back at the ranch.

3. One-liners (see p. 185) may be added to these frozen pictures to aid the guessing or to clarify the context. The pictures may also be set in motion (see pp. 165–66).

4. Family and group portraits may be depicted. It may be an historical family (John F. Kennedy's family) or group (the First Continental Congress), a newsworthy family or grouping (Olympic medalists), or a literary family or group (Laura Ingalls Wilder). If the groups show how they prepare themselves for the picture-taking event, interrelationships and feelings can be shown.

Frozen pictures in role drama

Frozen pictures (sometimes called *tableau*) is an extremely useful activity in role drama (see Chapter 11). The activity's purpose is to slow down the drama, giving students time to reflect on ideas or capsulize thinking. A point frequently emphasized by many writer–practitioners is that frozen pictures in role drama should not be a guessing game. Instead, they are interpreted and discussed by the observers and are a catalyst for reflective thinking.

Frozen picture of Washington Crossing the Delaware.

Variations

1. Sometimes the pictures are referred to as photographs from the past (as in a photograph album or historical painting). Or they may be visions of the future to show a group's wishes, dreams, hopes, aspirations, or predictions.

2. As another variation, the people posed in the frozen picture may quietly speak a single private statement that reveals their character's inner thoughts of the moment. ("I'm frightened.") Or, they may voice questions they have. ("I wonder how long our journey will take?") This technique is useful in determining how involved or committed the students are to the topic. If they can respond in thoughtful ways, the leader knows they can proceed meaningfully to the next stage of the drama. Since the aim in this instance is to get to the deeper feelings of the people in the pictures, you may need to stipulate beforehand that comical or flippant statements are not appropriate.

3. Sometimes a series of perhaps five or six pictures is created by a group. The series tells a story (see example of this technique on page 4), or explains the events leading up to a particular situation (see the accident picture example in the next section), or forecasts an event in the future. A series of pictures is also very useful for demonstrating fights and battles in order to control students' physical contact with each other.

"Setting pictures in motion" or "Coming to life"

This activity sets a frozen picture in motion on cue. For example:

"When the music begins, your idea of 'slithy toves' will come to life and 'gyre and gimble in the wabe.' When the music stops, the still picture of the Jabberwocky's home will return" (3,18,24,29). (Numbers refer to anthologies listed in this text's final bibliography.)

"In this short poem, 'The Shopgirls' (20), we are told that when the shopgirls leave the stores and the working day is over, certain things in the store come to life. What might some of these things be and how would they move? What do they do all night? What position might they freeze into at daybreak?"

"This picture shows an accident of some sort. In your groups decide how this situation might have happened. Then create a series of five pictures to show the events leading up to this moment.

Another way to set a picture in motion in a dramatic way is to perform it in sequence. Each child in each group is assigned a number. When you call "1" s, they move, then "2" s add on to the "1" s, and so on. If you reverse the counting, the picture can return slowly to its frozen position once again. For example:

"For your 'rumpus' (Maurice Sendak's *Where the Wild Things Are*), you will all be frozen as a 'wild thing,' I'll start the music, and when I call your number you can move. When I call your number the second time, you'll freeze."

"Now that we've studied early railroad building in the United States, we can create our own railroad crew. In each group decide who will be the one who lays the ties ('sleeper'), the one who holds the spike ('shaker'), the one who hammers, the one who carries the water, and the supervisor. When you've worked that out, I'll give a number to each."

Intra-group pantomimes

This game is a little complicated and is usually too difficult for children below third grade to play, but it is highly popular with older students. Divide the class into several groups of five or six persons. In each group, three or four members pantomime ideas for two members to guess. The instructions might be "Pantomime all the words you can think of that begin with the letter *r*." Other topics might be rhyming words (*at: hat, cat, flat,* and so on); verbs; household chores; toys; ways we use water; and consonant blends (*st: stand, street, stop,* and so forth).

The three pantomimers do not confer with each other; each thinks of his or her own ideas and enacts as many of them as time permits. The two guessers work as quickly as possible and write down the ideas. If an idea cannot be guessed, the pantomimers *or* the guessers may say, "Pass," and the pantomimers go on to another idea.

A time limit of one or two minutes for each topic may be imposed. Afterward the children might discuss the ideas that were "the most humorous," "the most difficult to guess," or "those that appeared on every group's list." Avoid introducing competition by counting the number of words on each list. You can also avoid competition by giving each group a different topic to work on.

The advantage of this method is that the audience in each group is small and the time limit encourages the children to pantomime quickly. Even the most reticent children will find it difficult not to get caught up in this game, since attention on them will be minimal.

Hint: Caution the children to work quietly so that other groups cannot hear their ideas. This reasoning usually makes more sense to them than just being quiet, and this game can get a little noisy.

Musical scenes

Many musical selections, both with lyrics and without, provide interesting material for pantomime scenes created to musical accompaniment. Folk songs and ballads that tell a story are likely candidates. Many selections with descriptive titles such as tone poems and ballet suites are also useful. The scene does not have to fit the title; scenes created from "Grand Canyon Suite," for example, do not have to take place in that setting.

At first some students may feel more comfortable using puppets to show movement to music. (This was a popular activity for Jim Henson's Muppets in television guest appearances.) Or students might prefer to create a shadow pantomime. For this the pantomimers perform behind an old sheet; a bright worklight shines on the pantomimers' backs to cast their shadow on the sheet. If possible, videotape these experiments so students can see how their work appears to the viewers.

Without saying a word

This activity can be played by older or advanced classes. In groups the players prepare a familiar story (for example, "The Three Bears," "Little Red Riding Hood") to show to the class. However, they must carry out all their preparations, including the selection of the story, casting, rehearsing, and finally the performance *totally in pantomime*. Writing notes or mouthing words is not allowed.

To make the activity a little easier, brainstorm some titles with the group and list them on the chalkboard. Be sure that everyone knows each story listed. The groups may select from this list as they plan; however, they are not allowed to go to the board and point out a title. When all the groups are ready, you too can enter the playing by guiding the sharing of stories with pantomimed instructions, indicating who goes first, leading the audience's applause, and so forth.

This game is a real challenge, but the rewards make it worthwhile. Both you and the students may be amazed to discover how much you can communicate with others without using any words at all. When the stories are shared, do not be surprised if one or two people in a group are acting out a story different from that of everyone else in their group. It demonstrates the difficulty of accurate communication. When the entire activity is ended and talking is allowed, you may need to allow for some moments of chattering as students check out all the pantomiming they were not sure of.

Additional Topics

The following topics may be used with several of the methods discussed in this chapter. Children can choose their own topics; or you may assign them, perhaps giving ideas written on cards.

Who am I (are we)?   Act out community helpers, storybook or nursery rhyme characters, historical or literary characters, famous scientists, people in current events, and so on.

What am I (are we)?   Children can pantomime animals, inanimate objects, machinery, toys, plants, and the like.

What am I (are we) doing?   This may be as simple as acting out verbs (*running, skipping, jumping*) or more complete ideas, such as making a cake, driving a car, or milking a cow. Pantomimes may be more challenging and add conflict, such as testing a water bed before purchasing, washing an unwilling dog, or setting up a tent in a windstorm.

What am I (are we) seeing, hearing, tasting, smelling, touching?   Pantomimers react to various sensory stimuli, which may cover such topics as seeing a ghost, listening to loud music, tasting unsweetened lemonade, smelling ammonia fumes, or touching a hot iron.

What's the weather?   Players enact clues for the audience to guess the seasons or the climatic conditions. They may act out seasonal sports or daily chores related to certain times of the year, putting on appropriate clothing for the weather (hot, cold, rainy, windy) or demonstrating various natural disasters.

What am I (are we) feeling?   Students act out various emotions. As an additional challenge, limit them to using only certain parts of the body to show emotion (face, hands, feet, or back). You can hold up a sheet to make just the particular body parts visible. Or use expressionless masks, below.

Emotions can also be combined with the "doing" pantomime: Show an action and how you feel about doing it (for example, a household chore you do not like to do). Extend the idea by acting out a brief scene showing more than one emotion or a scene in which something happens to change the feeling. For example, "You are happily packing a picnic basket when you suddenly notice that it's raining. Now you can't go on the picnic and you are disappointed."

Where am I (are we)?   Pantomime being in various locations, such as a zoo, a hospital, a desert island, a haunted house, a carnival midway, an

Masks made of paper plates, with stapled darts for chin and forehead and string or elastic for ties. (See also photo, p. 55).

elevator, and so forth. You may also use particular cities or countries studied.

Let's get ready to go.   Pretend to pack supplies for various adventures, such as going on a fishing trip, preparing for a hike, loading a covered wagon, equipping an explorer's ship, preparing for a space launch, and so forth.

Transportation   Players pretend to travel in various ways: on foot or skates, by bicycle, bus, airplane, and so forth. Categories may include modern (electric car, spaceship), historical (horse and buggy, high-wheeler bicycle), foreign (rickshaw, camel), or fantastic (flying carpet, seven-league boots).

Dress up   Pretend to be certain people dressing in their appropriate clothing for what they are to do: baseball player, ballet dancer, knight, astronaut, desert nomad, or Egyptian priest. Historical and literary characters are good for this game, too.

Foods   Pretend to grow, harvest, or prepare and eat familiar and unusual foods: corn on the cob, an ice-cream cone, pizza, a hot dog, lobster, spaghetti, wild rice, coffee beans, peanuts, coconut, and so forth. Students can also do the four basic food groups: fruits and vegetables; bread and cereal; dairy products; and meat, fish, and poultry or other protein.

Health and hygiene   Players can demonstrate various good (or bad) habits, such as brushing and flossing teeth, getting fresh air and exercise, washing clothes, and cleaning house.

Energy and water conservation   Students demonstrate various ways to conserve electricity and water at home and school, and in business and industry (for example, turning off unneeded lights, repairing leaky faucets, and turning heat or air-conditioning down).

Occupations   Children can act out various jobs, perhaps pantomiming what they would like to be when they grow up. Consider also community helpers, occupations in Colonial times, occupations in other locations or countries.

Tools   Demonstrate various tools people use to perform certain occupations or tasks: kitchen, carpentry, sewing, household, doctor's, teacher's, and so on. Tools from the past (and in some cases still in use) might include a blacksmith's bellows, a weaver's loom, and a pioneer's butter churn.

Machines   Demonstrate simple tools—such as levers, wedges, and pulleys—as well as more sophisticated machines, such as electrical appliances or construction equipment. Students may demonstrate operating the machinery or becoming the machines. This topic can also include human organs—such as the heart, lungs, or stomach—since they resemble machines.

Sports   Children enact favorite sports or portray favorite athletes. The sports may be categorized into team sports, Olympic events, winter sports, and so forth.

Animals   Different groups of animals may be pantomimed: pets, farm animals, zoo animals, circus animals, mammals, amphibians, or mythical animals.

Biography   Enact a famous or historical person performing a typical activity or acting in a famous event. Students may focus on various categories, such as Famous Women (Sally Ride, Barbara Jordan, Maria Tallchief), Minority Heroes or Heroines (Martin Luther King, Jr., Mary McLeod Bethune, César Chavez), or Famous Scientists (Albert Einstein, Marie Curie, George Washington Carver).

Inventions   Pantomime using or being the invention. The class guesses the inventor as well as the invention (Eli Whitney, cotton gin; Robert Fulton, steam engine; Samuel Morse, telegraph; and so forth).

Musical instruments   Pantomime the instrument of choice or one from a category, such as orchestral, marching-band, percussion, woodwind, and brass. Instruments associated with a particular country or culture (for example, Scottish bagpipe) might also be considered.

Safety   Pantomime the dos and don'ts of various activities: use of playground equipment, bicycle riding, water sports, camping activities, household or school activities, or rules for dealing with natural disasters.

First aid   Demonstrate techniques for treating cuts, insect bites, removing a foreign body from the eye, aiding a choking victim, treating frostbite, giving first aid for burns, and the like.

Festivals and holidays   Act out various activities associated with holidays in the United States (Fourth of July, Thanksgiving, Memorial Day); celebrations (Christmas, Hanukkah, Halloween, Valentine's Day); other cultures and countries (Chinese New Year, Mexican birthday, French Bastille Day). The audience guesses the custom and the country.

Word pantomimes   Several games can be played using categories of words or parts of speech. For example, in an opposite game the audience guesses the word that is the opposite of the one pantomimed (*hot, cold*). This game may also be played with homophones, words that sound alike but are not spelled alike (*weigh, way*). The guesser should spell both words. Other words might be those with long vowel sounds, spelling words, and vocabulary words.

Countries and customs   Students enact a custom, and the audience guesses both the custom and the country: British afternoon tea; Spanish or Mexican bullfight; Japanese kite-flying contest.

Sign language   Learn some Indian sign language (see Robert Hofsinde (Gray-Wolf), *Indian Sign Language,* New York: Doubleday, 1956); finger

In an "Opposite Game," the answer to this pantomime is "hot."

spelling; American Sign Language (see Mary Beth Sullivan and Linda Bourke's *A Show of Hands,* New York: Harper & Row, 1985); or other nonverbal language systems. Use these in place of pantomiming.

FOR THE COLLEGE STUDENT

1. Play some of the pantomime activities suggested in this chapter. Afterward discuss the special skills required of the pantomimer and the interpreter in acting out and guessing the nonverbal messages. How successful were you in doing each?
2. After playing some of the pantomime games, discuss which pantomime types would be most useful for different grade levels. Also discuss which curricular topics might be particularly suitable for the different types of pantomimes.
3. Create ten pantomime activities, using various curricular topics in each. Vary the types of pantomime activity you use.
4. Now select one of the pantomime activities you have written and guide your classmates or a group of children in playing it. Consider the various techniques you can use to guide the playing, to help the audience interpret the pantomimes, and to evaluate the playing. Discuss the activity afterward.
5. Create your own type of pantomime, perhaps creating a variation on a type mentioned in this chapter. Teach it to your classmates.

8

Verbal Activities
and Improvisation

In this chapter we will look at a number of verbal activities and simple improvisations. In general, the activities progress from the easier to the more difficult. Many will be incorporated into story dramatization, role drama, and extended lessons in later chapters.

BEGINNING VERBAL ACTIVITIES

Sound Effects

Creating sound effects can be an excellent learning experience for all ages. The voice is a marvelous instrument of sound that has an extremely wide range of possibilities, when we take the time to explore it. Without saying a word at all, there can be great flexibility of communication.

Children will enjoy doing this kind of experimenting. And you will soon discover that there are many places in the curriculum for this activity. While students have fun, they will also be learning facts, experimenting with the physics of sound, and creating settings and environments of the mind. Sound effects can be highly dramatic by themselves or when added to more elaborate productions, such as "sound mimes" (see p. 176).

Sound Effects from Literature.   There are many excellent stories and poems that focus on sounds. Simply narrate the material (as you did before in narrative pantomime) and pause for the students to make the sounds in the appropriate places, thus exercising the children's listening and interpretive skills.

The list of literature that follows covers a broad range of subjects for you to choose from. For example, the delightful books of Margaret Wise Brown tell stories about a little dog Muffin who, for different reasons in each book, must guess about all the sounds he hears. Many sounds are ordinary, but others are challenging and may require some discussion. What would "butter melting" sound like? Or a grasshopper sneezing? "The Devil's Pocket" has continuing echo sounds, and *Paul Revere's Ride* provides opportunities for an entire drama of sound effects. Children are intrigued by the various sound possibilities and usually have a greater appreciation of the literature after working with it in this fashion.

Tips

1. Some sounds are best made by one student or by just a few, whereas other sounds will require the entire class. Experiment to see what procedure will give the best results.
2. Control the sounds by using an indicator for volume control. Some leaders use an arrow made of wood or cardboard or an oversized pencil. One teacher used a cutout picture of an ear on a stick and simply raised and lowered it to indicate on and off and intensity of volume.
3. It is probably best not to let students operate the volume control—at least not at first.
4. Do not try to do too much at a time. Children may get tired working on a long selection in one sitting.
5. Try tape recording the selections after they have been rehearsed a few times so that students can hear themselves. It will be easier for them to evaluate

Follow the arrow to know when to make the sound and how loud it should be.

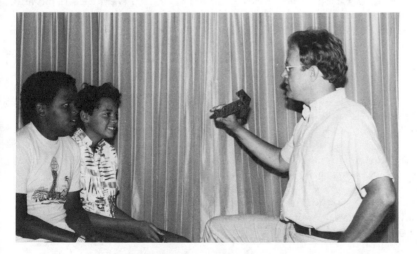

their work this way. Consider these like radio dramas, where one's imagination can soar, visualizing entire scenes based on narration and sound effects. Older students will enjoy added information from *The Magic of Sound,* by Larry Kettlekamp (New York: William Morrow, 1982). Chapter 4, "Fun with Sound Effects," tells how to make, amplify, and record a variety of sounds.

6. Try adding some musical sounds or other nonvocal sounds for variety. Rhythm-band or Orff instruments have endless possibilities. Experiment also with objects in the classroom that make noise. One fourth grade class decided the most realistic sound for rain was achieved by running their feet over the little bits of gravel that had accumulated under their desks on a particularly muddy day!

Suggested Literature for Sound Effects. (*Note:* Letters at the beginning of each entry indicate suggested grade levels. Numbers in parentheses correspond to numbered anthologies listed in this text's final bibliography.)

Y–M *Bam Zam Boom!* Eve Merriam. New York: Walker, 1972. Demolition day brings the excavating and rebuilding of a city apartment house.

Y–M "The Bed," Pura Belpre (38). The squeaks of an old-fashioned bed frightens several characters in this Puerto Rican folk tale.

M–O *Clams Can't Sing,* James Stevenson. New York: Greenwillow Books, 1980. A delightful story of two clams who prove they can contribute to the orchestra concert. This one lets you pull out all your creative stops when it "gets fancy."

Y–M *Country Crossing,* Jim Aylesworth. New York: Atheneum, 1991. An old car, a freight train, and a peaceful countryside meet in the late night in this captivating picture book.

Y *Country Noisy Book,* Margaret Wise Brown. New York: Harper & Row, 1940. Muffin the dog hears farm and countryside sounds in this classic story. Other books in the series include: *The Noisy Book* (1939), *Quiet Noisy Book,* (1950), *Winter Noisy Book* (1947).

M–O "The Devil's Pocket," George Mendoza (5). Two boys have a "Twilight Zone" adventure with echo effects after throwing a penny into an old abandoned quarry.

Y–M *Klippity Klop,* Ed Emberley. Boston: Little, Brown, 1974. Prince Krispin and his horse Dumpling meet a dragon in a cave.

M "Louder than the Clap of Thunder," Jack Prelutsky (17). A child claims no sound is as loud as his father's snoring.

Y *Mr. Brown Can Moo! Can You?* Dr. Seuss. New York: Random House, 1970. Mr. Brown makes all kinds of sounds from a bee buzzing to a hippopotamus chewing gum.

Y–M "My Family's Sleeping Late Today," Jack Prelutsky (35). A child tries different sounds to wake his family.

Y *Night in the Country,* Cynthia Rylant. New York: Bradbury, 1986. The sights and sounds of a country night are recorded.

Y *Noisy,* Shirley Hughes. New York: Lothrop, Lee & Shepard, 1985. All kinds of sounds from doors slamming to airplanes zooming.

Y *Noisy Counting Book,* Susan Schade and Jon Buller. New York: Random House, 1987. Sounds in a pond are counted out with humor.

Y–M *Noisy Gander,* Miska Miles. New York: E. P. Dutton, 1978. A young gosling does not understand why his father honks at everything—until a fox enters the barnyard.

Y–M *Noisy Poems,* collected by Jill Bennett. New York: Oxford U. Press, 1987. Opportunities abound for making all manner of sounds from eating spaghetti to imitating machines.

O *Paul Revere's Ride,* Henry Wadsworth Longfellow. New York: E. P. Dutton, 1990. There are opportunities for such sounds as feet climbing wooden stairs, startled pigeons, and horse's hoofs on sand in this picture book of the classic poem. Try making a shadow play.

Y–M *Plink Plink Plink,* Byrd Baylor. Boston: Houghton Mifflin, 1971. A young boy imagines all the things night sounds could be.

Y–M *Sounds All Around,* Jane Belk Moncure. Chicago: Children's Press, 1982. This book teaches some basic concepts about hearing sounds, from the ping of a toaster to fireworks.

M *Too Much Noise,* Ann McGovern. Boston: Houghton Mifflin, 1967, 1992. An old man tries to find the solution to too much noise in his house.

Y *Wake Up Bear,* Lynley Dodd Gareth. Milwaukee, Wisc.: Stevens Publishing, 1988. Everyone tries to wake up bear with different sounds.

Original Sound Effects Materials.   You can also compose some materials of your own for sound effects. Try creating a group story with the students or encourage them to write their own.

The stories can be based on a number of curricular materials being studied. For example, stories can be based on the seasons, holidays, or weather sounds; or the sounds heard in certain locations, such as a supermarket, seaport, zoo, school, or foreign city. Consider a natural disaster and the preparations and safety precautions surrounding it. An event, such as a space launch, could be created.

Example   The following dramatic incident is based on the surrender of Lee to Grant at Appomattox from information in a social studies text:

Let's imagine it is the afternoon of April 9, 1865.

It's very quiet. . . .

All eyes are looking down the dusty road to the courthouse.

A blue jay calls. . . .

An annoyed squirrel answers back. . . .

In the distance young children shout and begin a game of tag. . . .

The muffled sound of horses is heard . . .

and a gray figure riding a gray horse approaches. . . .

All sounds cease. . . .

Slowly, the gray horse, Traveller, passes the line of waiting Northern soldiers. . . .

He stops at the gate of the McLean house. . . .

General Lee's footsteps on the wooden stairs are clear and brisk. . . .

Now another figure on horseback rides into view. . . .

While the watching men softly sing "Auld Lang Syne" . . .

General Grant disappears into the house . . .

and the battle-weary country waits for peace.

For speech improvement, some teachers of young children have focused stories on sounds many children have difficulty pronouncing, such as "s," "sh," "th," or "r." The sounds can represent specific things, such as "s" the hissing of a snake, "sh" waves on a shore, "th" air escaping from a balloon, and "r" the sound of a car motor. The sounds can be combined in a story about the adventures of a snake who travels by boat, balloon, and car to seek his fortune.

Another variation of sound effects is to select favorite stories and assign certain sounds to each of the characters. Each time the character is mentioned in the story, the sound is made. Consider the characters' looks and personality in order to determine the most appropriate sounds. (For example, Papa Bear's and Baby Bear's growls would be different. Gold-ilocks' sound might be a tinkling bell or a giggle. Finger cymbals might be the sound for a Princess; a drum might signal the villain; and so forth.) This is a valuable characterization lesson for both drama and for literature study.

Sound Mimes. Older students will enjoy creating sound effects for pantomime dramas and scenes. For this activity, one group of students performs the sound effects for the pantomime players. They must watch carefully and fit the sounds to the movements.

For an even more challenging activity, have the sound effects people create sounds for a story while the pantomimers follow the sounds along with appropriate actions. This is a little more elaborate than the sound pantomimes on page 96, since an entire scene or story is being told. Some students may wish to work out their scene and sound effects before presenting them, while others might prefer to improvise on the spot.

Sequence Reading Games

As with the pantomime sequence games, sequence reading can also be created for verbal activities. Actually, a sequence reading game is similar to reading a short play script. With these materials you can encourage appropriate interpretive reading of the lines, pointing out the opportunities for variety in vocal inflection, pitch, dynamics (loud and soft), timing, pauses, and so forth. And, since sequence reading depends on responding to one's cue, there is a strong incentive to listen, a highly important but often overlooked language arts skill.

As with the pantomime sequence games, verbal sequence cards are made up with a cue and a line to read (and perhaps an accompanying action to perform). Cards are shuffled and distributed. The first card might say

> You begin the game.
> Stand and say, "Good morning, ladies and gentlemen. Welcome to the Fourth Grade TV Personality Show!" (Bow and sit down.)

The next player will have a card that reads:

Cue: "Good morning, ladies and gentlemen. Welcome to the Fourth Grade TV Personality Show."
You: Stand and say, "Brought to you by Multicolored Jelly Beans." (Sit.)

Three children may have this next card:

Cue: "Brought to you by Multicolored Jelly Beans."
You: Stand and applaud. Then sit down.

Often it takes a run-through reading first for the children to familiarize themselves with the material and get into the spirit of it. Usually they ask to repeat the game so that they can switch cards and perfect their delivery. Even after just one playing there is usually an automatic improvement in reading. Soon children will ask for more than one card, inspired by the challenge of keeping track of several cues. Once children are familiar with sequence reading, they can transcribe material on cards themselves or even create their own material. It is a good idea to laminate the cards so they will survive repeated playings.

As students become more adept at playing sequence games, the cues can be very brief, perhaps one word. For example,

Card 1: This is the house that Jack built.
Card 2: *house*
This is the malt that lay in the house that Jack built.
Card 3: *malt*
This is the rat that ate the malt that lay in the house that Jack built [and so forth].

Sequence Reading Games from Literature. There are a number of stories and poems with interesting dialogue or statements in a series that

Interpretive reading skills are encouraged in verbal sequence games.

provide excellent material for sequence reading. Although children enjoy reading almost any text from script cards, some materials are more effective than others. For example, first-person narratives (either prose or poetry), in which the writer is the speaker, work well. In Judith Viorst's *Alexander and the Terrible, Horrible, No Good, Very Bad Day* (see bibliography following this section), a little boy recounts his day's miserable adventures. In Shel Silverstein's popular poem "Sick" little Peggy Ann McKay lists her numerous physical ailments as reasons why she shouldn't have to go to school—until she discovers it is Saturday. Children delight in interpreting these speakers' humorous lines, which are familiar complaints to them.

Stories that relate cause-and-effect adventures are interesting because they build suspense. In Remy Charlip's classic, *Fortunately,* a fortunate happening follows each unfortunate one in "good news/bad news" format. *If You Give a Mouse a Cookie* by Laure Joffe Numeroff tells of the step-by-step chores you will have to perform should you fall prey to a mouse's initial desire.

Literature that is written totally in dialogue begs to be read aloud. In Trinka Hakes Noble's *The Day Jimmy's Boa Ate the Wash,* a mother questions her child about a field trip to a farm. The child dutifully responds to each question, revealing an increasingly chaotic adventure.

Some materials will not require specific cue lines. Alphabet and number books, enjoyed by younger children, are one example since "two dogs" obviously follows "one cat" in numerical order. In like manner, a "B" word or phrase follows an "A" word or phrase.

Riddle books also need no cue. Readers determine if the answers they hold fit the riddle just read. For example:

Card 1:   Why does an elephant hum?
Card 2:   Because it doesn't know the words.
          Why does the chicken cross the road?
Card 3:   To get to the other side.
          Why does . . . [and so on].

Incidentally, the first reader will appreciate getting to read the answer to the final riddle. This may be placed at the top of the first card.

The abundance of riddle books, many of which correlate with content areas, range from the subject of dinosaurs (see Noelle Sterne's *Tyrannosaurus Wrecks*) to homographs (see Giulio Maestro's *What's a Frank Frank?: Tasty Homograph Riddles*) and provide an almost infinite source of material.

Materials written in rhyming couplets can be read using the rhyming word as the cue for every other line. For example, the nonsense rhyme from *Alice's Adventures in Wonderland* (46) might be prepared as follows:

Card 1:   You begin: "Twinkle, twinkle little bat,"
Card 2:   "How I wonder what you're at."
Card 3:   [at] "Up above the world you fly,"
Card 4:   "Like a tea-tray in the sky."

Older children will enjoy sequence reading games based on books with trivia information. Many of these books have short commentaries interspersed, as if the reader is reacting to the information. These side comments can be included in the sequence reading to create a dialogue encounter. Often students are motivated to create their own scripts from these books.

Suggested Literature for Sequence Reading Games. Following are some suggestions from literature. In most cases they can be used just as they are written. (*Note:* Letters at the beginning of each entry indicate suggested grade levels. Numbers in parentheses correspond to numbered anthologies listed in the final bibliography that begins on page 300.)

Y *A My Name Is Alice,* Jane E. Bayer. New York: Dial Press, 1984. A collection of animals introduce themselves and the things they sell. Steven Kellogg's illustrations are wonderfully witty.

M *Alexander and the Terrible, Horrible, No Good, Very Bad Day,* Judith Viorst. New York: Atheneum, 1972. A young boy enumerates everything that goes wrong for him in one day. Available in Spanish.

Y–M *Alfred's Alphabet Walk,* Victoria Chess. New York: Greenwillow Books, 1979. Alfred sees many things on his walk, including "a herd of hungry hogs hurrying home."

Y–M *Animalia,* Graeme Base. New York: Harry N. Abrams, 1986. An alphabet with tongue twisters and wonderfully detailed pictures of fantastic animals inhabit this treasure.

M–O *Ask Me Anything about the Presidents,* Louis Phillips. New York: Avon, 1992. Fascinating facts from Benjamin Harrison's fear of electricity to Jimmy Carter's wearing of a pair of women's high button shoes are included.

M–O *Astronauts: Space Jokes and Riddles,* Charles Keller. New York: Simon and Schuster, 1985. A witty collection of puns and word play. The author has several other joke books; topics include dinosaurs, dentists and doctors, and sports.

Y–M *Because a Little Bug went Ka-CHOO!* Rosetta Stone. New York: Random House, 1975. A domino effect of events is created when a bug sneezes.

M–O *Bringing the Rain to Kapiti Plain,* Verna Aardema. New York: Dial Press, 1981. An African Nandi tale, written in the style of "The House That Jack Built," tells how a herdsman helps end the drought.

M *Can I Keep Him?* Steven Kellogg. New York: Dial Press, 1971. A boy has a humorous conversation with his mother about having a pet.

M *The Day Jimmy's Boa Ate the Wash,* Trinka Hakes Noble. New York: Dial Press, 1980. A dialogue between mother and child about a class field trip to a farm. Sequels: *Jimmy's Boa Bounces Back,* New York: E. P. Dutton, 1984 (use a frozen picture at the end); and *Jimmy's Boa and the Big Splash Birthday Bash,* 1989.

M *Don't Forget the Bacon,* Pat Hutchins. New York: Greenwillow Books, 1976. A little girl struggles to remember a grocery list. In the end she forgets the bacon!

O *Encyclopedia Brown's Record Book of Weird and Wonderful Facts,* Donald J. Sobol. New York: Dell Publishing/Delacorte Press, 1979. The facts and information in this book are frequently tied together so that many parts read like a script.

There is ample opportunity for several games from this collection. (Sequels available with topics of animals, crimes, spies, and sports.)

M *Fortunately,* Remy Charlip. New York: Four Winds Press, 1980. For each unfortunate happening, a fortunate one follows.

M–O *Geographunny: A Book of Global Riddles,* Mort Gerberg. Boston: Clarion, 1991. Useful bits of information are coupled with punning and other word play.

M *George and Martha,* James Marshall. Boston: Houghton Mifflin, 1972. These delightful stories are told with so much dialogue they work well for sequence reading. Several sequels exist.

M–O "Grey Goose," traditional (26). A gray goose is too tough to be killed and eaten. Twenty-five lines can be done, one to a card, with the chorus of "Lawd, lawd, lawd" said by everyone after each line. Add some pantomime for even more fun.

O *Hail to Mail,* Samuel Marshak. New York: Henry Holt, 1990. A certified letter is sent to a man who keeps moving from place to place around the world. Lengthy, but the entire story should be told.

M–O *Hello, Mr. Chips!* Ann Bishop. New York: E. P. Dutton, 1982. This joke and riddle book takes a look at the world of computers.

M–O *Hush Up!* Jim Aylesworth. New York: Holt, Rinehart and Winston, 1980. A nasty horsefly lands on mule's nose and creates a domino effect of trouble. Try pantomime with this one also.

Y–M *I Can Read with My Eyes Shut!* Dr. Seuss. New York: Random House, 1978. A reader delights in his accomplishments.

M *"I Can't," Said the Ant,* Polly Cameron. New York: Coward-McCann, 1961. A broken teapot creates a problem for kitchen inhabitants. Leader can read longer narrated passages. May edit to shorten. The sequel, *The Green Machine* (1969), tells of a reckless automobile creating havoc along country gardens.

Y *I Don't Want to Go to School,* Elizabeth Bram. New York: William Morrow, 1977. A little girl is reluctant to go to her first day of kindergarten.

M *If I Were in Charge of the World and Other Worries,* Judith Viorst. New York: Atheneum, 1981. Try the title poem as well as "Fifteen, Maybe Sixteen, Things to Worry About."

Y–M *If You Give a Mouse a Cookie,* Laure Joffe Numeroff. New York: Harper & Row, 1985. Once you give a mouse a cookie, he will want one thing after another until we return to the beginning. If you add at the end, "And you know what happens if you give a mouse a cookie," you can read the story all over again. Sequel: *If You Give a Moose a Muffin,* 1991.

Y *Is Your Mama a Llama?* Deborah Guarino. New York: Scholastic, 1991. A baby llama asks his friends what their mothers are. They answer in rhyme. Leave the answers blank for readers to guess.

M–O *Jokes to Tell Your Worst Enemy,* Scott Corbett. New York: E. P. Dutton, 1984. There is much to choose from in this mixture of jokes, short stories, and poems. Mix and match or focus on one subject—such as the sections entitled "History Rewritten Mother's Way" (for example, Paul Revere's mother will not let him go out for his famous midnight ride).

M–O *The Judge,* Harve Zemach. New York: Farrar, Straus & Giroux, 1969. This comical story shows various prisoners warning a judge of a horrible monster. *Suggestion:* Add "Hear ye! Hear ye! The court is now in session" and "Here comes the Judge" (the latter repeated three times) at the beginning. At the end, pantomime the monster (three students linked together) eating the judge with the line "There goes the Judge" repeated three times.

Y *The Lady with the Alligator Purse,* Nadine Bernard Westcott. Little, Brown, 1988. An old jump-rope rhyme in picture book format prescribes pizza to cure an ailing child.

M–O *"Let's Marry," Said the Cherry,* N. M. Bodecker. New York: Atheneum, 1974. A poem tells, in short, rhymed couplets, the wedding plans for the cherry and the pea.

M–O *Lightning Inside You: and Other Native American Riddles,* edited by John Bierhorst. New York: William Morrow, 1992. Over 120 riddles have been translated from twenty Native American languages.

M *Magic Letter Riddles,* Mike Thaler. New York: Scholastic, 1974. By adding and subtracting letters, you can find the answers to these word riddles.

M–O *Marvin K. Mooney Will You Please Go Now?* Dr. Seuss. New York: Random House, 1972. Various modes of transportation are suggested for Marvin's departure.

M–O "The Meehoo with an Exactlywatt," Shel Silverstein (15). This is a combination of a knock-knock joke and the old Abbott and Costello "Who's on first?" routine—with repetitive possibilities as well.

M–O "Messy Room," Shel Silverstein (15). A complainer discovers the mess is his!

M *The Moon Clock,* Matt Faulkner. New York: Scholastic, 1991. A young girl confronts bullies in a dream world and loses her cowardice. Story is told in dialogue balloons.

Y–M *My Mom Travels a Lot,* Caroline Feller Bauer. New York: Frederick Warne, 1981. A little girl lists the good and bad consequences of her mother's being away from home.

Y *One Was Johnny,* Maurice Sendak. New York: Harper & Row, 1962. This forward and backward counting rhyme gives some actions to add for extra fun.

M *The Pain and the Great One,* Judy Blume. New York: Dell Yearling Books, 1985. An older sister and younger brother share their feelings about each other.

M–O "Peter Perfect, The Story of a Perfect Boy," Bernard Waber (19). This is a running commentary about a boy who, we find out at the end, does not exist at all.

M *Pierre: A Cautionary Tale,* Maurice Sendak. New York: Harper & Row, 1962. A little boy who always says "I don't care" decides to care when a lion eats him. Let one child play Pierre (with complete script if needed) to say the "I don't care" lines.

Y–M *The Popcorn Book,* Tomie de Paola. New York: Holiday House, 1978. Children make popcorn while reading facts about it. Intersperse the popcorn maker's comments with the facts being read, just as the book does.

M "Sarah Cynthia Sylvia Stout," Shel Silverstein (41). Disaster strikes when Sarah won't take out the garbage.

M *The Sheriff of Rottenshot,* Jack Prelutsky New York: Greenwillow Books, 1982. Almost all the poems in this collection are useful for sequence reading games.

M "Sick," Shel Silverstein (41). Little Peggy complains she's too ill to go to school—until she discovers it's Saturday.

O *A Surfeit of Smiles,* Norton Juster. New York: William Morrow, 1989. Two characters venture into the world of similes, with commentary in between. David Small's illustrations are an additional treat.

M *The True Story of the 3 Little Pigs by A. Wolf,* as told to Jon Scieszka. New York: Viking, 1989. The Wolf tries to defend himself. Available in Spanish, *El Cuento Verdadero de los Tres Cerditos* (1991).

M *Tyrannosaurus Wrecks,* Noelle Sterne. New York: Thomas Y. Crowell, 1979. Dinosaur riddles make an entertaining word study.

M–O "Whatif," Shel Silverstein (15). A child speculates on all the horrible things that can happen to a kid. It is amusing but has undercurrents of seriousness.

O *What's a Frank Frank?: Tasty Homograph Riddles,* Giulio Maestro. New York: Clarion Books, 1984. This collection of homographs (two words spelled the same way but with different meanings) provides material for a fun language arts lesson.

M *Where in the World Is Henry?* Lorna Balian. Nashville: Abingdon Press, 1972. In this question and answer game, a mother and child cover an interesting geography lesson. ("Where is the city?" "The city is in the state," and so on.)

Y–M *Where's My Cheese?* Stan Mack. New York: Random House, 1977. A story about a piece of cheese that travels from one person to another is told in simple dialogue.

Original Sequence Reading Games.   You will soon find many of your own sources for sequence games; you may even be inspired to make up your own. And the possibilities for incorporating other areas of the curriculum are numerous.

A review of famous statements from literature, history, or other sources can form a sequence game. Note that the next reader in sequence names the speaker of the previous quote.

Card 1:   You begin: "I cannot tell a lie."
Card 2:   George Washington. "Give my liberty or give me death."
Card 3:   Patrick Henry. "We have not yet begun to fight!" [and so forth]

Or after a study of mythology:

Card 1:   You begin: "If Athena can weave better than I, let her come and try."
Card 2:   Arachne. "I knew I should have used a superglue instead of wax!"
Card 3:   Icarus. "The only man I'll marry is the one who can outrun me." [and so forth]

The following extended example is from a sixth grade social studies lesson on exploration in the New World. Note the addition of pantomime to many of the cards and that cues are not included.

1.   You begin the game. Stand and say, "The time is the late 1400s. The place is Europe. Curtain going up!" Sit.

2.   You stand, walk around the circle, and call out, "For sale, for sale, our latest shipment of spices, silks, perfumes, and gems! For sale, directly from the Indies. Come and get it while it lasts!" Return to your seat.

3. You stand and say (shaking your head sadly), "Too bad we can't have more." Sit.

4. You jump up and say excitedly, "Ah, but we could if we had a sailing route to the Indies." Sit.

5. You stand, clap your hands as if you're trying to get someone's attention, and say, "Children—recite today's geography lesson." After two people recite, you sit.

6, (two cards) You and another person will stand and recite together: "Roses are
7. red, violets are blue. The earth is flat, and that's the truth." Then bow and sit.

8. You stand and say slowly, "Very interesting." Sit down slowly.

9. You stand and say, "But not true!" Sit.

10. You stand and say, "And it doesn't even rhyme." Sit.

11. You stand and say, "Mama mia, have I got an idea! I'll go west (point one way) to get to the east" (point the other way). (Wait to sit down until someone says, "Noooo!")

12, 13. (two cards) You stay seated and yell, "Nooo!"

14. You stand and say, "Everybody knows the earth's flat as a pancake. And if you go too far, horrible sea monsters will get you." Then pretend to be a sea monster, growling and showing claws and teeth. Sit.

15. You walk slowly around the circle, pretending to be very tired and say, "Poor Columbus left Italy and finally went to Spain—to King Ferdinand and Queen Isabella. They gave him three ships and a crew." Return to your seat.

16. You stand and rock back and forth on your feet and chant, "Sailing, sailing, over the ocean blue. And when we arrive—if we get there alive—it'll be 1492." Sit.

17. You stand, look around, put your hand up to your forehead as if you are shading your eyes and shout, "Land ho!" Sit.

18. You stand, pretend to be near death, and gasp out the words, "Thank goodness, I thought we'd never make it." Then stagger and fall down.

19. You stand, pretend to plant a flag in the soil, and say, "I name this island San Salvador and claim it for the king and queen of Spain." Sit.

20, (two cards) You stay seated and cheer, whistle, clap hands, and so on. (There
21. will be two of you doing this.)

22. You stand and say, "Columbus and his crew stopped at other islands in the Caribbean Sea also." Sit.

23. You stand and say, "What do you know? We're the first ones to ever take a Caribbean cruise! Think I'll go for a swim." Then pretend to dive into water. Sit.

24. You stand and say in a big, deep voice, "I have named this island Hispaniola, and on it I have built a fort. Guard it well, men! I'm going back home." Then walk around the circle and sit back down.

25, (two cards) You stand, salute, and say, "Aye, aye, sir." Sit. (Two of you will do
26. this.)

27. You stand and say, "Now it's 1513 and I'm Balboa. I have crossed the Isthmus of Panama, and I claim this body of water for Spain. I name it the Pacific Ocean—meaning peaceful (Yawn)—boy, it sure is . . . (then lie down and fall asleep and snore once).

28. You stand, pretend to ride a horse around the circle, and then say, "I'm Cortés. I've spent the last four years conquering Mexico in the name of Spain." Sit.

29. You stand and say, "The year is 1532. Pizarro's the name, and exploring's my game." Then say in a loud whisper, "Listen! I've heard that there's lots of gold and silver down in South America. The king of Spain has agreed to help me get it. What do you say?" After De Soto shakes your hand, you sit.

30. You stand, go over to Pizarro, shake his hand, and say, "The name's De Soto. I think we'd make a good team." Then return to your seat.

31. You stand and march to the center of the circle, and announce in a big voice, "They marched toward the heart of the Inca Empire." Then return to your seat.

32. You stand and say in a frightened voice, "Who are these men who steal from us?" Sit.

33. You stand and yell, "Our towns are burning! Run for your lives!" Then pretend to be hit and fall dead.

34. You stand and say, "The emperor will save us!" Then pretend to be hit and fall dead.

35. You stand and raise your hands up as if asking for silence and calm, and say slowly and in a big voice, "I am the emperor. I am God. I have thirty thousand soldiers, and the Spaniards have only a few men. Why is everyone so afraid?" Then fold your arms across your chest and sit down slowly.

36. You stand, cup your hands to your mouth, and call to the emperor, "Hey, Emperor! How about dinner at our place?" Then turn your head and laugh behind your hand. Sit.

37. You stand and announce, "And so the emperor and five thousand unarmed Inca warriors went to a feast. The emperor came in a golden chair carried by slaves. The warriors were killed by the Spaniards." Sit.

38. You stand and shout angrily, "Why do you do this terrible thing?" Sit.

39. You stand and shout, "Gold! We want gold!" Sit.

40. You stand and say, "I will have this room filled with gold if you will let me go free." Remain standing until you hear someone say "What do we do now? Kill him." Then fall dead—but do it in slow motion.

41. You stand and say, "Gold and silver came from all parts of the Inca Empire. At first the Spaniards were glad. Then they worried about what to do with the emperor." Sit.

42. You stand and say in a loud whisper, "What do we do now?" Sit.

43. You stand and say very seriously, "Kill him." Sit slowly.

44. You stand and say, "Thus ends a sad chapter in history. Land and wealth gained but at the cost of human suffering. Curtain going down!" (music)

BEGINNING IMPROVISATION

In creative drama, dialogue is usually played *improvisationally*. This means that it is created spontaneously, as the students respond to the dramatic situations they are involved in. Improvisation is one way to achieve a more natural delivery of dialogue than the recitation of memorized script. It is also an excellent exercise in learning to think on one's feet. No one knows exactly what will be said; therefore, the spontaneity of improvisation captures everyone's attention—even the players themselves.

In this next section the activities will build progressively from simple responses to those requiring more extensive improvisation.

One-Liners

One-liners are fairly simple to do, since students need to say or create only one line of speech. Following are a variety of ideas for one-liner activities.

One-liners with pictures

1. Keep a file of pictures of people and animals in interesting poses or situations, or exhibiting unusual feelings. Pictures should be large enough for everyone to see easily. Large ads from magazines, calendar pictures, and posters work well for this activity.

2. Show pictures to the children and ask them what they think the person might be saying. Ask them to pretend to be the person in the picture, saying the statement the way they think the person or animal might say it. If pictures have more than one person, ask the students to say what they think each might be saying.

One-liners with props

1. Interesting props can also stimulate one-liners. Comedian Jonathan Winters (later imitated by Robin Williams) became famous with his ability to create imaginative comments when browsing through an old attic or a trunk of interesting and unusual cast-off clothing (for example, hats, shawls, and spectacles) or other items (for example, a hula hoop, caulking gun, or perfume atomizer).

"This case calls for some super detective work!" (one-liners with props)

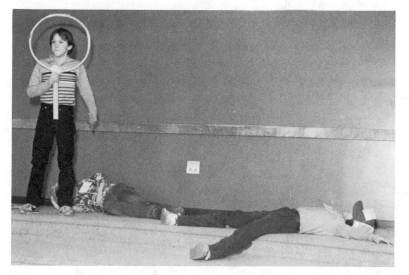

2. Borrowing this technique, students can select a prop, then demonstrate a use for it while saying an appropriate one-liner. *Example:* A folding yardstick can be shaped into several things: (a) a fishing pole, (b) the letter "Z," or (c) a triangle. One-liners that can accompany these uses might be
   a. "Shucks, been here over three hours and haven't had a nibble."
   b. (holding letter against chest) "Coach, I'm gonna get in there and win the game for old Zorro U."
   c. (holding triangle around face as a picture frame) "The family doesn't know it, but I can see everything that goes on around here!"

Ad talks

1. This game is intended for third grade and up. Intriguing statements are clipped from magazines and pasted to cards. Some examples include: "We're all in this together." "I sure wish I could have a lot more." "It'll knock your socks off." "Yeah, but station wagons are so dull." "Is your house being watched?" Again, students can participate in finding their own statements and making their own cards.

2. Use the cards in any of the following ways:
   a. Students sit in a circle. Go around the circle and let each one read his or her card, pretending that they make sense or have some logic. The statement may be said to the person on the speaker's right or left or to the entire group. It helps if you explain that many conversations are fragments of somewhat unrelated thoughts, especially in large groups. This is a good way to introduce Ad Talks, but you'll want to follow up with one of the games below.
   b. Distribute several cards or "dialogue packets" to each student. A volunteer begins with the first statement. Whoever feels his or her card is a good response reads next. (The first to stand gets to say the next line.) If no one thinks he or she has an appropriate card, you can say, "Let's change the subject." Often the sequence of cards results in an abstract conversation, but students do not seem to mind, particularly if they like the lines on their cards. Somehow the dialogue they have been dealt

Statements clipped from a variety of sources and placed on cards provide good material for the "Ad Talks" games.

empowers them to speak. The game continues until all the cards are read or until the students decide their cards are no longer appropriate.

c. Mixing an equal number of questions and answers in the dialogue packets can produce interesting results. (*Example:* "How much time do we have?" "You'll never know." or "Would you let this doctor operate on you?" "What an idea!")

d. Try using different types of voices with the cards: computer or robot, salesperson, politician, and so on.

e. Distribute alphabetized cards randomly. The alphabet determines the next card read. ("Announcing something you may not want to hear!" "*Be* cool." "*Can* you really manage without money?" "*Decide* for yourself." "*Exactly!*")

Oral presentations in character

Announcements, brief speeches, or other presentations may be made as a character. The characters may be vaguely drawn, as a "salesperson," "television announcer," or "official." At other times the characters may come directly from literature, history, or other sources. For example, Toad in *Wind in the Willows* (95) might explain why he finds motor cars so fascinating; and Governor John Winthrop might try to convince the doubting people of Massachusetts that the water in the New World is pure enough to drink. Some children enjoy giving presentations in character, even though they might find it difficult to do so as themselves. Being able to clothe themselves in another character may eventually give them the confidence to express their own thoughts in future situations.

Storytelling

Storytelling is an excellent verbal activity to help students imagine and create plots. It also encourages the building of details, plot prediction, and the making of inferences.

Students may build group short stories using the round-robin technique, with volunteers adding another line to the story. Let children say "Pass" if they cannot think of an idea to add. Be prepared to participate yourself and to keep the story interesting.

When ideas flow freely and students are comfortable with storytelling, you may need to set limits on each one's contribution. Using an egg timer or a bell can make it into a game. A ball of knotted yarn is another possibility. As the "yarn is spun" the ball is unraveled. When the knot is reached, the ball is passed to another student.

Older or advanced students enjoy being stopped in mid-sentence, which forces the next storyteller to end the thought. This technique also challenges the group to listen closely and to mesh their creative thinking with that of another person.

Storytelling with wordless picture books. An easy way to begin storytelling is to use wordless picture books. Children interpret what they see happening in the pictures, using their own words and sometimes even adding dialogue.

Not all wordless picture books tell a story, so choose carefully. You may also need an opaque projector to enlarge the pictures in smaller books.

Some examples are listed below. (*Note:* Age levels are indicated at the beginning of each entry. Numbers in parentheses correspond to numbered anthologies listed in the final bibliography that begins on page 300.)

Y–M *Amanda and the Mysterious Carpet,* Fernando Krahn. New York: Clarion, 1985. When a magic carpet is delivered to Amanda's house, there are surprises in store.

M *The Angel and the Soldier Boy,* Peter Collington. New York: Alfred A. Knopf, 1987. Toy pirates, a soldier, and a toy angel have an adventure during a little girl's dream.

M–O *Arthur's Adventures in the Abandoned House,* Fernando Krahn. New York: E. P. Dutton, 1981. A young boy explores an abandoned house and captures some crooks in an ingenious way.

Y–M *The Bear and the Fly,* Paula Winter. New York: Crown Publishers, 1976. A bear family has difficulty getting rid of a pesky fly.

Y–M *Changes, Changes,* Pat Hutchins. New York: Macmillan, 1971. A wooden man and woman create needed objects out of miscellaneous wood pieces to solve the many difficulties they run into.

Y–M *The Chicken's Child,* Margaret A. Hartelius. New York: Doubleday, 1975. A chicken hatches an alligator egg and adopts it as her child.

M–O *The Damp and Daffy Doings of a Daring Pirate Ship,* Guillermo Mordillo. New York: Harlan Quist, 1971. Pirates encounter one obstacle after another in seeking treasure.

Y *Deep in the Forest,* Brinton Turkle. New York: E. P. Dutton, 1976. Like Goldilocks, a curious bear cub visits a cabin in the woods and finds porridge, chairs, and beds to try.

Y *Do You Want to Be My Friend?* Eric Carle. New York: Thomas Y. Crowell, 1971. A lonely mouse discovers another mouse.

Y–M *Ernest and Celestine,* Gabrielle Vincent. New York: Greenwillow, 1982. This popular series tells about the friendship between a bear and a mouse and how they cope with life's problems. Sequels available.

Y–M *First Flight,* David McPhail. Boston: Joy Street Books, 1987. Boy's teddy bear turns into a real full-sized bear who fears flying. The boy comes to his rescue.

M–O *Free Fall,* David Wiesner. New York: Lothrop, Lee & Shepard, 1988. A boy's dream produces surrealistic episodes and interesting characters.

Y–M *Good Dog, Carl,* Alexandra Day. New York: Green Tiger Press, 1985. An unusually intelligent dog, with great patience, babysits a small child and keeps it out of danger. Sequels include *Carl Goes Shopping* (New York: Farrar, Straus & Giroux, 1989), *Carl's Christmas* (1990), and *Carl's Afternoon in the Park,* (1991).

M–O *The Gray Lady and the Strawberry Snatcher,* Molly Bang. New York: Four Winds Press, 1980. The gray lady runs from a strawberry thief until, in the heart of the forest, he discovers blackberries.

M–O *How Santa Claus Had a Long and Difficult Journey Delivering His Presents,* Fernando Krahn. New York: Dell Publishing/Delacorte Press, 1970. Droll-looking "angels" come to Santa's rescue.

Y–M *The Hunter and the Animals,* Tomie de Paola. New York: Holiday House, 1981. A hunter makes friends with animals and destroys his gun.

Y *Lily at the Table,* Linda Heller. New York: Macmillan, 1979. Lily creates a fantasy world with the food on her plate.

M *Mighty Mizzling Mouse and the Red Cabbage House,* Friso Henstra. Boston: Little, Brown, 1984. Mouse builds a house from a red cabbage, but Rabbit has other ideas for it.

M–O *The Mysteries of Harris Burdick,* Chris Van Allsburg. Boston: Houghton Mifflin, 1984. This series of black-and-white surrealistic pictures, each with its own caption, provides much material for creative storytelling. As an added challenge, see if a story can be made out of several of the pictures in sequence.

Y *Pancakes for Breakfast,* Tomie de Paola. San Diego: Harcourt Brace Jovanovich, 1978. A woman has many interruptions getting pancakes made.

M *Sir Andrew,* Paula Winter. New York: Crown Publishers, 1980. A dapper donkey can't help admiring himself, in spite of little disasters.

M *Who's Seen the Scissors?* Fernando Krahn. New York: E. P. Dutton, 1975. A tailor's scissors fly away and have a cutting adventure through the town.

Storytelling with pictures

1. Pictures of interesting people or animals involved in unusual situations can also stimulate storytelling. At first you may need to start out the story with a rousing or imaginative beginning to get creative juices flowing. (Picture of a man all bandaged up: "This is Melvin Q. Batts. Nothing ever goes right for poor Melvin. One day. . . .") You may also need to introduce the conflict and help students focus on the story's conclusion.

2. As a variation, use several pictures with a related theme or setting. After beginning the story with one picture, add other pictures to stimulate the continued storytelling.

3. As another variation for round-robin storytelling, create a packet of storytelling cards. Paste pictures of interesting people, props, transportation, locations on 5″ × 8″ cards. Shuffle and turn face down; students draw from the pack and must incorporate the item in the story.

Storytelling in character. Once children are accustomed to creating stories, another dramatic dimension can be added. They can pretend to be characters, with appropriate attitudes, doing the telling.

1. There are many literary sources that show storytellers in action. For example, in the story *Frederick,* by Leo Lionni (New York: Pantheon Books, 1967), the little poet-mouse tells stories to help his friends and relatives forget their hunger. What sort of stories would a little mouse tell to entertain an audience of mice? Pa Ingalls entertains his children with short adventures from his past in Laura Ingalls Wilder's series of Little House books. Make up stories to tell that are appropriate to Pa.

2. There are also possibilities for storytelling in other areas of the curriculum. Some student teachers were doing a lesson on cowboys in a second grade. They all gathered in one corner on a rug with the lights dimmed, pretending to be around the campfire at night, telling stories about their day's activities. Three children were given the role of "Chuckwagon Charlie," who periodically gave the listeners some "bowls of stew" to eat quietly while the storytellers entertained them. Other examples: Elders of long ago telling myths or

stories around a campfire; soldiers relating harrowing escapes in war campaigns; or pioneers telling of hardships as well as happy times in moving west.

3. For yet another variation, select pictures, newspaper articles, or facts from the *Guinness Book of Records* and have students tell the story as if they were the person involved. ("You want to know my recipe for the hottest chili this side of the Rio Grande? Well, it goes something like this. . . ." "We hostages weren't allowed to talk to each other, so we used a kind of sign language. . . .")

4. Point of view stories can be told. For example, "Tell the story of 'The Three Billy Goats Gruff' as if you were the troll." Refer to sources such as Jon Scieszka's *The True Story of the 3 Little Pigs! by A. Wolf* (New York: Viking, 1989).

More storytelling variations

What's happening here? Use interesting and colorful pictures with people or animals involved in unusual situations or conflicts. The picture may show the middle of the story, but how did the story begin? How will it end? Again, a story could be told from the point of view of one of the characters.

What's the word? When students show skill in storytelling, they may wish further challenges. Try telling stories using new vocabulary words, spelling words, foreign language words, and so forth.

Math manipulations Tell stories using mathematical operations from simple counting ("*One* day, Big Bird decided to take a walk. *Two* monkeys decided to go along. Suddenly *three* friends yelled, 'Help!'") to other calculations, such as multiplication by 2 ("Once there were *two* kings who lived in neighboring countries. They each had *four* daughters. For *eight* years everything was fine. Then one day, after all the princesses had reached the age of *sixteen,* a very strange thing happened. . .").

Alphabet story Tell a story with each sentence beginning with a letter of the alphabet in sequence. ("*A* story about a cat. *B*oy, was he an ornery cat. *C*ats are often ornery, but this one was especially bad.")

What's that sound? Tell a story suggested by a series of sounds. (Open a desk drawer, shut a door, and scream.) What story does that suggest? Or start with one sound to begin the story and continue the story suggested by each added sound.

Prop stories Make up a story about a curious or unusual object such as a strangely shaped stone, a piece of jewelry, or a document written in an unknown language. Focus on answering who, what, where, when, and why questions in building the story. Also, make the object important in some way (for example, having lost this object, a certain person's life is now in danger).

Skeleton stories Make up explanations or stories using a skeletal framework of props, pictures of people, or settings to stimulate ideas. To establish a more dramatic context: "These are the only pieces of evidence left at the scene of a crime; what meaning can you attach to them?" "These (object, photo, piece of costume) were discovered on the abandoned space-

A panel is questioned by the class while the leader moderates.

ship. Can you explain why?" "These are the items that were in the time capsule. What do they tell us about the people who left them there?"

Questioning Games

The following games, adapted from television, develop questioning skills and critical thinking. The format for all the games is similar. Several children form a panel and the rest of the audience asks the questions. The panel may be fairly large, perhaps as many as eight, who take turns answering the questions. The leader serves as the moderator–host, similar to the host of a game show.

What's my line?

1. This game can be useful for a unit in career education. In this adaptation of the television show, all the members of the panel are assigned the same occupation and take turns answering the questions. The audience tries to guess the occupation within twenty questions. Only yes or no answers are allowed; an occasional maybe is permitted (in consultation with the leader–moderator).

2. A questioner is allowed to question the panel as long as yes answers are given. If a no response is given, another questioner is chosen.
   Variation: Use occupations of the future (flight attendant on a spaceship) or occupations of the past (town crier, court jester, stagecoach driver).

To tell the truth

1. A panel of students pose as a particular famous person who may be living (current events), historical (social studies), or fictional (literature). Children might also play inanimate objects such as a particular food product, a means of transportation, an invention, and so forth.

2. All the panel members must be knowledgeable about the character, which may necessitate some research. One panel member is designated the true character and must give accurate answers to the best of his or her ability. Other panel members are allowed to give inaccurate answers.

3. The audience poses questions to determine which one is the character. These questions are not limited to yes or no responses. Number of questions may be limited, or a time period may be imposed.

Liars' club

1. In this game a panel is presented with an unusual object. One panelist has been told what the object is; the others must create believable explanations. (As a variation, you may choose not to give any of the panelists the true information beforehand.)

2. Some students may know what an object is. If so, they may either give the real explanation or make up a plausible one. In the spirit of fun rather than competition, a vote might be taken among audience members on the most believable explanation before the object's true identity and use are told.

3. Objects for discussion may be antiques, unusual gadgets, or new products on the market. Some suggestions are an eyelash curler, rug beater, Chinese yo-yo, Braille stencil, knitting stitch holder, candle snuffer, vegetable steamer, and the like.

4. To establish a context for this game, students might pretend to be archaeologists trying to identify how the object might have been used by a particular culture they have been studying. Or, they may be museum directors who must determine the true identity of an object in order to label it appropriately for a museum display.

   Variation: "Language Liar's Club" can be played by guessing definitions of words. Panel members offer their definitions, with only one person knowing

Props for "Liar's Club" (clockwise): stereoscope, darning egg, button hook, wooden potato masher, and (center) antique vaporizer.

the correct one. Suggested words with made-up definitions might be *epee* (a small hairpiece), *topography* (the subject of a speech), *brouhaha* (a colorful kerchief), and *serendipity* (hair-styling gel). A commercial game with similar rules is called "Balderdash" (New York: The Games Gang, Ltd., 1984).

I've got a secret

1. Again, borrowing from television's past, this game can easily be adapted for classroom use. Several on a panel share a secret for the audience to guess.
2. Panel may answer only yes or no. Limit to twenty questions.
   Examples:
   Category: Fictional character from Mother Goose. "This secret involves something the person did while dressed in a certain way." (Wee Willie Winkie—ran through town in his nightgown)
   Category: Character from American history. "This secret involves a message this person delivered. Who is the person and what was the message?" (Paul Revere; "One if by land and two if by sea.") Or "This secret involves something this person had that was made of wood." (George Washington's false teeth)

Discussions

Discussions are designed to share information, compare thoughts, and mull over problems. These may be teacher-led discussions with the entire class or small group discussions followed by a larger group meeting.

Often in drama discussions children are cast into roles. They may be detectives, explorers, elves, servants, or whatever the situation calls for. For example, children might be the royal relatives making a list of names for the queen's new baby, explorers making an inventory of supplies needed for an expedition, investigators comparing notes on clues to solve a crime, or all the king's men discussing ways to put Humpty Dumpty together again.

Brainstorming is a useful technique in discussing. In brainstorming, ideas are pooled as quickly as possible. No criticism is made of any idea; all are initially accepted without judgment. Later, the best ideas can be winnowed out.

Interviews

Interviewing is a way of seeking information. Interviews in drama may be set up in a variety of ways.

1. *Leader interviews the class.* Example: Leader plays the role of a captain of an exploring party and interviews the children who apply to be members of his or her expedition, questioning them on their qualifications for the job. One or two children might be the leader's assistants.
2. *Children interview the leader.* Example: Children are citizens questioning the head of the city council about his or her recent proposal to raise taxes. Again, one or two children could be the leader's assistants.
3. *Children interview each other in pairs.* Example: A police detective asks a witness for any descriptions he or she has of crime suspects. Usually the pairs switch roles and replay so they can have experience both in questioning and in

answering. The leader moves among the pairs, listening and assisting with ideas when necessary. A large group discussion follows so that some of the most important ideas can be shared: "What was the most crucial piece of information you discovered?"

4.   *A large group interviews a panel.* Example: An audience of reporters ask questions at a news conference of scientists who have made an important discovery. Leader plays the role of moderator. (See Panel Interviews below.)

Good questioning is important in any interview. Therefore, it is helpful to discuss possible questions before playing out the interview. You might say, "If the king were to come here, what would we want to ask him?" Actually, this process is similar to preparing the children for any classroom visitor. The class decides on the most useful questions to ask, and inappropriate or unnecessary questions are eliminated. However, this planning is doubly important in drama because it gives you (and any children who will be playing the interviewees) an opportunity to hear the questions and consider the answers you might give.

Panel interviews

Another variation of the interview is the panel interview. It allows for the most participation from the class, with students playing both the interviewer and interviewee. But unlike the private paired interviews, the class can hear each other's ideas.

Panel interviews may be set up as follows:

1.   Groups of five to eight students take turns being panel members. The rest of the students are audience questioners.

2.   The leader serves as the moderator–host, similar to the host of a talk show. This role allows you to ask questions, keep order, and express gratitude for information shared.

3.   Establish a context for the interview to enhance the drama. Perhaps it is taking place in a television studio, at a meeting or a conference, or in a judge's private chambers.

4.   To help panel members identify with their role, props or simple costume pieces may be employed, such as nameplates, badges, headbands, or hats. Audience questioners may have small notepads and pencils.

Experts' panel interview

1.   Panel members are declared to be experts on a subject. The purpose of giving students expertise is to allow them the security to give their opinions freely. After all, *they* are the experts. Unusual topics are used to enhance self-confidence, since there are no specific answers and no precedents to follow.

     Examples: Santa Claus's elves answering questions on how they make certain toys; tooth fairies explaining how and why children's teeth are collected and used; owners and trainers of fleas for a flea circus; people who knit small socks for birds; or people who have ridden in an alien spaceship.

2.   The context for any of the above might be a television talk show. Or, for variation, the experts on bird socks might appear before an audience of business people interested in opening a franchise. Newspaper reporters could

question the spaceship riders at a press conference, and a pet owners' club might be interested in pet condominiums. The leader might play the role of program chairperson or a public relations person.

3. Although the topics may seem superficial at first glance, it is interesting to note that they often develop into full-blown curricular projects. For example, the topic of bird socks has produced ideas for unique clothing for other animals, raised awareness of environmental concerns, and encouraged creative projects on product development and marketing, including catalogues and advertisements.

Advisers   Playing the role of an adviser is similar to being an expert, although an adviser often deals with personal or political issues. In this role children give their opinions on how to solve problems or deal with troubling situations.

1. *Juvenile jury.* This variation of an old radio and television show features a panel of children who give advice on other children's problems. The audience poses certain questions such as, "My little brother always wants to play with my toys and I don't want him to. What can I do?" Such problems can sometimes be more easily solved by peers than by adults trying to impose rules. Although children frequently repeat advice they have heard from adults, it sounds more acceptable when a peer gives it.

2. For further ideas to play consider the various fields in which advisers are useful: politics, medicine, government, education, and economics. An advisory panel might present new laws, discuss health issues, consider environmental problems, or propose educational reforms.

Character panel interview   A panel interview is useful for seeking information about various persons, real and fictional. The procedure is as follows:

1. Panel members all may play the same role (so that varying ideas can be presented), or they may have different roles.

2. The audience questioners may be themselves or may take on a more specific role for themselves (for example, "I'm the town baker"). They should identify themselves before asking their questions. As you call on them, you might ask, "Excuse me, may we have your name and occupation?"

The following suggestions are only some of the many possibilities:

   a. Characters from a story are questioned about their actions and motivations for behaviors not explained in the stories. For example, the panel might all be Goldilocks. The audience ask whatever questions they wish: "Describe the bear's house." "Did you get punished when you got home?" "What were you doing in the woods all by yourself?" (It doesn't matter if the characters' stories aren't in agreement. Children readily accept different interpretations from the various Goldilocks.)

   b. The panel may be comprised of several characters from the same story. For example, Sleeping Beauty might be asked, "What was it like to be asleep for so long." "Were you glad when the prince woke you up?" "Is he the prince you would have chosen?" The thirteenth fairy might be asked, "Why were you so upset about not being invited to the christening?" "Why did you wish the princess to be killed—and by a spinning wheel?"

c. Panel members may be characters who have a common trait or behavior. Perhaps they are clever at solving problems like Tom Sawyer, Harriet the Spy, Pippi Longstocking, or Br'er Rabbit. Perhaps the audience would like to question them about how they would solve a particular problem. Their answers should be presented as their character might respond.
d. Panel interviews can also take the form of a guessing game. Assign roles or identities to the panelists in secret. They answer questions anonymously for a given time period. By the kind of answers they give (and perhaps by the way they speak and conduct themselves), the audience tries to determine who they are.

Debate

Improvised dialogue is often most easily generated and most dramatic when there are problems to be solved or when conflict is present. Problems require discussion in order to find a solution. Conflict encourages people to explain their position and to persuade others to their point of view. Some students participate more and become more involved when you focus on the problems and conflict inherent in a topic.

The next activities are set up to encourage debate. As before, you can facilitate in debate by playing a moderating or mediating role. This role is a neutral one and guides the players to consider relevant questions. At times, this role is a specific character, like Willy Wonka or Captain Jones in the examples below.

Simple debate: Method I

1. Divide the class in half, and present each with an opposite viewpoint to uphold. You can easily play this at the desks, which simplifies organization.
2. You play the moderator or mediator. With this format you can use a number of situations. Some suggestions follow.
    a. *Opposites game:* One side makes all the positive statements they can think of, while the other half responds with negative ones. Ideas can be called out by volunteers on either side of the room alternately. The statements may be made in response to each other or simply presented randomly. For example:

Yes.	No.
It's a beautiful day.	There's rain in the forecast.
Ice cream.	Spinach.
Vacation.	Schoolwork.
I love to watch television.	The set's broken.

    b. *Literature example:* In Roald Dahl's *Charlie and the Chocolate Factory* (51), Willy Wonka has difficulties with several children. One little girl, Violet, swells up like a blueberry and turns purple after disobeying orders not to chew the experimental gum. The Oompa-Loompas, or factory workers, have to take her away to the juicing room. Willy, the owner of the factory, is upset with Violet for disobeying his rules, but he would like to have her problem solved, too.
        Although Violet really has no choices given to her in the book, you can use the situation for a simple debate with half the class being Oompa-

Loompas trying to convince the other half of the class, who play Violet, that being juiced is her only option. Violet argues for other solutions.

You, playing Willy, can call on those who have ideas to express. You may also pose questions to each side, if this assistance seems helpful. ("What will happen to Violet in the juicing room?" "What sorts of machines and equipment do you have in there?" "Violet, why did you disobey the orders?" "Has this ever happened to you before?")

c. *Social studies example:* A similar arbitration scene might be played between the Pilgrims and the crew of the *Mayflower,* based on information in Wilma Hays's *Christmas on the Mayflower* (New York: Coward-McCann, 1956). Captain Jones wants to help the Pilgrims get settled before leaving them to fend for themselves in a new country. But he is also worried about his crew. They are anxious to get home because it is December and the sailing will be difficult. Each day the crew members become more hostile. Both the crew and the captain had wanted to be home for Christmas, but now it is impossible.

One half of the class plays the Pilgrims; the other half plays the ship's crew. You can play Captain Jones and moderate the two sides of the argument, encouraging a discussion of the various reasons for going or for staying.

Simple debate: Method II

1. Present an idea to the class for the scene. (You can use the preceding examples, but here is a new one: A creature on the moon who wants to accompany a reluctant astronaut back to earth in the spaceship.)
2. (Optional step; useful if children need assistance) Brainstorm with the students some of the different reasons the space creature would give for wanting to go to earth. Then brainstorm some of the reasons the astronaut would give for not being able to take the moon creature.
3. (Optional step; useful if children need assistance) Now pair the students and let them rehearse or try out the scene briefly—at their desks—all talking at the same time. (It can be a little noisy, but you will survive.) Switch roles and repeat.
4. Let the students share their ideas as follows:
   a. Select several volunteers for sharing. You might have five pairs in front of the class. (If children are shy, you can have two astronauts talking with two moon creatures, thus making conversational groups of four.)
   b. Give each pair (or group) a number. The pair (group) may talk when you call out their number.
   c. Call numbers randomly and give each pair (group) a few moments to share.

There are several advantages to this procedure for sharing. First of all, a number of students are allowed the opportunity to share, so they do not have to wait long to get a turn. Second, you are in control of the sharing. If some students have little to say, you simply call another number to relieve the pressure on them. Some students, if they cannot think of something to say, may begin to giggle with embarrassment or possibly start to fight. By being able simply to call another number, you can bail them out. (You can call their numbers again after they have had a little break to collect their thoughts.) This procedure also makes it easy to cut off those who would go on forever if you let them.

Extra challenge. Highly verbal students will enjoy this additional challenge: They must pick up the thread of the previous pair's (or group's) conversation and continue it. This forces them to listen carefully to the rationale of other players and develop it further.

Character panel debate

This format, similar to the character panel interview on page 195, can be used as a structure for presenting different viewpoints. The following are some possibilities for you to consider:

1. a. You (or a competent student) pretend to host a television talk show or a public forum.
   b. All the panelists (four to six students) are the various stepmothers from folk tales and fairy tales who feel they have been given a "bum rap." They tell their side of the story and try to convince the audience they are not as bad as they have been portrayed.
   c. The "audience" questions the details of their stories. (You can also use this with other characters and personages in literature or history: villains, witches, traitors, and so forth.)

2. a. Again, you host or moderate a talk show or forum. Choose a character usually assumed to be a villain, and see how he or she might be looked at in a new light. For example, in "Little Red Riding Hood," is it possible that the wolf might be a sympathetic character?
   b. Panelists could be his supportive mother, an employer, or a Boy Scout leader who speak on his behalf and answer questions the audience poses. To keep the tension, an equal number of panelists should speak on behalf of Little Red Riding Hood and her grandmother.
   c. The audience ask questions of either "side."
      Note: It is best to do this one without having the original characters present. They tend to become protective about the usual interpretation of their character and get in the way of the group's being able to talk about them in new and different ways.

3. a. A panel of members of the Virginia Company might try to convince the audience to settle in the New World.
   b. The audience knows about the hardships and failures of the earlier colonies, however, and is reluctant.

4. a. You may also assign characters and viewpoints to the panel and the audience.
   b. Write instructions and pertinent data for each character on note cards and distribute them. If the class does not know who is receiving what instructions, the scene can be even more realistic.

Example: "A Town Debate"

1. A town meeting is called; you might play the mayor.
2. Two panelists present the side of those who want a new factory built. One might be the president of the company, and the other a local contractor who will do the building. Both emphasize the number of jobs that will open up in the community, which has an unemployment problem.

3. The other two panelists might represent environmentalists. One has data about the company's past record of waste-disposal abuse, and another believes the plant location will pose unsolvable problems.

4. Members of the audience are the citizens of the community. Some are unemployed and hope for new jobs. Some work for the construction company which will do the building, and they want to be loyal to the company. Some are concerned because they live next to the plant site. The remainder are not sure how they feel about the issue.

FOR THE COLLEGE STUDENT

1. Collect stories and poems suitable for sound effects activities.
2. Create your own sound effect story. Base it on a curricular topic.
3. Lead your classmates in one of the sound effect activities, using a sound arrow to guide their sounds.
4. Adapt a story for a sequence reading game.
5. Write a sequence reading game, basing it on a curricular topic.
6. Collect interesting pictures, props, and one-liners useful for stimulating verbal activities.
7. Try round-robin storytelling with your classmates, using some of the techniques mentioned in this chapter.
8. Lead your classmates in one of the questioning games, interview activities, or debates. Play the role of moderator or mediator.
9. Create your own verbal game or adapt some of the ones presented in this chapter.

9

Improvised Scenes
and Stories

As children become familiar with drama work, they want to create scenes and stories on their own. The leader's role in this work is to help them with topics and guidance in creating plot lines.

The first half of this chapter will cover one technique you can use to help students create and play pantomime stories of their own. An outline of the process follows.

STEPS IN THE PROCESS OF CREATIVE PLOT BUILDING

Outline

1. Present an intriguing idea that can be played in pantomime. The playing may be solo, in pairs, or in groups. You may play a role yourself.
2. Guide the students through a series of approximately five discussion questions to assist them in planning their own stories. The questions help them create a beginning, a middle, and an end to their stories as well as a conflict and a resolution.
3. Side-coach the unison playing of the stories. (Sometimes half the class plays for the other half, and then players and audience switch.)
4. Follow-up discussion may be with the leader in role. Other verbal activities are also possible.
5. Replay (optional).

Now let us look at each step a little closer.

Choosing an Idea

The topics for a creative story, whether fact or fiction, can come from a number of sources as you tap your own imagination.

> *Literature.* "The little boy in *Harold and the Purple Crayon* (Crockett Johnson [New York: Harper & Row, 1955]) has such interesting adventures with his magic crayon. Let's pretend that you have a crayon like his and you're going to draw an adventure you'd like to have. . . ." (solo or individual playing)
>
> *Science.* "As the world-famous team of Dr. Pinna and Dr. Lobe, the ear experts, you will need to use your secret invention to make yourself small enough to travel in your patient's ear to find the source of the problem. . . ." (pair playing)
>
> *Music.* "Listen to this music called 'Neptune' from *The Planet Suite* by Holst. Imagine yourself a space explorer and this music is what seems to be coming from a new planet you're about to land on. What kind of place do you think the planet will be?" (group playing)

Discussing Ideas

Discussion questions essentially develop character, setting, plan of action, conflict, and resolution. In other words the children need to plan who they are, what they are going to do, what problems they might have, how they will solve them, and how the story will end. The specific wording of these questions, however, will depend on the topic and on the leader's objectives in using the material.

Discussion Outline.   The discussion format usually involves five questions, although you can combine several short or related questions into one. Generally the *first* question introduces the idea; the *second* and *third* questions build the adventure; by the *fourth* question, the conflict is introduced; and with the *fifth* question, a solution is planned and the story is brought to a close.

With individual playing, the children plan their ideas in a large group discussion. With pair and group stories, however, the children will have to discuss their ideas together. It is also possible to play an idea individually first and then as pair and group work in replayings. Three examples of discussion outlines follow.

Individual playing

TEACHER: Now that we've read about *Harold and the Purple Crayon*, it might be fun to go on our own magical adventure. Let's suppose you have a crayon like Harold's that will draw anything you want.

1. Where would you like to go on your adventure?
2. How will you get there? Do you need to take any supplies with you?
3. What are some of the things you'd like to see and do? What unusual things might happen to you?

In a creative story, children make up and act out their own plots.

4. Harold's trips are not without some problems. What kinds of problems could happen to you on this adventure?

5. But with a magical crayon Harold usually figures a way out of any problems and gets back home safely. How do you think you could solve your problems, and how will you return home?

Paired playing

TEACHER: It's Halloween. You and a friend have decided to visit a haunted house. At least you think it's haunted.

1. What might be some of your reasons for going?

2. You're going at night and it's a bit chilly. What things will you need to take with you? What route will you take?

3. How will you go about investigating the house? What are some things you want to check? What do you think you might find?

4. What problems might you run into in a haunted house? At least there will be the two of you to face them together; maybe you'll even be able to help each other out. What do you think could happen?

5. Anyone who visits a haunted house is probably confident enough to survive anything. Let's suppose your venture turns out all right. Bring back a souvenir, though, to prove you were really there. We'll find out what your souvenir is after you return.

Small group playing

TEACHER: Let's suppose that it's Boston, 1773, and you are the group of people called the Sons of Liberty, who object to the high tax on tea. You disguise yourselves as Indians, board a tea freighter at night, and throw the tea overboard.

1. Now, what are your plans for disguising and arming yourself for tonight? Your disguise should be good enough to fool the British.

2. Next you need to plan your strategy for getting down to the harbor and out onto the ship without being spotted. How will you do that?
3. Once you get to the harbor and get on board the ship, how will you take it over and get to the tea? How will you take care of the crew?
4. It's always good to be prepared for problems. What sort of problems do you anticipate, and how will you solve them?
5. After the mission is completed, you'd better lay low—maybe even go into hiding. How will you do that?

The Leader's Role.   Some ideas can be enhanced by your playing a role in the drama. In the drama about the Boston Tea Party, for example, you might be an older patriot who says:

> "My friends, I'm afraid my age and infirmities prevent me from joining you this night. This 'tea party' you're planning should make quite a surprise for the British. I'm glad I have this shop for you to meet in. You should be safe here."

Or in Palmer Brown's poem "The Spangled Pandemonium" (3,24)[1] you might be the mayor of the town who is concerned for everyone's safety with this animal on the loose. Perhaps you have called in the children as expert "spangled pandemonium" catchers and say to them:

> "As the mayor of this town, I want you to know we're all counting on you. Our fair city has never had a crisis like this before. But I've been assured by the people who have hired you before that you're the ones for this job."

Hints on wording discussion questions

1. Keep questions limited to five, or the discussion may last too long.
2. Remember that the questions follow the story line format. There must be a beginning, a middle, and an end to the stories, with a conflict and a resolution.
3. The questions should help the children think of *action* they are going to pantomime. Avoid topics where characters interact, particularly with dialogue, or the children may have nothing to pantomime.
4. Keep the questions following the chronological order of the story, moving it forward. Do not back up and change the direction of a story or ask questions that are not directly related to it.
5. Ask questions that are open-ended and encourage embellishment of ideas. If a question can be answered with just a yes or no, it will build minimal plot.
6. Ask intriguing questions that will draw the students into the idea:
   a. Give the children importance. You might open a discussion, for example, by saying that Paul Bunyan has the flu and has called on them for help feeding the hungry lumberjack camp. Children might become expert goblin catchers, called upon by the person in Rose Fyleman's poem "The Goblin" (3) to rid his home of this noisy creature. Or the President might

---

[1] Numbers in parentheses refer to the numbered anthologies and books listed in this text's final bibliography.

send them on an important mission back into history to discover needed answers to pressing problems.

b. Add tension to the questions to build interest. In the Halloween adventure outlined earlier, for example, there is the suggestion that the house may be haunted. Or those who go on adventures with the magic coin from *Half Magic* (59) must always be sure to double their wishes, since it can grant only half ones. Or perhaps there is the pressure of time: A job must be finished by midnight, or a magic spell will wear off.

7. It is helpful to word the questions tentatively so that the students can change their story as they hear more ideas discussed. For example, "What *do you suppose* you'll do next?" leaves the way open for flexibility.

Do not try to get answers from everyone on every question. Discussion should continue only as long as it is motivating the students and the ideas are flowing. Most students will want to get to the playing as soon as possible.

The importance of the class-wide discussion is for the evolving of numerous ideas, the cross-fertilization of thinking, and the expanding and elaborating of creativity. Students may hear ideas that will mesh with theirs; or they may hear an idea they like better than their own. You too may even be inspired with new ideas. Discussions are most valuable when this kind of creative process is taking place.

Discussions also help you see the ideas the children have so that you can better organize the playing and interpret what you see the children playing. Because a child mentions that her balloon ship will develop a leak, you can understand why she is swirling and sinking during the playing.

As students gain skill in this kind of story building, they may not always need a lot of discussion time. You may be able to give the entire outline of your discussion questions and let them plan it all in one gulp. It is not unusual for some students to give you their entire story after you ask the first question. They may be several steps ahead of you!

Playing and Side-Coaching

Preview Playing.   You may want to have children preview part of their ideas before playing their entire story. For example, how will they get into their armor before going off on their adventure as a knight? Or before a story on skydiving, you may want children to check out the procedures and maneuvers a diver goes through to have a safe and stable fall with both arms and legs apart. Such maneuvers must be automatic for the skydiver; preview playing would thus simulate actual conditions.

Instructions for Playing.   At first, students may create brief stories of perhaps only 30 seconds to a minute in length; gradually, with a topic that interests them, they should increase their playing time to three minutes and possibly even longer. Since not all students' stories will last the same length of time, it is best to instruct them to sit down when they have finished their story and quietly watch others.

Even though students are making up their own beginnings and endings for their stories, you should give signals for both. Your signals will add more to the playing if you make them as imaginative as possible.

For example, in an adventure about Miles Standish and a party making the first trip to the shore of the new land, you might play one of the Pilgrim fathers who stays behind on the *Mayflower:*

> "Goodman Standish and friends, be at rest about those of us who would remain on board ship. We will be safe. But, good brothers, be vigilant. The shore looks peaceful, but dangers would lurk. Do not tarry."

When most of the students have ended their playing, you can narrate or side-coach an ending for those still playing if it looks as if they need help in finishing. (Some can go on forever if you let them!) It is also wise to narrate or side-coach an ending if you see the playing deteriorating at any time.

Side-coaching hints

1. As before, music will play an important part in encouraging the students' ideas and providing a background for their dramas.
2. Since students have created their own stories to play, they should not need more than just a few reminders of the various stages of their plot—the beginning, the action, the problems they may be encountering, and the solutions they may have. Many will be too engrossed in their playing to pay much attention to side-coaching.
3. Side-coaching is usually needed more for individual playing than for pair and group playing. When students work with each other in these stories, they rely more on their classmates than on you for assistance.
4. It is usually best to word the side-coaching tentatively, since the students' ideas are all different and you really do not know all the details of each story. Also, the students are not moving through the various stages of their stories at the same speed.

   "It *seems as if some* people have already left on their mission. . . ."

   "I *wonder if anyone* has run into a problem yet. . . ."

   "You're all such clever detectives, I'm sure you'll all be able to *find the clues you need* to solve the case. . . ."
5. Do not interject any new idea in the side-coaching. If you call out ideas such as "Look out for that shark!" or "Suddenly you discover gold!" you will only confuse the playing. These ideas are appropriate to narrative pantomime but would be interruptions in these original stories.

Discussion Follow-Up with Leader-in-Role

When the playing has ended, many students will want to tell you what happened in their stories, elaborating on the ideas they mentioned earlier. There may be times when you will ask them to write their experiences in story, diary, or newspaper-article format; or you might have them draw a picture or just discuss what happened.

However, you will not want to miss the opportunity to extend the story or plot idea through discussion. If you play a role, you have the chance to explore many additional ideas and concepts with the students.

Ideally in your questions you want to extend the story and build on the students' creativity. It is often helpful to use props, pictures, costumes, or anything else that will stimulate ideas. In the following example, the creative story has been based on Mary Ann Hoberman's poem, "The Folk Who Live in Backward Town" (24,31). The children's stories have centered on a day in the life of one of these people, who "take their walks across the ceiling" and "only eat the apple peeling," among other unusual behaviors. The leader plans to play the role of a visitor to the land and to ask the following questions:

1. "I'm afraid I'll have a problem during my visit, and I always like to be prepared. What are some things I should be especially careful about?" (The leader is prepared for the fact that some children may give their responses in backward sentences.)

2. "I understand you've had a recent campaign to find a slogan for your town. What were some of the suggested slogans?"

3. "Say, here's a sign I just found over there. I can't read it, and I wonder what it's for. Can anyone tell me?" (The sign could spell DANGER backwards and perhaps could be held upside down. The children have to read it and then explain its importance.)

4. "I have a gift here (hold imaginary box) from the mayor of my town to the mayor of yours. Where's the mayor?" (Someone will probably volunteer.) "I don't know what it is, Your Honor, so I guess you'll have to open it to find out. I hope it's something you can use." (The child opens the gift and tells what it is. If this proves popular, there can be more gifts and more mayors, or council members, or other dignitaries.)

5. "I'd like to take back some photos of your town to show my friends and neighbors. Have we got some people who wouldn't mind having their picture taken? I like action shots, so you'll need to be doing something. Who'd like to be first?" (This can be done in groups like the frozen pictures in Chapter 7.)

Opinions, evaluations, or descriptions may also be explored. You may even introduce new problems to be solved. The following examples are from a variety of topics:

1. Newspaper or television reporter talking to the survivor of a plane crash: "The rescue team said they had no trouble finding you. You were a big help to them. What exactly was it that you did to help them find your location?"

2. Head elf to apprentice elves who have done good deeds: "I have to write your good deed down in this record book and then evaluate its importance on a scale of one to five, with five being the highest. What was your deed, and how important would you say it was?" (The children's ratings can be negotiated.)

3. Government official to secret agent: "There's one expenditure here in your report that I can't quite figure out. It's listed as 'miscellaneous,' but the amount you've given is $1,035.74. You'll have to justify that, I'm afraid."

4. Dr. Timepiece talking to children who have just gone through a time machine to another period of history: "I'm trying to perfect my machine. What improvements would you suggest?"

5. Wizard whose lost wand the children have found: "You deserve a reward for your efforts. What would you like—within the power of my wand—to have as

your prize?" (Any outlandish request can be labeled "outside the power of my wand.")

6. Royal monarch to an early discoverer: "This is the only map we have of the territory you have just explored. On the basis of your explorations, what changes will need to be made?"

Discussion with Verbal Children. It is generally best to ask questions of the group as a whole and then call on volunteers. If students are highly verbal, you need to move quickly from one student to another. Another alternative is to use paired interviewing. If the majority of the class is highly verbal, you will want to utilize other verbal activities, such as panels of experts (p. 194) or even verbal scenes (discussed at the end of Chapter 9).

Discussion with Reticent Students. If the creative story has been intriguing and the questions are captivating, often even the shyest person will want to become involved. However, it is a good idea to be prepared with simple questions that can be answered yes or no for students who find it difficult to speak up in a classroom ("Did you have an exciting adventure?" "Did you find what you were looking for?" "Were you scared?" and so forth). Even nodding or shaking the head in answer to a question can be a big undertaking for some children.

As another precaution it is helpful for you to have an "out"—a reason you can give in case a child appears ready to speak and then freezes up at the last moment. For example, as a "newspaper reporter" you might say to an inventor, "I can understand your not wanting to talk to me; this invention of yours is probably top-secret stuff."

Replaying and Sharing (Optional)

Once the students have tried an idea they like, they may ask to play it again. They may have new ideas. Some may want to include ideas they have heard from others. Or they may want to work with a partner after playing solo. They may also desire to share their ideas by playing them for the rest of the class.

Before sharing or replaying, you can take the opportunity to have them evaluate their work by asking what they might like to change or what they particularly liked about their previous playing.

SAMPLE LESSON PLAN: THE BORROWERS
(lower elementary)

Objectives

1. Experience a creative movement and creative verbal experience based on literature.
2. Create a story with a beginning, a middle, an end, a conflict, and a resolution.

3. Deal with the concept of size relationships: small borrowers in normal-sized home.
4. Imagine problems that could be encountered in a given situation and create appropriate solutions for those problems.
5. Have opportunities to reflect on questions related to experience.

Preparation and materials

1. Space: area in center of room with desks around edge of room
2. Supplies
   a. Small objects, such as small metal pillbox, fancy beaded ballpoint pen, small decorative mirror. One prop for final discussion: small pair of child's plastic craft scissors, for example
   b. Music: "Arabian Dance" from Tschaikovsky's *Nutcracker Suite*
   c. Copy of Mary Norton's book *The Borrowers* (48)
   d. Pictures from the text (enlarged, if possible)
3. Length of session: 45 minutes (approximately)

Motivation

Recall the book if they already know it or simply tell them briefly about the tiny people who live under the floorboards of a person's house. When the people in the house are asleep at night, the little people search for and "borrow" small objects from the house to furnish their own miniature home. Show illustrations so that children can see objects such as postage stamps, thimbles, and pins being used in the Borrower's house in unique ways.

Discussion questions

1. "Suppose you were a Borrower, and you needed some new things for your home. Look at these objects and tell me what you think you might be able to use them for." (Children's answers might include such ideas as: the pillbox as a baby bed, the pen as a decorative column for the porch, or the mirror as a skating rink for the children.)
2. "Suppose that tonight's the night for the borrowing trip. You're going to get these objects—or perhaps something else. What equipment will you need to take with you on your trip?" (You could use string and safety pins to hook various objects with and to climb up the drapes. You could use a wagon from a dollhouse to carry things in. Better have cotton to stuff in the dog's ears so he won't hear us and start barking.)
3. "What other things will you be looking for tonight?" (I need a new picture for the wall. My rug is worn out and I want to get a handkerchief for a new one. I want a swimming pool, and there's a soup bowl in the china cabinet that would be perfect.)
4. "Borrowing is a dangerous business. Homily, you know, always worries about her husband, Pod, when he goes on one of these missions. And Arrietty had to wait a long time before she was old enough to go with him. What's so dangerous about borrowing, and what particular problems do you think you might run into?" (Household pets could hurt you. If you got near a bathtub filled with water and fell in, you might drown. If anyone sees you, you'll have to move out and go to another house because they'll be after you for sure.)

What could Borrowers use these items for? (doily, decorative comb, picture frame, plastic fork, magnifying glass, and locket)

5. "How will you be able to avoid these problems and get home safely with all your new furnishings?" (I have a map of the house with all the danger points marked. I'm just gathering the stuff together tonight and will make another trip tomorrow to carry it back; I always wear dark clothes so it's harder to see me.)

Directions for playing

"I can see you have all your ideas worked out, so we'll get ready for the mission. I'll dim the lights so it will be more like nighttime. Now, you have all your gear ready, so you'll just be resting and waiting for the household to go to bed. When you hear the clock strike one o'clock, you'll know you can be sure everyone's asleep. Remember that you must be as silent as possible or you might wake someone up, and you know what that will mean. When you have reached back home, just sit down quietly in your playing space and wait for others to finish.

"We will need to do this in two shifts—so shift one will work from one o'clock until three o'clock; shift two will work from three o'clock until five o'clock." (Designate who is in which shift.)

Side-coaching (as needed). (Start the music.) "It's very quiet now and almost one o'clock. . . . Everyone's gone to bed. . . . " (Strike a metal platter for the clock.) "It's time! . . . Quietly you begin your adventure. . . . I believe some people are checking their equipment for one last time. . . . Some have already started out. . . . I hope you'll be able to see well enough. . . . It's so dark this time of night. . . . There are so many dangers out there, too. . . . Oh, oh, I think someone may have had some difficulty. . . . All we can do is hope they'll be okay. . . . Borrowers are used to living by the skin of their teeth, so I guess they'll do all right. . . . Ah, it looks as if some have been successful and have all the things they came for. Good. . . . Some appear to be heading home (over half the children are now seated). . . . It seems to be very close to three o'clock and time for the second shift to take over. . . . I hope everyone is nearly finished or they'll run out of time. . . . " (Strike the "clock" three times.) "Three

A Borrower assists her "injured" partner in a creative story.

o'clock and everyone who's left needs to hurry home. And it's been such a tiring night, you all fall exhausted into bed." (Fade out the music.)

"Now, while the first shift rests, the second shift will begin their work." (Repeat the playing as above.)

(Turn up the lights.) "Well, that was an exciting adventure. Let's hear about what happened to you. What was the scariest part for you?" (Discuss.)

Leader-in-role

"Now, let's suppose I'm a Borrower from another house and I've come to visit you. I've never been borrowing before, and my parents sent me here to talk to you so I could learn. They told me you're the most famous Borrowers and you know all the ins and outs of this business. Will you help me with some questions?"

1. "How did you get to be so good at borrowing?"
2. "What was the closest call you ever had in borrowing?"
3. "Can you tell or show me what you're most proud of having borrowed?"
4. "What's the most important thing I should know about borrowing? Do you have any secret tricks you could tell me about?"
5. "My parents told me you're planning to have a garage sale soon. What things are you planning to get rid of? Why?"
6. "I found this on your doorstep." (Show scissors or other small object.) "I wasn't sure if you'd lost it or if you have it out there for a reason. What is it used for?"
7. "What personal characteristics are important in being a Borrower?"

("Out" for reticent children: "Excuse me, I should have remembered that it isn't always safe to talk; someone could overhear us and then your life would be in danger.") "Thanks for talking to me. I have to go home now. I know you've had a very busy night, so I'll let you get a little sleep. 'Bye."

Quieting activity

(as leader) "And so the Borrowers put away their things, fluff up their pillows on their beds, lay their heads down, and quietly go to sleep." (Play restful music such as "Aquarium" from Saint-Saëns's *Carnival of the Animals.*)

SAMPLE LESSON PLAN: ROBOTS
(upper elementary)

Objectives

1. Experience creative mechanical movement and creative verbal experience based on topic of robots.
2. Gain practice in creating a story with a beginning, a middle, and an end.
3. Deal with the concept of a mechanical robot's possibilities for work.
4. Imagine problems that could be encountered in mechanical devices and create appropriate solutions.
5. Provide opportunities to respond to character questioning related to the experience.
6. Provide opportunity to become more familiar with computer concepts such as programming, GIGO (garbage in/garbage out), and user friendly.

Preparation and materials

1. Space: area in center of room with desks around edge of room
2. Supplies: ad statement cards; small nondescript piece of machinery
3. Books: catalog advertising of a personal robot, or use one of the robots discussed in *Robots* by Gloria Skurzynski (New York: Bradbury Press, 1990.)
4. Music: use any "mechanical-sounding" music plus some quieting music
5. Visual aids: pictures of robots

Warm-up. Introduce the advertisement for a personal robot that rolls on rubber wheels, has a stationary tray-type arm, a manual grasping hand to carry objects, flashing eyes, and a tape-recorded voice.

1. Do a warm-up activity being robots doing calisthenics or aerobic dancing to music. (Give the opportunity to move as the robot would move, translating calisthenics designed for the human body over to a robot's body.) Divide students into two groups, taking turns with brief exercise

activity. Try interpreting how a robot would do toe touches, jumping jacks, knee bends, and so on.

2. Do ad talks (see p. 186) using a robot or a mechanical voice.

Discussion questions

1. "Suppose you were a robot. What type of job might you do? Where do you work?" (Children's answers might include: in an office doing odd jobs, in a house doing simple housework tasks or belonging to a kid like me who has him as a servant.)

2. "What are all the things you have to do in a day's time? What's your typical day like?" (Deliver mail, run copy machine, get coffee, dust, empty wastebaskets, run a vacuum cleaner; it follows me around to carry my books, brings me breakfast in bed, does my paper route.)

3. "Suppose today, as you're in the middle of all your work, something goes wrong. What might that be? And what happens to you and all your work?" (I could start doing things all wrong and pour coffee in the mailbox and run lots of blank paper; I'm cleaning because a lot of company's coming, and I'm trying to mop and spill the bucket of water and short all my circuits and go haywire; I throw the papers on the porches, but I got programmed wrong and the papers start breaking windows and knocking stuff around.)

4. "Oh, dear. Well, we'd better get things back to normal again. What could happen to stop all this damage and make things right again?" (I have to be sent out for repairs and get straightened out and finish the day; someone comes and blows me dry with a hair dryer and I still have to be fixed but at least I stop messing things up; some people tackle me and punch in the right code so I can do it right.)

5. "Now I'd like to know what robots do when they've finished a hard day's work. What would you do to relax?" (I watch TV in the lounge; I have my own room so I go there and listen to music; I like to play chess with myself and see if I can trick myself.)

Directions for playing

"I think we're ready to give this a try. Since there isn't enough space for everyone this first time, we'll take half of you for the first playing and half for the second. I'll play some mechanical-sounding music for you to pantomime to. Get in your places. And be sure you stay in your own space, especially since you said so many things would go wrong. I'll let you know when you're switched on. When you finish your story, just freeze where you are." (Music starts.)

Side-coaching (as needed). "Robots, get ready for a new day. You're switched on—now. . . . Oh, boy, a robot's day never seems to end. . . . It's work, work, work, all the time. . . . You've been thoroughly programmed . . . so many jobs are being done . . . I hope the people who own you are aware of the complete job you're doing for them. . . . Ah, and today is that special day when you're to do your special job . . . it's so very important that everything goes right . . . everybody's counting on you. . . . I think I see some things looking not quite right. . . . Is it possible? . . . Oh, I hope someone can save you from making such a mess of things. . . . Whew, good, I think some robots

Robots carry out their tasks.

must have been helped . . . they seem to be getting back to normal—or at least they've been stopped from doing any more damage. . . . Some are completely done in I see . . . and now almost all robots are finished. . . . We'll shut off the last few as the music ends." (Fade music out.)

The second group of players enact their stories.

Leader-in-role

"Now that you robots are back to normal again, I'd like to check with you on some things. Allow me to introduce myself. My name is McGillicutty, and I'm a marketing analyst. I've heard about you robots, and I want to talk directly to you about your capabilities so I'll know how to market you in this country."

(Students may use the "computer-sounding" voice used earlier in the ad-talk activity.)

1. "Just how user friendly are you? Is it possible to make you even more user friendly than you are? And if so, how might we do that?"
2. "Which of your parts need replacing most frequently? What is the cost for that?"
3. "I've heard it said that some of your early customers had complaints. For example, some said you didn't work fast enough; you were too noisy; and one even claimed you talked too much. Would you care to respond to any one or all of those complaints?"
4. "Oh, by the way, here's a small piece of machinery I found on the floor. I think it might be a part of one of you. Who claims it and would you explain it, please?"
5. "I understand you are the first model of personal robot and that there are others in design and manufacturing right now. How are the new models different from you, and are the differences significant?"

6. "One final question—and this is strictly personal and off the record. You can level with me. As a robot, do you ever have a desire to become even more human than you are now? Why or why not?"

(Other roles for verbal children: Instead of questioning in the leader role, you could set up a panel of robots who are questioned by the class playing prospective buyers. If they all like talking as robots, you might want to set up paired conversations with robots interviewing other robots for jobs. "Out" for reticent children: "I'm terribly sorry. Your manufacturer probably considers that classified information.")

"Thanks for talking with me. I have to go write my report. I know you've had a busy day, so I'll let you relax now."

Quieting activity

"Robots, please return to your packing cases. We need to have you sent out for servicing and overhauling after your experience today. You're all inside? Good. I'm shutting off all your power now." (Play restful music for a few moments.)

CREATING AND SHARING IMPROVISATIONS

After some experience in drama work, children eight years of age and above enjoy the challenge of improvising scenes and stories in small groups to share with their classmates. These scenes may be played either in pantomime or with dialogue; in pairs or in small groups. Particularly with the younger and inexperienced students, you may need to help with choice of material, who plays which part, and other organizational assistance.

If left to their own devices, children usually reenact stories that are fairly familiar to them, such as folk tales or stories they have seen on film or television. Some youngsters who have seen the famous MGM *The Wizard of Oz* film several times or Charlie Brown television specials, for example, can reenact many scenes verbatim. However, you will want to have a ready store of ideas for creating scenes in a variety of ways and with a number of kinds of stimuli. This second half of the chapter focuses on these materials.

Plot Structure

Plot structure becomes important in these activities as it provides parameters for the work. Children need to understand that stories basically have a beginning, a middle, and an ending. Remind them that since a "story" is being told, it should not ramble on indefinitely.

Particularly at first, students' work will often be short, rather episodic, or without a completed ending. This usually happens because the group has not been able to reach an agreement on the story line. (Remember, group decision making is not an easy task.) Another reason may be that as the students are actually playing the scene, new thoughts occur to them and they begin improvising additional ideas, without anyone knowing what is going to happen next. If their scenes have strong conflict, then arguments, shouting, or even a physical fight may be all they can think of to do. (And they sometimes cannot even bring *that* to a close!) A third reason is that they simply do not realize the importance of deciding on an ending. They keep on playing, even though some of them are becoming embarrassed and even panicked if they see no way out of their dilemma.

Pressing them to decide on an ending for their scenes as they plan becomes a major task. The author once instructed some children to be sure to plan an ending for their scene and then asked if they knew why it was important. One child's answer was, "So we'll all know when to quit." That says it pretty well, and is an explanation I often share with children.

In spite of your precautions there may still be times when students reach a dead end. The following strategies may be helpful.

1. You may walk up to them privately and quietly ask, as a reminder, "Do you have an ending?"
2. If an ending is not forthcoming, you may be able to narrate them out of the difficulty. *Example:* Some students were enacting scenes based on returning an item to a store's complaint department. One group could not settle its argument, so the leader narrated: "And so the complaint manager and the irate customer never got a chance to find out who would win the argument, for a bell sounded the closing of the department store. And to the strains of the Muzak playing 'We Wish You a Merry Christmas,' they all went home."
3. It may be possible to step into the scene as a mediating character and negotiate. In the above scene, for example, the leader might have stepped in as the store manager to help work out an agreement between the two.
4. Stop the scene and ask if audience members see a way to solve the *characters'* problem. Continue the scene with new suggestions or with new players.

Audience Behavior

Leaders need to encourage sensitive audience behavior. Some students are very supportive of each other. But there are those who will become impatient with their classmates. They think *they* would know what to say or do in the same situation, so they may call out instructions. "Maybelle, tell him you don't want to go!" "Psst, George, give him a shove!" Just a quiet reminder to anxious audience members will usually suffice, but you may also need to explain that prompting from the audience interrupts the players' thinking and bothers them more than it helps them.

Evaluating Scenes

When doing scenework in groups students sometimes say, "We need to rehearse more," or "We don't like what we're doing." Not all groups are ready to share their work at the same time. Often the best remedy is to let them continue improvising and working together rather than forcing them to share too quickly.

When students are ready, evaluation of scenes should include both the ideas presented and the performance itself. Encourage the class to reflect on the ideas, solutions to problems, or other insights that were presented. How effectively did the players demonstrate the activity's curricular goal?

In evaluating the performance, focus first on self-evaluation with such questions as

"What did you like about the (your) scene?"

"What moments were the most enjoyable for you? Why?"

"If you could do it over again, what would you want to change? Why?"

"How successful do you think the ending was to the (your) scene? Why?"

Some questions for discussion of pantomime scenes might include:

"What was the most understandable moment?"

"When did you have difficulty expressing yourself or understanding what was happening?"

"How clearly were the characters portrayed?"

"Were the characters and their feelings believable?"

"How satisfying was the ending?"

When students have developed a great deal of confidence in their ability to create scenes, you may want the audience members to give their evaluations. Positive evaluation is paramount, so your wording of discussion questions can guide this:

"What did you *like* about the scene?"

"What things were said by certain characters that were *especially believable?*"

"What lines of dialogue were *especially typical* of the characters?"

"During what moments did people *help each other?*"

Your own positive feedback will be important, especially if some students insist on being overly critical of classmates. Or if the scene could benefit from additional challenges, you may need to suggest these. However, continued playing and experiences in improvisation also can result in more involving and believable dramatization.

Topics for Scenes

Deciding whether scenework should be in pantomime or should include dialogue depends most often on the material selected. Some of the topics below can be played either in pantomime or as dialogue scenes. But you will also want to consider the groups' needs. Some children prefer to pantomime rather than talk, because they feel less attention is drawn to them. And yet, pantomime work is always a good challenge, even for the

"Just keep saying 'There's no place like home.'" Improvisation of a scene from a favorite story.

most experienced. On the other hand, when some children are given pantomime scenes to perform they ask, "Can we talk?" This usually means they are ready and see possibilities for dialogue in the drama. Be ready to adjust to their needs accordingly.

Favorite/familiar stories   An easy beginning for group scenes are re-enactments of familiar short stories such as folk or fairy tales, fables, or short episodes from longer books. They may be enacted in pantomime or include dialogue. As a stimulus, you may have some simple costumes and props on hand. For example, a bowl and a spoon may remind children of "Little Miss Muffet" or "The Three Bears." Or a piece of red material may suggest "Little Red Riding Hood." For older students, this activity can "advertise" literature to the class and serve as a book report.

Quickies   Acting out one-minute versions of familiar folk tales is a good exercise in focusing on story essentials. These may be done as pantomime or with dialogue. Children like to double up on parts, some playing several roles, including animals (if appropriate) and scenery. In fact, some students will enjoy the challenge of doing an entire folk tale by themselves, playing all the parts.

Scenarios   Scenes and stories may be based on outlines written on cards. The following samples show only some of the many possibilities.

1. You are having a picnic. After everything is laid out, it begins to rain. You must eat your picnic in the car. (Don't forget to take the picnic items into the car!)
2. Two friends are riding their bicycles. They pass an old house they think is haunted and decide to explore it. While they are exploring, something inside the house frightens them, and they race out of the house and head for home. Decide what the something is that scares them and let us see it in your scene.

Proverbs and sayings   Students in fourth grade and up can illustrate the meaning of proverbs. What stories do the following suggest? "Make hay while the sun shines." "A stitch in time saves nine." "A friend in need is a friend indeed." "Two heads are better than one." "All that glitters is not gold." "A fool and his money are soon parted." Consider proverbs and sayings from various cultures and discuss how the proverbs fit the values or beliefs of the culture. Encourage players to illustrate the broader meaning of the proverb rather than a simple literal enactment.

News story of the week!   Illustrate a current news event or human interest story. Have newspapers on hand to provide ideas for the stories and stimulate interest in reading.

Television shows   Students can act out scenes from teacher-approved television shows. If you study media, relate this activity to the structure of various types of shows: situation comedies, soap operas, variety shows, and so forth.

Television commercials   Commercials (either in pantomime or with dialogue) may be created. Relate this activity to a study of persuasive advertising techniques, such as bandwagon approach, testimony, appeal to status,

Fourth graders act out their version of a television commercial for cough medicine.

and the like. In addition to creating commercials similar to those frequently seen, try creating new types of commercials:

1. *Sell yourselves as a group.* What skills, abilities, or personalities do you have that are worth marketing? Who would you like to have hire you? What will you charge for your services? Do you guarantee your work?

2. *Recycle products.* Create a commercial for things that might otherwise be thrown away. What uses can you find for one large oversized glove, used bubble gum, a cracked mirror, or one old tennis shoe?

3. *Sell products from the past.* How might a guillotine, a suit of armor, a covered wagon, or a spinning wheel have been marketed if there had been television in earlier centuries? Or create commercials for products of the future, such as lifelike robots, personal spaceships, or wristwatch television sets.

You are there   Scenes of scientific or historical significance may be re-enacted. Facts about the events might be listed on cards, or the students might be encouraged to do research. Consider the following: the test drive of an early automobile; the Wright brothers' flight at Kitty Hawk; the first heart transplant; women granted the vote; Madame Curie's discovery of radium; the discovery of King Tut's tomb; Alexander Graham Bell makes the first telephone call; and so forth.

Fractured fairy tales and fables   See such resources as *Roald Dahl's Revolting Rhymes* (New York: Alfred A. Knopf, 1983); Jon Scieszka's *The True Story of the 3 Little Pigs! by A. Wolf* (New York: Viking, 1989) and *The Frog Prince, Continued* (New York: Viking, 1991); Judith Viorst's poems based on folk tales in *If I Were in Charge of the World* (New York: Atheneum, 1981); Arnold Lobel's *Fables* (New York: Harper & Row, 1980); Tony Ross's *Foxy Fables* (New York: Dial Press, 1986) for a different turn of events in traditional stories. Students may play these or be inspired to create their own versions.

The invention   Children act out their version of the discovery of such inventions as laughing gas, suspenders, the rubber band, fire, the mirror, the popcorn machine, fireworks, the wheel, potato chips, snowshoes, or bubble gum. For comparative purposes, refer to *The Invention of Ordinary Things,* by Don L. Wulffson (New York: Lothrop, Lee & Shepard, 1981), which tells the story behind the invention of such common products as the zipper, breakfast cereal, and the toothbrush.

Add on scenes   An interesting and challenging way to play scenes is to begin with one or two players setting up a problem situation. Other players spontaneously add on to the scene as characters who might logically appear next. Allow a few seconds for each new character to make his or her contribution. *Example:* A group of sixth graders began a situation with a person being stuck in a revolving door of a department store. Various characters added on to the situation with their ideas: a floorwalker who tried to keep things under control; sympathetic clerks with various ideas for calming the customer who began to panic; a harried mother with a child who refused to leave the store without going through the revolving door; and so on. (*Note:*

It is a good idea to quickly and privately check on each child's idea for the scene *before* they play it in order to weed out any inappropriate ones.)

Occasionally, these scenes reach a logical conclusion on their own. You may, however, have to ask for a wrap-up. Or, they can be stopped when everyone has run out of ideas. Another method is to call "Freeze" at any point and then discuss what has taken place.

Wordless picture books   Scenes may be made from wordless picture books that have several characters interacting. Students make up the dialogue they think would accompany the pictures. Some suggestions: *Alligator's Toothache,* Diane DeGroat (New York: Crown Publishing, 1977); *Arthur's Aventures in the Abandoned House,* Fernando Krahn (New York: E. P. Dutton, 1981); *The Damp and Daffy Doings of a Daring Pirate Ship,* Guillermo Mordillo (New York: Harlan Quist, 1971); *The Flying Grandmother,* Naomi Kojima (New York: Thomas Y. Crowell, 1981); *Robot-Bot-Bot,* Fernando Krahn (E. P. Dutton, 1979); *The Secret in the Dungeon,* Fernando Krahn (New York: Clarion, 1983); and *Mr. Top,* Fernando Krahn (New York: William Morrow, 1983).

Comics   Select cartoon strips from the Sunday paper or comic books with enough action that the basic plot of the situation is understandable. Block out the dialogue and have students create the story in their own words.

Talking pictures   Find dramatic pictures which show several people (or even animals or objects) in a problem situation. Students select the picture they want to work with and develop a scene around it. They may re-create the picture as a "frozen picture" and then present their solution. Or they may want to begin the scene prior to the picture. The same picture may be used by several groups and a comparison made of the different interpretations and solutions presented.

Scenes from ad talks   Use the ad talk cards explained on page 186. (Be sure the ad statements suggest story ideas and are not just casual comments.) Shuffle and distribute perhaps five to each group. Students are to build a scene around their ad cards in any order they choose. They may use as much additional dialogue as they wish. Post the cards for the audience to see while the scene is being played. This activity presents an intriguing challenge. It is often amazing to note how seemingly unrelated statements can be incorporated into a logical story line. You might even let several groups use the same cards and see what variations result. (The following cards were randomly drawn as an example: "She has a right to know." "Finally, a store that's open when you have time to shop." "Hey, Mom, let's take this one." "Let's make a deal." "I sure wish I could have a lot more.")

Stories from advertisements   Newspaper ads often stimulate one's imagination as to the story behind them. Items for sale or messages in the "Personals" section might pose possibilities. For example: "House for sale. Furnishings included. Vacating immediately. Best offer" might suggest a haunted house. Or "Lose ten pounds a week! Success guaranteed or your money cheerfully refunded." What really happens when someone is not successful?

Opening lines   Often the opening line of a story draws the reader in immediately. What is the rest of the story for openers such as the following?

1.   It seemed a perfect day for the event. Crowds were gathered for the momentous, historic occasion. One person in the crowd, however, seemed out of place.
2.   Silently and without warning it came on them like a thief in the night. Not until the following morning were they aware of what had happened.

Famous last words   Create story lines suggested by intriguing lines like the following:

"I have an idea that will revolutionize the world!"
"You never listen to anything I say."
"I told you we should have called the police."
"I know exactly what I'm doing."
"Sure Mom will let us keep it."

Keep talking!   What ways can students think of to deal with the following situations?

1.   Two television announcers try to fill in the time before a delayed space launch or a sporting event, but they have already said almost everything they can think of.
2.   A persistent salesperson tries to sell a product in order to meet a daily quota.
3.   A person gets on a crowded bus with a briefcase that is ticking.
4.   Two people are arguing. A third tries to enter as a peacemaker, even though she does not know what the argument is about.
5.   Two people who speak different languages try to communicate with each other about a problem they're having. A third is a translator. (Unless students can speak different languages they may use nonsense words or repeat a word like "applesauce." In the latter case, the emphasis would be on conveying language through gesture and vocal intonation.)

Random scenes

1.   Prepare sets of cards using the categories: settings, props, and characters. Picture cards work best.
2.   Groups select one or more cards from each category.
3.   Groups plan a scene using the cards selected.
4.   Shuffle the cards for an infinite variety of combinations.
     Settings. elevator, Island of No Return, museum at midnight, abandoned mine shaft, lost and found department, information desk, haunted house, tower with revolving restaurant, hijacked airplane.
     Characters. spy, detective, genie in a bottle, Frankenstein's monster, Superman or Superwoman, ghost, good fairy, Snoopy, statue that comes to life.
     Props. treasure map, magic wand, flying carpet, poison apple, cape to make you invisible, sneezing powder, singing harp, seven-league boots, old jalopy, air balloon with a slow leak.

What short drama could be created from this bag of props?

Prop stories

1. Keep a selection of interesting props, bits of costume, pieces of material, and the like. (Caution: Do not include weapons, such as swords or toy guns, since they do not encourage imagination—just violence.)
2. In a whole-group discussion, brainstorm some ideas for a couple of them. "Who might have owned this jewel box?" "What does this key unlock?" "Why is there only one glove?"
3. Select three or four props for each group to incorporate into a scene. The story must be built around these props.
4. *After* the stories are planned, students may be allowed to add other props and costumes to the scenes. But do not let them know this ahead of time or they will plan a different story.

   Example: A scarf, candlestick, and pocket watch might suggest this story: A woman (wearing the scarf) and her husband (carrying the pocket watch) are robbed. The only clue is the candlestick, which was dropped by the thief. The thief, who was the butler in disguise, is apprehended when his fingerprints are found on the candlestick.

Role-playing situations   Once students have had some experience with dialogue scenes and other drama activities, it will be easier for them to do the role playing suggested in many social studies texts. Students can dramatize various ways of handling personal and social problems. Sometimes the dramatizations show unacceptable behaviors, but usually the consequences of those behaviors are shown in the scene or in the discussion that follows. Searching for the most appropriate solutions becomes the goal.

Examples

1. Children have the habit of crossing an elderly couple's lawn. They angrily confront the children one day. What happens?

2. A group of children are throwing hard-packed snowballs at passing cars and shatter a windshield. The car stops, and the driver starts shouting at the group. What happens next?

3. A group of friends are bored and are looking for something to do. A couple of them suggest shoplifting for the fun of it. The others are not so sure. What does the group finally decide to do?

4. A group of friends are playing. Two children, new to the neighborhood, enter the scene and ask to play. Some of the children do not want to include the newcomers. How does the scene end?

Dialogue scenes from literature Poems often involve interesting dialogue encounters one can build on. Some suggestions are listed below. Particularly with younger children, you will need to play a role in the scene in order to model the activity.

M–O "Barter," Sara Teasdale (2). "Life has loveliness to sell. . . ." What would Life as a salesperson have to sell? What would Life say to try to convince someone to buy? What would you trade for Life's loveliness?

Y–M "Doorbells," Rachel Field (3,36). In addition to the people suggested in this poem, who might appear at the door and what do they want? How does the homeowner receive them?

M–O "Phizzog," Carl Sandburg (3). Create a dialogue scene in which you receive your newly made face and you want to exchange it. To whom would you speak? What bargain would you strike?

M–O "Southbound on the Freeway," May Swenson (18,26,29). A visitor from "Orbitville" mistakes cars for earth creatures and gives an interesting description of them. To whom is the visitor reporting and how does that creature respond? What other observations about earth can the visitor make?

M–O "Summons," Robert Francis (26). A person asks to be summoned if something important arises. What would be something important to summon a person to? How will the summoned person react?

O "Two Friends," David Ignatow (34). It seems that two friends who pass each other and talk hurriedly really do not listen to each other's comments.

M "The Zax," Dr. Seuss (33). Two Zax meet and neither will give way for the other—ever. The poem doesn't explain why. Create a scene that answers the question for us.

Dialogue guessing games Verbal students will like the challenge of this game.

1. Students work out a scene on their own, without identifying the characters in it.

2. You stop the scene periodically so that the audience can guess from the clues who the speakers might be. Here are two examples:

Example A:
"I don't want you coming around here again!"
"But what harm did I do?"
"Harm? What about the food you ate and the furniture you broke?"
"Well, the food wasn't my idea of terrific—and the furniture wasn't very well made anyway! . . ."

Goldilocks and Papa Bear

Example B:
"I know you can do it; I have a lot of faith in you."
"Well, I've sewn a lot of things, but this is a real challenge."
"Here's the design we have in mind."
"Ah, but five points are just as easy to make as six. . . ."

George Washington and Betsy Ross

FOR THE COLLEGE STUDENT

1. Outline lesson plans for two separate creative stories. One is to be based on fiction or fantasy; the other, on fact. One should be for individual playing; the other for a pair or a group. Refer to the sample outlines and lesson plans in this chapter.
   a. *Introductory materials.* Write out objectives, preparation and materials, and motivation.
   b. *Discussion.* Form five carefully worded discussion questions to help the children get a story line for their ideas. For each question, give three possible answers (speculative on your part) which three children might give you. When you have finished this section, check the five answers you have received from each child to see if each has a completed story line. If not, examine the questions again for possible problems.
   c. *Organization of playing.* Indicate whether any, and what kind of, preview playing is necessary. Give the directions for children to get organized. Give directions for beginning and ending the playing. Specify if you are in a role.
   d. *Side-coaching.* Write out in exact wording some side-coaching comments appropriate to the story idea. If you are side-coaching in a role, specify your character.
   e. *Final discussion in character role.* Explain your role for the final discussion. In words as your character would say them, write out five open-ended questions appropriate to the story and your role. Or suggest other verbal activities that would be appropriate for a follow-up playing of the idea. What roles could be given to highly verbal children? Include an "out" for the reticent child.
2. Lead your classmates in one of your lesson plans. Discuss afterward the effectiveness of the plan. What were the strengths? How might it be improved?
3. In groups, brainstorm ideas for pantomime and dialogue scenes based on literature or on other curricular topics. Keep a file of these materials. In addition to literature and textbook information, you might also want to consider newspaper clippings, pictures, music, slides, films, props, and costumes.
4. Select or create a dialogue scene and play it with a group of your classmates.
5. Select one of the scene ideas presented in this chapter and plan it out with some classmates. Share your scenes with the rest of the class. Include the evaluation process.

10

Story
Dramatization

A number of stories and various ways of dramatizing them have been presented throughout this text. The stories used for narrative pantomime focused on action, whereas the stories used for verbal activities and improvisation focused on dialogue. In this chapter, we will present some additional ways of approaching story dramatization. You and your students will eventually decide for yourselves what methods you want to use with the stories you choose to dramatize.

TRADITIONAL STORY DRAMATIZATION

Traditionally in creative drama, the term *story dramatization* refers to the process of creating an informal play from a story with the leader's guidance. The procedure generally includes the following:

1. Sharing a story or other piece of literature with a group of students
2. Planning the characters, scenes, and events
3. Playing
4. Evaluating
5. Replaying

The process used for creating dialogue is the improvisational method. There is no script and no memorization of lines. Furthermore, no one student is cast permanently in or owns any one role.

Short stories with simple plots are often played from beginning to end in the course of one class period. Longer or more complex stories, including short novels, are usually divided into scenes that are played and rehearsed separately, then spliced together for the completed play. The interchanging of roles and experimenting with ideas may take place during one class period or may extend over several days' or even weeks' time. The completed story-play is the result of the group's work, facilitated by the leader.

Selecting the Story

Several considerations should be made in selecting a story to make into a play. First, the story should be of good *literary quality.* (There is a bibliography at the end of this chapter to get you started.) The story should also be one that appeals to both you and the children. However, stories used for initial attempts at dramatization should be less complex than ones children are able to read and listen to. It should be fairly obvious that reading or listening to an enjoyable story is not as demanding as dramatizing one.

Second, there should be plenty of interesting *action* in the story that can be played without elaborate staging. Thirdly, the *dialogue* should be interesting, but not so difficult that the children become frustrated in their attempts to improvise from it.

Lastly, the *characters* should be believable. There should also be enough characters (or the possibility of adding characters) to permit a significant number of children, if not the entire class, to be involved in the playing.

Presenting the Story

Stories may be presented to the class in a variety of ways. They may be read or told in your own words. Picture books are usually shared visually with the children, particularly if the illustrations help in seeing action and characterization. There may even be times when you will want to share audio recordings or filmed versions of a story.

Most experts would agree that folk tales should be shared orally whenever possible, as they were originally told rather than read. Besides, oral telling allows you to maintain eye contact with the audience, helping you judge how the children are reacting to it.

Whatever method you use, you must focus on helping the children understand the action of the story and the interaction of the characters so that they can re-create it and expand upon it in their dramatization.

Dialogue

An important part of the presentation of the story is the dialogue. Children usually listen very carefully to the dialogue in the stories that are read or told to them, repeating it in their playings and improvising upon it.

Adding dialogue to the storytelling often helps the children see verbalizing possibilities. Changing indirect dialogue to direct dialogue is particularly useful. For example, a line might read:

> As the young man went down the road he met an old woodcutter. He asked the old man if he knew the way to town. The old man told him to follow his nose.

By adding direct dialogue as you tell the story, the above passage might be changed to:

> As the young man went down the road, he met an old woodcutter. "Excuse me, sir," he asked, "I wonder if you could tell me the way to town?"
> The old man answered, "Follow your nose, follow your nose. You can get to almost anywhere you want if you just follow your nose!"

However, dialogue that is too complicated should be simplified. Otherwise children might be frustrated trying to remember it. Even if you encourage them to "tell it in your own words," they may feel compelled to re-create the original wording and experience failure in the attempt. For example in telling the story *Bartholomew and the Oobleck* (see sample lessons in this chapter), I find it best to omit the magicians' lengthy, poetic chant and simply say, "While they mixed the oobleck, they said their magical chants."

Casting the Story

Consider the possibility of adding roles to the story so that every child may take part when all the scenes are finally spliced together. Crowd or group scenes, for example, are common in the theatre and are useful for adding more players. Guards in palaces are popular because they generally remain stationary (important to teachers) but have status (important to children).

There may also be special effects or other technical aspects children can perform. If these effects add to the overall dramatic impact of the play (e.g., a drum roll, flashing lights for a storm), children can be as proud of these parts as they would be of playing a character role.

Usually it is not effective to cast children as inanimate or immobile objects such as trees unless they are important to the plot or move in some dramatic fashion. The trees in *Petronella* (see bibliography at the end of this chapter), for example, grow magically from a comb, which makes them significant enough to play. Trees that move in a windstorm and create frightening effects are another example.

"I'll show you I'm not afraid," says the Captain of the Guard in *Bartholomew and the Oobleck.* (triple-casting of one character)

Because you will be playing the story several times, and because you will want each playing to build on the previous one, it is important to establish a solid beginning. The following suggestions should help.

1. At first, cast the most competent students in major roles in order to establish an appropriate model. Shy or slower students can benefit from seeing the story enacted by others before they undertake it themselves.

2. Double and even triple casting (two or three students playing one character) will also be useful. This technique will allow more students the opportunity to play the story and will provide the security needed for improvising freely. It is helpful to remember: "What one can't think of to say, the other one usually can." Shyer students or students with handicaps and special needs can also benefit from the assistance of their classmates, even if just in moving about the room.

3. You may assist with the main role, particularly in first playings with younger children and even with some of the most competent older students. This technique allows you to walk the students through the story, mapping out the playing areas as you go along. If you are also using the technique of double and triple casting, you can easily and unobtrusively tag along in replayings and still be available to help as needed. (*Note:* In traditional story dramatization the leader usually stays on the sidelines. We have found it helpful to enter the playing, though it is still our goal to remove ourselves as soon as the children seem ready to go it alone.)

Aids for Organization

A main concern with story dramatization is "How will I keep things organized?" It is a legitimate concern, but with some careful planning, many difficulties can be alleviated.

Following are a number of organizational suggestions to consider. They are designed to help you remember the story line as you play it and to avoid having all the students moving and talking at the same time. The techniques usually evolve quite logically as you work with the stories. In time you will find the techniques that work best for you and your students, as well as for the stories that will become your particular favorites.

1. Briefly review the plot of the story before you start to play it or write a simple outline on the chalkboard or a chart.

2. Organize space carefully. You will usually want to have the major scenes take place in the middle of the playing circle or in the front of the classroom. However, other areas of the room, such as the corners, will be useful for additional scenes. It is particularly helpful to place the scenes around the room, sequencing them in the same order that they appear in the story.

   You will need to think this organization through ahead of time. It may be helpful to map it out on the chalkboard for everyone's reference. Later as you feel more comfortable and flexible and as the children gain experience, you will want to consult them for their ideas on mapping out the scenes. Create specific locations using classroom furnishings. For example, a teacher's chair can become the "king's throne," or a teacher's desk might become a "banquet table."

3. Make the students' desks a part of the drama whenever possible. Use them as "homes" for the citizens of the town, "stores" for shopkeepers, or "horses" for the king's army. Keep children seated at their desks (or on a rug) until their scene is ready to be played. During these sitting-out periods, refer to the students as the "audience" so they will not feel left out or neglected. They may also be able to assist with some sound or lighting effects when they are not involved in the actual playing of the story.

While part of the class acts the story, the rest wait for their cue at the desks.

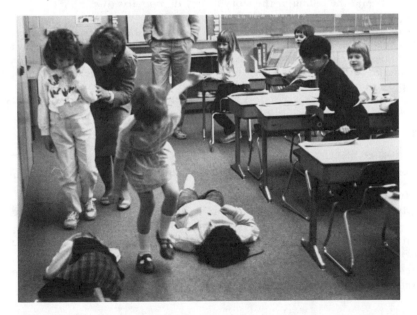

Paper plates form headbands for the story *The Mitten* by Alvin Tresselt (mouse, boar, fox, wolf, and cricket).

4. Look for the natural controls within the story. Sometimes the characters rest or take a nap. Sometimes they are in a frozen position due to enchantment (as in "Sleeping Beauty") or other spells. Often they "return to their homes" in which case you can send them back to their seats. Capitalize on these moments to give legitimate quiet periods. You may even be able to incorporate such moments into the telling of the story if they do not already exist.

5. Designate characters in some way so that you—and they—can remember who is playing which part. If you separate and group the students in various parts of the classroom, it will help everyone visualize the layout of the story and remember the characters. Another technique is to make simple name tags or headbands with pictures of characters on them, as shown in the above photo. Simple costuming with hats, props, and pieces of fabric is also useful but may take more time. You may wish to add these after initial playings and when you are sure the children want to continue playing the story.

6. Narrating and playing a role yourself also helps organization. (See next section.)

Organization through Narration and Leader-in-Role

Two additional techniques (both of which have been discussed in earlier chapters) will be indispensable to you in dramatizing a story. They are *narration* and *playing a character role*. *Narration* helps you guide the dramatization from *outside* the story. When you play a character role, you guide the playing from *within*. And you can use both techniques interchangeably in the same story dramatization (like wearing a belt and suspenders at the same time!).

Ways to Guide Using Narration.   Narration can help you in the following ways:

1. Open the story:
   "Once upon a time there was . . ."
2. Guide the story if it lags or if the children forget the sequence of events:
   "And then the bear started off down the road. . . ."
3. Control the action if problems arise:
   "Finally the people decided to stop arguing and did something about the situation. . . ."
4. Add pantomime ideas if the children need suggestions:
   "The rabbit looked at himself in the mirror and admired his new clothes."
5. Encourage dialogue:
   "The king and queen argued about their daughter's leaving home. The king was against it, but the queen was for it."
6. Provide transitions for scenes, indicating passage of time or change of environment:
   "The next morning the old lady went out to the smokehouse. . . ."
7. Close the story:
   ". . . and he never went looking for trouble again."

Ways to Guide by Playing a Character Role.   Playing a character in the story can help you:

1. Carry the dialogue, initiating interaction:
   "We seem to have lost our way. Can you give us directions to get to the nearest town?" "We've got some things to sell. Let us show you some of them."
2. Progress the plot:
   "I don't know about you, but I'm getting hungry. Maybe there's a place around here where we can get something to eat."
3. Cue the entrance of characters:
   "Over there's someone who may be able to help us."
4. With management control:
   "As the king's prime minister, I must remind you that you cannot go into the throne room until you are quiet. And you must bow to the king before you speak. Are you ready?"
5. Reactivate involvement, offering new situations for students to react to and new challenges for them to solve:
   "This letter just arrived, and it's addressed to you. I'm sure everyone here would like you to read it aloud."
   "Say, excuse me, but do you have a peddler's license? I'm the inspector here in this town, and we don't allow door-to-door peddling unless someone has a license. I'll have to ask to see yours."

What role do I play?

1. You can play the main role, although it is best to have one or two students double-cast with you. Often this character is in the story from beginning to

Leader can assist students in dialogue by playing a character role.

end, and by playing this part you are available in all scenes. This technique is useful with shy students or those who need considerable assistance. If the child(ren) double-cast with you are able to take over entirely, you simply back off and shadow them so that you're available if needed. Even when students are experienced in story dramatization, you may be able to revitalize a story by playing a character role yourself. Once you guide the children through a story by playing a role, they will usually be ready to take over by the second or third replaying.

2. You may choose to play a secondary role, such as a king's prime minister or a friend to the central character. If these roles do not already exist in the story itself, they can usually be easily added.

3. You may step into a scene in a spontaneously invented role to assist if students have forgotten the sequence of events or to reactivate the students' involvement if the playing is becoming too mechanical or superficial.

It is important to note that all the above techniques are used in order to sustain the drama from the moment the dramatization begins through to its end. Children are usually anxious to dramatize, but in their haste they may find themselves suddenly stopping in the middle of their work and asking, "What do I do now?" or "What do I say now?" The believability is lost at this moment and imaginative flow comes to a screeching halt. If you have elected to remain on the sidelines, your only alternative is to become an off-stage prompter. But by using the above techniques you can help the children sustain the drama reality and avoid (or at least minimize) these interruptions.

At the same time, we hasten to add that there is nothing wrong with stopping and regrouping if you've gotten off to a bad start. While there is certainly nobility in the captain going down with a sinking ship, it would be better to head for the shore and set sail again with the leaks caulked!

Evaluation

Evaluation of the dramatization should be made after each playing. The emphasis should focus on the positive elements that have been observed in order to ensure that they will be repeated in subsequent replayings.

Consider such questions as "Would someone who doesn't know the story be able to follow it from our play?" "When was the story most understandable?" "In what parts of the story was the action clear?" "What parts of the dramatization were most interesting (or exciting, sad, or other predominant emotion)?" or "When were the characters most believable?"

When the evaluation is made, it is best to use the characters' names rather than the children's names. This practice can be encouraged when children comment on their own playing or when speaking about the contributions of others.

TEACHER: The *king* really seemed to care about his subjects.
CHILD 1:   The *soldiers* all talked at the same time. I think they should wait for each other.
CHILD 2:   I spoke the *captain's* orders in a gruff voice, but I tried to show that he was a kind person by smiling just a little.

Replaying the Story

During evaluation, additional ideas may be suggested and incorporated into replayings. You and the class may find ways to include sound effects, lighting, or music that the children can operate for themselves.

Consider alternative procedures for replayings after the children have become familiar with the story. For example, middle and older grade children, particularly, may be able to divide into smaller groups, each presenting its own rendition of a replaying. Some children become fascinated with the narrator role and ask to play that part. These changes and additions should grow out of group creative process, facilitated, rather than imposed, by you.

CIRCLE STORY DRAMATIZATION

Many stories can be dramatized easily and quickly using a method I call *circle story dramatization*. The name has been given for two reasons: The stories have a circular pattern and the staging is circular. This method emphasizes involving all the students in playing the basic plot of the story in an orderly manner. In a sense, this method is rather like organizing a game, since less emphasis is given to the more subtle points of dramatization.

Circle story dramatization is very suitable for young children, who want to play as many parts as they can and act out all the action and excitement immediately. Even for many older groups this technique can be useful, especially if the students are eager to see quick results in their efforts at making a play.

One type of story that fits this method has one or two main characters and an indefinite number of one other character type. The characters are often stereotypical, with little variation in personality. For example, in "The Conjure Wives" (see end-of-chapter bibliography), there is a voice and perhaps a leader witch, but all the rest of the characters are simply a group of greedy witches.

Another type of story that fits the circle story method particularly well is the cumulative story. Often one or two main characters interact with different characters in successive incidents. The dialogue is frequently repetitive. "Henny Penny" is a classic example of this type.

Some stories have cumulative episodes within them, making them suitable for circle story dramatization. Dr. Seuss's *Bartholomew and the Oobleck*, for example, becomes cumulative when Bartholomew goes off in search of a solution to the oobleck problem. Jay Williams's *Petronella* must complete three tasks, for which she is given three magical gifts. These stories are more complex, often having more scenes and characters that are more fully developed. These features make the stories of interest to middle to older children. Yet their structure permits some circular arrangements to make for easier staging.

For circular staging, seats may be placed in a circle, students may sit in a circle on a carpeted area, or the action may take place in the circle around the outer aisles of the room. Even the most active students understand and sense order in a circle, which aids class management.

In playing circle stories, you, with perhaps one or two other students, assist in playing the main part initially. The rest of the children are cast in the roles of the other characters and placed in the circle arangement according to their appearance in the story. If you want maximum control with a simple story, you can probably keep the majority of characters seated in the circle throughout the story. For example, in *Where the Wild Things Are*, children can become the trees that grow in Max's bedroom, then hold hands and make the waves of the ocean, and finally become the Wild Things, all while remaining in a circle.

Extension activities may be added to circle story dramatization using any of the techniques presented throughout this text. These activities explore the story in greater depth or extend the story's implications. Sometimes these activities cover related curricular areas, such as writing.

Sample Outlines for Circle Story Dramatization

Following are sample outlines for two circle stories with some extension activities. They are not intended to be prescriptive but are descriptions of what has been done with children. Feel free to add your own touches to the suggestions and to adapt the methods to similar and favorite stories of your own.

FAT CAT
by Jack Kent
(New York: Parents' Magazine Press, 1971)

Synopsis

In this Danish tale, an old woman leaves her pot of gruel in the care of her cat. Instead of just watching the pot, he eats the gruel and the pot. When the old woman returns and complains, he eats her, too. As he goes for a walk, he meets various characters whom he also eats. He finally meets his match when he encounters the woodcutter, who slices him open, frees all the eaten characters, and bandages the cat's stomach.

Selected Variants

"The Cat and the Parrot," Sara Cone Bryant (29).[1] This variant is from India.

The Greedy Fat Old Man, Paul Galdone. New York: Clarion, 1983. Called an American tale, this variant replaces the cat with a fat man who falls from a tree and shatters into pieces at the end.

"Kuratko, the Terrible," in *The Shepherd's Nosegay,* retold by Parker Fillmore, edited by Katherine Love. New York: Harcourt, Brace and Company, 1958. In this Czech version, Kuratko is a chicken adopted by an old couple as their child. He grows up to have an insatiable appetite, eating everyone in sight. A cat comes to the rescue and receives the chick to eat as his prize.

Presenting the story

Read the story and show the pictures. Allow the children to join in the refrain, "What have you been eating, my little cat? You are so fat." You might also want to let them chant the cat's repeated listing of all the people he has eaten. This will be good rehearsal for the dialogue and for remembering the characters and the order of their appearance in the dramatization. Be sure to notice the last picture, without text, where two Band-aids are on the cat's stomach.

Casting

Fat Cat: You play the cat along with two other children.

Old Woman, Pot, Skohottentot, Skolinkenlot, Lady with pink parasol,

---

[1] Numbers in parentheses refer to the numbered anthologies and books listed in this text's final bibliography.

After children are familiar with a story, the leader can play a minor role. . .

Parson, Woodcutter: These may all be double-cast.

Birds in a Flock and Girls Dancing: Any number.

Setting the stage

Seat the children in a circle. Two children who are the pot face each other in the middle of the circle and join hands to make the shape of the pot. The two old women are next to the pot. The cats are nearby napping on the floor.

Playing the story

Note: The following script outline is intended to help you see possibilities, *not* to dictate how the story must be played. As much as possible, the children should carry the story.

Narrate an opening: "Once there was an old woman who was cooking some gruel in a pot while her cat slept nearby."

Cat: "Ummm, that smells good, old woman." (to other cats) "Doesn't that smell like the best pot of gruel the old woman has cooked in a long time?" (After the Old Woman leaves, cats pretend to eat the gruel.) "Yum, yum, this is so good. I just have to have some more." (Discover the pot is empty.) "Oh, my, it's all gone." (One of the cats will probably suggest eating the pot. You might pretend at first that it sounds absurd to you.) "Eat the pot? On top of a full stomach? Nawww." (suddenly) "Okay, why not?"

(After eating the pot, line up the cats. Have them put their arms around each other's waists. Put the two children playing the pot behind the cats to signify they have been eaten. You stand behind the cats, giving them the lead.) "Oh, look, here comes the Old Woman. We could be in big trouble."

. . . or let the children take over by themselves. ("The Cat and the Parrot")

(The Old Women returns and asks where the gruel is. The cats say they ate it and that they are now going to eat the Old Woman, too.) "Do you have anything to say before we eat you?" (Add the Old Woman to the lineup.)

Cat: "Umm, I'm feeling a bit full. How are you feeling? Let's go for a little walk. That should help settle our stomachs." (Lead the lineup around the circle. Hold your stomach and pretend to have a little trouble walking.) "Hello, Skohottentot." (Lead children in the chant: "What have you been eating, my little cat? You are so fat." Lead the cats in saying what has been eaten.) "We ate . . . and now we are going to eat YOU." (Add Skohottentot to the lineup.)

Follow the above pattern for the rest of the characters:

Skolinkenlot
five birds
seven girls dancing
lady with the pink parasol
parson with a crooked staff

Cat: (As you get bigger, walk slower and heavier; the children will follow your lead. Comment on how full you feel.) "Oh, dear, I don't think I could eat another thing." (polite burp) "Excuse me." (If the children who have been eaten tend to get a little noisy, stop for a moment.) "Oh, oh. Our stomach is getting a bit too rumbly. We'll have to stop and sit down for a moment until it settles down." (Pretend to pop an antacid tablet or a mint in your mouth. This usually calms the children down so that you can proceed.)

(Cat meets the Woodcutter. Chant repeats. When the cat says he is going to eat the Woodcutter, the latter cuts the cat's stomach open with the axe.)

Narrate, if needed, to control Woodcutter's actions: "The Woodcutter raised his axe high and slowly and carefully sliced open the cat's stomach." (You and the cats hold on to each other and slowly sink down to the ground.

The rest of the characters, since they are in your stomach, will probably sink with you.)

Narrate to control, if needed: "And when the woodcutter cut the cat's stomach open, out came the parson with the crooked staff, who went back to his church (seat); the lady with the pink parasol, who went back to her park bench; the seven girls dancing, who went back to their playground; the five birds in a flock, who went back to their roost; Skolinkenlot and Skohottentot, who went back to their homes; and last, the old woman came out with the pot and took it home. And the cat? Well, let's see." (To cats on the floor.) "How are you feeling?" (Commiserate with them. If the Woodcutter does not offer a bandage, as is shown in the last picture of the book, encourage the cats to ask him for help. Be contrite.) "Oh, sir. We do hate to trouble you, but would you have a couple of little Band-aids we could borrow?" (with relief) "Thank you." (Patch yourselves up.) "Ah, there, that's better. I don't think we need to eat any dinner tonight, do you?"

Narrate ending: "And that's the story of the Fat Cat." (Lead everyone in applause.)

Extensions

Creative movement. Create a dance for the seven dancing girls.

Verbal solo. "You are the old woman. Give us your recipe for gruel. Why do you think the cat was so attracted to it?"

Leader-in-role. The Old Woman is concerned. As much as she would like to keep her cat, he's eating her out of house and home. But who can she give him to? She insists he must be treated well. And with his eating talents, surely he ought to be able to perform some worthwhile service. What ideas do the children have?

Character panel interview or paired interviews. Fat Cat's experience was written up in the newspaper and now he is a celebrity. *Cat Lovers' Magazine* wants to interview him, and there is even some talk that a movie might be made of his life. Reporters are here to find out more about him. Afterward the interviews may be written up as newspaper articles.

BARTHOLOMEW AND THE OOBLECK
by Dr. Seuss
(New York: Random House, 1949)

This story has a more complex plot and greater variety of characters than "Fat Cat," yet the circle method still works. We have used the story with children in second grade through middle school, though obviously the older students are able to bring more embellishments to it. A few additional activities are presented in this sample plan for illustrative purposes. The story is used again on pages 245–47 with the segmented story dramatization method so you can compare the two methods.

Synopsis

King Derwin of Didd complains to his page boy, Bartholomew, that he is bored with the weather. The problem is turned over to the magicians, who suggest that "oobleck" would be a good solution, though they have never made it before. As the oobleck begins to fall the following morning, the king is delighted and declares a holiday. But the joyousness is short-lived when it is discovered that the oobleck is green, sticky, and falling in greater abundance hourly. Only the king's magic words "I'm sorry" stop the oobleck and restore sanity to the Kingdom once again.

Introduction

Option A.   Begin with a discussion of sticky substances. "What is the stickiest thing you can think of?" "Did you ever get stuck in something really sticky?" Children might share experiences of times they got gum stuck in their hair or walked on hot, sticky tar or ate sticky candy.

Option B.   Discuss things children may have wished for that did not turn out as well as they had thought. Children might share experiences of times they got toys, articles of clothing, or food products that were not as good as had been advertised or a trip they took that turned out less than satisfactory.

Warm-up activity

Option A.   "Let's pretend that you have something on your desks, a little substance of some sort, and you try to brush it away. Whoops, it sticks to your hand. No problem, just brush it away with both hands. Uh-oh, your hands stick together. Try to pull them apart. Now what can you do?" Here you might want to let the children suggest some ways to get their hands unstuck, try them, and see what might work. Children might hold one arm around their heads or neck and pull mightily; some might step on a hand; some might blow warm air on their hands to soften the substance. You can also narrate a few more tries, getting the children more stuck to other parts of their body until they are totally stuck to themselves. Then wave your "wand of unstickiness" and set them free. Or if they get unstuck themselves, you can congratulate them on their cleverness.

Option B.   Do a count-and-freeze pantomime of acting out a wish that turns bad. Or, if you prefer, small groups can present scenes demonstrating one student's experience.

Presenting the story

Tell the story to simplify the dialogue. You might want to show the pictures as you tell it.

Casting

Bartholomew: You can play Bartholomew with perhaps one or two other students. (I use a boy and a girl to demonstrate nonsexism.)

Magicians: Three to five students.

Bell Ringer, Trumpet Blower, Captain of the Guard: Three students for each.

King: Two can play this role; or if you prefer, use a king and a prime minister or a king and queen.

Townspeople and People in the Palace: The rest of the children can be divided into these roles. The book's illustrations show various occupations in the kingdom, and mention is made specifically of musicians, the laundress, and a cook in the palace. You may invent others. Students will feel special if you let them choose an occupation. Tell them to be acting out their routine tasks when they become stuck in the oobleck.

Setting the stage

Place the students around the room in the circular pattern. The throne room is at the front of the classroom. On the king's right (as he sits on his throne) are the magicians in corner #1 as if "offstage." On the king's left in corner #2 are the three bell ringers. In the back of the room are the three trumpet blowers (corner #3) and the three captains of the guard (corner #4). Seated at the back desks are the people of the kingdom, and at the front desks are the people of the palace.

Playing the story

Note: As before, the following script outline is intended to help you see possibilities, *not* to dictate how the story must be played.

Narrate an opening: "Once upon a time, in the kingdom of Didd, there lived King Derwin who was bored with the weather. One day he was overheard complaining to his pages."

(option) *Bartholomew:* (to King Derwin) "Your majesty, isn't it a beautiful day today? Just look at that sun!" (Bartholomew and the king discuss the weather. If the king does not remember to call the magicians, Bartholomew can suggest it.) "If you're sure you want the magicians, your majesty, we'll whistle for them." (Get the special whistle that only the magicians can hear. Escort them to the throne room with the admonition to bow before speaking to the king. The dialogue between the magicians and the king is simple enough, but if needed, you can explain to the magicians what it is the king wants. Escort them back to their work place.)

Narrate: "And so the magicians went to work making oobleck while everyone else in the kingdom went to sleep." (If they need help thinking of actions to perform, narrate how they take down bottles from the shelves, pour and stir the different ingredients, whisper magic chants, and so on.) "They worked far into the night and finally they finished with their task and went to sleep. The following morning, the king got up early and looked out the window and was delighted with what he saw." (Pause in case the king has something to say.) "But Bartholomew woke up, looked out the window, and wasn't sure how to react."

Bartholomew: (ad lib with the other Bartholomews) "Gosh, do you see what I see? What do you think? I wonder what the king thinks about it."

The magicians work long into the night creating "oobleck."

Report to the king, exchange dialogue about declaring a holiday, and make your way over to the bell ringers. You might pretend you have to wake them up. Encourage the other Bartholomews to knock at the door (repeat in other corners). The bell ringers will not be able to ring the bell because of the oobleck. You try to help, but nothing works. Everyone now realizes there is no cause for a holiday. Instead you must warn the people of the kingdom about the danger.

Urgency grows as the oobleck falls harder and faster. Pretend you have to be careful where you walk as the oobleck is increasing. Go to the trumpet blowers to ask them to sound the trumpet warning. Students usually remember that oobleck gets stuck in the trumpet. So, off to the captain of the guard to call out the king's army. The captains usually remember to eat the oobleck to show they aren't afraid of it.

Your job as Bartholomew is to keep asking for help and be surprised when oobleck gets in the way. Standard lines such as, "Somebody has to do something" or "Uhh, I don't think I'd do that if I were you" will probably come naturally to you as the students play their parts.

You may need to suggest returning to the palace. As you go past the back desks in the classroom, comment on the various people in the kingdom, the jobs you see them doing, and how they are stuck in oobleck. Stop and talk briefly to a few. "What were you doing at the moment it started to fall?" "How long have you been stuck like this?" "We're trying to get help." "Yes, it's another one of the king's ideas."

Repeat with the people of the palace at the front desks.

As you go to the throne room the king (and partner) will be stuck. Encourage the Bartholomews to tell how bad things are in the kingdom. The king tries to think of some magic words. Bartholomew loses patience with him.

Bartholomew: "You've got to do something. And if you don't you're not fit to be a king at all." (Turn to leave.)

Trumpet blowers try to get the "oobleck" out of their instruments.

Narrate: (if the King needs help) "And if you listened closely, you could hear the king say softly, 'I'm sorry.'"

Bartholomew: (ad lib to the other pages) "Did you hear what I heard? Did he really say he's sorry? Look! The oobleck's melting!"

Narrate an ending: "And no one knows why, but as soon as those magic words 'I'm sorry' were spoken, the oobleck began to melt. And then there was cause to celebrate." (Involve everyone in a final moment.) "The bells rang, the trumpets blew, and the guards marched, and everyone cheered ("Hip, hip, hooray!") in honor of the day the oobleck came *and went.*"

Lead the class in applause for themselves.

Quieting activity

Have children stand at the side of their desks. Say, "As the king said those magic words, 'I'm sorry,' no one knows why, but the oobleck started to melt. Just like snow on a warm, sunny winter day, the oobleck got smaller and smaller until it disappeared completely, bit by bit. And, now, as I count to three you will melt like a piece of oobleck into your desks." (music optional)

Extensions

See the additional activities for this story in the next section.

SEGMENTED STORY DRAMATIZATION

Another method of story dramatization I call *segmented story dramatization.* For segmented story dramatization, a story or even an entire book becomes a stimulus for creating numerous separate (or segmented) drama activities.

Technically speaking, any piece of literature or topic can be handled with this method.

The method has evolved from two basic sources. First, as is commonly done in the rehearsal of a play, the script is worked on part by part. Similarly, segmenting a story breaks it down into more workable rehearsal units. The segmented activities are the same as those that have been described in preceding chapters.

The second source for segmented story dramatization comes from improvisational theatre techniques that encourage in-depth exploration of characters and situations. As is true with improvisation, many of the activities in segmented story dramatization (see the sample lessons beginning on page 245) extend beyond the original story line and may introduce new characters or new situations. For example, in "The Emperor's New Clothes," there is a solo verbal activity which asks the emperor's mother (an invented character never mentioned in the original story) how her son became so interested in clothes and whether he has always acted the way he does now. Such an activity encourages children to explore the many possible dimensions of the story characters and the motivations for their behavior. A student, pretending to be the emperor's mother, for example, may answer that the royal family once fell on hard times and the emperor, as a child, really had only one change of clothing. Now he seems to be trying to make up for his earlier deprivation. Another student might explain that her son has always enjoyed clothes. In fact, as a baby he cried to have his diapers changed even when they did not need to be; and as a toddler he would cry if his outfits were not changed each hour.

Creating and Wording Segmented Activities

In segmented story dramatization, both pantomime and verbal activities are developed. Each of these categories is subdivided into solo and then pair and group activities. This grouping makes it easier to see what the activities' basic requirements are and to help you sequence them from the easier to the more difficult.

The number of activities you develop will depend on your own inventiveness as well as on the children's interests and abilities. The children may have their own ideas to add, too. Since you will often have an abundance of ideas, each story will probably provide material for several lessons.

Generally the activities in the sample provided are worded simply and briefly and can be stated as instructions in their present form. In some instances you may need to add side-coaching instructions or other elaborations as you see the children's response to them.

Even though brief, the activities include careful wording to make them intriguing. For example, the words *special* and *urgent* lend significance to the activity so that students become more involved. The wording frequently includes cues to signal playing and other management controls. For example, students may be instructed to play while the leader counts, the music plays, the drum beats, or the tambourine rattles. And, finally, in the dialogue activities there are often conflicts to solve, a useful technique (see Chapter 8) in encouraging dialogue flow.

Use with Younger and Older Children

Younger children, who are more interested in seeing things in "wholes," may not be interested in extended playing of segmented activities. They will, however, enjoy the additional challenges of a few of these activities combined with circle story dramatization.

Older students are able to bring many creative ideas to these activities. They find them challenging and react to them as they might to new games to play and new puzzles to solve. For them, especially as they become more experienced, you will be able to offer an activity and let them work it out on their own. They will even have ideas of their own to suggest for activities.

Playing the Activities

It is generally best to begin by playing some solo activities, both pantomime and verbal, at the desk. They often serve as a warm-up to the pair and group activities. For pantomime solos, the students all play simultaneously. Many of these are brief scenes that benefit from the addition of musical background or side-coaching.

The verbal solos are usually short responses of a sentence or two. For these you can call on as many volunteers as you wish. Some children will be able to deliver quite a lengthy speech, however, so you may need to limit some of the responses ("Tell us in just one sentence"). If there are more volunteers than you have time for, try pairing the students and letting them share their ideas with each other. You may wish to play a role in the verbal solos, perhaps as a newspaper interviewer or other information seeker, in order to give students a person to respond to. As you play, you will probably think of additional interview questions to ask, giving further challenge to the students. As the children see these interviews being modeled, they may ask to play the role of the interviewer themselves. If so, just change the activity to a paired interview. Likewise paired interviews might inspire character panel interviews.

For the pair and group verbal activities, follow the procedures discussed in Chapters 8 and 9. Some of the more complex group activities may take an entire drama period to complete.

Most students will probably want to play all the pair and group activities eventually, especially if the activities are intriguing and creatively challenging. As an alternative procedure, to be used only if students are experienced, you may let individual pairs and groups select their own activities to work on independently.

To end the drama period, you might select a pantomime solo activity at the desk for a quieting experience.

It is possible to select favorite activities, arrange them chronologically according to the story, and create an improvised play. However, the exploration into the various aspects of the story through the activities themselves is often satisfying by itself.

BARTHOLOMEW AND THE OOBLECK
(segmented story dramatization)

(*Note:* See pages 238–42 for the story synopsis and for the circle story method of playing this same story.)

Pantomime solo

Simple pantomime. "You are Bartholomew blowing the whistle that only the magicians can hear." (Take it from its special hanging place, blow some of the dust off it, now blow, and so on.)

Simple pantomime. "You are the bell ringer trying to ring the bell that is stuck in oobleck; now be the trumpet blower trying to play your horn even though a large blob of oobleck just fell into it; and now you're the vain captain of the guard combing your moustache very carefully with a tiny moustache comb."

Slow motion. "You are a small drop of oobleck. As I count to ten, grow slowly into one big blob and begin to ooze out of your desk. When I reach ten, become a frozen blob of oobleck."

Simple Pantomime/Frozen picture. "You are a villager working at your occupation. As the oobleck starts to fall, you try to continue your work in spite of increasing difficulty. By the time the music comes to an end, you will become completely frozen."

Sensory pantomime. "Be Bartholomew investigating the first piece of oobleck to fall from the sky. Use all your senses (sight, touch, taste, smell, hearing) in examining it." (Discuss reactions.)

Simple pantomime. "Be the king seeing the first drops of oobleck falling; now be Bartholomew seeing the oobleck fall. How or why did your reactions differ?"

Verbal solo

Interview. "You are Bartholomew. Explain to us what it is like working for King Derwin. What do you like the most about your job? What do you like the least?" (Leader could pretend to be a reporter or perhaps a family member back home.)

Interview. "You are King Derwin of Didd. Why is it so important to you to have a change in the weather? What other things bore you?"

Interview. "You are King Derwin's mother or father. He seems to be bored with many things. What was he like as a child growing up?"

Oral presentation. "You are one of the magicians. Explain the positive qualities of oobleck now that you have created it."

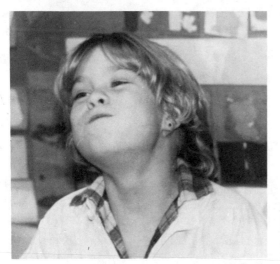

"You are the captain of the guard tasting and then eating the oobleck. Your mouth gets stuck, but you still try to say one very important sentence. What is it?"

One-liner. "You are the captain of the guard tasting and then eating the oobleck. Your mouth gets stuck, but you still try to say one very important sentence. What is it?"

Oral presentation. "You are a weather forecaster for the Kingdom of Didd. You do not know the story of the oobleck, but you notice that the weather patterns appear to be different tonight. Give your report."

Pantomime in pairs and groups

Mirror activity. "In pairs, one of you will mirror the captain getting ready for work in the morning, combing his hair, his moustache, shaving, and so forth." Switch roles.

Count-and-freeze pantomime. "You are one of the people living in the Kingdom of Didd. Think of an appropriate occupation for yourself. As I count to ten, you will perform your duties and slowly become stuck. We will guess what job you are doing."

Build-a-place pantomime. "Create a room for King Derwin of Didd. Remember that he is often bored, so there are probably a lot of things in the palace for his amusement."

Frozen picture. "Create frozen pictures of the various scenes you think might have happened when all the people became stuck in oobleck."

Verbal activities in pairs and groups

Discussion. "The magicians have a discussion over what kind of weather to make. In addition to oobleck, they find that there are some other possibilities in their book of magic that sound even more interesting. Let's hear some of that discussion in groups of five."

Improvised scene. "Suppose the king has called on the magicians to help with another problem he has. And suppose the results are as disastrous as the oobleck incident. In groups of five prepare a brief scene showing what the king's other problem was and what happened that time."

Simple debate. "A secret meeting has been called. Two factions of the kingdom of Didd discuss the possible dethronement of King Derwin. One faction believes the king has exercised poor judgment on too many occasions; the other feels that the king has many good qualities. Let us hear some of that debate." Divide the class into two groups. You play a mediating role, perhaps as Bartholomew or a prime minister.

Simple debate. "The children and the adults of the kingdom of Didd are not in agreement about the oobleck. The children have found it to be fun and interesting, while the adults find it intolerable. What arguments does each side have?"

Experts' panel interview. Oobleck exterminators are being questioned by townspeople and members of the court about the details of their work.

Leader-in-role/Advisory groups. "The king is in desperate need of your advice. As you know we have a large supply of oobleck that will not melt. What can be done to get rid of it? (or: "What new uses can it be put to?") Please give this urgent matter your attention. I shall return for your answer soon." Divide class into several small groups.

Character panel interview. "The magicians have been ordered to appear before a higher court of magicians because of their role in the disastrous oobleck incident. What are their reasons for doing what they did? The higher court will vote whether to judge them innocent of wrongdoing or to revoke their magician's license."

Related activities

1. "You are the castle minstrels. Create a ballad of the oobleck story." Use "Greensleeves" melody, "Scarborough Fair," or another ballad tune students may be familiar with.
2. "Prepare some pages of the magicians' magic book. Include a recipe for oobleck."
3. "Write an entry for Bartholomew's diary about the day the oobleck fell. Also write an entry for the following day."
4. "King Derwin has decided to make an apology to the kingdom. Pretend you are the king and write the apology."

THE EMPEROR'S NEW CLOTHES
by Hans Christian Andersen

Selected sources

The Emperor's New Clothes, translated and illustrated by Erik Blegvad. New York: Doubleday, 1974. Small ink drawings, alternating black and white pictures with full color ones.

The Emperor's New Clothes, retold by Riki Levinson. New York: Reading, Dutton, 1991. The illustrations by Robert Byrd depict animal characters; the emperor is a lion.

See also (12,23,36,39).

Variant

The Principal's New Clothes, Stephanie Calmenson. New York: Scholastic, 1989. In this retelling of the Andersen tale, a clothes-conscious school principal is tricked into wearing his T-shirt and shorts to school but is a good sport about it.

Synopsis

A vain emperor, who is particularly fond of his wardrobe, is visited by two rogues posing as weavers. They claim to be able to weave fabric invisible to those unworthy of the office they hold. Of course, all pretend to see the imaginary fabric in order not to lose their jobs. A parade is held to show off the emperor's new clothes, but only when a small child innocently calls out, "But the king has nothing on!" do the people finally realize the swindle and their own gullibility.

Pantomime (solo at desks)

Frozen picture. "You are the emperor who loves clothes, and you are posing for your latest portrait. How will you pose to show off all the new garments you're wearing? As I count to five, pose in five different positions that will show the garments to best advantage."

Frozen picture. "You are the emperor, proudly walking in the procession, listening to all the appreciative comments of the admiring crowd. Then you hear the voice of the child saying you have no clothes on. You freeze. How will you look? After you've paraded a few moments (in place), I'll say the child's line and stop the music. That will be your cue to freeze." (Play processional music.)

Quieting activity. "The rogues wove their cloth at night by candlelight. Be one of the candles slowly melting and then burning out as daybreak approaches."

Slow motion. "Suppose that when the emperor doesn't get his way, he throws a temper tantrum. Demonstrate one of his temper tantrums—silently and in slow motion as I count to ten."

Creative pantomime. "The emperor returns to his palace after the procession. Think of how he must feel, and then think of three things he might do. As I count to three, pantomime each of your three ideas."

Verbal (solo at desks)

Interview. "Suppose you are the emperor's son or daughter. What birthday present are you getting for your father this year? How do you know he'll like it?"

Interview. "Suppose you're the emperor's mother or father. How did your son get so interested in clothes? Has he always been like this?"

Oral Presentation. "You are one of the rogues, giving your description of the fabric you have woven. You might include comments on the lovely patterns, the careful attention to detail, the unusual color combinations, and so forth. Give us your sales pitch."

Pantomime in pairs and groups

Creative pantomime. "You are the two swindlers setting up your loom. You're unpacking it and setting it up carefully for this special job. The court is watching you, so look professional."

Mechanical movement. "In groups of eight to ten, create and become the special loom on which the marvelous fabric is to be woven."

Creative pantomime. "You are the swindlers putting on a good show of how diligently and carefully you work at weaving, cutting out, and sewing these garments. As the music plays, put on your best performance."

Creative pantomime. "You are the rogues when you are certain that no one is watching you work. What will you do to pass the time and to entertain yourself, locked up in the workroom?"

Mirror activity. The emperor is being dressed for the great procession by the two rogues. (Three mirrored by three.)

Frozen picture. "In groups of ten create a frozen picture of the procession during that crucial moment. Decide who each of you is and how you feel about it. As you are posed I will come around and tap you on the shoulder. At that moment you will say one thing you are thinking."

Conducting an orchestra. "The band is rehearsing for the procession. A conductor leads as you each play a different instrument." Use groups of six: one conductor and five band members. (March music such as Elgar's "Pomp and Circumstance" might be used.)

Verbal activities in pairs and groups

Improvised scene. "The emperor has learned his lesson about listening to clothes swindlers. But today new swindlers come to town. What will they try to sell to the emperor? Will it have unusual qualities as the special cloth did? Remember that the emperor may be harder to convince this time."

Improvised scene. "You are the old minister visiting the rogues. When you cannot see the material, you make up excuses. What are they? You'd like to leave but the rogues keep showing you more things to admire. How will you finally get away from them?"

Debate. "You are an official who is delegated to visit the weavers and see how the work is coming along. You don't trust them and you don't really believe their story, but you don't want to say so to the emperor. What else will you use as your excuse to the emperor to get out of going on this mission? He is very insistent."

Improvised scene. "Suppose the emperor's wife (or brother), who is given a meager supply of funds for clothing, would like a new outfit. She tries to get money from the minister of finance who claims no more money is available. The emperor's wife shows him her pitiful wardrobe as evidence that she needs a bigger clothes allowance. What other arguments will she give? How will the minister of finance handle her request?"

Improvised scene. "You are the citizens of the kingdom where the emperor spends huge sums on clothing. There are a number of community projects that need tending to. You go as a committee to the emperor to present your case on behalf of the kingdom. The emperor and his advisers reluctantly decide to fund one of the projects. Let's play the scene and find out how the emperor decides which project will be funded."

Debate. "The rogues have received an order of knighthood to wear in their buttonholes and the title of Gentlemen Weavers. Now that they have left the kingdom, they would like to sell this prize. They bargain with a used goods merchant for the best price they can get for this medal. The merchant is suspicious."

Debate. "The emperor has spent the entire kingdom's treasury on clothes for himself. Now he must go to the bank for a loan. He must try to convince the bank president that he will be a good credit risk. The bank president is a shrewd operator."

Improvised scene. "The kingdom's garment workers are exhausted from trying to keep up with all the new clothes orders the emperor demands. We hear them complaining as they work. The scene ends when they decide to go on strike." (groups of five)

"You are a clothing designer who has just designed a new outfit for the Emperor."

Debate. "You are a clothing designer who has just designed a new outfit for the emperor to wear. It is the most unusual design the emperor has ever seen. Convince the emperor to order this outfit from you, even though the emperor is not sure it's suited to him."

Character panel interview. "The emperor holds a press conference some time after the incident with the rogues. Reporters still have questions about what happened, but they must be diplomatic in asking them so as not to embarrass or anger the emperor. The emperor may enlist the aid of his minister or other officials in answering the questions."

Related activities

1. "Write out the parade marshal's plan for the procession. Who will be in it, what will be the parade route, and what will be the order of people in the procession?"
2. "You are one of the people in the emperor's kingdom. Write a letter to a friend in another kingdom, telling of the incident. Make it sound as if you knew all along about the swindle and were never taken in."
3. "Make a catalogue of clothing that the vain emperor would be attracted to. Draw the designs and describe their special features."

THE PHANTOM TOLLBOOTH
by Norton Juster
(New York: Random House, 1961)

Synopsis

Milo, a boy who is bored with school and with life, finds a mysterious package in his room. He opens it to find a tollbooth, a small electric car, and a curious map. Joined by a watchdog named Tock and a boastful Humbug, Milo travels to many lands and adventures. The three companions are able to restore the princesses, Rhyme and Reason, to the Kingdom of Wisdom and to reunite King Azaz of Dictionopolis and Mathemagician, his brother and the ruler of Digitopolis. In the process, Milo learns that there are a great many things that are exciting in life if one just takes the time to see and experience them.

(*Note:* The book emphasizes a great deal of play on words and mathematical references that require some sophistication to understand. A feature-length animated film version was made by Chuck Jones for Universal Studios in 1969.)

Pantomime solo

Creative pantomime. "Be the watchdog Tock carefully winding yourself with your left hind leg."

Sensory pantomime. "Pretend that you are picking off your initials from the letter tree and eating them. Use your face to show what they taste like. Are they sweet, sour, bitter, salty, mushy, hard, sticky, or cold?" Afterward students might explain their reasons for their interpretations.

Noiseless sounds. "The awful DYNNE expresses its emotions to extremes. As I count three, be the DYNNE (1) collapsing in a fit of hysterics, (2) sulking in the corner, and (3) sobbing uncontrollably. But each emotion is to be done in slow motion and without any sound."

Creative pantomime. "You are Milo almost ready to say the word *but*. Instead, you hold it in your mouth to drop it into the cannon as the ammunition that will break open the sounds for Silent Valley. While I count to five, pantomime how you think this might have looked."

Simple pantomime. "You are Canby. Let us see you being as tall as can be, short as can be; generous as can be, selfish as can be; strong as can be, weak as can be; graceful as can be, clumsy as can be; fast as can be, slow as can be; and happy as can be, sad as can be." Add other actions the students suggest.

Frozen picture. "You are the Dodecahedron with twelve sides or faces all showing different emotions. As I count to six let's see half of those faces one by one."

Verbal solo

Sound effects. "Be Milo sighing a deep sigh of boredom so great 'that a house sparrow singing nearby stopped and rushed home to be with his family.'"

Interview. "Milo is bored in spite of all the things he owns that he can play with. Tell us, Milo, what are some of the things you have and why don't you enjoy playing with them?"

Oral presentation. "The Whether Man welcomes Milo but speaks very fast and repeats everything several times. Pretend you're this person and let us hear one of your welcoming remarks to Milo and Tock."

Oral presentation. "The Lethargarians in The Doldrums have strange laws and a daily schedule they follow. Be one of the Lethargarians, speaking the way you think they might sound, explaining one thing about the way you live."

Storytelling in character. "Be the watchdog Tock who goes ticktick, not ticktock, all day. Tell us about the sad story of your name, becoming increasingly sad as you speak, until you are sobbing. I know it's painful for you to tell this story, so perhaps several of you could take turns." (Use the round-robin technique.)

Oral presentation. "Be one of the merchants in the Word Market. What are you selling and what is your sales pitch?"

Discussion. "Suppose we are all people who have landed on the Island of Conclusions. What conclusion did you jump to to get here? Does anyone have an idea for getting away from here?"

Sound effects.   After Milo's word was shot from the cannon and released the Soundkeeper's vaults, all the sound of history rushed forth. Read this paragraph in Chapter 13, and have each student imagine one sound or saying (like a one-liner) he or she thinks would have been released. Then wave the sound arrow over the class slowly from one side to another. As the arrow passes over them, the students say their sound or statement. You might want to try this a second time, letting the students continue to make their sound or repeat their saying, building in intensity and then settling back down as the sounds disappear over the hill and all returns to normal.

Oral presentation.   "At the end of the story the Humbug says he has arranged a lecture tour. Pretend you are the Humbug giving a small lecture. To whom will you speak and what will be your topic?" This activity could be done as a pantomime, since the Humbug is such a blustery fellow; or it might be a short speech delivered spontaneously or a prepared speech students take time to develop. Perhaps you will want to give students individual choices in these possibilities.

Pantomime in pairs and groups

Count-and-freeze pantomime.   "Milo meets many strange and unusual people on his journey. Select one, think of something he or she might do, and demonstrate it for us."

Count-and-freeze pantomime.   "Suppose the Terrible Trivium captured you. What neverending task will he have you do? Demonstrate your task."

Frozen picture.   "In groups of five create a frozen picture of one of the scenes in the book." Some possibilities are Milo assembling the Tollbooth with some children being the booth itself; Tock flying with Rhyme, Reason, Milo, and Humbug after the Castle in the Air is destroyed; scenes from the celebration carnival at the end; and so forth.

Conducting an orchestra.   Create the colorful symphony with all the imaginary instruments. Play a rainbow, a sunset, a storm, or any other scene you and the students decide upon. Even though the music is seen and not heard in the story, it might be helpful to play a selection from Grofé's *Grand Canyon Suite* or Respighi's *Pines of Rome* in the background. See if the entire class can be involved in this one. You or a student might be Chroma the Conductor. Another playing could be with Milo as conductor, losing control and causing a week's time to be played. Chopin's "Minute Waltz" might be useful for this second playing.

Walking game.   Whole class creates the main street in the city of Reality. Remember that there are crowds of people rushing along with their heads down or driving in cars and trucks, seeming to know where they are going and what they are doing, even though there are no buildings. Use the procedure explained on page 93, starting with just a few children, making sure they can move about without touching each other, and carefully adding a few people at a time until the entire class is participating. Music will help; play a fast piece or something at a fast speed. Khachaturian's "Sabre Dance" is one possibility.

Since this scene will change when Rhyme and Reason are returned, you might play it twice, with a "before" and an "after." The "after" scene will be much slower, of course, with people seeing and reacting to the world around them which should reappear as they react to it.

Without saying a word (p. 187). "In groups you are the people of Silent Valley creating a pantomime scene to explain to Milo in your own way what happened to your community to bring on the absence of sound."

Build-a-place pantomime. "Create Mathemagician's workshop, including some of the items mentioned in Chapter 15 as well as other ideas you may have."

Verbal activities in pairs and groups

Sound mime. Read the section in Chapter 11 where the awful DYNNE appears out of the bottle. Notice that it begins small and gets larger, growing hands and feet and a large frowning mouth. At the end it drinks what is in the bottle in three gulps. In pairs, one will be the DYNNE growing while the other creates the sound effects to go with it.

One-liners. "You are the people in the marketplace when the fight between Humbug and Spelling Bee upsets all the word stalls and everyone's speech becomes scrambled. Let us hear one of the comments you might say."

Character panel interview. "A panel of five will be King Azaz's advisers. Remember that you each give short answers, saying the same thing in slightly different ways. The interviewers will ask some simple questions of you. We'll rotate who answers first each time." Some questions might be "Do you feel important working for King Azaz?" "What's the best advice you've ever given to the king?" and "What is the most important word in the English language?"

Language liars' club. Have a panel of word experts guess the definitions of words. Use some words mentioned in the book such as *quagmire, flabbergast,* and *upholstery.*

Simple debate. "On one side of the debate are the people who grow down and on the other are the people who grow up. What advantages do you see for your condition?" Leader plays Milo and moderates.

Storytelling in character. All children pretend to be the Spelling Bee, creating a story using spelling words. Use round-robin storytelling, with each child adding on a sentence incorporating one spelling word. Example: "Once upon a time there was a king who lived in a castle (c-a-s-t-l-e)."

Sound effects. There are a number of interesting sounds in Chapter 11 that could be created. You might divide the class into small groups and assign them each a sound to create. For example: "a blindfolded octopus unwrapping a cellophane-covered bathtub"; "a square-wheeled steam roller riding over a street full of hard-boiled eggs"; "a handful of fingernails being scratched across a mile-long blackboard"; "a fast-moving freight train being derailed into a mountain of custard." Students could make up their own ideas to add to this list. You may wish to make an entire project of this chapter, working on many sounds individually and then reading it as a radio drama with sounds, tape recording it or performing it live.

Paired interview. "Milo, Tock, or Humbug are being interviewed by the Senses Taker. Remember that our heroes are anxious to escape from the demons that protect Ignorance, but the Senses Taker has an unending list of questions and must record the answers in five different places." (The Senses Taker's report could be carried into a writing activity.)

Dialogue guessing game. "Select two people in the story and create a conversation between them. The rest of us will try to determine who you are by what you say and how you say it. The people may or may not have met each other in the book, so the conversation can be invented. For example: Faintly Macabre does not speak with Officer Shrift in the book, but they could have an imaginary conversation for this activity."

Related activities

1. "Write a letter or a message that might have been sent to the Sound-keeper from one of the people in Silent Valley."
2. "Write a diary entry for Milo of one of the incidents he experienced."

FOR THE COLLEGE STUDENT

1. Select a story suitable for circle story dramatization. Refer to the following story bibliography or select your own. Plan out the dramatization using the sample outline format given in this chapter. Present the story to your classmates or to a group of children and lead them in the dramatization. Afterward, discuss the effectiveness of the activity with your classmates. What changes or alternative procedures might be used with the story?
2. Select a story or a book for segmented story dramatization. Refer to the following story bibliography or the list of books in the final bibliography, or select your own. Proceed as above, playing a representative sampling of the activities you design.

STORY BIBLIOGRAPHY

The following materials are arranged in alphabetical order by title. Numbers in parentheses correspond to numbered anthologies listed in this text's final bibliography. The following symbols are used to indicate the age level they might be best suited for:

Y   Young children in kindergarten, first, and second grades
M   Middle-grade children in third and fourth grades
O   Older children in fifth and sixth grades

*Y[2] "The Adventure of Three Little Rabbits," author untraceable (36). Little rabbits get stuck in some spilled syrup and almost become rabbit stew. Easy for circle story dramatization.

M–O *Aladdin and the Wonderful Lamp*, Carol Carrick. New York: Scholastic, 1989. This retelling of the old tale is beautifully illustrated and makes the classic tale more approachable for all ages. See also (12).

O "All Summer in a Day," Ray Bradbury (6). Children on Venus anxiously wait for the sun, which shines for only one hour every seven years.

*M *Anansi and the Moss Covered Rock*, retold by Eric A. Kimmel. New York: Holiday House, 1988. Anansi's trick with a rock that makes everyone faint backfires.

M *Anatole*, Eve Titus. New York: McGraw-Hill, 1956; Bantam, 1990. In this ever-popular story, a clever mouse becomes a cheese taster in Duval's cheese factory in France. Other *Anatole* stories are equally appealing.

M *Angus and the Mona Lisa*, Jacqueline Cooper. New York: Lothrop, Lee, & Shepard, 1981. Angus, a cat of French ancestry, gets into an adventure with Interpol and the theft of the Mona Lisa.

*Y *Are You My Mother?* P. D. Eastman. New York: Random House, 1960. A baby bird hatches and goes off in search of its mother, mistaking many things for her.

*Y *Ask Mr. Bear*, Marjorie Flack. New York: Macmillan, 1932, 1986. Danny seeks the help of animals for ideas of a birthday present for his mother in this picture book classic.

*M–O *The Bremen Town Musicians*, Paul Galdone. New York: McGraw-Hill, 1968. See also (3,4,25,29,36). On the way to Bremen to become musicians, four animals encounter a band of robbers and wealth to keep them secure the rest of their days. "Jack and the Robbers" in this bibliography is a variant of this tale.

O "The Case of the Sensational Scent," Robert McCloskey (61). Robbers, a suitcase containing $2,000, a skunk, and after-shave lotion create an unusual detective adventure for Homer Price.

*Y–M *The Cat on the Dovrefell: A Christmas Tale*, George Webbe Dasent. New York: G. P. Putnam's Sons, 1979. The trolls who visit Halvor mistake a bear for a cat. This picture book version by Tomie de Paola makes the story easy for young children to understand.

Y–M *The Cock, the Mouse, and the Little Red Hen*, Lorinda Bryan Cauley. New York: Putnam Publishing, 1982. This is a retelling of the story of the Little Red Hen who does all the work. In this version she saves the cock and the mouse from being the fox family's dinner.

*M "The Conjure Wives," Frances Wickes (36). Selfish witches are turned into owls in this story.

*Y–M *The Country Bunny and the Little Gold Shoes*, DuBose Heyward. Boston: Houghton Mifflin, 1937, 1974. This is an old favorite that has been reissued. A little country girl bunny proves that she can grow up to be an Easter Bunny. It can be played as a circle story, particularly for the scenes with the twenty-one little bunnies. Because it is a longer story, you will probably need more than one session to play it.

M *The Cuckoo's Reward*, Daisy Kouzel and Earl Thollander. New York: Double-

[2]Starred entries are suitable for circle story dramatization.

day, 1977. A cuckoo helps save the grain from fire in this Mexican folk tale. In Spanish, the story is *El Premio del Cuco,* also by Doubleday, 1977.

O *The Devil's Bridge,* Charles Scribner, Jr. New York: Charles Scribner's Sons, 1978. The devil promises the people of a French town that he will build them a bridge for the price of a human soul.

M–O "The Doughnuts," Robert McCloskey (3,29,61). Homer Price, an enterprising boy, has an adventure with a doughnut machine that just will not quit making doughnuts.

*Y–M *Drakestail,* Jan Wahl. New York: Greenwillow Books, 1978. See also (4). A very clever duck, with the help of some unusual friends, outwits a greedy ruler and becomes king in this traditional French folk tale.

O *Duffy and the Devil,* Harve Zemach. New York: Farrar, Straus & Giroux, 1973. A devilish imp, in the manner of Rumplestiltskin, helps Duffy, a servant girl, with her chores. She so impresses Squire Tovel that he marries her. And then the trouble begins.

M *The Elephant's Child,* Rudyard Kipling. New York: Walker, 1970. A little elephant, who has "'satiable curtiosity,'" finds out some answers to his questions but gets a long nose doing it in this mythical explanation of the elephant's trunk. See also (3,14).

*Y–M *The Elves and the Shoemaker,* Freya Littledale. New York: Four Winds Press, 1975. The age-old Grimm Brothers' tale of the poor shoemaker who was aided by kind elves. See also (25,39) and *The Shoemaker and the Elves* in this bibliography.

O *Everyone Knows What a Dragon Looks Like,* Jay Williams. New York, Four Winds Press, 1976. Only the road sweeper believes the old man who claims to be a dragon who can save the city from the Wild Horsemen of the North. "Things are not always what they seem."

M–O *The 500 Hats of Bartholomew Cubbins,* Dr. Seuss. New York: Random House, 1938, 1988. The remarkable adventure of a young boy whose hat won't come off in spite of the king's demands.

M–O *The Fool of the World and the Flying Ship,* retold by Arthur Ransome. New York: Farrar, Straus and Giroux, 1968. This Russian tale recounts the adventures of a family's youngest son, whom they consider a fool. Through kindness and the help of friends, he marries the czar's daughter. Uri Schulevitz's pictures won the Caldecott medal. See also (4).

*Y–M *Foolish Rabbit's Big Mistake,* Rafe Martin. New York: G. P. Putnam's Sons, 1985. This is a retelling of an East Indian tale similar to Henny Penny. Pictures by Ed Young make this a memorable edition.

*Y *The Gingerbread Boy,* Paul Galdone. New York: Seabury Press, 1975. See also (3,25). The classic story of the little cookie that runs away from all who chase him, until he meets a fox. Variants include *Journey Cake, Ho!* in this bibliography "Johnny-cake," (39); and "The Pancake," (3,29).

*M–O *The Golden Goose,* Jacob and Wilhelm Grimm. New York: North-South Books, 1988. The sight of many people stuck to Simpleton's goose makes a sad princess laugh; but her father won't give her in marriage until the lad accomplishes some difficult tasks. Compare the second half of the story to *The Fool of the World and the Flying Ship.* See also (4).

O *The Golem: A Jewish Legend,* Beverly McDermott. Philadelphia: J. B. Lippincott, 1976. A rabbi in Prague creates a clay figure to help suppress an uprising against the Jewish community.

Y–M *Hansel and Gretel,* Jakob and Wilhelm Grimm. Several translation/retellings in picture books include: Elizabeth Crawford/Lisbeth Zwerger (New York: William Morrow, 1979); Ruth Belov Gross/Winslow Pinney Pels (New York: Scholastic, 1988); Susan Jeffers (Dial Press, 1980); Rika Lesser/Paul O. Zelinsky (New York: Dodd Mead, 1984); and James Marshall (New York: Dial Press, 1990). The classic tale of two children who are left alone in the woods and encounter a witch. See also (23,40).

O *Harald and the Giant Knight,* Donald Carrick. New York: Clarion Books, 1982. In medieval times, knights take over Harald's father's farm for their training ground. Harald, who once admired the knights, scares them away with a huge reed knight. Sequel: *Harald and the Great Stag,* 1988.

M *Heckedy Peg,* Audrey Wood. New York: Harcourt, Brace Jovanovich, 1987. A mother must win back her seven children from a witch who has captured them.

*Y *Henny Penny,* Paul Galdone. New York: Seabury Press, 1968. The old tale of the hen who thinks the sky is falling when an acorn drops on her head. *Chicken Little* by Steven Kellogg (New York: William Morrow, 1985) is a modernized version older children will enjoy. See also (25,29).

M *Horton Hatches the Egg,* Dr. Seuss. New York: Random House, 1940. Horton, an elephant who hatches an egg for lazy Maizie bird in spite of numerous odds, is eventually rewarded for his faithfulness.

M *The House on 88th Street,* Bernard Waber. Boston: Houghton Mifflin, 1962. In this popular story, a crocodile who is more human than animal is discovered by a family who have just moved into their new home in New York. Other *Lyle* stories may be of interest also.

*M "How Jahdu Took Care of Trouble," Virginia Hamilton (1). In this African-American trickster tale, Jahdu outwits Trouble and frees everyone from the huge barrel they have been caught in.

M *How the Sun Made a Promise and Kept It,* Margery Bernstein. New York: Charles Scribner's Sons, 1974. In this retelling of a Canadian myth, the sun is captured and the animals take on the task of freeing it.

M *Jack and the Beanstalk,* Joseph Jacobs. Several outstanding picture books include Lorinda Bryan Cauley (New York: G. P. Putnam's Sons, 1983); John Howe (Boston: Little, Brown, 1989); Steven Kellogg (New York: William Morrow, 1991). See also Appalachian versions: *Jack and the Bean Tree,* Gail E. Haley (New York: Crown Publishers, 1986), and *Jack and the Wonder Beans,* James Still (New York: Putnam Publishing, 1977).

M–O "Jack and the Robbers," Richard C. Chase (13). This is an Appalachian version of "The Bremen Town Musicians."

*Y *Journey Cake Ho!* Ruth Sawyer. New York: Viking, 1953. The journey cake escapes Johnny as well as a variety of animals in this Appalachian retelling of "The Gingerbread Boy."

M–O *Kassim's Shoes,* Harold Berson. New York: Crown Publishers, 1977. Kassim finally agrees to throw out his old shoes but everyone keeps returning them.

*Y–M *King Bidgood's in the Bathtub,* Audrey Wood. New York: Harcourt Brace Jovanovich, 1985. The king loves his bath too much; the page boy is forced to pull the plug.

M *King Midas and the Golden Touch,* retold and illustrated by Kathryn Hewitt. New York: Harcourt Brace Jovanovich, 1987. This Greek mythological tale is of the king who loved gold too much for his own good. See also "The Golden Touch" (3,12,29,36).

*M–O   *The King's Fountain,* Lloyd Alexander. New York: E. P. Dutton, 1971. A king wants to build a fountain without understanding that it would cut off the water supply to the people. A poor man fails in his attempts to find someone to persuade the king to reconsider and must speak to the king himself.

O   *The King's Stilts,* Dr. Seuss. New York: Random House, 1939. When the king's stilts are stolen by the evil Lord Droon, the king becomes too depressed to protect the kingdom from its main enemy: large birds called Nizzards. Eric, the pageboy, comes to the rescue.

*M–O   "The King's Tower," Harold Courlander (28). In this Latin American tale, a foolish king desires to reach the moon.

*M–O   *The Lady Who Put Salt in Her Coffee,* Lucretia Hale, retold and illustrated by Amy Schwartz. San Diego: Harcourt Brace Jovanovich, 1989. This story, which originally appeared in a children's magazine over a hundred years ago, tells of the efforts of many people who try to change the taste of Mrs. Peterkin's coffee after she mistakenly puts salt in it.

M–O   *Legend of the Bluebonnet,* Tomie de Paola. New York: Putnam Publishing, 1983. A Comanche Indian tribe, in the midst of famine, is saved by the sacrifice of a young girl's warrior doll.

O   *The Legend of Sleepy Hollow,* Washington Irving, retold by Robert D. San Souci. New York; Doubleday, 1986. A trick is played on a schoolmaster who goes courting in this American legend.

M–O   *The Legend of William Tell,* Terry Small. New York: Bantam, 1991. The medieval Swiss legend of the brave marksman is told dramatically and with fine illustrations.

M   *Liang and the Magic Paintbrush,* Demi. New York: Holt, Rinehart and Winston, 1980. In this Chinese tale a young boy has a magic paintbrush he uses to help the poor and outwit a greedy king. Another version, *Tye May and the Magic Brush,* by Molly Bang (New York: Greenwillow Books, 1992), has a female hero.

*Y–M   *The Little Engine That Could,* retold by Watty Piper. New York: Platt & Munk, 1961; Scholastic, 1979. A little engine is able to take the stalled, larger train over the mountain to deliver toys.

*Y   *The Little Old Lady Who Was Not Afraid of Anything,* Linda Williams. New York: Thomas Y. Crowell, 1986. When a disassembled body cannot frighten a little woman, it becomes a scarecrow.

*Y   *The Little Rabbit Who Wanted Red Wings,* Carolyn Bailey. New York: Platt & Munk, 1978. A little rabbit discovers that what we wish for may not always be the best for us.

Y–M   *Lon Po Po: A Red-Riding Hood Story from China,* Ed Young. New York: Philomel, 1989. Three sisters outwit a persistent wolf in this Caldecott medal winner.

*Y–M   *Madeline,* Ludwig Bemelmans. New York: Viking Penguin, 1939; Puffin, 1977. Madeline lives in a Paris convent with eleven other little girls. After she is rushed to the hospital for an appendectomy, she becomes the envy of her friends.

M–O   *Many Moons,* James Thurber. New York: Viking Penguin, 1943, 1970. See also new edition with pictures by Marc Simont, 1991. Princess Lenore is ill from eating too many raspberry tarts but can be cured, she says, if she can have the moon. The court jester finds a solution.

*Y–M   *Mike Mulligan and His Steam Shovel,* Virginia Lee Burton. Boston: Houghton Mifflin, 1939, 1977. Mike Mulligan's unique solution to collecting the money for digging the basement of the town hall with his steam shovel, Mary Anne, makes an old story remain ever popular.

*Y *Millions of Cats,* Wanda Gag. New York: Coward-McCann, 1928, 1977. A little old man discovers many more cats than he expected to.

*Y *The Mitten,* Alvin Tresselt. New York: Lothrop, Lee & Shepard, 1964. A little boy's lost mitten becomes a haven for several animals until a Bear tries to enter. The circle can resemble a mitten's shape. Another version of the same title is by Jan Brett (New York: Putnam Publishing, 1989).

*Y–M *Mother Goose and the Sly Fox,* retold by Chris Conover. New York: Farrar, Straus, & Giroux,, 1989. In this handsome picture book, Mother Goose outwits a fox and saves her little goslings. Similar to "The Wolf and Seven Kids" by the Brothers Grimm.

M–O *Mufaro's Beautiful Daughters,* John Steptoe. New York: Lothrop, Lee & Shepard, 1987. This African tale resembles Cinderella with its two sisters, one spiteful and the other gracious, and a king who seeks a bride.

*Y *Mushroom in the Rain,* Mirra Ginsburg. New York: Macmillan, 1974. A mushroom expands when numerous animals seek shelter under it.

O *The Nightingale,* translated by Eva Le Gallienne. New York: Harper & Row, 1965. This Hans Christian Andersen tale is of the Chinese emperor who orders the nightingale to stay in court and sing its beautiful song.

M *No Help at All.* Betty Baker. New York: Greenwillow Books, 1978. This humorous Mayan Indian legend is about West Chac, the rain god of the West, who helps a young boy one day and then asks for his help in return. But everything the boy does is "no help at all," except by accident.

O *The Nose Tree,* Warwick Hutton. New York: Atheneum, 1981. A princess/witch tricks three poor soldiers out of special gifts they have received, until the young men use a few tricks of their own.

M–O *Of Cobblers and Kings,* Aure Sheldon. New York: Parent's Magazine Press, 1978. Because of his common sense, a cobbler rises from one important position to another until he becomes grand chancellor of his country—where the people no longer have shoes!

O "Old Dry Frye," Richard Chase (9). In this Appalachian folk tale, an old preacher dies accidentally, but everyone tries to get rid of the body, afraid they will be accused of his murder.

M–O "Old One Eye," Richard Chase (9). In this Appalachian story, an old lady unwittingly frightens robbers who plan to steal her money. It is fun to add a general store scene in the beginning where the robbers hear about the old lady's riches.

*Y–M *The Paper Bag Princess,* Robert N. Munsch. Toronto: Annick Press, 1980. A princess rescues a prince but decides not to marry him when he proves to be shallow.

*Y *A Pet for Mrs. Arbuckle,* Gwenda Smith. New York: Crown Publishers, 1981. A woman seeks a cat's advice in finding a perfect pet. After traveling the world over and interviewing all manner of exotic creatures, she settles on the cat who says, "I thought you'd never ask."

*O *Petronella,* Jay Williams. New York: Parent's Magazine Press, 1973. A princess rescues a prince in this turnabout tale.

*Y–M *Petunia,* Roger Duvosin (21). A goose thinks she has knowledge because she owns a book, even though she cannot read. Other *Petunia* stories are equally popular.

M–O *The Pied Piper of Hamelin,* retold by Sara and Stephen Corrin. New York: Harcourt Brace Jovanovich, 1988. An illustrated story version of Robert Browning's poem of the piper who rids the town of rats but who gets his revenge when the town refuses to pay. See also (4,12,29,40).

*Y–M *Quail Song,* Valerie Scho Carey. New York: G. P. Putnam's Sons, 1990. Coyote wants to learn Quail's song in this retelling of a Native American folk tale. Add more characters by having Quail's children and other animals.

O "The Quest of the Hammer," Abbie Farwell Brown (29,36). Thor, the strongest of the Norse gods, reluctantly dresses as a giant's bride in order to retrieve his magical hammer. For another version see "The Theft of Thor's Hammer," by Ingri and Edgar D'Aulaire in *D'Aulaires' Norse Gods and Giants* (Garden City, N.Y.: Doubleday, 1967).

M–O *Rip Van Winkle,* Washington Irving. Retellings with illustrations include John Howe (Boston: Little, Brown, 1988); and Thomas Locker (New York: Dial Press, 1988). The American tale of a man who falls asleep for twenty years to return to a world that has forgotten him. See also (36). Compare with "Urashima Taro and the Princess of the Sea" in this bibliography.

M *The Seven Chinese Brothers,* retold by Margaret Mahy. New York: Scholastic, 1990. Seven brothers with extraordinary powers punish a cruel emperor and free the people from his reign.

*Y–M *The Shoemaker and the Elves,* Cynthia and William Birrer. New York: Lothrop, Lee & Shepard, 1983. This age-old Grimm's story tells of the poor shoemaker who is aided by kindly elves. Another popular version is illustrated by Adrienne Adams (New York: Charles Scribner's Sons, 1960). See also *The Elves and the Shoemaker* in this bibliography.

O *Six Chinese Brothers,* Cheng Hon-tien. New York: Holt, Rinehart and Winston, 1979. Brothers who have special powers take the king's pearl to cure their ailing father. Because they look alike, they are able to trick the royal executioner and eventually gain the king's respect. Paper-cut illustrations accompany.

M–O *Snow White,* retold by Josephine Poole. New York: Alfred A. Knopf, 1991. The illustrations by Angela Barrett are realistically and richly drawn in dark colors in this Grimm Brothers classic tale.

M–O *The Sorcerer's Apprentice,* Inga More. New York: Macmillan, 1989. This beautifully illustrated picture book of a timeless legend tells of the apprentice who tampers with magic and creates more problems than he solves.

O *The Sorcerer's Scrapbook,* Michael Berenstain. New York: Random House, 1981. A wizard, a sorcery school dropout, tells his story of how he came to help a duke capture a unicorn. Told in a humorous way, the story gives some of the lore and myths of medieval times.

O *The Squire's Bride,* P. C. Asbjørnsen and Marcia Sewall. New York: Atheneum, 1975. See also (36). An old squire wants to marry a young woman who has other ideas. She tricks the squire's servants into dressing a donkey for the wedding.

M–O *The Stone in the Road,* Stephen Seskin. New York: Van Nostrand Reinhold, 1968. Efforts to find gold under a huge stone present this story's conflict. It has a medieval setting. See also "Stone in the Road," (36).

*M–O *Stone Soup,* Marcia Brown. New York: Charles Scribner's Sons, 1947. Three soldiers teach some villagers how to make soup out of stones, with a few vegetables and meat added for flavor.

*M–O *A Story—A Story,* Gail E. Haley. New York: Atheneum, 1970. In this African tale Anansi must capture and give to the sky god a leopard, hornets, and a dancing fairy whom men never see in order to have all stories be his.

*M *The Story of Jumping Mouse,* John Steptoe. New York: Lothrop, Lee & Shepard, 1984. In this retelling of a Native American legend, a young mouse travels to a far-off land. His hope and sacrifice carry him through many dangers, and he is eventually rewarded by being transformed into an eagle.

Y–M *The Story of the Three Little Pigs,* Joseph Jacobs. Attractive picture book versions include: Margot Zemach (New York: Farrar, Straus and Giroux, 1988); Erik Blegvad (New York: Atheneum, 1984); and James Marshall (New York: Dial Press, 1989). This is the story of two foolish pigs and one smart pig who outwit a greedy wolf. See also (25,39,40).

M–O *Striding Slippers,* Mirra Ginsburg. New York: Macmillan, 1978. A shepherd makes magical striding slippers to help him in his work, but those who steal them seem unable to control them. Students will love pretending that their shoes are walking where they themselves do not want to go.

*M *The Talking Eggs,* retold by Robert D. San Souci. New York: Dial Press, 1989. Kind Blanche receives riches while her greedy sister is punished in this Southern American tale. The eggs and the farm animals are as fun to play as any part.

Y *The Three Billy Goats Gruff,* Marcia Brown. San Diego: Harcourt Brace Jovanovich, 1957. This is the age-old story of the goats who outwit the troll under the bridge. Other picture book versions include: Paul Galdone (New

"Little pig, little pig, let me come in. . . ."

York: Clarion, 1973) and a modernized version Janet Stevens (New York: Harcourt Brace Jovanovich, 1987). See also (4,25,29,36,39).

O *Three Strong Women*, Claus Stamm. New York: Viking Penguin, 1962, 1990. In this Japanese tall tale, a wrestler meets his match with a strong family of women who train him to become a champion. Illustrations in the new edition are by Jean and Mou-Sien Tseng.

M *The Ugly Duckling*, Hans Christian Andersen, retold and illustrated by Lorinda Bryan Cauley. New York: Harcourt Brace Jovanovich, 1979. This is the touching story of a "duckling" who is rejected by all other animals until he happily discovers that he is actually a swan. See also (25,29).

M–O "Urashima Taro and the Princess of the Sea," Yoshiko Uchida (3,7). Urashima is enticed to live in the sea and spends much more time there than he at first imagines. This Japanese folk tale compares with "Rip Van Winkle." See narrated example in Chapter 5 of this text.

M–O *The Wave*, Margaret Hodges. Boston: Houghton Mifflin, 1964. In this Japanese story Grandfather knows a tidal wave will follow a small earthquake. He burns his rice fields to warn the unsuspecting villagers of the danger.

*Y *Where Can an Elephant Hide?* David McPhail. New York: Doubleday, 1979. Morris the Elephant wants to be able to hide like the other animals. But their methods of camouflage do not work for him.

*Y *Where the Wild Things Are*, Maurice Sendak. New York: Harper & Row, 1963, 1987. Max is sent to his room for punishment and imagines that he goes off to a land inhabited by Wild Things. Let children in the circle be the trees that grow in Max's bedroom, the ocean Max sails, and the Wild Things.

*M *Why Mosquitoes Buzz in People's Ears*, Verna Aardema. New York: Dial Press, 1975. This African tale demonstrates a domino effect when communication is misunderstood.

O "The Wise Old Woman," Yoshiko Uchida (30). In a Japanese village a cruel lord banishes anyone over age seventy-one from his village. A young

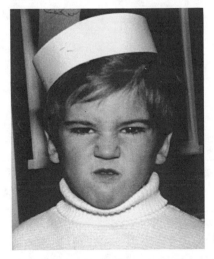

A "Wild Thing" gets ready to roar its terrible roar.

farmer disobeys and hides his mother, who later saves the village with her wisdom.

O "The Youth Who Wanted to Shiver," (Grimm) Eric Carle (8). A young man wonders what shivering is and goes through some harrowing experiences in order to find out. But only when he is doused with a pail full of minnows and cold water in his warm bed does he understand!

11

Leader-in-Role
and Role Drama

Throughout this text there are many examples of the teacher playing "a role." For example, in the brief activities on page 99 the leader momentarily pretends to be a toy-workshop manager in one instance and a garage mechanic in another. Roles are also suggested for some narrative pantomime stories on page 138. Even in story dramatization discussed in Chapter 10 the leader frequently plays a part. It has long been a recognized practice for the teacher to participate in drama with the children.

In recent years, however, creative drama in the United States has been greatly influenced by a British educational drama technique often called "leader-in-role" or "role drama."[1] Dorothy Heathcote, now retired from the University of Newcastle-upon-Tyne in England, is usually credited with developing the technique, while many others, including such scholar-practitioners as Gavin Bolton, Cecily O'Neill, Norah Morgan and Juliana Saxton, and Carole Tarlington and Patrick Verriour have further explained and adapted it.[2] This chapter will address the topics of leader-in-role and role drama, examining the philosophy and guidelines for its use.

[1]Morgan and Saxton explain that role drama is also known as "contextual drama, a role play or a drama structure." See Norah Morgan and Juliana Saxton, *Teaching Drama: A Mind of Many Workers*. (Portsmouth, N.H.: Heinemann Educational Books, 1987), p. 119. Tarlington and Verriour, among others, tend to use the terms *teacher-in-role* and *role drama* interchangeably. See Carole Tarlington and Patrick Verriour, *Role Drama* (Portsmouth, N.H.: Heinemann Educational Books, 1991), p. 9.

[2]Readers are encouraged to refer to additional sources in order to expand upon the

GENERAL CHARACTERISTICS OF LEADER-IN-ROLE

Whenever the leader plays a role, the students are usually playing roles also. For example, the teacher may be the leader of a spaceship expedition; the children might be the ship's crew. The leader's role may be lesser in status if he or she decides to play a second-in-command position or one of the crew. If the group is experienced, the leader may even allow one of the children to be the captain.

Whenever the leader plays a role in any drama activity, the underlying stance is that of a facilitator as opposed to an actor. In a sense it is like guiding and participating with students in an "enlarged" version of childhood dramatic play. Just as children might say to one another, "You be the storeowner and I'll be the customer" or "You be the robber and I'll be the cop," so does the leader signal a drama when he or she says:

> "I'll be the salesperson who comes to your door."
>
> "Would you like to be the newspaper reporter or the person being interviewed?"
>
> "Let's suppose you're Goldilocks and I'm your parent."

It is because of the leader's insight into the material's possibilities for dramatic encounters that children accept adults into their play, not that the leader brings "acting" into the drama. The concept of a leader not playing a role in the theatrical sense of the word may seem strange to those who think they are "supposed to act" in anything called drama. Some leaders mistakenly begin performing, perhaps in a stereotyped or showy manner. However, anyone falling into this trap will quickly learn that it is counterproductive. For one reason, children are more inclined to watch rather than participate when the teacher performs. They may become embarrassed, especially if the teacher overacts. And, even if the teacher is a skilled actor, there is the risk of intimidating the students. The moral is: Keep the role playing low-key and believable. Let the stories, situations, and activities themselves produce the drama.

The leader also uses the role to monitor the students' behavior, making requests or giving commands as part of the drama. For example,

> "All those who seek audience with the king must bow before His Majesty."
>
> "The rules of this wagon train are that we work together for the good of all. Those who are not committed to our journey endanger the lives of everyone else. Are we agreed to continue and to abide by the rules?"

This technique is generally more effective than the usual reprimands used in classroom management.

---

ideas presented here. See the "Drama in Education" section of the bibliography in Chapter 1 as well as other resources noted at the end of this chapter.

ROLE DRAMA—WHAT IS IT?

A role drama is a series of dramatic activities, most of which are leader-in-role, based on a single topic. In some ways it is like a lesson plan with multiple activities the leader chooses from as he or she sees the drama unfolding. It may also be described as a play that develops scene by scene. Consider the following:

MRS. FRISBY AND THE RATS OF NIMH

A fourth grade class has read *Mrs. Frisby and the Rats of NIMH* by Robert C. O'Brien (New York: Atheneum, 1971) and are beginning their drama explorations of it. Today the leader begins by asking the children if they can pretend to be the rats who have escaped from the labs at NIMH and are now living at the Fitzgibbon Farm planning their future. He will pretend to be a rat along with them. They agree, and he tells them, with a touch of mystery in his voice, that a letter has arrived for them. He reads the following:

N I M H
National Institute of Mental Health
1000 Maze Avenue
Government City, USA 10001

March 22, 1992
Resident Rat Colony
Fitzgibbon Farm

Dear Friends:

My assistants, Julie and George, join me in expressing our sincere concern at your sudden departure from our laboratory. Unfortunately, our studies were interrupted when you left.

Surely by now you realize the tremendous abilities we gave you—abilities you would never have had without our intervention. And now we have a proposal. We have many more ideas for your development, growth, and education. There are many more advantages we could give you. But—of course—we need your cooperation.

We are sure you will not want to pass up this opportunity. A van from NIMH is ready to pick you up as soon as you send the word. Please let us know as soon as possible when we might come to get you.

Sincerely,

Dr. I. M. Schultz
Chief Researcher

A discussion immediately ensues as to whether the offer should be accepted. Some are curious about the details of the offer. The teacher says he wonders also, but the letter doesn't say exactly what the researchers have in mind. The majority of the "rats" express the view that they are not interested in returning to NIMH; they enjoy their freedom too much. One "rat" reminds the group that Mrs. Frisby, the fieldmouse, is counting on them to help her, so they dare not leave—even if they wanted to—until Mrs. Frisby's sick child, Timothy, is well enough to travel. The teacher asks if that is their final decision or if they want to invite a representative from the lab to discuss the offer further with them. They choose the latter alternative.

The leader stops the drama momentarily and asks if the children want him to play the researcher role or if some of them wish to. They decide they want to play the role. He selects four volunteers and speaks with them briefly and privately, reminding them of the great opportunity and responsibility that will be theirs if they can convince the super-intelligent rats to return to the lab. They must not underestimate the rats and their abilities. Then he gives each a large shirt to wear as a lab coat and writes an identification badge (stick-on nametag) with the inscription: "Researcher #_____." The four children come to the front of the room to sit on "lab" stools and the drama begins again as they are questioned by the "rats" about the new research plans. The leader plays a mediating role, briefly clarifying and expanding on questions and points made by both the rats and the researchers, but only when the children have difficulties expressing themselves.

As the discussion evolves, the rats want to know what sorts of experiments the lab intends to undertake. The lab researchers aren't sure; the teacher says the plans probably cannot be revealed yet because of government security precautions. The researchers agree and continue their persuasive stance, making promises and negotiating various perquisites "if only the rats will return" to the lab. The rats ask for various promises generally related to no cages and higher quality of life in the laboratory. When one researcher promises one luxury too many, the other three make a qualification and say, "We'll have to check with Dr. Schultz on that."

At this point the leader stops the drama and suggests that the rats form small groups and draft a letter of reply to NIMH, spelling out their demands and expectations; the lab researchers are to write a report to Dr. Schultz, detailing the status of events as they interpret them. The children readily agree and they busily move to the task.

The above example is a description of one hour spent on a role drama; the writing activity that followed took an additional half hour. In role drama the leader sets up imagined situations that focus on a problem, enters into a role related to the topic, engages the students in their role, and the drama begins. There is no specified plotline as there is with a story or play that has a known beginning, middle, and end. Instead, the drama is a series of dramatic encounters that explore the various facets of the conflict. The leader creates activities and related roles, sometimes with the students' input. He or she bears the responsibility of moving the drama forward by creating new activities that probe the problem further and build on information discovered in the previous activities. There is a sense of

Children pair up to interview witnesses for clues.

progression, though not necessarily chronological, since there are times when the group may want to consider earlier events related to the story or to make predictions about future events. In addition, the leader structures the drama so that students play a variety of roles over time. This allows them to look at the conflict from differing viewpoints. Sometimes the students are grouped into one role; at other times they may interact in pairs or work in smaller groupings. Depending on the students' interest, the drama may last for an entire class period or extend over several days' time. Leader and students together decide when the conflict is solved in a satisfying manner and the drama feels ended.

A major part of role drama are the discussions and reflections (out of role) on the issues raised by the drama. These discussions take place periodically as the leader deems appropriate and are designed to further cement the learning benefit. Because the students have tried on a slice of life, they and the leader usually have insights they need and want to share.

"What qualities are needed in a good researcher?"
"Is a person ever justified in not keeping a promise?"
"What does commitment to a cause mean?"

There is no one way to structure a role drama. Indeed, the same topic may be played one way with one group and an entirely different way with another. Now let's take a look at another role drama and the directions it might take. (See also the example on pp. 293–95.)

"THE OLD WOMAN IN THE SHOE"

Suppose a leader selects the nursery rhyme "The Old Woman in a Shoe" as a topic for a group of young children.[3] Her goal may be twofold: to explore a piece of literature and to use the main character's problem as a learning experience. She decides to take on the role of the woman and approaches the children as if they are experts who can help her. She might start the drama with a statement such as the following:

> "Good morning. I'm sure you've heard of me. I live down the street in a shoe and have a lot of children. I've been told you're very helpful boys and girls and that you might have some ideas of how I might take care of all the children I have. I just don't know what to do. It was an awful mess at our house this morning getting everyone off to school. Everyone was getting in everyone else's way. The children almost missed the school bus. What could we do to get things organized better?" (Note: To add even more tension, the leader could add that she has a job which she may lose if she arrives late.)

With this opening, the stage is set for an interesting discussion. Usually the children have many ideas about how they think a household should be run, based on their own experiences. The "woman" might even write down their ideas on the chalkboard to show that she considers them important and "so I can remember them." This procedure also makes an excellent writing/reading lesson.

Even though the "old woman" role is from literature, the discussion easily edges into a variety of curricular topics. In the above instance, the discussion focuses on household management. However, as the children discuss they may suggest other directions the leader can pick up on. For example, someone may suggest that older children can help with the chores and take care of the younger children. Now the group can explore such questions as: "What chores are suitable for what age groups?" "How does one look after babies and toddlers?" and so on. Another might suggest that the family cut expenses by raising some of its own food, which could lead to an exploration of gardening and farming.

The questions posed continually encourage the children's thinking and motivate them to find answers to an intriguing problem. As long as the leader asks questions requiring the children's advice and remains interested in their responses, the children will instruct her (and each other) about numerous strategies for running a household efficiently. The questions and responses (dialogue) also develop the "old woman" role, making her a real person with a real problem, worthy of the children's attention.

The leader tries not to let the problems be solved too easily and does not accept glib or inappropriate answers. Not only does this keep a degree of dramatic tension evident, it also encourages the children to think more deeply.

---

[3]Notice that although this example begins by focusing on young children, the drama later develops into more sophisticated dimensions which are suited to older children. The level of difficulty is not necessarily determined by the topic.

Therefore, as she listens to the children's suggestions she might need to gently remind them that she has a limited income:

> "Move to a bigger house? I don't think we could afford to do that. Some days all we have to eat is broth and bread. Can you think of something else?"

or that she has limited space in her home:

> "Living in a shoe is pretty cramped. We can't even fit everyone around the eating table at the same time."

If the children give advice she doesn't wish to accept, she can say simply, "I don't think I could do that. Do you have another idea?" As an example, a child once suggested, "You could give some of your children away." As shocking as the answer seemed, the teacher didn't pass judgment by saying, "What a terrible thought!" or "Be serious!" Instead, she quietly said it hadn't occurred to her. Remaining objective can be tough at times, but children need to have a chance to weed out their own inappropriate suggestions and discover their best ideas. More often than not, the children themselves will give reasons for rejecting lesser ideas and selecting better ones. As it happened, another child quickly said, "But you couldn't do that; you love them all, don't you?" The leader assured them she did indeed love all her children and giving them up would be too painful. As a result of her delayed response, dramatic tension was enhanced and the children were pressed into deeper thinking. No doubt, they learned more in the process than if the teacher had squelched the initial response too quickly.

A discussion continues as long as it seems productive and the children are interested. If time runs out, the topic can be picked up on another day. Additional ideas can also be introduced; the old woman could return later and ask for further assistance.

> "How can I keep my children entertained?"
>
> "What are some inexpensive, nourishing meals I can serve that children will like? They're such picky eaters."
>
> "What are some toys you like to play with—that don't cost a lot of money—that I might be able to get for my children?"

If the children—or even the leader for that matter—lack some needed information to pursue a topic further, the drama can be stopped just as children do in their pretend play so they can discuss the information they need in order to continue. ("How do you plant potatoes?" "How can simple toys be made by hand?" "Where can we find good recipes that are nourishing?") They may even decide to take time to research the questions and return to the drama another day with their newfound knowledge.

Role dramas do not have a preconceived beginning, middle, and end; they evolve as the leader and the children see new possibilities and new questions to explore. The leader bears the responsibility of keeping the interest and motivation level high but may pick up new threads of development whenever meaningful potential arises. And, although the leader has questions in mind that she wishes to ask, she may also take her cue from what she senses to be the children's interest.

"Is that right? You can have fun without spending money? Tell us about that."

"He thinks we need to rearrange the living quarters in the shoe. What do the rest of you think?"

One can also stop at any time and simply ask the children if they wish to continue. They may have other ideas they want to explore or other roles they want to play. This break also gives the leader thinking time to consider the next move.

During the drama, the leader constantly assesses the group's progress with the topic, looking for the deeper concerns the topic offers and designing ways to explore them. For example, suppose the leader wants older children to address the subject: "What circumstances might force a person to use a shoe as a home?" If so, in groups the children could improvise scenes (or a series of frozen pictures) to show how they think it might have happened. Or, suppose the leader wants older children to consider: "What do the city officials think about one of their residents living in a shoe?" If so, investigative reporters might question a panel of officials at a news conference.

Planning a Role Drama

In creating role drama, there are some suggested procedural steps one can follow. (*Note:* We will omit the kinds of role drama that begin with the leader saying, "What shall we do our drama about today?" since that more open-ended approach requires additional techniques in structuring and questioning. Instead, we suggest that beginners select topics from literary sources in order to have some stimulus and structure to fall back on. As confidence increases, one can move in other directions.)

Returning to our topic of the Old Woman in the Shoe, let's look at the various considerations we might make in structuring the role drama. Depending on the age of the children and their experience with drama, you may choose to let them take part in some of the various planning stages.

One of the first planning questions is, "What are the areas of learning suggested by this simple rhyme?" Some that come to mind are household organization; disciplining of children; everyday life of household managers and children; parents' responsibilities; children's responsibilities; effects of living in cramped quarters; shelters and makeshift housing; shoemaking; providing food and clothing in large quantities; and so on.

The next step is to focus the topic on human conflict. In our earlier discussion we chose to focus on the question, "How does a mother cope with so many children to care for?"

Next, we might brainstorm a list of the various groups and individuals who could be affected by the problem, such as the mother, the children, other relatives, the school system, the health-care system, social services, public safety officers, realtors, neighbors, to name a few. We also consider what their viewpoint of the problem might be and what kinds of "meeting" scenes might take place. The following list begins to emerge, all of which include problems to solve:

The mother	Seeking help in getting the house organized more efficiently
	Telling the children there isn't enough money for birthday (or holiday) presents this year
The school	Teacher telling the mother the children's grades are suffering because of difficulties with studying and homework
The neighbors	Meeting with the mother to complain about the children's unruly behavior
Relatives	Confrontation between relatives who want to help the family and those who feel they have to solve their own problems
Children	Meeting to discuss if they should quit school and work to support the family
Social services	Meeting to discuss a complaint that the children are not being taken care of properly
Public health officer or fire marshal	Meeting to condemn the shoe as a home; eviction of family

Now the leader selects one of the above situations, chooses a role for him or herself, and selects a group role for the children. (One may also create a more complex arrangement and select two different people from the above list who confront each other. For example, one might play the role of a social worker and approach the relatives (students), to enlist their aid in solving the woman's problems.)

Finally, the leader writes a brief introductory speech for the drama. This little "script" should explain who the leader is and who they (the children) are and what the meeting is about. Why have they been called? It is best to have this opening statement clearly in mind in order to stay on course.

Activities Played in Role Drama

The leader keeps the drama evolving not by developing a story line but by structuring activities that probe events and people's reactions to those events. The most frequent type of activity is the "meeting" or encountering of key persons in the drama. The meetings that are the most intense are those in which the person's actions and motives are questioned or in which the group persuades them to some view.

Variety is a key factor in maintaining the group's interest throughout an extended role drama. If the leader keeps the drama activity variables (see page 27) in mind, she or he can structure activities that are interestingly varied. For example, a whole group discussion might be followed by an individual movement activity so that children experience both movement and speech as well as variety in grouping.

Props to stir the imagination: ornate box, message, wooden cup, necklace, keys in a velvet pouch, and a small vial with mysterious liquid.

Props can also enrich a drama. An intriguing box, an ornate key, a curious picture, a piece of clothing, garner interest and hold attention. Note the use of the letter in the Mrs. Frisby example earlier, as well as the lab coats and identification tags. Other dramatic elements can be useful, such as darkening the room and lighting a candle or holding a flashlight, whispering, discovering a secret document, receiving an unexpected message or phone call, using slow motion movement. These and similar effects have been used in the examples throughout this text.

As the drama proceeds, the leader injects dramatic tension periodi-

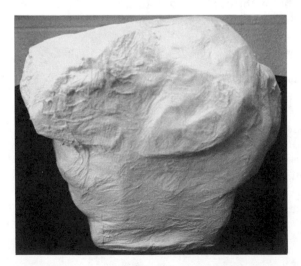

A large papier-maché tooth might have belonged to a giant, a prehistoric animal, or one of the gods.

cally to keep interest high. Secrecy, mystery, problem solving, and urgency all are ways to make an activity more dramatic. Although props can help, the wording of the leader's comments throughout the drama also lend tension:

"Be very careful, this is a touchy situation."
"I trust that you will all keep this confidential."
"What does the mayor think about this?"
"An election is coming up soon; we don't want a scandal on our hands."

There are times when one needs to lure the children into the drama before delving into activities with deeper meaning. This is called "building belief" or "commitment" to the drama. These activities may take place as preliminaries or at any time during the drama when it is deemed helpful. These activities may be drawn from any suggested throughout this text. Some possibilities for the Old Woman in the Shoe lesson are:

Solo narrative pantomime   "Let me tell you what my day is like living in a shoe with all those children. You pantomime as I describe it."

Count-and-freeze pantomime (solo or pairs)   "Demonstrate a household chore that children are capable of doing."

Frozen picture (small groups)   "Demonstrate some of the difficulties the family experiences with so many living in little space."

Related drama activities can also be used throughout the drama. Following are some categories with specific suggestions for the Old Woman in the Shoe drama.

Artwork   You can encourage drawings, illustrations, posters, murals, or maps. *Examples:* "Draw a picture of the kind of shoe you think would make the best house." "Draw a floor plan of the shoe house."

Writing   Students can experience writing letters, diaries, historical accounts, newspaper articles, autobiographies, descriptions, lists, or story endings. *Examples:* "Write a house-for-sale newspaper advertisement describing the shoe's best features." "Write a condemned notice for the shoe house."

Types of Roles

The type of role played by the leader is usually determined by the selected literature and the goal of instruction. However, some beginning leaders find it easier to begin role dramas by examining the kinds of roles that are available. They can then select the type of role they personally feel most comfortable with and select literature that presents that role. This next section looks at some role types and possible topics which can be used with them.

"I Don't Know" or "I Need Help" Role.   One role that seems easy for beginning leaders and that works well with young children is the helpless person in need of assistance. (See initial question for "The Old Woman in the Shoe.") Children are usually eager to give advice to an adult because it makes them feel significant. And, since they are so used to being told what to do and how to do it, they relish this unique opportunity to share their knowledge and ideas with someone who genuinely needs their help.

Teachers are frequently quite surprised to discover that even young children do know a good many things and often have a great deal of insight into problem-solving and philosophical issues when given the chance. Children are also more inclined to seek out further answers through research when there is a compelling reason to do so; that is, when someone we know needs this information.

Some examples of helpless roles are a person who just inherited a pet dinosaur and doesn't know how to care for it; Little Bo Peep who has problems losing things—today it's her sheep; Winnie-the-Pooh's mother who needs help convincing her son not to eat quite so much honey. In fact, anytime the leader says "I don't know. What should we do?" she or he is playing this role.

Authority Role.   In the authority role, the leader is in command and can give orders. In fact, it is very similar to a teacher's regular role in the classroom. The authority role can sometimes be overpowering and threatening to children if you overplay it and begin throwing your weight around. Without thinking of the consequences in real life, some children are eager to "do away with" a despot in drama. Fortunately, they are usually in the minority and are pulled back by the rest of the group. Nevertheless, it is best for the authority role to be played in an impersonal and businesslike attitude that suggests: "This is what needs to be accomplished, and I'm the one who's supposed to see that it gets done."

Some examples of the authority role are chief of detectives in charge of a crew investigating a crime; newspaper editor sending reporters out to interview people; and a leader of an expedition.

Second in Command.   This is a "mid-authority" position. The person has been sent to give orders for someone else, which makes the role less powerful than the authoritative role. The attitude here is: "These are the orders, and I'm here to see they are carried out. It's not my idea; I'm just doing my job."

The second-in-command role also allows you to say, "I don't know; I wasn't told." This is particularly useful if the children press you for further information and you can't think of a response. There is also a certain dramatic tension created whenever the leader, in whatever role he or she is playing, says, "I don't know."

Because you are not in a high-authority position in this role, some children may refuse to do your bidding. If so, you can caution, "I suppose you can refuse if you want, but what will I tell the (*authority role*)?" This kind of response generally encourages the children's compliance in the drama because of the *implied* but unstated threat: "I'll see that the one in charge hears of your refusal. There may be a later consequence of your decision!"

In playing this role, you cannot be blamed for the demands being made. However, you may need to remind the group of this fact if someone suggests a "kill the messenger" solution. After all, you are only the bearer of the news. A deferential approach on your part generally gets support from the group.

Another way to play this role is to present a letter (see earlier example for *Mrs. Frisby and the Rats of NIMH*), a decree, a proclamation, a written or tape-recorded message, or other materials that are prepared beforehand. Thus, the problem is presented through the material, giving you a chance to step back and gauge the reactions.

Some examples of the second-in-command role are vice-president of a company; prime minister of a government; and spokesperson for an individual or group.

One of the Group.   In this case you play the same role as the children. You talk with them on an equal basis and your opinions are not more important than theirs. The words *we, us,* and *our* are useful because they remind you and the children of your equal status with them.

"What will we say to the king when he arrives?"
"What should we do with our supplies?"

As you play the one-of-the-group role, the children may choose one of their peers to be the leader or a leader may emerge spontaneously.

"Derrick should be the one to speak to the king."
"I know how to drive a tractor."

You need to go along with this move since you have given up your teacher-authority position for the moment. However, you can still be the voice of wisdom and moderation and guide by modeling appropriate behavior.

A common way to use this role is to begin the drama in a higher role, give the group a problem to discuss, then leave and unobtrusively slip back into the group as one of them.

Some examples of the one-of-the-group role are the rats in *Mrs. Frisby* setting up their new society; survivors of a shipwreck stranded on an island; and space pioneers setting up life on another planet.

Devil's Advocate.   This role can be played while being in the one-of-the-group role. In it you question or perhaps even challenge the decisions the group makes. The children are thus pressured into defending their ideas and decisions and clarifying their thinking. You may feel pressured into defending your position also. If you are too persuasive of your position, the group will possibly abandon their original decision and side with you. This move places you back in the authority position. Therefore, it is best to challenge on small points first and gauge your power over the group carefully.

Some examples are a rat in *Mrs. Frisby* who wants a monarchy while others are focusing on a democracy; an explorer who loses faith in the expedition; one who rejects the group's desire to befriend aliens.

Antagonist. In this role the leader becomes an opposing force that challenges the group. (See officer role example on page 3.) This role can become threatening to children causing them to turn against you. For this reason, beginners would be wise to play a potentially strong person in a weakened position (e.g., a witch who has lost her power; a ghost who would like to find a friend; or a general who is weary of war).

In the antagonist role one may also provide some built-in protections for the children. For example, a teacher once pretended to be "someone" delivering a package to the home of the three little pigs. Of course they immediately assumed she was the wolf in disguise, as she speculated they would. Although the wolf is an adversarial character, we know he was outsmarted by the wise pig in the original story and therefore he carries a weakened status. During the drama the children tried all manner of suggestions to get the leader to leave the package so they wouldn't have to open the door. Thus the imaginary house and the door were another protection; as long as they didn't open the door, they were safe. (And, she never threatened to blow the house down!) In addition, the leader "protected" the children further by showing she could not hear them as they talked together. She did this by speaking loudly—as one would through a closed door—and by not making eye contact with them directly. This allowed them to whisper their strategies to each other in secret and gain emotional support from each other. Eventually she walked away in defeat and returned as Mother Pig to congratulate them on their cleverness.

Other examples are a neighboring ruler (or giant or dragon) who threatens the kingdom; the boss of a company who exploits the workers; and Rumplestiltskin who demands the queen's baby.

Multiple Roles. A leader may play more than one role in the course of one activity or may switch roles during an extended role drama.

For example, in a role drama based on the book *Company's Coming* by Arthur Yorinks (New York: Crown Publishers, 1988), a leader played Shirley who asked her relatives for their opinion on whether she should have invited the aliens to dinner. Next, as an official at the Pentagon she asked her staff of experts to explore ways of dealing with the aliens. Later, as a supervisor at the F.B.I. she rehearsed undercover techniques with investigative agents. In this drama the children changed roles each time the leader did.

As indicated earlier, the leader can also open a drama in one role, leave the group, return in the one-of-the-group role to discuss the problem, leave again, and return in the original role to deal with the group's decision.

A photograph can be useful in helping children develop roles from a different time period.

Each new activity in the drama also offers opportunity to play different roles. Keeping all the types of roles in mind can be helpful in determining the various activities one can structure.

Children in Role

Most often, particularly in beginning work, all the children play their role as a single group.[4] In The Old Woman in the Shoe example, the children were themselves, although they were addressed as if they had the expertise to advise the woman about her problem. In later activities described above it was suggested that they might be neighbors of the old woman, newspaper reporters, or city officials. In some instances, one group of children might play a role that interacts with another group of children playing another role just as was done in many of the verbal activities in previous chapters.

If a child asks to play a certain role, it is permissible and even desirable for you to take him or her aside and discuss the qualities demanded by the role. (See the example of this in *Mrs. Frisby*, described earlier). Another strategy is to suggest a scene that might take place. "Shall we bring the city

[4]For a more detailed look at students' playing of roles, see Morgan and Saxton who explain five stages of "becoming someone else." Norah Morgan and Juliana Saxton, *Teaching Drama: A Mind of Many Wonders* (Portsmouth, N.H.: Heinemann Educational Books, 1987), pp. 30–35.

officials in to question them?" If the children agree, and you plan to have them play the roles, first discuss what questions they think should be asked. Then, whether you or the children play the role, you will be better prepared with answers. (See also "Interviews" in Chapter 8.)

A Final Note

The technique of role drama was developed not so much for teaching the aesthetics of drama as it was to stimulate thinking, discussion, and problem solving among the students. As such, role drama has been referred to as a learning medium and recommended as a way to make school curricular subjects more dramatic and immediate. However, many of the goals of role drama parallel theatre goals, though attention may not always be called to that fact. For example, in the hands of a competent leader, role drama is very often emotionally charged and can be as dramatically exciting as theatre. Secondly, since children are immersed in and respond to the drama of the moment in a believable manner, phony theatrics and superficial acting usually do not emerge. Thirdly, commitment and believability are encouraged in role drama just as they are in good theatre. Hence, role drama can be as valuable for a theatre arts curriculum as it is for other curricular purposes.

FOR THE COLLEGE STUDENT

1. Select a piece of literature to use for a leader-in-role activity, keeping in mind the various types of roles you can take. Plan an introduction for your role and present yourself to your classmates or to a group of children. Lead the discussion in your role for a few minutes. Record the encounter or recall it afterward. Evaluate the results, considering what worked well and where you might improve the activity in the future.

2. Select a piece of literature to use for a role drama. What conflict or conflicts are suitable for dramatic exploration? What activity would you use to begin the role drama? List activities that might be used to build belief and commitment to the drama. Create an outline similar to the one beginning on page 272, exploring the various directions the role drama could take. Play a part of the drama with classmates or a group of children. List the universal questions the literature poses for reflective discussion during and after the drama.

3. Keep a file of literature to use for role dramas. The bibliography which follows can help you get started.

BIBLIOGRAPHY OF SELECTED LITERATURE FOR ROLE DRAMA

The following materials are presented to give you some beginning ideas for creating your own role dramas. Note the variety of genre and style. Numbers in parentheses refer to the numbered anthologies and books listed in this text's final bibliography.

M–O *Be a Perfect Person in Just Three Days,* Stephen Manes. New York: Clarion, 1982; Bantam, 1984. A young boy tries to follow the instructions in a library book in order to better himself. The premise is interesting to pursue even without the book. How would one go about such a task? What is a perfect person? Are there drawbacks to being one?

Y–M *Cloudy with a Chance of Meatballs,* Judi Barrett. New York: Macmillan, 1982. In this modern tall tale, a town is turned into food and the people are forced to leave. Although it is said the people are too frightened to return, suppose an expedition were undertaken. What preparations would have to be made for the return trip? Will the journey be successful? How might the story end this time? Although the tone of the book is humorous, reflective discussions can be centered on such questions as being displaced due to natural disasters and the courage required to begin life anew.

M *Company's Coming,* Arthur Yorinks. New York: Crown Publishers, 1988. A spaceship lands in a couple's yard and two small aliens emerge. They seem harmless enough, so the wife asks them to come to dinner at six o'clock. Stop the story here (or later when they return with a box) and play a role drama to find out what happens. Another drama could also focus on the aliens' problem of overcrowding on their planet and their search for a new galaxy. Reflective discussions might center on dealing with the unknown and ecological issues.

O *The Forgotten Door,* Alexander Key. Philadelphia: Westminster Press, 1965. In this intriguing science-fiction story a boy from another world falls through a forgotten door into this world. Because he is different, both he and the family who befriend him must deal with the fears and prejudices of the less tolerant citizens of the community. Explore the various circumstances the story suggests before revealing the book's ending. Reflection might center on the effects of fear and prejudice on the people who hold them.

Y–M *The House on East 88th Street,* Bernard Waber. Boston: Houghton Mifflin, 1962, 1975. Upon moving into a new apartment, the Primm family finds a crocodile, named Lyle, in the bathtub. This popular book has generated sequels of Lyle's encounters with neighbors, repair persons, and other New Yorkers. Role dramas can explore these and other invented situations. Under Lyle's frightening exterior is a very loveable and caring creature, leading to reflections on how looks may be deceiving.

Y *The Hungry Thing,* Jan Slepian and Ann Seidler. New York: Scholastic, 1990. A strange-looking beast arrives in town with a sign that reads "Feed me." Only the children are able to decipher the meaning of the "gollipops" and "hookies" it asks for. A role drama might explore other messages from the Thing as well as who it is, where it comes from, and what to do with it. Sequel *The Hungry Thing Returns* offers more ideas.

Y–M *The Island of the Skog,* Steven Kellogg. New York: Dial Press, 1973, 1976. Mice set sail from city life and arrive at an island paradise, only to discover that it is already inhabited by a mysterious creature. Before reading the book's ending, play a role drama to discover who or what the creature is and whether there can be peaceful coexistence. How do people organize to respond to outside threats?

M *Jack and the Beanstalk,* John Howe. Boston: Little Brown, 1989. At the end of the story we might question what should be done with the giant who has fallen to his death. What damages occurred when he landed? Should Jack be punished or praised for his deed?

O "Jabberwocky," Lewis Carroll (3,18,24,29). Who is the strange creature in this nonsense poem? What has it done? Why is the young man sent to slay him? Who is the one who sends the young man on this mission? More questions than answers in this poem make it an excellent source for role drama.

M–O *Johnny Tremain*, Esther Forbes. Boston: Houghton Mifflin, 1943. Johnny is a silver apprentice in Boston in 1773. After his hand is severely injured in an accident and he is no longer able to work as a smith, he becomes involved in revolutionary activities. The characters and situations in this historical novel provide excellent material for additional exploration through role drama. The book's handling of incidents can be used for comparative purposes afterward. Or, scenes that are presented briefly can be played out more completely. Other historical novels listed in the final bibliography are equally useful.

Y–M *The Jolly Postman or Other People's Letters,* Janet and Allan Ahlberg. Boston: Little, Brown and Company, 1986. This unique little book consists of real letters to and from well-known fairy tale characters. The letters themselves may form the basis of several role dramas or may stimulate additional ideas. Many writing possibilities also exit.

Y–O *The Lorax,* Dr. Seuss. New York: Random House, 1971. This fantasy tale has almost become a manifesto for children's ecological concerns. Explore the before and after situations presented by story as well as the future predictions. The material is suitable for all ages.

Y–M *The Missing Mother Goose,* Stephen Krensky. New York: Doubleday, 1991. As this book of original stories based on the Mother Goose demonstrates, the rhymes lend ideas for role drama because of their open-endedness. For example, the author wonders why Old King Cole was such a "merry old soul" and why would a cow jump over the moon? Role dramas could also explore ways to help Little Boy Blue stay awake so he can keep his job. And, is it possible that the spider is purposely trying to scare Little Miss Muffett? What can we do to take care of Humpty Dumpty and see that he doesn't fall again? Why did Tom, Tom the Piper's Son steal a pig? and so on. See *Dramathemes* by Larry Swartz (Portsmouth, N.H.: Heinemann, 1988) for an extended role drama outline on the rhyme "One Misty Moisty Morning."

Y–M *The Missing Tarts,* B. G. Hennessy. New York: Puffin, 1989. This almost wordless picture book explores the Mother Goose Rhyme, "The Queen of Hearts." The queen visits other nursery rhyme characters looking for the tarts the knave stole and discovers that he has given them to the hungry children of the Old Woman in the Shoe. Before sharing the book's ending, what other directions might the story take?

M–O *The Money Tree,* Sherry Stewart. New York: Farrar, Straus & Giroux, 1991. A money tree, which grows in Miss McGillicuddy's yard, seems to be of greater interest to her neighbors than it is to her. A role drama could explore what will happen the following year. What will Miss McGillicuddy and the town do if a money tree grows again; or, how will they manage if it doesn't? Discussions on wealth, happiness, and life goals are all possible.

M–O *The Mysteries of Harris Burdick,* Chris Van Allsburg. Boston: Houghton Mifflin, 1984. This unique book consists of surrealistic-looking pictures with captions that serve as story starters. One activity based on this book is described in Chapter 1 of this text. An extended role drama might be based on any one of the pictures. For an extended role drama outline focusing on an investigation of Burdick's disappearance referred to in the forward of the book, see *Dramathemes* by Larry Swartz (Portsmouth, N.H.: Heinemann, 1988.)

M–O *Old Henry*, Joan W. Blos. New York: William Morrow, 1987. An elderly gentleman moves into a dilapidated house, but makes no attempt to improve it the way the neighbors had hoped. Before revealing the book's ending, explore the various encounters that might occur due to the citizens' and Old Henry's dilemma. Discuss conflict of goals and its effect on interrelationships.

M–O *The Pied Piper of Hamelin*, Robert Browning. Many editions. This classic story provides rich opportunities for drama based on the problem: How can we get the children back to Hamelin? Reflections on broken promises and revenge may emerge. See *Role Drama* by Carole Tarlington and Patrick Verriour (Portsmouth, N.H.: Heinemann, 1991) for an extended role drama outline.

M–O *Rip Van Winkle*, Washington Irving. Several editions. An American legend of a man's twenty-year sleep. Explore the various problems posed when a man suddenly leaves his family and community. And, what problems are created after his just as sudden return? What of his story? Who were the old men in the glen and was there some reason why Rip was selected for this experience? How might one go about trying to make up for lost time?

M *Rumplestiltskin*, Jakob and Wilhelm Grimm. Many editions. Carol Tarlington and Patrick Verrior, in their book *Role Drama* (Portsmouth, N.H. Heinemann, 1991), tell a variation of this story and stop at the point where the little man allows the queen additional time before giving up her baby. The children are asked to be advisers to the queen and help with her decision. An outline of an extended role drama is presented.

M "Sarah Cynthia Sylvia Stout," Shel Silverstein (41). The girl in this poem refuses to take out the garbage. The speaker in the poem says her fate cannot be told, so a role drama could explore what happens to her. Possibilities also exist for going backward, looking at the events that led up to her refusal. Although this is an outlandish poem, reflection might be made on tasks that can become overwhelming.

M "Something Big Has Been Here," Jack Prelutsky (35). A curious "something," with feet size 956, has visited. In one class a teacher set up a detective agency and said a letter had come from Mr. Prelutsky, the poet, asking for advice. The class interviewed witnesses. No clear picture emerged. An "anonymous phone tip" said something outside the agency door might provide a clue. A large footprint and a papier maché tooth were examined, although the children also thought the "tooth" could be part of a bone or the creature's egg. File folders with unique pictures in them were produced as previous cases that might provide clues. Although the mystery was never solved, the children wrote letters describing what they thought the creature was and offering advice on ways to cope.

M *The Shrinking of Treehorn*. Florence Parry Heide. New York: Holiday House, 1971; Dell Publishing, 1980. A young boy notices that he is shrinking, but he cannot seem to get the attention of adults to help him solve his problem. What solutions might a role drama reveal? Question for reflection: How believable is Treehorn's dilemma? What parallels does it suggest?

M–O *The Stranger*. Chris Van Allsburg. Boston: Houghton Mifflin, 1986. In this unique story, a stranger, after being injured in an accident, suffers from amnesia. He stays with a farm family until he realizes his identity as Winter and is obliged to return to his work. By omitting the conclusion, a role drama can focus on exploring who the man might be. Or, accepting the fact that he is Winter, what might happen if he does not regain his memory?

M–O *Tuesday*, David Wiesner. New York: Clarion, 1991. This is a wordless picturebook—for the most part. On Tuesday, frogs fly; the next day, pigs. Meanwhile, detectives are checking out clues. Reporters and mystified people compare observations regarding the mystery that is never explained. The process of investigating can be more interesting than any answer that may be revealed. A discussion of mysteries and their appeal can follow.

12

Planning
Drama Lessons

Throughout this text many drama activities and even some lesson plans have been presented. Virtually any of the single activities in each chapter can be incorporated into classroom teaching at any time and with various curricular subjects. Some of the activities can be played in a relatively brief time period; others may range from forty-five minutes to an hour. Some activities, such as the segmented stories and role dramas, have been shown to cover several class periods.

Various situations exist for teaching drama. Some teachers may feel they can grab only precious minutes throughout the day; others see ways to accomplish multiple curricular goals through drama and have no difficulty finding time. Others may have the luxury of being able to teach drama lessons that last for a full hour and even longer. Some may prefer to do themed drama over several days' time, spending perhaps twenty or thirty minutes each day on an activity. In any case you will want to design lesson outlines that are more than just a series of activities. This chapter is designed to help you in sequential lesson planning.

CONSIDERING GOALS

Some teachers may be in educational situations where creative drama is taught as a theatre art. A major emphasis will then be on drama goals such as artistic discipline, pantomime skills, or improvisation.

Even with an emphasis on theatre goals, the classroom teacher is usually expected to combine drama with other areas of the curriculum. For this reason, lessons often have a curricular-related topic such as Pilgrim life, westward movement, seasons, or current events. Or the drama may be used in conjunction with writing activities.

If personal development goals are a major concern, they must also be taken into consideration as you plan the lesson. Perhaps the children need assistance in listening to one another, and you decide to use pantomime activities as a way of focusing their attention on each other. Perhaps you want them to work in small groups to develop socialization skills and cooperative behaviors. All these considerations are taken into account as one plans drama lessons.

SELECTING AND SEQUENCING THE ACTIVITIES

For beginning teachers one approach is to select a topic and brainstorm a list of possible activities. Cover as wide a range as possible, noting all the types of activities presented in this text from simple activities to leader-in-role. Then select the most appropriate ones for your students and sequence them according to level of difficulty.

For an hour's lesson, anywhere from three to five activities may be planned, even though they may not all be used. Alternative strategies should also be included. Being overprepared will give you more flexibility as you see the group's response to the lesson.

The lesson should be built just as the structure of a story or a play takes shape. The first activity may be considered a warm-up. For the specialist who teaches only drama, this activity may be crucial in developing rapport with the group. Warm-up material should not be too difficult for the children to do and should put everyone in a relaxed mood, ready to work together. The activities should build commitment and belief in the topic, a particularly important concern for role drama.

If you are working with a class that is already "high" at the beginning of the period, it might be appropriate for the initial material to expend excess energy and calm the children down. In this case it should also be highly structured and highly controlled.

One activity should be used as the core of the lesson; this is generally the most challenging activity. Then the lesson should taper off and end with a quieting activity.

As the activities progress they should become more challenging. To analyze levels of difficulty, you might consider again the chart on page 28 in Chapter 2. For example, suppose you choose a pantomime activity from the many presented in Chapter 7. According to variable 3 on the chart, pantomimes are easier verbal activities. But they are also considered advanced, according to variable 5, if they are shared with classmates as an audience. At the same time, the topic of the pantomime also determines its difficulty. Therefore, it would probably be easier for students to perform a pantomime of their favorite sport in a count-and-freeze pantomime (p. 161) than it would be to participate in a group frozen picture (p. 164) of a current event. The former relies on the students' individual playing (variable 4: solo playing) and something they are familiar with (variable 7: minimal informational content), whereas the latter requires group decision making (variable 4: pair and group work) and a knowledge of current events (variable 7: high data content). Although each activity is a pantomime, other variables affect the level of difficulty. While you need not adhere slavishly to a thorough analysis of each activity you choose to do, an overall consideration of the variables will help you select and sequence your activities for students' maximum success.

You also need to determine (perhaps even as the lesson is progressing) just how much time and effort should be put into a given activity. It may take more than one playing to achieve the depth of involvement desired. Or, children may take a longer time committing themselves to the topic. At the same time, if the children are not responding to the material and you cannot see a way of combatting the problem, then the activity may simply need to be dropped.

Remember that some activities can be handled as run-throughs or trial runs. Other times, you will want to develop deeper concentration. In the latter case the material will need to be slowed down and divided into smaller, more workable units.

Whenever an activity is repeated, a new challenge should be added. Otherwise there is the danger that the activity will "plateau" and become stale. Ultimately, an activity with numerous repetitions and no new challenges simply becomes boring.

The end of the drama lesson should have a relaxing and calming effect on the group. The children should have a chance to reflect on the experience they have just had and to absorb it. Particularly if the class is to move on to seatwork after the drama lesson, a quiet ending is almost mandatory.

SAMPLE LESSON OUTLINES

Following are two sample lesson outlines for two different grade levels. They are presented to show variable approaches to lesson planning. The outlines provide the leader with flexibility and opportunity to make decisions according to the group's response during the playing.

The first outline focuses on five activities only. Even so, it is not likely that the entire lesson could be covered in an hour's time frame and possibly not in a single day. The second outline has multiple activities; both outlines include alternative suggestions for some activities. The lessons may also be used over a span of several days, spending perhaps twenty minutes each day on an activity. Time will also vary according to how familiar students already are with the information.

WINTER (SNOW)
Grade Level: K to 3

Objectives

1. Gain an understanding of the winter season and the various activities connected with it.
2. Experience creative movement in enacting winter activities.
3. Communicate and interpret nonverbal messages through pantomime guessing games.
4. Dramatize a folk tale with opportunities for pantomime and verbal interaction.
5. Experience characterization of selfish and generous qualities in the trees and the helplessness of the wounded bird.

Preparation and materials

1. Copy of *The Snowy Day,* by Ezra Jack Keats (New York: Viking Penguin, 1962).
2. Copy of the folk tale "Why the Evergreen Trees Keep Their Leaves in Winter" by Florence Holbrook (36).[1]
3. (optional) Pictures of people engaged in various wintertime activities.
4. (optional) Paper headbands for characters in the story dramatization of the folk tale.

Motivation and warm-up activity: The Snowy Day *(play at desk or other limited area)*

1. Open session with comments about winter and snow appropriate to the experiences of the children.
2. Read and show pictures from the book, a narrative pantomime story about a small boy who has his first memorable experience in the snow.
3. Narrate or side-coach the story, which includes dressing for snowy weather, building a snowman, making a snow angel, and being a mountain climber. The ending is the return indoors, taking off outdoor clothing, going to bed, and dreaming of a wonderful day in the snow. (*Suggestion:* End the playing with Peter in bed so that the children are seated. Omit playing the book's ending of going outdoors again on the following day.)

Half-and-half pantomime: snow activities *(pantomimers in front of the class; guessers at their desks)*

1. Discuss with children snow or winter activities not included in *The Snowy Day.* Show pictures of people engaged in winter activities such as ice skating, skiing, and feeding birds. Children add their own ideas to the discussion.
2. Divide class in half. One group performs a winter activity for the other group to guess. Depending on the maturity of the children, you may tell

---

[1]Numbers in parentheses refer to numbered anthologies and books listed in this text's final bibliography.

them what to pantomime or let them decide. Or have activities written on a few cards and let them draw one card.
3. Switch groups perhaps three times.

Story sharing: "Why the Evergreen Trees Keep Their Leaves in Winter" (at desks or in the story corner)

1. Tell or read this folk tale of a little bird with a broken wing who cannot fly south with the other birds as winter approaches. When it seeks shelter in the trees, it is rejected as being too small and unimportant. Only the evergreens offer help. When the wind blows in the winter and causes all the trees to lose their leaves, the frost king tells it to spare the leaves of the evergreen trees because of their kindness to the little bird.
2. End with a brief discussion of their reactions to the story and various characters.

Story dramatization

1. Review the story if you read it on a previous day.
2. Act out the sensory and emotion pantomimes and some of the brief verbal interaction from the story at desks or in a circle.
   a. Children are the various birds flying south for the winter. You briefly side-coach and narrate a few words about the various kinds of birds, the flapping of wings for the birds' takeoff, soaring to higher altitudes, and circling around one more time to encourage the little bird to join them or to say good-bye.
   b. (Continue side-coaching.) "Now you're the little bird with a broken wing trying to fly, sadly watching your friends leave. You feel the cold and puff out your feathers to protect yourself from the wind."
   c. "Now you are the trees—the birch, the oak, or the willow—standing proudly, feeling very important. You don't like strangers. Uh-oh, it looks as if someone's coming."
   d. Children continue to play the trees. You play the little bird (either by yourself or with a couple of children). Approach some of the trees and ask for permission to make a home in their branches. Some children may forget that they are the trees who say no to the little bird. (They may feel sorry for the bird, especially if you are convincing.) If this is the case, you can say "Oh, you must be one of the friendly evergreen trees."
   e. Now you can narrate or side-coach the trees briefly through the experience of having the cold and wind touch their leaves, making them shake loose and fall a few at a time. You can play the wind yourself, coming near them and touching a few trees at a time ("This row" or "This table"). This is a nice control feature, as the trees must wait until you give them a signal. (*Note:* Little children may literally fall to signify the leaves falling. Be prepared to side-coach a slow motion fall should this be the case.)
   f. "Now you are the friendly evergreen trees who are much kinder to the little bird. They offer their branches, protection from the north wind, and even berries to eat. And here comes the little bird with the broken wing." Again, you (by yourself or with two more children you select quickly) play the bird and interact briefly with a few of the trees.

The birds fly south for winter.

> g. To end these warm-ups, you can briefly narrate the ending of the story: "And so, the little bird was protected by the friendly evergreens and the frost king rewarded them. And that is why to this day evergreen trees keep their leaves in winter."

3. If the children want to continue, you may wish to put the story together as a small playlet. You may decide to play the wounded bird with the children in order to help with the dialogue. Or if the children are verbal and feel confident, you may only need to narrate a little from the sidelines.

Cast (in order of appearance)

Wounded bird	Two children (You may choose to play with them.)
Birds	Three children
Unfriendly trees	Groups of two or three each for an oak, a birch, and a willow
Wind	Two children
Wind sound effects	Played by the same three children who were the birds
Frost king	Two children

Evaluation and reflection. Questions such as the following might be asked:

1. "Was the story clear?"

The wounded bird asks the maple trees for shelter.

2. "Could we see a difference in the two kinds of trees—the selfish and the generous?"
3. "How many different tree shapes, or kinds of trees, did we see?"
4. "How could we tell the bird was wounded?"
5. Reflect on helping others; discuss rewards and punishments.

Replaying of the story, switching parts. If the children enjoy playing the story, consider additions such as the following:

1. A scene showing how the bird's wing was wounded
2. A scene between the birds when the wounded bird's problem is discovered
3. A scene at the end, showing the return of the birds in the spring who discover the young bird well again

Quieting activity: melting snow statue. (This may be played at desks or in larger areas.) Children are snow statues melting in the warm sun: "Your right arm melts the fastest and starts to slide down your round body. Now your left arm starts to slip. The sun gets higher in the sky and starts to melt your head. Your face starts to run, and your head begins to roll off. Then your shoulders begin to slump and your back begins to curve. You're only about half as tall as you once were. The sun is getting warmer, and now you're beginning to melt faster. You sink into a large lump. Now the lump starts to spread out until you are just a puddle of water."

If children are in larger areas of space, after a moment of relaxation you (as the frost king) may touch the children, one by one, as a signal to return to their seats.

ABRAHAM LINCOLN
Grade Level: 4 to 6

Objectives

1. Gain an understanding of some of the events in the life of an important American historical figure, recalling information previously studied.
2. Experience pantomiming and interpreting pantomime of occupations of Lincoln's time.
3. Dramatize in groups an interpretation of an episode in Lincoln's life demonstrating personal characteristic of honesty.
4. Explore through role drama Lincoln's open door policy with the common people.
5. Explore reasons one might seek audience with a President.
6. Reflect on personal qualities of a great President, as well as the problems and dangers faced by leaders of a nation.

Preparation and materials

1. Copies of Abraham Lincoln biographies. Suggestions:

   True stories about *Abraham Lincoln,* Ruth Belov Gross. New York: Lothrop, Lee & Shepard, 1973.

   Lincoln: A Photobiography, Russel Freedman. New York: Clarion, 1987.

   . . . *If You Grew Up with Abraham Lincoln,* Ann McGovern. New York: Four Winds Press, 1966, 1992.
2. Copy of the poem "Nancy Hanks," by Rosemary Carr and Stephen Vincent Benét (3)
3. Picture of the Lincoln Memorial in Washington, D.C., or other Lincoln statues
4. (optional) Other pictures of Lincoln which might motivate or illustrate points in the lesson

Introductory activity: "Nancy Hanks"

1. Read the poem by Rosemary Carr and Stephen Vincent Benét. It is written as if Nancy Hanks, Abe Lincoln's mother, is speaking. It suggests that she comes back to today's world and wonders how her son made out.
2. Leader plays the role of Nancy (or Tom, Lincoln's father) and interviews the rest of the class, who are to convince you that Abe did, indeed, "get on." If students are capable, you may let them play Lincoln's parent with you or even handle the interview alone while you play a moderator. Nancy should pretend to find it difficult to believe all the information about Lincoln. Her objections might include: "But when I died, Abe and his pa were barely making it in that log cabin in Indiana. How could he have become a President?" "But we were so poor, Abe couldn't even go to school more than just a few days. Where'd he learn to read and write?" Other points of information she might ask: "What happened to Tom,

Abe's father?" "What did Abe look like when he grew up?" "Do you have a picture of him?" and so on.

Pantomimes of jobs Lincoln held

1. Review a number of jobs held by Lincoln during his lifetime (rail splitter, postmaster, carpenter, peddler, surveyor, sawmiller, lawyer, storekeeper, farmer, riverboat driver, and President). Nancy Hanks could ask to see these jobs, if desired. Methods of playing the pantomimes can be almost any one discussed in Chapter 7. Reflection afterward could be: "How might any of these jobs have helped Lincoln be a better President?" "What occupations today would be useful for a prospective President to have experienced?"
2. Pantomime alternatives:

   Option A. Build-a-place pantomime of Lincoln's log cabin in Indiana or a general store where Lincoln worked. Refer to texts above for data and illustrations.

   Option B. In groups, create frozen pictures of famous scenes in Lincoln's life.

Group scenes: "Honest Abe"

1. Review or read to the class some of the stories or legends about how Lincoln got the nickname "Honest Abe." There are several stories, including his walking six miles to return six pennies to a woman who overpaid him for some cloth and the amount of time he spent working to pay off a library book he inadvertently damaged.
2. Students may reenact one of these scenes, showing their version of what they think might have happened. Or students might create a new story, based on data they know about Lincoln and the time period in which he lived, to demonstrate how someone might come to be known as a particularly honest person.
3. Groups of approximately five students each discuss and plan a scene. Share scenes in front of the classroom. Scenes may be in pantomime or may include dialogue.
4. Reflection afterward might be on how honesty might guide one's life as a President or any leader.

Role drama: The Open Door Policy

1. Review or read about Abraham Lincoln's belief that everyone should have a right to talk to the President. There were always crowds of people to see him, and he made every effort to see as many as possible.
2. Discuss: What kinds of people would come to see the President, and what reasons would they have? How would Lincoln be able to talk to so many people?
3. Students interview each other in pairs. They should find out who the other person is and what reasons he or she has for seeing the President. If this proves difficult, or if research is necessary, you could stop at this point. Each student (or in pairs or small groups) can find as much detail as possible about people and their problems appropriate to the time period. You may decide to focus on the Civil War period particularly. Students can find photographs of persons in various sources and write

an autobiography of themselves (or their family or other group they wish to play). This may take several days' time. As you work with the students in developing their characters, you will gain insight into the responses you (as Lincoln) can give to them. The situations the students may encounter in their research could include: a mother interceding for her young, sixteen-year-old son, who fell asleep on guard duty and is awaiting execution; two newspaper reporters claiming to have evidence of inferior goods being sold to the Union army; friends from Springfield, Illinois, who wish to bring greetings; and so on.

4. Set the scene in the White House (the front of the classroom) and the waiting room (students' desks). Discuss with the students what other aspects of the setting are needed to help them believe in what they are doing. Where do they think the President should sit? Behind a desk? In a large chair? What nonverbal messages are conveyed with both? You might also have them close their eyes and try to imagine not only how the room looks but also what the atmosphere might be like. Is it quiet or noisy? What sounds might they hear? Is it tense or relaxed? and so on. Another useful strategy is to go around the classroom, placing your hand on each student's shoulder and asking for expression of one thought that comes to mind as the waiting for the President continues.

5. When the group is ready, you might enter as the President's aide and announce: "Due to pressing governmental business today, the President's visitation hours must be postponed by one hour. Furthermore, today's interview time must be cut short. Therefore, only the most crucial requests can be presented. Please consider whether your concerns are truly worthy of the President's time today or whether your visit with him could be put off until another day. Thank you very much." If desired, you might add, "Are there any questions?" However, since this is a second-in-command role, you can be vague in your answers.

6. The students may whisper to each other at this surprised turn of events. This might be a good time to stop the drama by entering as yourself and reflect on the following questions with them: What were their feelings when they heard the announcement? How worthy did they think their reason for seeing the President was? Would they defer to others' needs to see the President?

7. This might be an appropriate time to discuss the different needs each student or group has and see if they might be prioritized in some manner. For example, are they personal or do they affect a larger group of people? What do the solutions depend on? money? political strategy? an act of Congress? Listing and categorizing may be done. If the group agrees to prioritizing, this may become the order of their encounters with the President.

8. The President will now see the visitors. This would be a good time to use the stop-frame technique. The leader should explain she will enter as Lincoln and then say, "Stop frame." All will freeze and the first person to her right will say aloud, but briefly, what he or she is thinking at that very moment. (Comments may range from: "At last!" to "My, how tall he is.") The leader also speaks her thoughts (for example, "So many people, and I am due to meet with my Cabinet in thirty minutes.")

9. Now the students may present their ideas in the order established earlier. A time limit may be set for the visits. Some interviews may also have to be "postponed" to a later date if the allotted time ends before students have a chance to present their ideas. You will need to end each visit

tactfully, diplomatically, and appropriately. The drama may end when all the scenes have been presented. Further dramas may center around any of the issues raised by the visits. For example, students may want Lincoln to meet with the young soldier's commanding officer; moving the action back in time, they may wish to develop the drama around the boy's life prior to his being drafted; and so on. Or, any of the following activities may be undertaken.

10. Additional activities might include:
    a. Write a newspaper article of the student-in-role meeting with the President. Depending on the reason for the meeting, the article may be for the Washington newspaper or the student-in-role's hometown newspaper.
    b. Create frozen pictures of each group with the President (a student may play the role this time) to accompany the newspaper article.
    c. President Lincoln needs help deciding whether his open door policy is taking too much time away from other matters (as some of his advisers are saying) or whether it is an important practice to continue. The students may be in role as friends whom he trusts. *Alternative:* This may also be done as a simple debate with Lincoln moderating the two viewpoints voiced by members of his staff.
    d. Students may write a letter of thanks to the President for having seen them; or they may write a letter they would like the President to send them, following up on the reason for the meeting. It might be helpful to look at letters from the period for examples of style.
    e. Reflect on how accessible a President should be to the people. Is today's situation different from or similar to Lincoln's day?
    f. Make comparisons between the White House of today and during Lincoln's day. What descriptions or photos can be found of the White House during Lincoln's presidency? How many and what kinds of changes have been made to the President's home over the years?

Quieting activity: Lincoln statue

1. Show class a picture of the Lincoln Memorial or other Lincoln statue. On a count of ten, the students slowly transform from themselves into the statue. This activity may be used whenever a quiet, concluding moment is wanted.
2. *Alternative:* Class could slowly become a statue of Lincoln at any stage of his life in an important moment. As the students are frozen, you (or the students themselves) can quietly comment on the various positions and perhaps identify some of the scenes.

EVALUATION IN CREATIVE DRAMA

In teaching creative drama it is important to assess children's progress along the way. Only then will you know the successes of your program and be able to plan the direction of subsequent lessons.

The most widely used method of evaluation in creative drama is class discussion, similar to those included throughout this text. If videotape equipment is available, you may want to use it periodically to help children evaluate themselves and to assist you in looking at the class more carefully. However, your school system may require you to make a more formal, written evaluation.

Cautions in Evaluating

Although it cannot be argued that teachers must check students' progress in all educational ventures, there are some cautions to remember. First of all, many educational goals are difficult to pinpoint, let alone define. Drama is no exception. Often in the process of exploration learning, undefined goals emerge and are achieved unexpectedly. Ironically, those serendipitous opportunities or objectives may turn out to be even more significant than any of your predefined ones.

In addition, if you design a drama activity around, or limit it to, only one or two skills or objectives, you may overlook the larger goals of instruction, the chance to explore drama experiences that emerge spontaneously, or even the opportunity to just play with ideas in a creative way. Furthermore, as is the case with many educational endeavors, some drama goals will be beyond precise measurement. In the attempt to measure a skill in a precise way, one can lose sight of other possible outcomes.

Being alert to these potential problems can save considerable time and frustration. The mark of a creative and effective teacher is one who lets the children and their needs define the direction of the lessons rather than the other way around. You should also be alert to the learnings the children make *when they happen* rather than looking for them *only* when you schedule yourself to do so.

Teacher Evaluation

Every teaching situation is different and will probably require a little different format. The following checklist is presented as a *sample* only. It is not intended that all items are required for any one activity or lesson. Nor is the list complete for all activities, since it does not include specific curricular objectives. For example, if your class has studied pioneer log cabins and then constructs a cabin in the pantomime game Build a Place, you would probably expect that students will include furniture and household goods appropriate for the setting and the time period. You could then include that objective in the day's evaluation. Finally, many of the goals will need special consideration or adaptation depending on individual children's needs, such as the gifted, those with handicaps, or those with other individual differences.

Since you will be involved in playing with the children during the drama lessons, it will be necessary for you to evaluate them at a later time, preferably as soon after a lesson has been taught as possible. A periodic assessment is usually as effective as keeping a daily record and should enable you to see students' growth and progress more readily.

On the sample checklist below you may simply place a *check* for the items a child demonstrates favorably and record a *minus* for those that are not favorably performed. Those that are not applicable may simply be left blank. Or you may prefer to use a rating scale (for example: 1 poor, 2 fair, 3 good, and 4 superior), marking only those items that are applicable.

By placing all the students' names lengthwise along the top of the checklist, you should be able to make your report on one sheet. Another option is to observe only a few students at a time in any one assessment. The latter should be less overwhelming than trying to evaluate every student after each lesson.

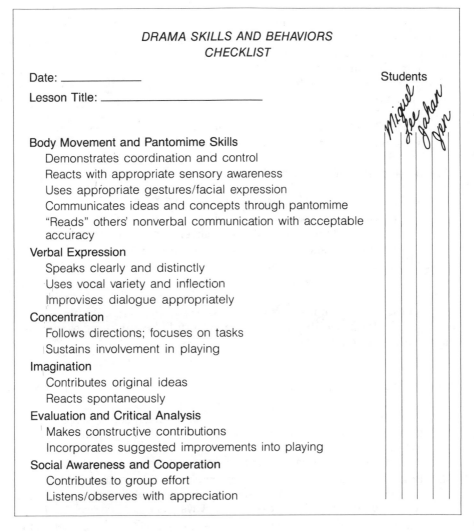

DRAMA SKILLS AND BEHAVIORS CHECKLIST

Date: _____

Lesson Title: _____

Students

Miguel Lee Johan Gen

Body Movement and Pantomime Skills
- Demonstrates coordination and control
- Reacts with appropriate sensory awareness
- Uses appropriate gestures/facial expression
- Communicates ideas and concepts through pantomime
- "Reads" others' nonverbal communication with acceptable accuracy

Verbal Expression
- Speaks clearly and distinctly
- Uses vocal variety and inflection
- Improvises dialogue appropriately

Concentration
- Follows directions; focuses on tasks
- Sustains involvement in playing

Imagination
- Contributes original ideas
- Reacts spontaneously

Evaluation and Critical Analysis
- Makes constructive contributions
- Incorporates suggested improvements into playing

Social Awareness and Cooperation
- Contributes to group effort
- Listens/observes with appreciation

Children's Self-Evaluation

In addition to the teacher's evaluation instrument, it is important that the children's self-evaluation, as individuals and as a group, be encouraged.

Aesthetic judgments are developed as they are given voice. Children need opportunities to make and defend their points of view with each other. And since not even so-called educated critics of the arts would agree with each other, children may not either. Neither should group consensus be considered the final word in the matter. Lone defenders of a viewpoint are often proved more accurate or insightful at a later date.

Likewise it is also true that tastes change and develop. Over a period of time, we all change our minds and directions about what appeals to us and what bores us. We may adopt the popular style of the day and then later reject it with as much energy as we first embraced it. Children, too, need opportunities to experiment with varying artistic ideas before they can come to any conclusions about their judgments.

For self-evaluation, young children may be questioned orally in a brief conference. However, older students may write a periodic self-evaluation. Students may

1. Circle "usually," "some of the time," or "hardly ever" for each item.
2. Write out their answers, perhaps even indicating "why" or "why not."

Questions might be similar to these:

1. "Do I participate and contribute to the activities?"
2. "Do I stay focused and concentrate when I am playing?"
3. "Am I a good observer or audience member for my classmates?"
4. "Do I participate and contribute to group planning?"
5. "Am I careful to consider my classmates' feelings?"
6. "Do I offer original ideas?"

These evaluation formats should not result in using creative drama as a routine drill. Rather, drama experiences should be enriching to the entire curriculum and enjoyable for all.

FOR THE COLLEGE STUDENT

1. Select a curricular theme or topic. Brainstorm with a group of your classmates the many drama activities the theme suggests. Working together or individually, select perhaps five activities from your list for a drama lesson, sequencing them appropriately. Use the sample lesson outlines as a model.
2. Design and teach a lesson to your classmates or to a group of children. What changes did you make in the lesson plan as a result of the group's responses? Afterward, analyze your successes and ways you could improve.
3. Discuss with your classmates various ways of evaluation one might use in creative drama. Refer to evaluation methods used in other curricular subjects. Which ones might serve as useful models for creative drama?
4. Check your local area or state to see if creative drama evaluation procedures exist. Perhaps evaluations from other geographical areas are available to you

for comparison. What features of the evaluations do you like? What suggestions for improvements can you make?

5. Construct your own evaluation checklist
   a. For a general use in creative drama.
   b. For a specific lesson plan.

   Use the evaluation checklist after working with your classmates or with a group of children. Discuss and compare your findings with your classmates.

Story and Poetry Anthologies and Books for Dramatization

Throughout the text, numbers in parentheses have referred to these correspondingly numbered anthologies and children's novels.

(1) *The All Jahdu Storybook*, Virginia Hamilton. San Diego: Harcourt Brace Jovanovich, 1991.

(2) *All the Silver Pennies*, ed. Blanche Jennings Thompson. New York: Macmillan, 1967.

(3) *The Arbuthnot Anthology of Children's Literature*, 4th ed., May Hill Arbuthnot, rev. by Zena Sutherland. Glenview, Ill.: Scott, Foresman, 1976.

(4) *Best-Loved Folktales of the World*, compiled by Joanna Cole. Garden City, N. Y.: Doubleday, 1982.

(5) *The Crack in the Wall and Other Terribly Weird Tales*, George Mendoza. New York: Dial Press, 1968.

(6) *Classic Stories 2*, Ray Bradbury. New York: Doubleday, 1990.

(7) *The Dancing Kettle and Other Japanese Folk Tales*, Yoshiko Uchida. New York: Harcourt Brace Jovanovich, 1949.

(8) *Eric Carle's Story Book; Seven Tales by the Brothers Grimm*, New York: Franklin Watts, 1976.

(9) *Grandfather Tales*, Richard Chase. Boston: Houghton Mifflin, 1948.

(10) *Gwot! Horribly Funny Hairticklers*, George Mendoza. New York: Harper & Row, 1967.

(11) *The Hat-Shaking Dance and Other Tales from the Gold Coast*, Harold Courlander and Albert Kofi Prempeh. San Diego: Harcourt Brace Jovanovich, 1957.

(12) *Hey! Listen to This,* ed. Jim Trelease. New York: Viking, Penguin, 1992.

(13) *Jack Tales,* Richard C. Chase. Boston: Houghton Mifflin, 1943.

(14) *Just So Stories,* Rudyard Kipling. New York: Henry Holt, 1987.

(15) *A Light in the Attic,* Shel Silverstein. New York: Harper & Row, 1981.

(16) *Mouse Tales,* Arnold Lobel. New York: Harper & Row, 1972.

(17) *The New Kid on the Block,* Jack Prelutsky. New York: Greenwillow Books, 1984.

(18) *A New Treasury of Children's Poetry,* ed. Joanna Cole. New York: Doubleday, 1984.

(19) *Nobody is Perfick,* Bernard Waber. Boston: Houghton Mifflin, 1971, 1991 .

(20) *On City Streets,* ed. Nancy Larrick. New York: Bantam, 1968.

(21) *Petunia the Silly Goose Stories,* Roger Duvosin. New York: Alfred A. Knopf, 1988.

(22) *Piping Down the Valleys Wild,* ed. Nancy Larrick. New York: Dell Publishing, 1968.

(23) *The Random House Book of Fairy Tales,* adapted by Amy Ehrlich. New York: Random House, 1985.

(24) *The Random House Book of Poetry for Children,* selected by Jack Prelutsky. New York: Random House, 1983.

(25) *Read Me A Story,* Sophie Windham. New York: Scholastic, 1991.

(26) *Reflections on a Gift of Watermelon Pickle,* eds. Stephen Dunning, Edward Lueders, and Hugh Smith. Glenview, Ill.: Scott, Foresman, 1966.

(27) *Ride a Purple Pelican,* Jack Prelutsky. New York: Greenwillow, 1986.

(28) *Ride with the Sun,* ed. Harold Courlander. New York: McGraw-Hill, 1955.

(29) *The Riverside Anthology of Children's Literature,* 6th ed., ed. Judith Saltman. Boston: Houghton Mifflin, 1985.

(30) *The Sea of Gold and Other Tales from Japan,* Yoshiko Uchida. New York: Charles Scribner's Sons, 1965.

(31) *Sing a Song of Popcorn,* Beatrice Schenk de Regniers. New York: Scholastic, 1988.

(32) *Six by Seuss,* Dr. Seuss. New York: Random House, 1991.

(33) *The Sneetches and Other Stories,* Dr. Seuss. New York: Random House, 1961.

(34) *Some Haystacks Don't Even Have Any Needle,* compiled by Stephen Dunning, Edward Lueders, and Hugh Smith. Glenview, Ill.: Scott, Foresman, 1969.

(35) *Something Big Has Been Here,* Jack Prelutsky. New York: Greenwillow, 1990.

(36) *Stories to Dramatize,* Winifred Ward. New Orleans: Anchorage Press, 1981.

(37) *The Tales of Uncle Remus,* as told by Julius Lester. New York: Dial Press, 1987.

(38) *The Tiger and the Rabbit and Other Tales,* Pura Belpré. Philadelphia: J. B. Lippincott, 1965.

(39) *Tomie de Paola's Favorite Nursery Tales.* New York: G. P. Putnam's, 1986.

(40) *Treasury of Children's Classics in Spanish and English.* William T. Tardy. Lincolnwood, Ill.: National Council of Teachers of English, 1985.

(41) *Where the Sidewalk Ends,* Shel Silverstein. New York: Harper & Row, 1974.

(42) *Windsong,* Carl Sandburg. New York: Harcourt Brace Jovanovich, 1960.

(43) *Yertle the Turtle and Other Stories,* Dr. Seuss. New York: Random House, 1958.

BOOKS FOR DRAMATIZATION

The following longer books are highly recommended for extended dramatization work. They are only a representative sampling of the fine literature available for today's children. Some are older classics that remain as viable today as when they were first printed. Others have been selected for their historical and geographical settings, relationship to other areas of the curriculum, social themes, and their variety of heroes and heroines.

The books are listed alphabetically according to title. Suggested grade levels are listed at the left.

(44)　O　*Across Five Aprils,* Irene Hunt. Chicago: Follett, 1964. A young boy grows up in Southern Illinois during the Civil War period in this award-winning novel.

(45) M–O　*The Adventures of Tom Sawyer,* Mark Twain. New York: William Morrow, 1989. The American classic of a Missouri boy's adventures on the Mississippi River in the 1880s.

(46) M–O　*Alice's Adventures in Wonderland,* Lewis Carroll. New York: William Morrow, 1992. This new edition of Alice's adventures is illustrated from the recently discovered original wood engravings. Another edition is illustrated by Michael Hague (New York: Holt, Rinehart and Winston, 1985).

(47) Y–M　*A Bear Called Paddington,* Michael Bond. Boston: Houghton Mifflin, 1958. A charming humanlike bear arrives in London and is adopted by a family. Sequels are also available.

(48)　M　*The Borrowers,* Mary Norton. San Diego: Harcourt Brace Jovanovich, 1981 (renewed). Life is full of adventures for the little people who live under the floorboards of the house and borrow small objects to furnish their home. Sequels are also available.

(49) M–O　*By the Great Horn Spoon!* Sid Fleischman. Boston: Little, Brown, 1963. A young boy and his aunt's butler stow away on a ship headed for California gold in this humorous, historical fiction adventure.

(50) M–O　*Caddie Woodlawn,* Carol Ryrie Brink. New York: Macmillan, 1973 (revised). The author reminisces about her tomboy grandmother as a young girl on the Wisconsin frontier in the 1860s.

(51)　M　*Charlie and the Chocolate Factory,* rev. ed. Roald Dahl. New York: Alfred A. Knopf, 1973. A young boy wins the opportunity to tour a famous and unusual candy factory owned by the equally famous and unusual Willy Wonka. Also available in Spanish, 1987. Sequel is *Charlie and the Great Glass Elevator,* 1972, which is also available in Spanish.

(52) Y–M　*Charlotte's Web,* E. B. White. New York: Harper & Row, 1952. Wilbur the pig, with the help of his barnyard friends and most particularly Charlotte the spider, develops into a most unique animal.

(53) M–O　*A Christmas Carol,* Charles Dickens. New York: Simon and Schuster, 1982. This edition of the classic story of Scrooge is beautifully illustrated with full-color plates.

(54) Y–M　*Christmas on the Mayflower,* Wilma P. Hays. New York: Coward-McCann, 1956. A dramatic conflict is presented when the crew of the *Mayflower* wants to return to England before the safety of the Pilgrims in a new land is assured.

(55) Y–M *The Courage of Sarah Noble,* Alice Dalgliesh. New York: Charles Scribner's Sons, 1954, 1974. The true story of a little girl who bravely accompanies her father into the Connecticut territory in the early 1700s.

(56)　O *Danny the Champion of the World,* Roald Dahl. New York: Alfred A. Knopf, 1975. Danny and his widowed father manage a filling station and live in a nearby caravan in England. Their love and respect for each other is a strong theme throughout the book along with a marvelous adventure of poaching pheasants.

(57)　O *The Great Brain,* John D. Fitzgerald. New York: Dial Press, 1967; Dell, 1988. This popular autobiographical account of the author's brother, a lovable schemer, has its setting in the late 1800s in Utah. The sequels are equally appealing.

(58)　M *The Great Cheese Conspiracy,* Jean Van Leeuwen. New York: Random House, 1969. A gang of mice, who have learned about burglaries from old gangster movies, decide to rob a cheese store.

(59) M–O *Half Magic,* Edward Eager. San Diego: Harcourt Brace Jovanovich, 1954. Four children discover a magical coin that grants them only half a wish.

(60) M–O *Henry Huggins,* Beverly Cleary. New York: William Morrow, 1950, 1978. The ever-popular antics of a young boy and his dog Ribsy are presented with humor and warmth. Available in Spanish, 1983.

(61) M–O *Homer Price,* Robert McCloskey. New York: Viking Penguin, 1943, 1976. A young boy in a small midwestern town manages to capture robbers with the help of his pet skunk and to solve a problem of too many doughnuts, among other adventures.

(62) M–O *How to Eat Fried Worms,* Thomas Rockwell. New York: Franklin Watts, 1973. Billy Forrester makes a bet that he can eat fifteen worms in fifteen days for $50. The plot centers on the many schemes the other bettor uses to keep Billy from being successful.

(63)　M *The Indian in the Cupboard,* Lynne Reid Banks. New York: Doubleday, 1980. A young boy, Omri, discovers that he can bring his plastic toys, including an Indian and a cowboy, to life by placing them in a cupboard. In the sequel, *The Return of the Indian* (1986), Omri is able to transport himself into his toys' world. *The Secret of the Indian* (1989) continues the exciting adventures.

(64)　M *James and the Giant Peach,* Roald Dahl. New York: Alfred A. Knopf, 1961. Inside a magic peach, James finds many insect friends, and together they have a fantastic journey across the Atlantic from England to New York.

(65)　O *Johnny Tremain,* Esther Forbes. Boston: Houghton Mifflin, 1943. Johnny, a young silver apprentice in Boston, struggles to maturity during the 1770s in this classic book of historical fiction.

(66)　O *The Legend of King Arthur,* Robin Lister. New York: Doubleday, 1991. Told from the perspective of Merlin the wizard, fourteen tales with full color illustrations are told about the legendary king.

(67) M–O *Little House* series, Laura Ingalls Wilder. New York: Harper & Row. These several books document the classic and true stories of an American pioneer family in various midwestern locations. They also inspired a long-running and popular television series.

(68) M–O *Lupita Mañana,* Patricia Beatty. New York: William Morrow, 1981. When 13-year-old Lupita's father dies, she and her brother journey to the

United States to find work. Posing as a boy, she struggles to evade the immigration police with determination and courage.

(69)   M *Mary Jemison: Seneca Captive,* Jeanne Le Monnier Gardner. San Diego: Harcourt Brace Jovanovich, 1966. This is the exciting biography of a courageous white girl who was captured and adopted by Seneca Indians in the late 1700s.

(70)   O *Mrs. Frisby and the Rats of NIMH,* Robert C. O'Brien. New York: Atheneum, 1971. Laboratory rats from the National Institute of Mental Health seek to make a better world for themselves.

(71) Y–M *The Mouse and the Motorcycle,* Beverly Cleary. New York: William Morrow, 1965. A mouse named Ralph has interesting adventures with a toy motorcycle. Sequels of Ralph's adventures are also available.

(72)   O *My Brother Sam Is Dead,* Christopher and James Collier. New York: Four Winds Press, 1974. An American family in Connecticut during the Revolutionary War are on opposing sides—the Tories versus the Patriots. Events before, during, and after the war change many of their attitudes.

(73)   O *My Name Is Not Angelica,* Scott O'Dell. Boston: Houghton Mifflin, 1989. Sixteen-year-old Raisha is a sheltered house slave, who is troubled by the suffering she sees being endured by the other plantation slaves. With courage and determination, she vows to help them in this powerful story based on historical research.

(74)   O *Number the Stars,* Lois Lowry. Boston: Houghton Mifflin, 1989. Nazi soldiers are relocating the Jews in Denmark in 1943. Ten-year-old Annemarie Johansen's family aids their friends, the Rosens, in hiding and escaping.

(75)   M *Peter Pan,* Sir James Barrie. New York: Henry Holt, 1987. The classic story of a boy who does not want to grow up. Illustrations in this new edition are by Michael Hague.

(76)   O *The Phantom Tollbooth,* Norton Juster. New York: Random House, 1961. Milo has many adventures in a fantastical land. (See sample story dramatization in Chapter 10 of this text.)

(77) M–O *Pinocchio, The Adventures of,* Carlo Collodi. New York: Alfred A. Knopf, 1988. This edition of the famous puppet who longs to be a real boy is colorfully illustrated by Roberto Innocenti.

(78) M–O *Pippi Longstocking,* Astrid Lindgren. New York: Viking Penguin, 1950. Pippi, a superhuman girl whose widowed father is off at sea, has an independent life-style that intrigues the neighborhood children.

(79)   O *The Prydian Chronicles,* Lloyd Alexander. New York: Dell. A five-volume fantasy series, featuring high adventure and quiet wisdom. Titles include *The Book of Three, The Black Cauldron, The Castle of Llyr, Taran Wanderer,* and *The High King.* The fifth of these books, a Newbery Medal winner, can be read independently of the others.

(80)   O *The Pushcart War,* Jean Merrill. New York: Harper & Row, 1964. In a humorous spoof on the traffic problems in New York City, pushcart vendors, who are being overrun by the Mighty Mammoths (truck drivers), start a war with peashooters.

(81)   M *The Reluctant Dragon,* Kenneth Grahame. New York: Holt, Rinehart and Winston, 1983. A peaceable dragon is not interested in fighting a knight in this modern classic. See also (12).

(82) M–O *Robin Hood—Prince of Outlaws,* Bernard Miles. New York: Rand McNally, 1979. The legendary accounts of the outlaw-hero of England are pre-

sented with updated language. Full-color illustrations are by Victor Ambrus.

(83)   M *Sam, Bangs and Moonshine,* Evaline Ness. New York: Holt, Rinehart and Winston, 1966. Sam, a fisherman's daughter, makes up fanciful stories. Trouble begins when she tells her friend about her mermaid mother.

(84)   M *Sarah, Plain and Tall,* Patricia MacLachan. New York: Harper & Row, 1985. When their widowed father sends for a mail-order bride from the East, Caleb and Anna hope she will like life on the prairie—and them—well enough to stay.

(85)   M *Sarah Whitcher's Story,* Elizabeth Yates. New York: E. P. Dutton, 1971. Based on a true account, this story is of a pioneer girl in New Hampshire who becomes lost in the woods for four days.

(86)   O *The Secret Soldier,* Ann McGovern. New York: Four Winds Press, 1975; reissued 1987. A true story of a young woman who disguised herself as a man and fought in the Revolutionary War is recounted by a well-known historical writer.

(87)   O *Shadow of a Bull,* Maia Wojciechowska. New York: Atheneum, 1964. Everyone expects Manolo to be a great Spanish bullfighter like his father, but the boy makes his own choice in the end.

(88)   M *Tales of a Fourth Grade Nothing,* Judy Blume. New York: E. P. Dutton, 1972. Peter is convinced his life is worth nothing with a little brother like Fudge who does everything wrong, including eating Peter's pet turtle. Sequels available.

(89) M–O *This Time, Tempe Wick?* Patricia Gauch. New York: Coward-McCann, 1974. During the Revolutionary War, disillusioned Pennsylvania soldiers try to rob Tempe of her horse so that they can return home, but she outwits them in a clever way in this true story.

(90)   O *Treasure Island,* Robert Louis Stevenson. New York: Charles Scribner's Sons, 1981 (reissued). Young Jim Hawkins and the villainous but appealing rogue Long John Silver sail to a tropic isle and become involved in a climactic battle for treasure.

(91)   O *Tuck Everlasting,* Natalie Babbit. New York: Farrar, Straus & Giroux, 1975. Twelve-year-old Winnie Foster runs away from home, meets Jesse Tuck, an immortal, and falls in love. She plans to reunite with him at age seventeen but learns she must decide between mortality and immortality.

(92)   O *Twenty and Ten,* Claire H. Bishop. New York: Viking Penguin, 1952; Puffin, 1978. When Nazi soldiers search for ten Jewish children at a mountain retreat, twenty fifth grade French children hide them in a cave in this adventure based on a true story.

(93) M–O *Venture for Freedom,* Ruby Zagoren. New York: Dell Publishing, 1969. The son of an African king, Venture, was sold into slavery in America in the 1700s. This account is based on his autobiography.

(94) M–O *The Whipping Boy,* Sid Fleischman. New York: Greenwillow, 1986. Prince Brat, as he is secretly called by his subjects, is bored with palace life and forces his whipping boy, Jemmy, to run away with him. Their adventures with kidnappers, a circus bear, and a chase through rat-filled sewers change their lives and relationship.

(95) M–O *Wind in the Willows,* Kenneth Grahame. New York: Charles Scribner's Sons, 1983. This 75th anniversary edition with the original illustrations by Ernest H. Shepard, proves that the charming adventures of Mole,

Rat, Badger, and Toad never grow old. Toad's friends aid him in conquering his craze for motorcars and in gaining back his family estate from the Wild Wood animals. (See also the edition with illustrations by Michael Hague. New York: Holt, Rinehart and Winston, 1980.)

(96) Y—M *Winnie-the-Pooh*, A. A. Milne. New York: E. P. Dutton, 1954 (renewed). Winnie, a stuffed bear, and his animal friends have many delightful days. See also *The House at Pooh Corners* for more adventures.

(97) O *The Witch of Blackbird Pond*, Elizabeth George Speare. Boston: Houghton Mifflin, 1958. After leaving her home in Barbados, Kit Tyler feels out of place in a Puritan community in Connecticut. Her spirited personality arouses suspicion, and she finds herself accused of witchcraft.

(98) O *The Wonderful Wizard of Oz*, L. Frank Baum. New York: Holt, Rinehart and Winston, 1983: Puffin, 1983. A Kansas cyclone carries Dorothy and her dog Toto to the Land of Oz where she makes friends with a scarecrow, a tin man, and a lion.

(99) M—O *A Wrinkle in Time*, Madeline L'Engle. New York: Farrar, Straus & Giroux, 1962. Children search for their father who has been in outer space for over a year on a classified mission. Traveling through time, they land on the planet Camazotz, which is under the rule of a black force, IT, where their father is a prisoner. Sequels are *A Wind in the Door* and *A Swiftly Tilting Planet*.

Index